Flash® Catalyst™ CS5 Bible

Flash® Catalyst™ CS5 Bible

Rob Huddleston

WILEY

Wiley Publishing, Inc.

Flash® Catalyst™ CS5 Bible

Published by
Wiley Publishing, Inc.
10475 Crosspoint Boulevard
Indianapolis, IN 46256
www.wiley.com

About the Author

Rob Huddleston has been developing Web pages and applications since 1994, and has been an instructor since 1999, teaching Web and graphic design to thousands of students. His clients have included the United States Bureau of Land Management, the United States Patent and Trademark Office, the States of California and Nevada, and many other federal, city and county agencies; the United States Army and Air Force; Fortune 500 companies such as AT&T, Bank of America, Wells Fargo, Safeway, and Coca-Cola; software companies including Adobe, Oracle, Intuit and Autodesk; the University of California, San Francisco State University, and the University of Southern California; and hundreds of small businesses and non-profit agencies, both in the United States and abroad.

Rob is an Adobe Certified Instructor, Certified Expert, and Certified Developer, serves as an Adobe User Group Manager, has been named as an Adobe Community Expert for his volunteer work answering user questions in online forums, and also helps users as an expert moderator on Adobe's Community Help system.

He is the author of *XML: Your visual blueprint™ for building expert Web sites using XML, CSS, XHTML, and XSLT*; *HTML, XHTML and CSS: Your visual blueprint™ for designing effective Web sites*; *Master VISUALLY: Dreamweaver CS4*; and *Flash CS4 Professional and ActionScript 3: Your visual blueprint™ for creating interactive projects in Flash CS4 Professional*.

You can visit Rob's blog at www.robhuddleston.com, or follow him on Twitter at twitter.com/robhuddles. He lives in Northern California with his wife and two children.

For Kelley, Jessica and Xander. I love you more than I can say.

Credits

Senior Acquisitions Editor
Stephanie McComb

Project Editor
Chris Wolfgang

Technical Editor
TJ Downes

Copy Editor
Kim Heusel

Editorial Director
Robyn Siesky

Business Manager
Amy Knies

Senior Marketing Manager
Sandy Smith

Vice President and Executive Group Publisher
Richard Swadley

Vice President and Executive Publisher
Barry Pruett

Project Coordinator
Patrick Redmond

Graphics and Production Specialists
Jennifer Mayberry
Ronald G. Terry

Quality Control Technician
Jessica Kramer

Proofreading and Indexing
Christopher M. Jones
Word Co Indexing Services

Media Development Project Manager
Laura Moss

Media Development Assistant Project Manager
Jenny Swisher

Media Development Associate Producer
Josh Frank
Shawn Patrick
Doug Kuhn
Marilyn Hummel

Foreword

In October of 2007, I was sitting in a conference room with members of my team at the interactive agency I worked at. We had been asked if we were interested in meeting with some people from Adobe on some possible features for what was at the time called Flex Builder.

The timing was great because we had recently launched a pretty sophisticated Flex Web application for a car manufacturer, and we had pushed Flex Builder and the Flex framework to its limits. We were thrilled with an opportunity to present all of the issues we had to the team to hopefully work on in the next version.

We sat in the room and dimmed the lights, and the team's product manager, Steve Heintz, made a clarification on the presentation. We weren't going to see Flex Builder, but an entirely new concept codenamed *Thermo*. As we watched the presentation, the team showed features for this mythical application including:

- Converting artwork into components without needing to go through the laborious skinning workflow.
- Editing designs in Illustrator within context of the Flex application.
- Rigging interactions between components.
- Capturing user interactions without needing to understand Flex.
- Working with design-time data to build data lists and components.
- And all this while writing MXML and ActionScript using the Flex framework behind the scenes.

We were floored, but at the same time were very skeptical — an application like Thermo was exactly what we needed for our recent project where we had a separate team of designers sending over Photoshop files that had to be painstakingly processed and converted into Flex component skins. The process was time consuming and frustrating. Thermo was promising to take the pain out of that workflow, to have the designs and code be connected in an intelligent way, and to allow the designers and developers to each do what they do best. It seemed too good to be true.

With Thermo still in our minds, we hopped on a plane for Chicago to attend Adobe MAX 2007. It was my first MAX, and I was really excited to meet the product teams, evangelists, and community to talk about Flex, Flash and Creative Suite. We were sitting near the front during the keynote and then saw the public unveiling of Thermo.

Note
MAX is a developer's conference hosted every year by Adobe.

Foreword

"Wow. This is really going to happen," I thought to myself, anxious and salivating for what Adobe was demonstrating to the crowd. It was what everyone talked about the entire conference, and I was proud to have been an early contributor to the product in that first meeting. I was also equally excited when I was able to share that I just had been offered a job at Adobe as a product manager for Creative Suite integration with — you guessed, it — Thermo.

Just as before, I was still skeptical, or at least cautiously optimistic about Thermo, the code name for Flash Catalyst. It promised a lot, and there were big hurdles to overcome, but what struck me about it was how much it was needed.

Before I came to Adobe, managing a team of designers and developers always brought out tons of discussions on what was needed to make the RIA development process easier and more stream-lined. It was an issue echoed by the rest of the industry. Flex, ActionScript, Flash — they are all extremely powerful, but they weren't for the timid. You needed to immerse yourself in complex code in order to make significant progress in developing sophisticated applications.

Outside of my day job, I also teach at San Francisco State University. I conduct classes on Flash Professional and ActionScript and also work with students as they build their interactive portfolios to enter into the job market.

Seeing students that are new to Flash and interactive design was an eye-opening experience for me when I saw first-hand that getting started is very difficult. So much of Flash is driven by ActionScript and with the release of ActionScript 3.0, novice and intermediate coders were confused, baffled, and frustrated. Designers that wanted to move beyond print, video pros that wanted to create interactive portfolios, and Web professionals that needed to create exciting Web sites quickly were lost. As Thermo evolved into Flash Catalyst, we worked hard to make it easy to create fun and engaging interactive Web sites, without needing to know the complexities of ActionScript and programming.

Flash Catalyst is for anyone that has a desire to create amazing, interactive Web sites or applications. Regardless if you are an experienced interactive designer, expert ActionScript or Flex programmer, or someone new to interactive design with no coding skills, Flash Catalyst is where you can take your existing skills in design and development and create interactivity like never before.

This book will help you discover all of the great capabilities of Flash Catalyst, as well as how to successfully use it in your workflows with Creative Suite and Flash Builder to create great Web sites and applications using the Adobe Flash Platform.

I would like to thank everyone on the Flash Catalyst team for all of their hard work, long hours, and dedication to deliver a great product. Every person on the team makes me proud to be working on Flash Catalyst. In addition, I want to extend my thanks to the entire Creative Suite team for their faith and dedication to creating a streamlined workflow with Illustrator, Photoshop, Fireworks, and other Creative Suite tools.

I sincerely hope that you enjoy and have fun using Flash Catalyst as much as we had making it.

Doug Winnie

Principal Product Manager
Adobe Flash Catalyst and Flash Platform Workflow

Preface

Science-fiction author Arthur C. Clarke once wrote, "Any sufficiently advanced technology is indistinguishable from magic." Surely nothing quite fits that bill as well as the Web, which will mark its 20th anniversary in 2010. It can be difficult to think of any other invention throughout history that has changed the way in which we think, communicate, and learn as quickly as has the Web.

When I was in college in the early 1990s, I was one of the few students in my residence hall with a personal computer, and I had to apply to be one of the lucky few who had his computer connected to the university's network. I can clearly recall struggling through learning the archaic command system to send even simple e-mails. Today, my seven-year-old daughter is as comfortable on a computer as is her mother, and if not for her father's insistence on taking a picture to commemorate the event, would never remember sending her first e-mail to ask a family friend a survey question for a homework assignment.

My first introduction to Flash came when I was an instructor at New Horizons Computer Learning Center in Sacramento. I had been asked to learn it so that I could eventually start teaching it. That was Flash 4, and even then, it was pretty cool: I had never imagined that it could be so easy to draw a shape and get it to move across the screen.

At the time, however, I definitely considered myself more of a designer. ActionScript, even in its fairly primitive 1.0 incarnation in Flash 4, was something to be feared and avoided if possible.

Several years later, when Macromedia first coined the term *Rich Internet Application* and began talking about moving Flash beyond animation and annoying banner ads and into the world of full-featured application development, I was comfortable enough with ActionScript and the ideas behind it that I was no longer intimidated. However, like almost everyone else who made a stab at working with those early Flash applications, I was sorely disappointed by how difficult it was to create them in Flash. Surely there had to be an easier way?

Macromedia realized that they had now effectively split the Flash community in two:

- The designers on the one side continued to want to use the tool as it had been originally intended and wanted to continue to create artwork and animation.
- The developers desired ever-better scripting tools and ever-easier development environments.

To their credit, the folks at Macromedia realized fairly early on that one tool could never hope to satisfy both groups, and thus was born Flex: Flash for developers. Like most software platforms, Flex had some issues at first, but by the time Adobe released Flex 3, it was a mature application development platform.

Preface

Every year, Adobe hosts an annual developer's conference called MAX. At MAX 2007, held in Chicago, Adobe first showed the world an exciting new tool, at the time code named Thermo. I wasn't able to attend MAX that year, but I can clearly remember the almost-immediate buzz online about Thermo. Like many others, I watched, over and over, shaking videos taken from the audience of this cool new tool that would forever revolutionize the way Flex applications were designed.

It's amazing, looking back over the two years since I first saw those quick glances of Thermo, how far it has come. Now officially rebranded as *Adobe Flash Catalyst CS5*, the greater Flex community can at last get their hands on it. I hope that everyone enjoys using it as much as I have.

Adobe sells almost all of their products these days as a part of a suite, and they like to stress how the programs work together. While products like Dreamweaver and Flash Professional may work better when used in conjunction with other programs, Catalyst is unique in that it really cannot be used alone.

Your project designs need to be created in another application (such as Illustrator or Photoshop), and the project needs to be finished somewhere else as well (such as Flash Builder). Therefore, while this book seeks to be as complete a guide to Catalyst as is possible, you will likely find that you need to rely on other resources as well to fill out your knowledge of the other programs you'll be using.

The *Adobe Illustrator CS5 Bible*, *Adobe Photoshop CS5 Bible*, and *Adobe Fireworks CS5 Bible* are each excellent resources for those design tools. Likewise, the *Flash Builder and Flex Bible* will show you what you need to know to finish your project in Flash Builder.

Acknowledgments

S ince becoming an author myself, I've started reading the acknowledgments in other books, as I'm always curious to see who other authors take this space to thank. There are two over-riding themes on which we all agree.

First, books, whether they be novels or technical guides, cannot happen without a dedicated team of editors and staff at the publishing company. On each of my books, I have been fortunate to be able to work with a fantastic team of professionals at Wiley, and this time was no exception. Stephanie McComb first approached me to write this Bible and shepherded me through the early stages of the book, and to her I am grateful. Once the writing got underway, Chris Wolfgang took over as the project editor, and I can say without any hesitation at all that this would never have come together without her hard work and dedication to the project. I need to particularly thank her for her patience through some of the project's more trying moments.

One particular challenge in writing a book on a brand-new product is finding someone with the expertise to be the technical editor. When I was asked whom I thought might be a good choice, one name came to mind immediately, so I am likewise grateful to TJ Downes for his help and dedication in finding and correcting my errors, as well as for his friendship.

The second theme I read from other authors and that I find holds true is that books cannot be written without love and support from the author's friends and family. I am very fortunate to have a loving and most important, an understanding wife who is okay with me needing to write through weekends, and likewise two beautiful kids who understand that sometimes daddy needs to work on Saturday.

The Flash Catalyst team at Adobe is an amazing group of people. Steve Heintz took time out of his schedule to call and personally answer some questions about the product, and for that I am eter-nally grateful. Ryan Stewart, Adam Cath, Andrew Shorten, Doug Winnie, and the rest of the team have been patient with me, even when I bombard them on Monday morning with a weekend's worth of questions, and have provided invaluable insight. If Catalyst changes the way you work as much as I think it will, these are the people to thank.

Richard Buikema at New Horizons was once an incredible boss; now, he's a good friend, and I need to thank him for opening up a classroom to give me a quiet place to write.

Brian and Laura Armstrong and Olen Sanders generously agreed to appear in pictures in the fake maga-zines used in this book's tutorials, and Jake Stroh provided useful insight on Fireworks; they all have my deep appreciation. Leslie Gallagher continues to be one of the most fantastic friends anyone could have.

Finally, I need to thank Ruth De Jesus. Ruth graciously agreed to design the Magazines Direct site used as the project in the book, and she did an amazing job. If you need design work, I can't recommend Ruth enough; contact her via her Web site at www.impetuswebdev.com or www.ruthdejesus.com.

Contents at a Glance

Contents

Contents

Contents

Contents

Contents

Contents

Contents

Contents

Contents

Introduction

Creating beautiful graphic designs and user interfaces is an obviously creative pursuit that combines a large degree of both natural talent and learned skills. Writing code, however, is every bit as creative a process as design. There is no one right way to write code.

Design and coding, however, require quite different skillsets and talents, and while there are some whose talent at design matches their talent at code, most find they excel at one or the other.

Flash Catalyst CS5 seeks to bridge the gap between the two, providing a means by which designers can utilize their skills in Illustrator and Photoshop to create rich designs, but avoid having to get deeply into what they likely consider the fairly intimidating world of writing code. Catalyst also provides a means by which coders who may not be great at design — who likely consider Illustrator to be every bit as intimidating as their design counterparts think of Flash Builder — can take the designs created by others and implement them in their projects.

Flash Catalyst CS5 is the first version of this product. Many, if not most, people today are used to working in programs that have been around for years, if not decades. They are used to finding a lot of people who have a deep understanding of the program and what it can do, and used to finding many resources available for it. As the new kid in the Adobe product line, Catalyst does not yet have that user base or the number of resources available as of yet.

You are getting in on the ground floor of this exciting new product.

Who the Book Is For

Flash Catalyst CS5 is a product designed for people with little or no skill or desire to write code. It is aimed at designers — those people who love and use Illustrator and Photoshop — and provides them with a means by which they can create user interfaces for Rich Internet Applications without needing to know or learn code or the Flex framework. This book is targeted at precisely the same audience.

Catalyst does not let you edit code, so you will not find page after page of code samples here. Rather, Catalyst allows you to draw shapes, import images, add animation, and work with sound and video. This book, therefore, includes chapters on drawing shapes, importing images, adding animation, and working with sound and video.

How the Book Is Organized

This book is organized into six main parts:

- **Part I:** Rich Internet Applications and the Flash Platform
- **Part II:** Designing the Application
- **Part III:** Creating the Application in Catalyst
- **Part IV:** Exporting Projects into Flash Builder 4
- **Part V:** Build a Complete Project
- **Part VI:** Appendixes

In Part I, you'll find chapters that start you off right by letting you know what a Rich Internet Application is, why the Flex Framework was created, and how Catalyst fits in to the big picture. This part also discusses the other applications which you'll need in order to create Catalyst projects.

Part II gets you started in designing projects. Chapter 4 shows how you can use the drawing tools provided in Catalyst to create basic wireframes of applications, while Chapters 5, 6, and 7 take provide introductions to Adobe Illustrator, Adobe Photoshop, and Adobe Fireworks and show you how to use these programs to create the initial assets you will use in your Catalyst project.

Part III pulls those design assets together. In Chapter 8, you will learn how to import designs created in Photoshop and Illustrator into Catalyst. In Chapter 9, you begin converting those imported assets into *components*, the building blocks of Flex projects. Chapter 10 shows how to create *view states*, the pages that make up a complete Rich Internet Application, while Chapter 11 shows how you can leverage the fact that your project will ultimately end up in Flash Player to add animation. Chapter 12 teaches how to add sample data to your project, and Chapter 13 discusses adding Flash movies, sound, and video.

Part IV switches gears and moves into Flash Builder to show you how to complete the project. Chapter 14 introduces Flash Builder and the Flex framework, while Chapter 15 shows how to move the project from Catalyst to Builder. Chapter 16 shows how to return the project to Catalyst for further design work, and Chapter 17 discusses other export options. Chapter 18 introduces you to AIR, the Adobe Integrated Runtime, which allows you to use Catalyst as a part of a design process for creating desktop applications.

Part V provides a step-by-step tutorial for creating a complete project, from start to finish. Its chapters take you from creating the initial design in Illustrator to the completed project in Flash Builder, with detailed instructions and illustrations for each step along the way.

The files needed to follow along in each chapter, including Illustrator and Photoshop design files and Catalyst and Flash Builder Projects are included on the books Web site (`www.wiley.com/go/flashcatalystbible`). Completed versions of the project are also included so that you can see where you are going while you work.

Dive Into Flash Catalyst CS5

Most popular software used by professionals today has been around for a long time. Office workers spend large parts of their days using Microsoft Word, Excel, and PowerPoint. Those applications were introduced more than a quarter-century ago between 1983 and 1985.

Graphic designers may spend their days using Adobe Illustrator, which was developed in 1987, and Adobe Photoshop, which celebrated its 20th anniversary in a gala event in San Francisco in February, 2010. Even the Web, considered by many to still be new, will be about 20 years old by the time you read this, having been first developed in 1990.

Thus, while users may feel that they are constantly playing catch-up with a seemingly endless string of new versions, rarely do they have the opportunity to work with a brand-new application. If you are reading this book, however, that is precisely what you are contemplating: working with a never-before-seen application.

Using mature products that have existed since before many people began using computers, and in fact since before some of today's users were even born, has advantages, chief among them a strong base of experts who can teach and guide users through the program.

While Adobe marketing has decided to brand this new application as Flash Catalyst CS5, you should remember that it is in fact Flash Catalyst 1.0. While Catalyst will, in time, enjoy the same user base as more, shall we say, mature software, today you are no more or less an expert in the program than practically anyone else who is using it. By learning Catalyst now, you are truly getting in on the ground floor, a rare opportunity for many in today's software environment.

Rich Internet Applications

In 2002, software company Macromedia released new versions of its core design tools:

- Dreamweaver
- Flash
- Fireworks

These latest versions of the programs were designed to work together to create a new paradigm in Web design, which the company termed *Rich Internet Applications*, or RIAs.

The development of the Web is credited to a physicist named Tim Berners-Lee. He did not develop it with the idea of creating a tool by which companies could sell books or friends could reconnect with high school acquaintances. Rather, he was building a system for his fellow physicists that would allow them to more easily exchange research data.

This original Web, therefore, did not focus on design or interactivity. Under Berners-Lee's vision, the presentation of Web pages would be left largely to the software used to display these pages, software that we would eventually come to know as browsers.

Berners-Lee knew that his creation had widespread potential, well beyond the insular world of particle physics, and yet he also knew that a closed or proprietary system would be unlikely to succeed, so he opened his technology to anyone who wanted to develop on it. Over the course of the next few years, the Web grew fairly quickly out of its infancy until in 1994 and 1995, companies began to realize the enormous marketing potential offered by the Web.

Yet, despite, or perhaps because of its open nature and extremely quick adoption, the Web still suffered from its original lack of true design capabilities. Many companies and individuals expanded on HTML, the language of Web pages, or built new tools such as Dreamweaver to try to overcome these limitations.

Nonetheless, it was this lack of true design capability and the continuing struggle by developers to enable easy cross-platform and cross-browser Web interactivity that led Macromedia to conceive of RIAs.

At the heart of the RIA idea was Flash Player. Already a mature product, Flash Player was by 2002 the most widely installed software in the world — a position it holds to this day. However, most designers and indeed almost all users saw Flash as a cool means by which you could build animation for your site, but little else.

Macromedia, however, saw Flash as an ideal tool by which developers could create engaging, truly interactive applications for the Web, and because applications in Flash Player run the same on every operating system, developers could conceivably code once; they would not have to struggle through browser-specific issues or hacks like their Web design brethren or create multiple complete copies of their applications like desktop application developers.

While many were quick to embrace the idea behind RIAs, Macromedia did face one large obstacle. If one was to build an application targeting Flash Player, one had to work in Flash Professional. This program, however, was — and is — a very powerful design tool. Developers found building applications that did not primarily rely on animating artwork difficult at best.

Macromedia was thus faced with a choice: It could convert Flash Professional into a development and coding tool, and thereby abandon its large Flash designer user base, or leave it for designers and create something new altogether for developers. Fortunately, it chose this latter option, and thus was born the Flex framework.

Every Flex developer must constantly answer the question, "What is Flex?"

I have found that the simplest answer is the one based on its history: Flex is, at its core, merely Flash for developers. Flex provides a base of code developers can draw upon to create RIAs. Most if not all of the work in building a Flex application is done in code, using two primary languages:

- **MXML.** An XML-based tag language.
- **ActionScript.** The scripting language originally introduced into Flash over a decade ago.

While Flex opened a whole new world of exciting development opportunities and freed those developers who fear drawing tools and timelines from having to deal with those or other designer issues, it at the same time suffered from its lack of a design base.

While creating beautiful applications was certainly possible in Flex, the nature of those persons who tended to devote the time and energy to becoming a Flex developer made artistically designed applications the exception rather than the rule. Generally, as reluctant as developers were to explore complementary color schemes, designers tend to be just as reluctant to write code. Most people who spend their days performing magic in Illustrator or Photoshop would rather volunteer for jury duty or go get their driver's licenses renewed before they'd consider sitting in front of a code editor and writing 500 lines of MXML and ActionScript.

Adobe, after purchasing Macromedia in 2005 and adopting the Flex framework, recognized this problem. To many, Adobe has long been a design company, so few people were surprised when it announced plans in 2007 to develop a new application that would bridge that gap.

The Flash Catalyst Workflow

As I will make clear through the course of this book, Catalyst is fairly unique in that it's not designed as a true stand-alone application. While it's theoretically possible to create a complete application in Catalyst, few if any serious users will take that approach. Rather, Catalyst is designed as a kind of *middle-ware*, sitting between Adobe's design-oriented programs on the one hand and the developer-centric Flex framework on the other. Therefore, a typical Catalyst workflow both begins and ends outside of the program.

When you create an RIA in the Flex framework and plan to use Catalyst, you will need to begin with a design comp. This is a visual representation of your application's interface. The design will almost always be created in one of Adobe's two oldest applications:

- Illustrator
- Photoshop

Only once this design is complete will you be ready to open it in Catalyst, which you will use to begin the process of converting the static drawing into an RIA. Then you will need to finish the programming of the application in Flash Builder, Adobe's tool for working with Flex applications.

By separating these three parts of the workflow (creating a design comp in Photoshop or Illustrator, converting the drawings in Catalyst, and programming in Flash Builder) into three or four distinct applications, Adobe has built in to the system the possibility of dividing the work among specialists.

If you are a designer who avoids code as much as possible, you can take on the task of creating the design comp in the familiar environs of Illustrator. On the other hand, if you're a developer whose artistic skills begin and end with simple stick figures, you can have someone else create the design while you focus on your strength, writing code.

In this situation, the designer can easily bring his or her comp into Catalyst and convert it into the beginnings of a Flex application, as you not only do not have to write code in Catalyst but, in fact, you cannot write code in the program. Alternately, the developer can take the designer's Illustrator file, open it in Catalyst, and simply convert the art into the components she needs for the application. While Catalyst has much more of a designer feel to it, either group can use it.

If you happen to be the kind of person who is as comfortable with design as with code, then nothing will stop you from creating the entire project, start to finish, yourself. You merely need to begin with your design, use Catalyst to convert it to Flex, and then finish with programming in Flash Builder.

Introducing Adobe Illustrator

The initial design of your application will be done in a graphics tool. Catalyst supports importing designs from either Adobe Illustrator or Adobe Photoshop.

Illustrator, long the industry standard for vector-based design, provides a slightly richer toolset for creating designs from scratch than does Photoshop, which is a raster-based tool more suited for manipulating existing graphics such as photographs. Therefore, while a chapter of this book is devoted to creating designs in Photoshop, the focus here will be on working with Illustrator.

Why not Fireworks?

Adobe's third primary design tool, Fireworks, provides many of the same tools for creating comps as Illustrator. However, for technical reasons, Adobe was unable to provide the same importing and editing capabilities between Catalyst and Fireworks in this release as it did between Catalyst and Illustrator. In CS5, you can still import Fireworks-created documents, but you don't have as many options for working with the design as you do when dealing with those created in Illustrator or Photoshop.

The primary stumbling block was that Fireworks, a program Adobe acquired from Macromedia, has a radically different underlying architecture than Illustrator and Photoshop. The limited Fireworks-Catalyst workflow is likely to change over time, however.

Illustrator interface

Any introduction to Illustrator needs to begin with the interface.

1. **Launch the program.** The Start screen appears.
2. **Open an existing file or create something new (see Figure QS.1).** When beginning work on a Catalyst project, you should select Web Document.

FIGURE QS.1

The Illustrator Start screen

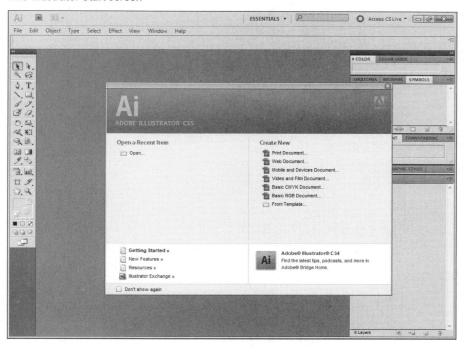

3. **Set up the basic parameters of your document.** Of particular importance are the width and height of the project (see Figure QS.2). Hopefully, you will have had discussions with everyone involved in the project — in particular, the developer and the client — as to what these dimensions should be.

FIGURE QS.2

Setting the dimensions of the project

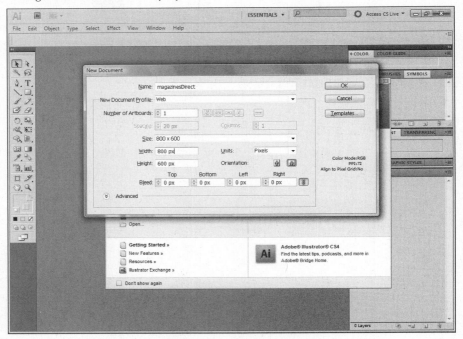

Cross-Reference
Chapter 5 presents a more detailed explanation of the other options in this dialog box.

4. **Click OK to save your settings.** You are ready to begin creating your design.

Illustrator artboard

The main area in which you work in Illustrator is the *artboard*. You can select tools from the Tools panel, which by default appears along the left edge of the screen. Additional options and controls are located in the other panels, most of which are grouped on the right edge of the screen (see Figure QS.3).

You are basically free to use whatever tools exist within Illustrator to create your design comp. For the most part, your imagination is the only limit as to what you can design.

One of the ideas behind the creation of Catalyst and the changes to the Flex framework that have been made to support it is that applications do not have preconceived notions as to what things should look like. Buttons, for example, need not be boring, gray rectangles, but can instead be drawn however you like. Of course, you should not sacrifice usability for making things cool: A button may be made up of blue brush strokes, but it still needs to be obvious that it is something with which the user can interact.

The Illustrator artboard

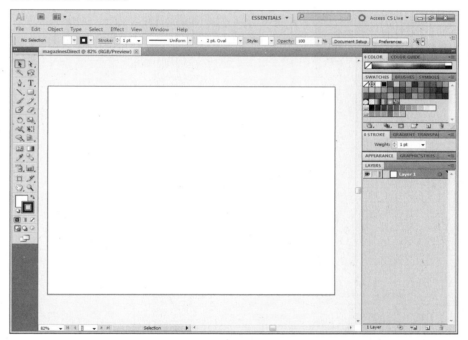

Illustrator tools

Illustrator contains a host of drawing tools, including paint brushes, shape tools, and line tools. All of them draw vectors shapes that can be freely edited.

Illustrator's most powerful tool is the Pen tool. The Pen allows you to create precise lines and curves (see Figure QS.4). While the Pen can be somewhat difficult to learn and master, once you are comfortable with it, you will likely find that it is also perhaps Illustrator's most useful tool.

In addition to the Pen tool, Illustrator contains a Paint Brush tool. The brush's biggest advantage is not the ease with which you can draw by simply clicking and dragging with the mouse, but rather the fact that you can use it with a wide variety of brush tips to create anything from simple strokes to painted shapes (see Figure QS.5).

Illustrator ships with nearly 30 brush libraries, each containing from a few brushes to dozens of them (see Figure QS.6).

FIGURE QS.4

Drawing shapes with the Pen tool

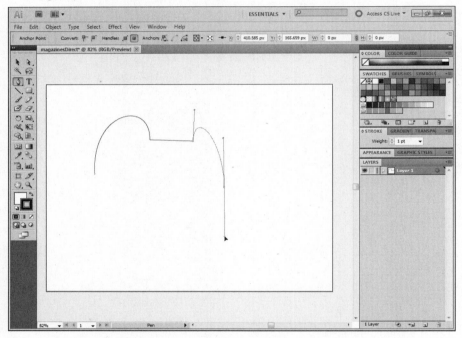

FIGURE QS.5

Drawing complex patterns with the Brush tool

Not everything need be drawn by hand. Illustrator contains a large set of shape tools that you can use to draw rectangles, rounded rectangles, ellipses, polygons, starts, and flares. With each of these tools, you can create a shape by merely clicking and dragging on the artboard (see Figure QS.7). You can adjust the fill and stroke size and color either before you draw a shape or after.

FIGURE QS.6

Selecting a new brush library

FIGURE QS.7

Drawing basic shapes

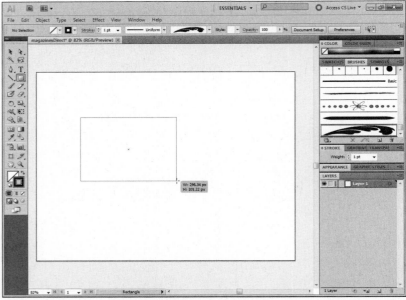

Importing into Illustrator

While most of your work in Illustrator will involve drawing new art, you can also import images for use in your design. Illustrator supports almost every image file format, including common image formats such as JPG and GIF and native files from other Adobe applications, including Photoshop PSD and Fireworks PNG files.

You can import files by following these steps:

1. **Choose File ⇨ Place (see Figure QS.8).**
2. **Select the image to import.**
3. **Click on the artboard where you want the image to appear (see Figure QS.9).** The image appears on the artboard. Its top left corner will be at the point at which you clicked.

FIGURE QS.8

The Place command

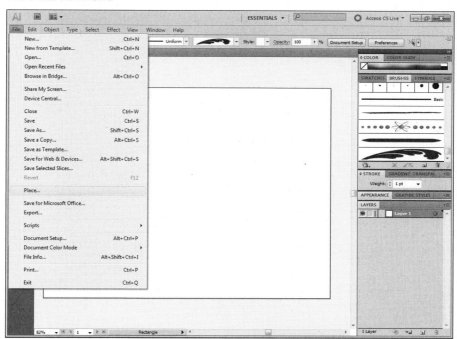

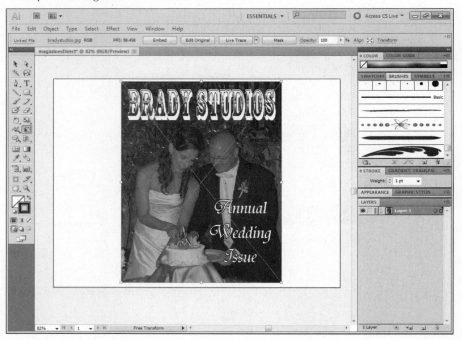

FIGURE QS.9

An imported image on the artboard

Using layers in Illustrator

Illustrator designs become quite complex very quickly. Therefore, it is important to keep the file organized with layers. By placing each piece of your design on its own layer, you can keep the art separated into editable parts.

Layers are automatically created with each new shape you draw, and you can organize and controlled via the Layers panel (see Figure QS.10). You can move layers freely up or down to change the stacking order of objects on the artboard, rename them to be descriptive of their contents, and show and hide them as needed using the panel.

Once you complete your design, you can simply save it as an Illustrator file. You do not need to do anything special to save the file in order to import it into Catalyst (see Figure QS.11).

FIGURE QS.10

The Layers panel in a complex project

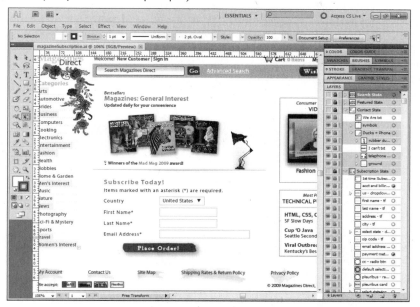

FIGURE QS.11

A completed design in Illustrator

Introducing Flash Catalyst

Once you complete your artwork, you are ready to import the piece into Catalyst and begin converting it from static art into the first stages of an RIA. Catalyst has been designed to look, feel, and behave similarly to other design tools such as Illustrator. In fact, as much as possible, Adobe's engineers borrowed names and even keyboard shortcuts from Illustrator. For example, the drawing area in Catalyst is known as the artboard, just as it is in Illustrator.

Also like Illustrator, Catalyst displays a Start screen when you first launch it (see Figure QS.12). The Start Screen provides options to create new projects from Illustrator, Photoshop or FXG files, or create a blank project into which you can draw using Catalyst's limited drawing tools. You can also open existing projects from here.

FIGURE QS.12

The Catalyst Start screen

Importing an Illustrator file into Catalyst

To import an Illustrator file to Catalyst, follow these steps:

1. **Click the option on the Start screen to create a new project from an Illustrator file.**

2. **Select the file you saved from Illustrator, which has an AI extension.** Catalyst then analyzes the file and displays a dialog box.

3. **Confirm the dimensions of the project.** These dimensions should already be set to the same values as the Illustrator file by default.

4. **Specify how Catalyst should treat objects in the file (see Figure QS.13).**

The Illustrator Import Options dialog box

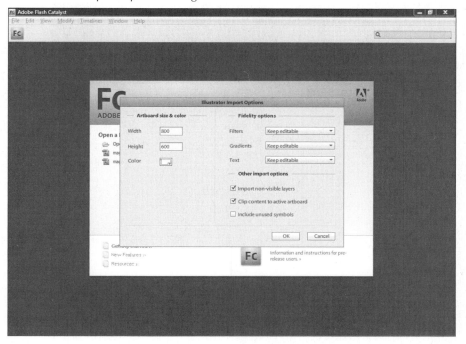

5. **Click OK in this dialog box. Catalyst imports the file onto its artboard (see Figure QS.14).** All of the layers you created in Illustrator will be converted to Catalyst layers.

   Depending on the options you selected in the Import dialog box, you should be able to move, resize, and even edit the objects on the artboard.

FIGURE QS.14

A file in Catalyst after import

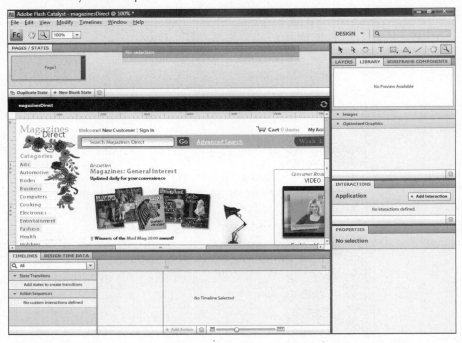

The Catalyst interface is similar to Illustrator's, albeit with fewer panels. The top panel displays the states or pages in the application. The right edge of the screen contains a toolbox, the Layers and Library panels, the Interactions panel, and the Properties panel. The Timeline and Design-Time Data panels stretch across the bottom. Floating somewhere on the screen is the heads-up display (HUD).

Note
You cannot customize the layout of panels in Catalyst.

Optimizing graphics

Your first step in beginning to work with the file will be to optimize the graphics.

Every object you see on the artboard is being represented in Catalyst by code. Most objects will take multiple lines of code, so very complicated designs could require tens of thousands of lines. You do not need to worry specifically about this code, and in fact you cannot edit it directly in Catalyst, but the fact that so much of it will likely exist is going to almost certainly slow Catalyst down.

Optimizing images is an effective countermeasure: When you optimize the image, you combine it within Catalyst into a distinct object that can be rendered more easily. You should optimize any image that does not need to be manipulated as the project runs. These would include logos and images being used as separators or merely visual flair. You can optimize an image by following these steps:

1. Choose the Select tool (the black arrow in the toolbox).
2. Select the object you want to convert.
3. Click Optimize Image in the HUD (see Figure QS.15).

Note

If you import a very large and complex Illustrator file, Catalyst is likely to run very slowly at first. This perfor-mance will improve quite dramatically as you proceed through the process of optimizing images and convert-ing objects to components. In the meantime, collapsing the Timeline panel by clicking its tab can help speed up the project.

FIGURE QS.15

Using the HUD to optimize an image

Creating components

Your next step in Catalyst is to convert objects or groups or objects to *components*. Components are the building blocks of a Flex application. Each distinct section of your application will likely need to be converted to a component.

Catalyst allows you to choose from a variety of predefined components such as buttons and data lists, but most of the time you will create custom or generic components. Just as you did when optimizing images, you define components by selecting their elements and then using the appropriate option on the HUD (see Figure QS.16).

FIGURE QS.16

Converting the main application elements into a custom component

View states

Traditional Web sites are made up of a series of pages, each representing a distinct state of the application.

Flex applications are run in a single file within Flash Player. Instead of breaking your application into separate files, you break it into states. For example, an e-commerce application in HTML would likely contain a product list page, a product detail page, a shopping cart page, and a checkout page. A similar Flex application would contain a product list state, a product detail state, a shopping cart state, and a checkout state.

You create and name states in the Pages/States panel at the top of the screen. Each state can either be a duplicate of the state to its left or a blank state. They can contain any content. You should also plan for states early in the design process, and create their assets on separate layers in Illustrator.

After importing into Catalyst, you can convert these assets into components, and then show or hide them as needed from one state to the next (see Figure QS.17).

A new state created in the application, displaying different components and layers

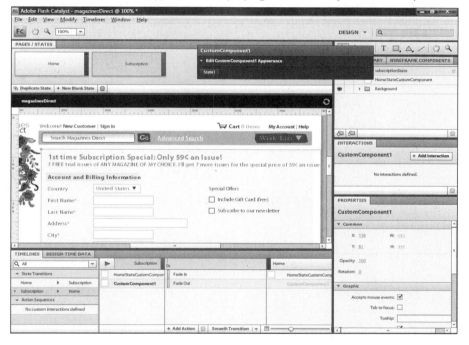

Interactions

At the beginning of this Quick Start, I described Flex as *Flash for developers*. Your application will eventually end up running in Flash Player. Therefore, any of the things you would normally expect to see and do in Flash can be done in Flex, such as how a user interacts with your application.

One fairly obvious place where clients might expect to see animation is in the transitions between states. Fortunately, Catalyst makes creating this animation easy.

State changes are most often triggered by a user action. For example, the user might click an Add to Cart button to switch to the cart state. As I mentioned earlier, you can use any artwork to create buttons; follow these steps to create a button:

1. **In Catalyst, select the artwork.**

2. **Choose Button as the component type in the HUD to create one (see Figure QS.18).** The button is created.

FIGURE QS.18

Creating a button component

3. **Use the Interactions panel to define what occurs when the user clicks it.** You can easily have the button trigger a state change by clicking Transition to State in the panel and then selecting the desired state (see Figure QS.19).

4. **Once the interaction is defined, create an animated effect to hide the elements that will be removed from the state and show those that are being added.** For example, you might have the old component slide off one edge of the screen while the new one slides in from the opposite edge.

   You begin setting up an effect like this by simply positioning the elements where you need them to either start or stop (see Figure QS.20).

FIGURE QS.19

Setting up a transition in the Interactions panel

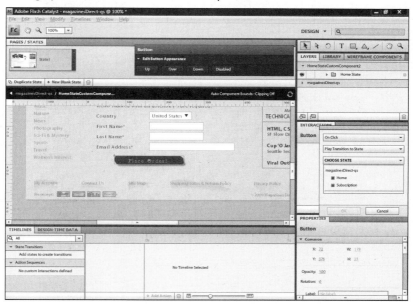

FIGURE QS.20

Getting ready to transition by moving components off the artboard

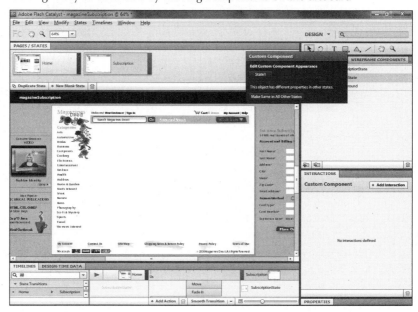

Tip

You can quickly zoom out to see the entire artboard by double-clicking the Hand tool in the tool bar in the top right corner of the screen. If you do this, make sure you select the Select tool again.

Tip

You can press and hold the Shift key while dragging the component to ensure that you drag it perfectly horizontally or perfectly vertically.

5. **Control the effects and timing of the component animation by using the tools provided by the Timelines panel (located along the bottom of the screen).** You can drag the bars that represent each component to change how long they animate and control their timing relative to other components (see Figure QS.21).

FIGURE QS.21

Using the Timelines panel

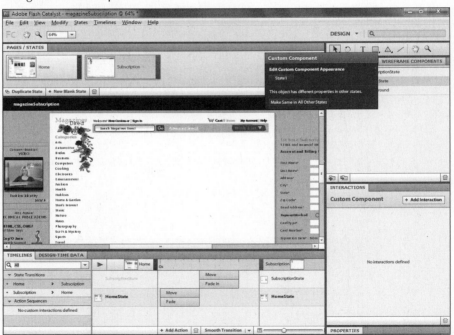

Once you complete your design work in Catalyst, you are ready to move to Flash Builder.

Introducing Flash Builder 4

Catalyst, as I mentioned, is designed to bridge the gap between the designer and the developer. In a team setting, the designer is likely to be an expert in Illustrator but know little code, while the developer would be the opposite: an expert in coding with little design skill. Flash Builder is the developer's tool in the Catalyst workflow.

While Flash Builder contains a design interface, you will spend most of your time in the program working in code. Flex applications are made up of MXML and ActionScript. The MXML primarily describes the look and feel of the application and is mostly what Catalyst generates, while ActionScript is a true programming language and is used to create the core functionality of the application.

Flash Builder is built on the Eclipse toolset. Eclipse is a powerful and popular open-source platform for developers. As Flash Builder is built for coders, it has a significantly different interface than Adobe's design tools (see Figure QS.22).

FIGURE QS.22

The Flash Builder interface

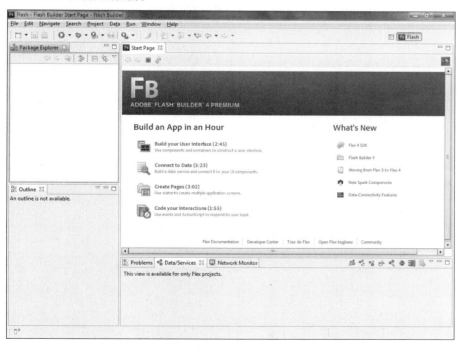

Catalyst projects are saved as FXP files, which is the main file format for Flash Builder projects as well. Therefore, you can import a Catalyst project into Flash Builder by choosing File ➪ Import Flex Project (FXP). A dialog box appears that you can use to navigate to the project you created in Catalyst (see Figure QS.23).

Once imported, you can view the project's files in the Package Explorer view or panel in the top-left corner. You can open files in either Design mode (see Figure QS.24), which provides a visual view of the project, or in Source mode, where you can work with code (see Figure QS.25).

Importing a project

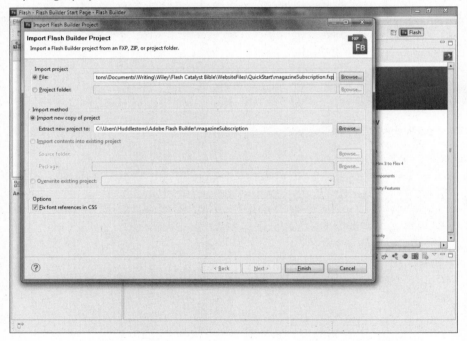

The project in Flash Builder's Design mode

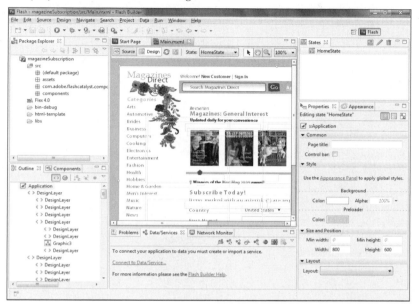

The project in Source mode

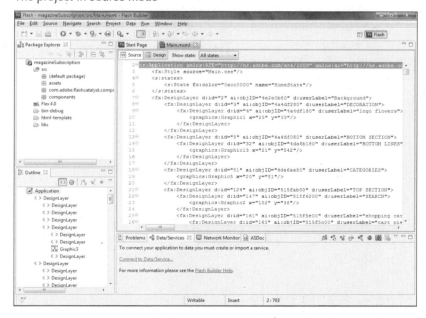

Summary

This Quick Start was designed to help you understand a little history as to why Adobe created Flash Catalyst and to see its unique workflow and reliance on other applications. You saw:

- How to create a design comp in Illustrator
- How to import the comp in Catalyst
- How to import the project into Flash Builder

Part I

Rich Internet Applications and the Flash Platform

Understanding Rich Internet Applications

The Web has changed. What began as a text-based system for scientists and academics to share information has grown into a vital part of life for many people. No longer can businesses afford to ignore it; for many, a simple collection of static HTML documents will no longer suffice. Users have come to expect a deeper, more involving Web experience; your users and your company or clients want Rich Internet Applications.

The idea of Rich Internet Applications, or *RIAs*, first came about in the early part of this century. One of the early proponents of the idea was a company named Macromedia. Macromedia developed its Flash Player technology — already the most installed piece of software in history, to provide designers and developers with a set of tools that could be used to create RIAs effectively. More important, Flash applications had the advantage of being completely cross-platform and cross-browser, unlike many other RIA technologies such as Ajax. Flash apps could be written and designed without regard to how they might perform on other machines or different browsers.

Moving Beyond HTML

Web pages are for the most part written in Hypertext Markup Language (HTML). HTML is a text-based language that allows developers to "mark up" text on their Web page with instructions as to how the Web browser should display text and other Web page items.

A brief history of the Web

HTML was invented in 1990 by Tim Berners-Lee, a scientist at the European Particle Physics Laboratory (CERN). Berners-Lee was seeking to develop a means by which CERN's visiting scientists could more easily and effectively exchange information, even across otherwise-incompatible computer systems. The fruits of his labor, first used by Berners-Lee and a colleague on Christmas Day of that year, was Hypertext Transfer Protocol (HTTP), HTML, and the first browser/editor, which he dubbed WorldWideWeb.

Over the next several years, these three inventions were expanded upon by many other Web pioneers. However, the technologies would not see widespread use until 1994, the year the Netscape Corporation released its Web browser, Navigator. Navigator was the first Web browser widely available to the public. That year and the following saw the founding of such companies as Yahoo! and Amazon and also the first hints of what the Web might become.

Unfortunately, those early days also saw the first hints of what in many ways remains the biggest challenge facing Web developers around the world: browser incompatibility.

After Netscape rejected its licensing offers, Microsoft developed its own browser, Internet Explorer (IE). Microsoft placed IE on the desktop of its soon-to-be ubiquitous Windows 9x operating system. Microsoft and Netscape would battle for the next few years for market dominance in what has become known as the Browser Wars.

This period marked a low point for Web developers, as both companies released version after version of their browsers. With each new release there were features not supported by the other company's browser. An early effort at providing basic animation on Web pages led Netscape to introduce the ill-fated `blink` tag. Microsoft responded with the equally ill-conceived `marquee` tag. As neither browser supported the other's innovation, neither tag took hold.

For some time during this period, Web design books and tutorials went so far as to advocate that developers create two separate sites; one that would display correctly in Navigator, the other in IE. Others focused on the non-too-reliable JavaScript solution of *browser sniffing* — using JavaScript to attempt to determine the user's browser and display browser-specific code.

All of the early versions of HTML shared one thing in common: a complete lack of capability to provide any interactivity for the users. As the Web grew in popularity and profitability, companies began demanding interactivity. This would include animation, games and ads or other areas of pages that could meaningfully respond to users. All of those capabilities existed for the development of desktop applications; why then, clients would ask, were they lacking on the Web?

Dynamic HTML

An early and for a time popular solution to this lack of interactivity was Dynamic HTML (*DHTML*). DHTML pages contain basic HTML markup, which can then be manipulated at runtime with JavaScript. DHTML offered designers a lot of freedom to create the kinds of interactivity their clients and bosses were demanding. For the first time, Web photo galleries could be created that allowed users to simply move a mouse over a thumbnail of an image and have a larger version of that image appear automatically.

Unfortunately, DHTML suffered from the beginning from the very problem facing everyone who tried to develop Web pages: varying browser support. If Netscape and Microsoft were at odds with their support for various HTML tags, it was nothing compared to the way they handled JavaScript.

In fact, JavaScript had been developed by Netscape, and for a time was not supported at all in Internet Explorer. Microsoft had developed a competing language known not-that-creatively as *Jscript*, which of course was not, in turn, supported by Netscape. Even after Microsoft tacitly acknowledged that JavaScript would win that battle and introduced support for it in its browser (it would eventually abandon Jscript), it continued to support JavaScript in a slightly different form than what was used by Netscape. As a result DHTML added lots of impressive features into pages, but development of it became a nightmare. At times, a developer had to write two complete scripts, one for Navigator, the other for IE, then use complicated browser-sniffing to determine which script should be run. These issues would ultimately doom DHTML.

Ajax

By the early part of this century, Netscape could no longer hold its position against Microsoft's market dominance with IE. DHTML eventually gave way to easier, more stable solutions. In large part, this was due to the end of the Browser Wars. In the late 1990s, Netscape was bought out by one-time Internet giant AOL. By the middle of the first decade of the 21st century, AOL would officially dissolve Netscape as a separate corporate entity. Navigator survives, but as little more than the official AOL browser; few if any users who are not AOL customers use Navigator.

The second factor that brought about the end of the Browser Wars was the establishment of Web standards.

Driven by a grass-roots effort of Web designers who were tired of having to deal with browser incompatibilities and having to develop and maintain separate versions of their pages, the Web standards movement advocated for a *code once* theory. HTML designers agreed that if one was willing to ignore browser-specific variations, it was possible to develop a page that would display near-perfectly across all browsers.

The advent of Cascading Style Sheets (CSS) provided a more powerful formatting platform for Web pages than had previously existed in HTML. JavaScript was also accepted as an open standard. These two progressions meant that it was at long last possible to develop pages guaranteed to display the same in the growing market of *standards-based browsers*: Minor fixes were still at times required for proper display in IE, but they were just that — minor — and more recent releases of IE promised ever-growing standards support.

At about the same time, developers noticed a little-used JavaScript method, *HTTPRequest*. They discovered that HTTPRequest could use JavaScript to make requests to Web servers. This enabled a designer to create pages that could, dynamically at runtime, retrieve data to update a small portion of a page. Prior to this, pages had to be completely refreshed every time they needed new data, a slow and inefficient process. As the data being retrieved with JavaScript was most often formatted using Extensible Markup Language(XML), this new method of feeding data into pages was termed *AJAX*, or Asynchronous JavaScript and XML.

In order to simplify the development of pages, advanced developers created Ajax libraries: code bases that enabled designers without a deep understanding of JavaScript to develop pages that used the technology. In time, libraries began to develop that had nothing to do with XML or even with retrieving data from the server, but instead merely relied on JavaScript, standards-based HTML, and CSS to dynamically redraw pages. Thus Ajax became the logical (and much more successful) successor to DHTML. Eventually, its name would be changed to reflect this reality.

Today the term Ajax is not an acronym for anything. Instead it is simply the name for this idea of using XHTML, CSS, JavaScript and XML to create interactive Web pages and for creating Rich Internet Applications.

Understanding the Flash Platform

In 1995, a small company developed *FutureSplash*, a set of tools that allowed designers to create vector-based animations. Shortly thereafter, Macromedia — at the time itself a fairly small, San Francisco-based software company — bought FutureSplash. Macromedia quickly changed the name of the animation tool to *Flash*, and began development of two separate but closely linked applications: Flash Player, a free browser plug-in to play Flash movies; and an authoring tool, known then simply as Flash, for creating those movies. In 2006, Adobe Systems purchased Macromedia bringing Flash under its umbrella.

Flash platform overview

What began as a simple animation tool has now grown into a complete platform of tools for creating animation, embedding video, and developing complete Rich Internet Applications for the browser and the desktop alike.

Flash Player

At the heart of the Flash platform is Flash Player. Still free, it remains the most-installed piece of software on Earth. As of June 2009, Flash Player is installed on more than 99 percent of all Internet-connected computers and it has started to expand into other devices as well. Adobe plans to offer support for Flash Player on smart phones by 2010 and is working on bringing it to televisions and any other device that can display Flash Player's content. Already, some digital cameras use Flash Player for their menu interface.

Flash Player relies on the ActionScript *Virtual Machine*. This technology allows Flash Player to deliver its content in exactly the same way across all browsers and operating systems. Those creating content for Flash Player never have to worry about browser and operating system incompatibilities: If a version of Flash Player exists for a platform, your content will run on it, and it will look and behave exactly the same as whichever platform you used when you created it.

Flash Player's release cycle is tied to that of Flash Professional. Thus, Flash Player 10 was released in October 2008, alongside Flash Professional CS4; Flash Player 11 is scheduled to be released in the spring of 2010 with Flash Professional CS5.

Adobe Integrated Runtime

In 2007, Adobe released Adobe Integrated Runtime (AIR). AIR allows developers to leverage existing skills and technologies to develop desktop applications. While it is possible to use a variety of languages to develop AIR applications, even including HTML and CSS, most AIR development is done with tools in the Flash platform.

Similar to Flash Player, AIR applications run within a virtual machine, thus they are not subject to operating system variations. Therefore, a developer using a Macintosh computer can create an AIR application and rest assured that it will work precisely the same way on a friend's Windows-based machine (so long as that user has AIR installed). If not, AIR can quickly be download and installed from Adobe's Web site for free. While the focus of this book is on developing Web applications, AIR development is covered in later sections.

Flash Professional CS5

Flash Professional has long been the primary design tool in the Flash platform. Originally, it was simply Flash. When version 6 (known as *MX*) was released, Macromedia began marketing both a Standard and Professional version. Two releases later, the Standard version was dropped, but the program has since maintained the Professional moniker.

Flash Professional is a full-featured, vector-based design tool. It includes a powerful set of drawing tools, as well as a timeline to create animation. Designers can import assets from other applications, including images from Adobe Photoshop or other imaging software and vector drawings from Adobe Illustrator, and then use these assets to create rich interactive environments. As of version 7, designers can also import video into Flash movies. In fact, over the last few years Flash video has become the de facto format for delivering video on the Web.

The Flex framework

As the idea of Rich Internet Applications began to take hold, Macromedia realized that Flash Professional had a problem. It was built around the idea of creating animation, not complete Web sites. While Macromedia briefly flirted with the idea of turning Flash Professional into a more developer- and code-centric tool, doing so would require sacrificing that core designer market for Flash. Therefore, Macromedia instead developed a new tool set for creating Rich Internet Applications, which would become known as *Flex*.

Flex is in many ways nothing more than an alternate way to create Flash content. Using Flash Professional, you can draw assets and animate them on a timeline. While coding support exists in Flash Professional, it is somewhat limited and no method exists to completely describe a site's assets in code. Flex, on the other hand, is entirely code-based. Flex applications are created using a combination of two languages. Visual assets are built using MXML, an XML-based markup language developed specifically for Flex. (MXML does not actually stand for anything.) Interactions, server data retrieval, and other dynamic aspects of a Flex application are built using ActionScript.

The Flex framework is open source, so anyone can download the Software Development Kit (SDK) from `http://opensource.adobe.com` and develop Flex applications for free. Anyone can also contribute bug reports and assist in the future development of the framework. The Flex framework is by necessity a key focus of this book, as Flash Catalyst is designed as a tool for the framework.

Flash Builder 4

While the Flex framework is open source and development of Flex applications is technically free, Adobe does offer a commercial Integrated Development Environment (IDE) for Flex. Originally known as Flex Builder, it was rebranded in early 2009 as *Flash Builder* to better fit the overall branding of the Flash Platform. Flash Builder is the tool of choice for professional Flex developers and indeed even for many developers creating applications in Flash Professional, due to the later tool's limited coding capabilities.

Flash Builder is built on the Eclipse toolset. Eclipse is itself an open-source IDE, used primarily by Java developers.

Cross-Reference
Flash Builder is covered in detail in Part IV.

Summary

As the Web has grown and matured so too have the needs of Web developers. Today's Web users expect more from the pages they visit, and Rich Internet Applications aim to satisfy that expectation with the help of such tools as Ajax and the Flash platform. In this chapter, you explored:

- A brief history of the Web
- The move from Dynamic HTML to Ajax
- The Flash Platform and its various tools and runtimes

Introducing Flash Catalyst

Since its creation, Adobe Flex has provided a powerful means for developers to create Rich Internet Applications. Unfortunately, many developers do not have design skills, and Flex developers had to hire an outside designer to create the visual interface for their application.

However, the developer still faced a problem once the design was complete: He would be given a visual comp (composition) of the interface, often created in a program such as Adobe Illustrator or Adobe Photoshop. Such a design format was not directly usable to the developer, as he would still need to completely render the design in the Flex framework.

Adobe designed Flash Catalyst to bridge this gap between the designer and the developer. By integrating Catalyst into their workflow, designers no longer have to pass off a mere visual representation of their design to the developer, with both parties hoping that the design could be effectively re-created in Flex.

Now, designers can do much more of the work. By importing their Illustrator or Photoshop comps into Catalyst, they can create the beginnings of the Flex project themselves, converting that design into a real, functional Flex project. This allows a design-challenged developer to focus on the backend and scripting aspects of the application.

Of course, this stereotype of the design-challenged developer and the development-challenged designer is not always the case. In fact, many people are as comfortable with visual design as they are with code. Catalyst can help them as well by providing a better workflow for implementing their designs.

Catalyst Projects

Catalyst is fairly unique in the software world in that it is designed to be a sort of middleman. Most projects will neither begin nor end in Catalyst. Instead, you or your designer will start out by designing a comp of the project in Photoshop or Illustrator and then importing that comp into Catalyst. Once your design work in Catalyst is complete, your project will most likely require further development in Flash Builder.

Note

That last point is an important one. When you work in Catalyst, you are not building a stand-alone file as you would in Photoshop or Microsoft Work. You are really building a starting point for a larger, more complex application to be built in Flex, so it's important that you understand a bit about Flex.

The Flex framework is designed around a *project-based model*. Rather than working on a single file as you would in other applications, this project-based model means that your application is going to be made up of many files. Flex projects contain multiple files. Simple projects may only contain a dozen or so files, while complex applications can potentially contain many hundreds or even thousands of files. Some of these files are the core MXML files that provide the basic code base for the application. Other files that often make up the bulk of the project are ActionScript files that provide the application with its processing logic.

The simplest way to look at these Flex-project files is this:

- MXML describes the visual components of the application (telling the application how it is supposed to look).
- ActionScript tells the application what it is supposed to do.
- Remaining Flex-project files are external assets, such as images and XML data files.

Tip

Web designers who are used to working in HTML can see several parallels here. MXML is similar in both form and function to HTML. Both languages primarily exist to define the structure and presentation layer of an application. In fact, MXML is tag based and looks very much like HTML, although MXML is actually based on XML. ActionScript is used in a Flex project somewhat like JavaScript is used in an HTML project, providing the application logic and processing code. In both cases, the application is rounded out with external asset files, such as images.

When you work in Catalyst, keep in mind that you are not really creating a Catalyst project per se; rather, you are creating the foundation for a Flex project. Ultimately, Catalyst is nothing more than a new tool to create MXML, the visual layer of the Flex application.

This is why you will see references to Catalyst *projects* throughout the program and this book, not files. Catalyst does create a project as a single file with an FXG extension, but this file is a package that hides much more complexity behind the scenes. Once you import the project into Flash Builder, you will begin to see the underlying complexity and how Catalyst really does create projects, not files.

Cross-Reference
See Part 4 for information on importing Catalyst projects into Flash Builder.

The Flash Catalyst Interface

Adobe developed Flash Catalyst on top of the Eclipse engine. Eclipse is the same powerful development environment used by Flash Builder (the primary tool for developing Flex applications), and by thousands of other developers using languages such as Java.

Eclipse is open-source, which gives those who want to use it almost complete freedom to do with it what they will. However, unlike its cousin Flash Builder, Catalyst was built with designers in mind. As such, its interface much more closely resembles other Adobe tools such as Photoshop than it does a traditional Eclipse workspace.

The Start screen

When you first launch Catalyst you will be presented with the Start screen (see Figure 2.1). This provides a useful starting point to launch a new project, import a project from another design application, or open a recent project.

FIGURE 2.1

The Start screen in Flash Catalyst provides a quick-launch point to get you started.

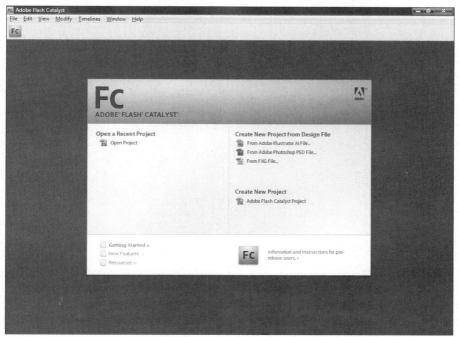

What about Fireworks and Flash Professional?

Experienced Web designers may be wondering about Adobe Fireworks. While it is possible to create Catalyst comps in Fireworks, you cannot work as easily between Fireworks and Catalyst as you can between Catalyst and Photoshop or Illustrator. See Chapter 7 for more details on using Fireworks and Catalyst together.

You might reasonably believe that Catalyst could work seamlessly with Adobe Flash Professional, as they are both obviously tools within the Flash platform. However, Adobe's concept of the Rich Internet Application workflow with Catalyst does not directly include Flash Professional, and in fact you will discover that the two have very different approaches. That is not to say, however, that some integration between the two is impossible, as is shown in Chapter 13.

If this is your first time using Catalyst, it might be easiest to select Adobe Flash Catalyst Project under the Create New Project heading. This opens a new project and allows you to jump right in to *wireframing* an application. A wire-frame is a rough design of a project, generally with simple shapes to illustrate where the project's elements will be. Wire-frames will generally lack final design elements.

Cross-Reference

For more information on wireframing in Catalyst, see Chapter 4.

Most of the time, however, you will be using one of the other options on the Start screen, like this:

1. **Choose one of the import options on the right side of the Start screen in the Create New Project from Design File section:**
   - From Adobe Illustrator AI File
   - From Adobe Photoshop PSD File
   - From FXG File
2. **To continue work on an existing project, you can do either of the following:**
   - Click the file name directly in the Open a Recent Project section.
   - Click Open Project to browse to the project file.

Cross-Reference

For more details on creating comps in Photoshop and Illustrator, see Chapters 8 and 9; for more information on exporting a project to Flash Builder, see Part IV.

The main workspace

After you open a project, whether new or from an existing design, you are presented with the main workspace in Catalyst (see Figure 2.2). As with other Adobe design programs, Catalyst relies on a series of panels to organize the workspace.

FIGURE 2.2

The Catalyst Design workspace. This view shows the workspace when opened for creating a new project.

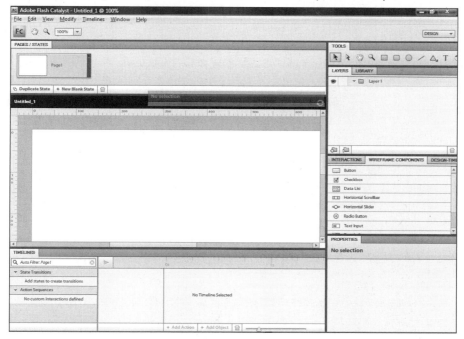

Menus at the top of the screen provide access to commonly used commands within the program. The menus provide many of the same options available in other similar design programs; I discuss their specific commands as they become relevant within the course of the book.

Design and Code workspaces

Catalyst provides two primary workspaces:

- Design
- Code

All of your actual work in the program will be done in Design. The Design workspace provides a set of panels that allow you to modify your project and its assets, as well as design a canvas to see what the project will look like when it's complete.

All Flex projects are ultimately code based. Catalyst merely provides a visual means by which designers can create this code; everything you do in Catalyst has a code equivalent. The Code workspace allows you to view the code that has been generated by the program, but you should note that it is read-only. You cannot edit code directly within Catalyst.

You can freely switch between Design and Code by choosing Window ⇨ Design Workspace or Window ⇨ Code Workspace, or by selecting one of the workspaces from the drop-down menu in the top-right corner of the screen. You can also toggle between them by pressing Ctrl-` (⌘-` for OS X).

Tip
The shortcut key is in the upper-left corner on most standard keyboards, immediately to the left of the number 1.

Design panels

Most of your work in Catalyst will be done via the panels in the Design workspace. If you are familiar with other Adobe applications such as Photoshop or Illustrator, the functionality of these panels should also be familiar:

- The Pages/States panel (see Figure 2.3), stretching along the top of the screen, provides a work area for adding and navigating to the pages in your application.
- A Tools panel in the top-right corner of the screen allows you to select Catalyst's basic drawing tools.

FIGURE 2.3

The Pages/States panel

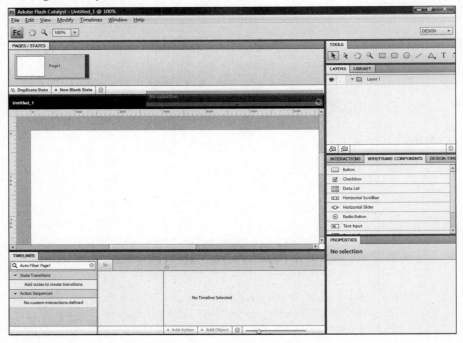

- The Layers panel immediately below the Tools panel displays the layers that make up your project (see Figure 2.4). Designers will already be using layers to organize the initial design comps in Photoshop and Illustrator, and those layers are imported and preserved in Catalyst.

  - The Library is grouped with the Layers and contains external assets such as images that will be used in the project.

FIGURE 2.4

The panels grouped along the right side of the interface include the Tools, Layers and Library, Interactions, Wireframe Components and Design-Time Data, and Properties panels.

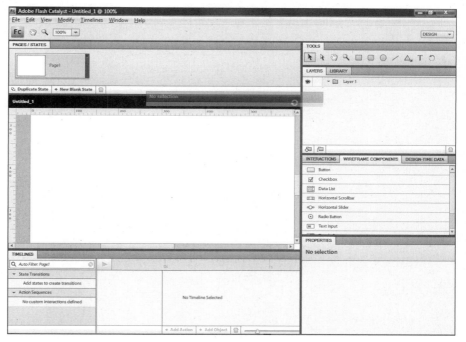

- The next set of panels also shares a group:

  - The Interactions panel is where you go to control the actions of the components in your project. For example, you can add instructions as to what happens when a user clicks a button.

  - The Wireframe Components panel contains a set of common Web tools such as buttons and sliders to use in wireframe comps in Catalyst.

  - Design-Time Data allows you to enter information to be used in repeating elements while you create the design.

- The Properties panel, the final panel on the right-hand column, allows you to modify an element that you have selected on the screen.
- The Timelines panel (see Figure 2.5), which stretches along the bottom of the screen, is your workspace for setting up animation.

FIGURE 2.5

The Timelines panel

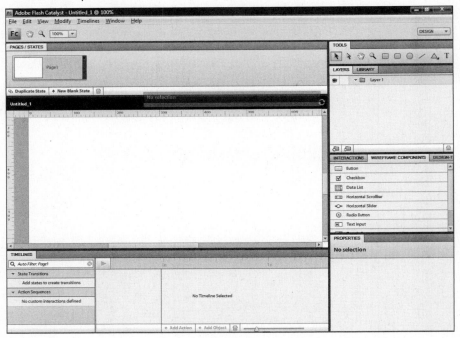

Code panels

The Code workspace provides two panels:

- Project Navigator
- Problems

The Project Navigator panel (see Figure 2.6) allows you to see the various files being created by Catalyst as you work. These are the files that make up your project and are used by the Flex developer to finalize the project in Flash Builder 4.

Cross-Reference

See Part IV for details on using Flash Builder 4 to finalize the project.

FIGURE 2.6

The Project Navigator panel is available only in the Code workspace.

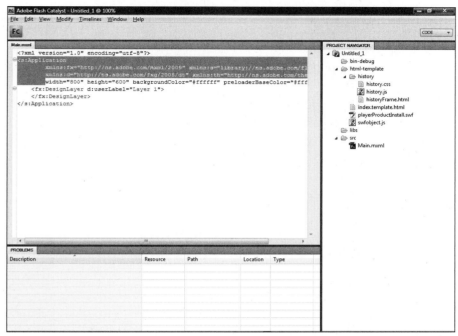

The Problems panel displays any errors that may be generated when you attempt to run the project. Errors may occur if you forget to complete a set of tasks (for example, creating a scrollbar but not specifying each of its required components).

The Heads-up display

The Heads-up display (HUD) floats on the screen whenever you are in the Design workspace. The primary purpose of the HUD is to convert selected artwork into a component such as a button or scrollbar.

You can freely move the HUD around on the screen to a location where it's easily accessible while still being out of your way. You cannot dock it on any edge of the screen — it will always be floating (see Figure 2.7).

The functionality of the HUD is duplicated. For example, you can right-click (⌘-click) an object on the screen to convert it to a component. Therefore, you may choose to disable it if you find that you constantly need to move it out of the way. The HUD can be disabled by clicking Window ➪ HUD or by using the F7 keyboard shortcut.

FIGURE 2.7

The HUD in Catalyst, showing the options to convert artwork to a component

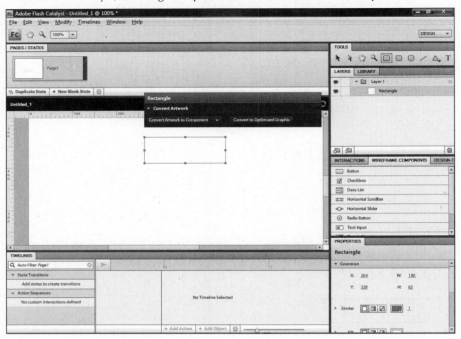

Customizing the workspace

Unlike most other Adobe design tools, Catalyst provides very little ability to customize the workspace. The panels are all set in predetermined locations and cannot be closed, moved, or rearranged.

You can, however, resize the panel groups by following these steps:

1. **Position your mouse over the edge of the panel set. A double-sided arrow appears.**
2. **Drag the arrow to resize the group.**

You have the following resizing options:

- Resize the Pages/States and Timelines panels up and down, and you can move the other panels left or right.
- Individually resize the panels along the right side up and down to provide more or less space for each.

Tip

Take caution when resizing the panels on the right. The panels can shrink to the point that some panels such as Design-Time Data disappear off the side of the screen. This can cause potential confusion when you need that panel and have forgotten that you merely resized it off the screen.

- Collapse or expand any panel by double-clicking the tab that displays the panel's name. This allows the panel to collapse so that only its tab is visible.

- If you are on a smaller screen and will not be using the Timelines panel, you can double-click on the word TIMELINES and the panel drops down to just its tab (see Figure 2.8). You can expand the panel again by double-clicking the tab.

FIGURE 2.8

Customizing the workspace. Here, the Timelines panel has been collapsed to its tab, and the panel group along the right side of the screen is resized to take up less space.

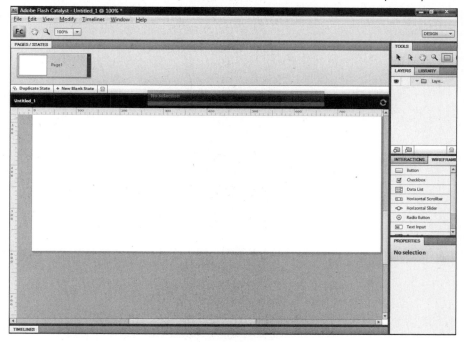

Getting Help

Help is provided within Catalyst using the Adobe Community Help system. When you click Help ⇨ Flash Catalyst Help, the Adobe Community Help application will launch. This stand-alone program, which is automatically installed with Catalyst or any other CS5 program, provides a central location for finding help.

The Community Help application displays help not only from the Adobe help files but also from community resources such as blogs. Users can also comment on help files, noting those items which might be confusing so that Adobe or other members of the community can clarify them.

Summary

Flash Catalyst has been designed to look and feel like other Adobe design products. While it provides some menu-based controls, most of the work is done through panels and the HUD. This chapter introduced the idea of creating projects (the main type of file used in Catalyst), provided an overview of that layout, and showed you how to use the application's help system.

Working with Other Applications

Today, most major software companies package their main programs into suites. Adobe is no exception. While Photoshop, Illustrator, and Acrobat are available as stand-alone products, almost everyone purchases them together as part of one of the Creative Suite packages. However, while they are purchased together, each program is designed to work alone. Adobe marketing talks about cross-suite workflows, but many a designer creates projects from start to finish in a single application such as Photoshop.

Catalyst is somewhat unique in that it's specifically designed not to work alone. It is the middleman in a Rich Internet Application (RIA) workflow. This workflow is not a marketing gimmick to sell more packaged software; it is the only way to work with Catalyst. Catalyst is not designed to be either the beginning or the end of a development process.

Catalyst was created to allow its users to take predesigned application comps and convert them into Flex projects. Therefore, in order to effectively work with Catalyst, you need other applications to sit at both ends of the workflow — design tools in which you create those comps and a development tool to finalize the project.

Adobe Creative Suite 5 Design Tools

Adobe's Creative Suite provides an integrated set of professional design tools. The main applications that will be used by Catalyst designers are Illustrator,

Photoshop, and Fireworks. Each will be discussed in-depth in later chapters, while this section will introduce new users to those elements that are shared by all three.

The CS5 Interface

Photoshop, Illustrator, and Fireworks all share many similarities in their interfaces (See Figures 3.1, 3.2, and 3.3). If you are comfortable using one, you will generally find that the learning curve for the others is dramatically lower. The primary Photoshop interface can be intimidating to the uninitiated.

FIGURE 3.1

The Photoshop CS5 interface

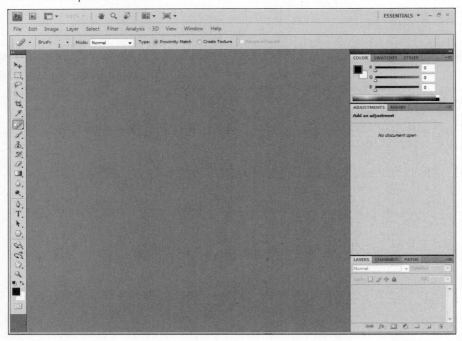

With almost 25 panels and close to 70 tools, many beginning Photoshop users become quickly overwhelmed by the sheer scope of the application. Illustrator has over 50 panels and 74 tools. Each program can take years to fully master.

FIGURE 3.2

The Illustrator CS5 interface

The focus of this book is on Flash Catalyst. There is no way, and no reason, to attempt to present a comprehensive overview of Photoshop, Illustrator, Fireworks, or Flash Builder here. Rather, this section is intended to provide a general overview of each software program.

Cross-Reference

Chapters 5, 6, and 7 delve deeper into each program, but with a focus only on those tools needed for creating comps for Catalyst.

Cross-Reference

See the Photoshop CS5 Bible, the Illustrator CS5 Bible, and the Fireworks CS5 Bible, all published by Wiley, for a much more comprehensive look at each program.

FIGURE 3.3

The Fireworks CS5 interface

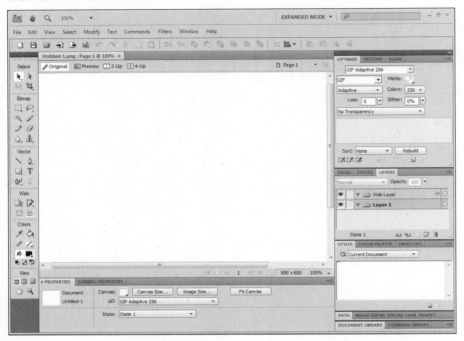

Tools

Photoshop, Illustrator, and Fireworks all group their main tools in the toolbox that runs along the left side of the screen (see Figure 3.4). Each program organizes its tools slightly differently, but all follow the same basic pattern of organizing them into groups based on what the tools do.

Not every tool is immediately available when viewing the toolbox. There are simply too many. If Adobe attempted to display all of the tools, the toolbox would be so large it would not leave room for the document. Therefore, each program groups certain related tools together. You can access the hidden tools by pressing and holding the mouse on any tool that displays a small arrow in its bottom right corner.

You can access each tool in a program via a single-key shortcut. For example, you can activate the Move, or Selection, tool in all three by pressing V on your keyboard. You can select the Zoom tool by pressing Z. These shortcuts are displayed next to the tool's name that appears when you mouse over, but do not click on, a tool.

FIGURE 3.4

The toolboxes, from left to right: Photoshop, Illustrator, and Fireworks

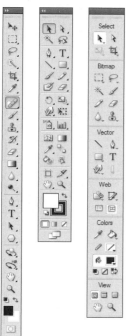

Panels

Almost all of your work in Photoshop, Illustrator, and Fireworks is done in panels. These panel sets are fully customizable. You can expand them so that they are visible (but also take up the most space, as seen in Figure 3.5) by clicking the small white double arrow in the top-right corner of the panel column.

You can also be collapse panels by clicking the same button, at which point they only display their icon and the panel's name. You can access the panel by simply clicking on either the name or the icon. If you need even more space, you can click and drag your mouse from the far-left edge of the panels and collapse them further to *iconic mode*, where only the icons are displayed (as shown in Figure 3.6).

You can access any panel that is not currently open via the program's Window menu, as shown in Figure 3.7. Simply click on a panel name in the menu to open it. A panel with a check mark next to its name indicates that it is already open and will close if selected.

FIGURE 3.5

The panels fully expanded in Photoshop

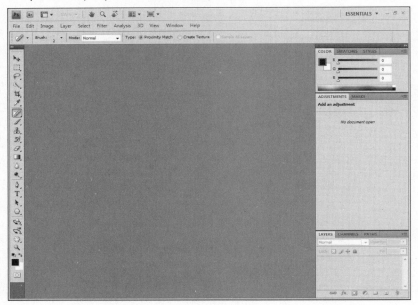

FIGURE 3.6

The panels in iconic mode in Fireworks

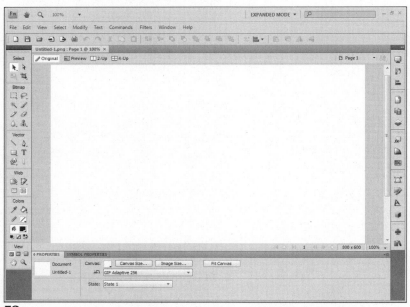

The Window menu in Illustrator, showing some panels to be open — those with check marks — and the rest closed

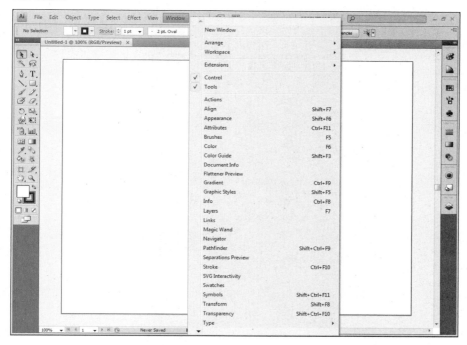

Workspaces

The arrangement of panels with the programs' interface is known as a *workspace*. The applications come with a variety of workspaces and allow you to customize your own as well (see Figure 3.8). You can access workspaces via the Workspace menu near the top-right corner of the application. You can freely switch between workspaces as you work.

The panels that appear by default in most of the workspaces are grouped together and docked, primarily along the right-hand side of the screen. You can undock any of these panels by simply dragging its tab away from the other panels. Once undocked, panels can be freely grouped and re-docked, either back along the right side of the screen or along the left and bottom edges.

Some experimentation is necessary to discover the arrangement of panels that best suits your needs. Once you have a panel arrangement that you like, you can click on the workspace dropdown list at the top of the screen and save your workspace, making it available at any time in the future.

You may discover that you need multiple workspaces, as some panel arrangements are better suited to some tasks than others. You can save as many workspaces as you need.

FIGURE 3.8

A custom panel arrangement in Fireworks. New panels have been opened, and panels have been moved to new locations on the screen.

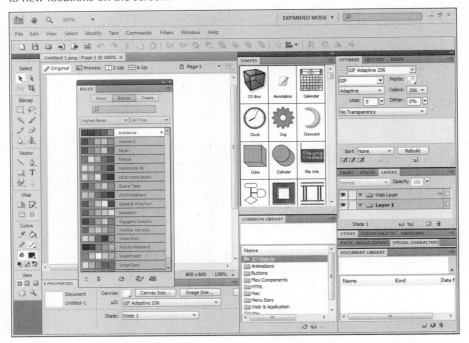

Choosing Your Comp Tool

You can create Catalyst comps using Photoshop, Illustrator, or Fireworks. The one you choose ultimately comes down to the program with which you are most familiar.

Vector versus raster graphics

You can create computer graphics in either of the following formats:

- Raster
- Vector

Raster graphics are made up of pixels. If you think of your computer screen as a large sheet of graph paper, each square of the graph is a pixel. By filling in each square with a color, you can create full-color images. However, these images are dependent on the resolution at which they were created. In order to double the size of the image, each colored pixel needs to expand to fill four squares or pixels; quadrupling the size of the image forces each pixel to fill eight pixels, and so on. Eventually, these ever-expanding squares will be noticeable in the image, causing the file to become *pixilated*. In addition, each of these size increases has a proportional impact on file size: Doubling the pixel dimensions of an image roughly quadruples the file size. It is therefore impossible to resize a raster-based image without affecting the file size and quality.

Vectors are created using a radically different approach. Rather than filling in squares, vectors define points and then use mathematical algorithms to calculate a line or path between the points. The path can either be straight or curved, and the space between the points can be filled with color. In a vector image, resizing is accomplished by moving the two points either farther apart or closer together and recalculating the math. Therefore, you can freely resize vector images without impacting either the file size or the quality of the image.

The ability to easily scale vectors might lead you to suspect that they are superior, but you should understand that they also have a distinct disadvantage from rasters. The area between points in a vector graphic can only be filled with a single color or gradient. Raster images, on the other hand, can change color from one pixel to the next. Therefore, rasters are *continuous-tone* images — for example, images such as photographs that may contain thousands or even millions of colors. Vectors, on the other hand, tend to be images that have large areas filled with single colors, such as illustrations.

Most graphics applications are either vector based or raster based. Adobe Illustrator was originally designed as a vector-based application, but today it contains a significant number of tools to work with rasters. Photoshop, on the other hand, was designed as a raster tool. But just as Illustrator now contains raster tools, Photoshop likewise contains many vector tools. All text is rendered in Photoshop using vectors, as are paths and shapes.

Tip
People new to graphics design often wonder about the difference between Photoshop and Illustrator. At its most basic level, it simply comes down to this: Photoshop is for creating and editing rasters, while Illustrator is for vectors.

Flex projects are designed to work in Flash Player. Catalyst creates Flex projects, so as you work in Catalyst, you are in essence designing a project for Flash Player. From its original version, Flash has been a vector-based tool; by extension, that means that Flash Player is essentially a vector-based display engine. However, it is a vector-based engine that has no trouble displaying raster-based images.

Adobe Flash Builder 4

Adobe Flash Builder 4 sits at the other end of the Catalyst development workflow, opposite the comp tools, as the endpoint in the application development process. You cannot begin the process in Flash Builder, as there is no way to import Builder projects into Catalyst. Instead, the Catalyst designer plans to hand off the project to a Flex developer, who then uses Builder to complete the development process.

As a Catalyst designer, it may not be important that you know or even own Flash Builder. Certainly, one-stop shops — designer/developers who wish to be able to deliver complete Flex projects to clients will need to understand and use both.

Many organizations, however, will likely employ designers to work on the comps in Photoshop, Illustrator, and Fireworks, and then take those comps into Catalyst, while separate developers will be responsible for taking the complete Catalyst projects and finalizing them in Flash Builder, as shown in Figure 3.9.

Flash Builder, like Catalyst, is built on the Eclipse development toolset. The Catalyst team at Adobe has gone out of its way to make Catalyst look and feel like Photoshop, Illustrator, and Fireworks and the other Creative Suite tools.

However, working in Flash Builder is a very different experience. Longtime developers will likely feel comfortable in Flash Builder; more comfortable than they will when being introduced to a program such as Illustrator. Designers may be intimidated by the code- and project-centric environment provided as a part of Flash Builder.

FIGURE 3.9

A project open in Flash Builder 4

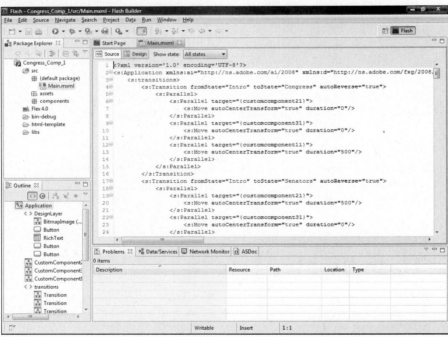

Cross-Reference

Flash Builder is covered in detail in Part V.

Summary

In this chapter, you were introduced to the basics of the other tools that you will be using alongside Catalyst. You learned:

- The similarities of Photoshop, Illustrator and Fireworks
- The differences between vector and raster graphics
- How to choose the right design tool
- The basics of Flash Builder 4

Part II

Designing the Application

Wireframing an Application in Flash Catalyst

C atalyst provides a few basic drawing tools. These are not designed to provide you with a complete drawing application; rather, they allow you to wireframe an application.

Wireframing is the process of visually laying out the basic framework of your application. In Catalyst, you can draw shapes and add common Flex components such as buttons and datagrids — features that the other Adobe design tools may lack.

The wireframe tools allow you to create an initial visual representation of your application. From there, you can move to Illustrator, Photoshop, or Fireworks to finalize the design before returning to Catalyst to create the actual project.

IN THIS CHAPTER

Creating a new Catalyst project

Using the Selection, Direct Select, Hand, and Zoom tools

Using the Drawing tools

Using the Transform tool

Understanding layers

Working with blend modes

Adding wireframe components

Running a project

Saving a project

Creating a New Wireframe Project

When you first launch Catalyst, you are presented with the Start screen (see Figure 4.1). If you want to wireframe your application, follow these steps:

1. **Select the Create New Project option in the lower-right corner.** A dialog box appears.

2. **In this dialog box, give the project a name (see Figure 4.2).** This will eventually be the name of the FXP file that Catalyst creates for the project, so be sure that it is a memorable name.

FIGURE 4.1

The Catalyst Start screen

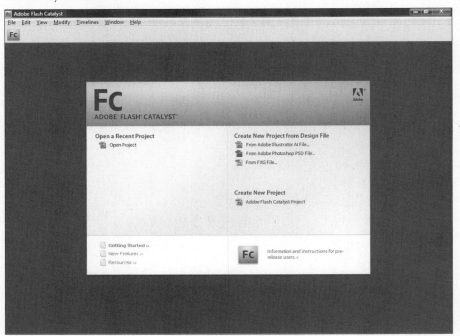

FIGURE 4.2

The New Project dialog box

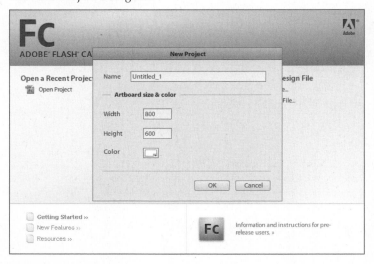

Sizing Your Projects for Display Online

There is no absolutely correct size to use for your projects. Most Catalyst projects are designed for display on the Web, and therefore must display in a browser. However, there is no way for you to accurately know the size of your user's browser. JavaScript can be used to detect the user's screen resolution, but many Web designers fail to realize that the screen resolution and the browser size are not necessarily the same, as many users do not maximize their browser. Even if you can detect the screen resolution and make the false assumption that that is the browser size, there is no simple way to use that information to have Flash Player resize the application to fit.

You need to set the application size based on your best judgment. Consider the application design: You do not want your application to either be much larger or much smaller than what is needed. Although you will never be able to be absolutely certain as to your users' screen and browser sizes, user testing may help you get a better idea.

You can also set the size of the artboard. The artboard determines the size of your project. All Catalyst projects use a fixed size. If you want to have your project scale to your user's browser window or screen size, you need to manually alter the application's settings in Flash Builder. You cannot choose to create a scalable project in Catalyst.

You can also set the background color of the project by clicking the Color Picker and selecting a color. The Catalyst Color Picker differs from those in other tools. You can either select from one of 40 preset swatches, or pick any color you want by selecting a base color from the spectrum and then setting the tint of that color.

To create a new Catalyst project, follow these steps:

1. From the Start screen, click Adobe Flash Catalyst Project.
2. Type a name for your project.
3. If desired, set a width and height for the project.
4. If desired, click the Color Picker and select a background color.
5. Click OK.

Using the Selection, Direct Select, Hand, and Zoom Tools

The first four tools in the Tools panel allow you to select objects and navigate within your project.

The Selection and Direct Select tools

The first tool on the panel, whose icon is a black arrow, is the Selection tool (see Figure 4.3). Use this tool to select objects on the stage so that you can modify their properties and to move objects on the artboard.

FIGURE 4.3

Selecting Objects with the Selection tool

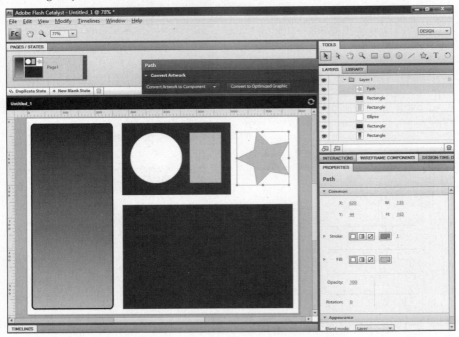

The white arrow to its right is the Direct Select tool. This tool does not do anything different from the Selection tool when dealing with shapes you draw directly in Catalyst; its primary purpose is to allow you to select items within a group.

Cross-Reference

For more information on using groups, see the section Grouping Objects.

The Hand and Zoom tools

The Hand tool lets you move the artboard on your screen. This tool does not move or select objects on the artboard as the Selection tool does; it simply repositions the artboard. The tool's usefulness becomes apparent once you zoom in on your project and need to view a different section of the artboard without first zooming out (see Figure 4.4).

The Zoom tool lets you zoom in and out to either get a more detailed look at small objects or to view your entire project. You can zoom in to get a closer look by simply selecting the tool and clicking a spot on the artboard. Press and hold the Alt (Option) key to zoom back out. You can zoom in to 1000 percent and out to 25 percent.

FIGURE 4.4

The artboard has been zoomed to a magnification of 200 percent, and the Hand tool is being used to move to a different part of the artboard.

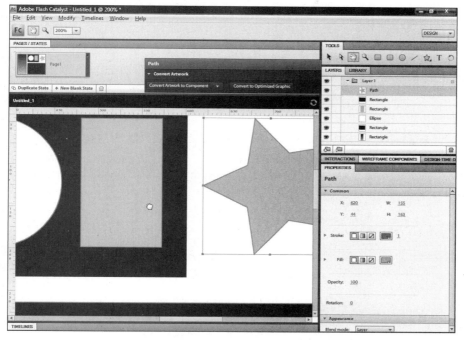

Catalyst Shortcuts

Photoshop and Illustrator users will be familiar with those programs' tool selection shortcuts and happy to find that the same shortcuts exist in Catalyst. With any tool selected, press and hold the Ctrl (⌘) key to temporarily switch to the Selection tool. Press and hold the Spacebar while using any tool to temporarily switch to the Hand tool. Pressing Ctrl (⌘) and Spacebar simultaneously gives you the Zoom In tool, while pressing Ctrl+Alt+Spacebar (⌘-Option+Spacebar) switches to the Zoom Out tool.

Most tools also have single-key selectors. Catalyst again uses the shortcuts with which Photoshop and Illustrator users are familiar. Press V at any time to get the Selection, or letter M to get the Rectangle tool. These shortcuts appear in the tooltips when you mouse over the tool on the Tools panel. Note that some tools, such as the Rounded Rectangle and the various polygons, do not have these shortcuts.

Tip

You can quickly switch to 100 percent magnification at any time by double-clicking the Zoom tool on the Tools panel. Double-click the Hand tool to jump to a Fit magnification — the level of magnification necessary to view the entire artboard.

Using the Drawing Tools

The Catalyst Tools panel includes eight drawing tools that allow you to draw rectangles, rounded rectangles, ellipses, lines, triangles, hexagons, octagons, and stars. A Text tool is also available.

Draw rectangles, rounded rectangles, and squares

You can draw simple rectangles using the Rectangle tool. As with other applications, you simply click the tool, then click and drag on the artboard to create a rectangle. Once you've drawn them, you can modify the rectangles using the Properties panel.

Rectangles with rounded corners can be drawn using the Rounded Rectangle tool (see Figure 4.5). Press and hold the Shift key while you drag with the mouse to create a perfect square using either tool.

FIGURE 4.5

Rectangles and rounded rectangles

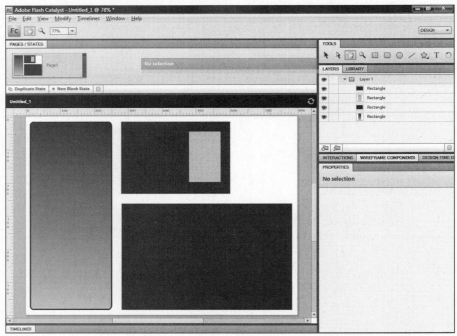

Tip

The values on the Properties panel such as the X and Y position, or the width and height, can be adjusted by clicking and typing a new value or by scrubbing the value. To scrub a value, simply click and drag. Dragging to the left decreases the value; dragging to the right increases it.

Note

The 0,0 point on the artboard in Catalyst, as in other Adobe design tools, is the top-left corner. X values count left to right, while Y values count top to bottom. A negative X value moves the object off the artboard to the left, while a negative Y value moves it above the artboard.

To create a new rectangle, follow these steps:

1. Click the Rectangle tool.

2. Click and drag on the artboard to draw a rectangle.

3. On the Properties panel, click and drag to scrub the X or Y value to move the rectangle on the artboard.

4. Click on the width property's value and type a new value.

5. Press Tab to move to the height property and type a new value.

Set strokes and fills

Each object you draw can have a stroke and a fill. *Strokes* are the outlines around objects, while *fills* place colors within it. Either strokes or fills can use solid colors or gradients. You can also set either the stroke or the fill to nothing.

On the Properties panel (see Figure 4.6), you will see three small boxes to the right of Stroke. The first sets the stroke to a solid color, the second a gradient, and the third removes it altogether.

A color picker appears to the right of these buttons when you select the solid-stroke option. Just as with the project's background color, this Color Picker (see Figure 4.7) presents 40 preset swatches and a spectrum from which you can select any other color. You can also enter a hexadecimal value for the color.

When you select the gradient stroke, you see a gradient map, which allows you to customize the gradient (see Figure 4.8). Color stops appear at either end just below the map. You can click on the colored square on the stop to change its color.

Dragging the stop sets its position within the gradient. You can add additional colors to the gradient by clicking the area below the map to add a new color stop. Drag a color stop away from the map to remove it.

When you select a solid color, a small number appears to the right of the Color Picker. Scrubbing this number allows you to create a thicker stroke. The stroke-width setting moves below the stroke buttons when you use a gradient.

FIGURE 4.6

The Stroke and Fill settings

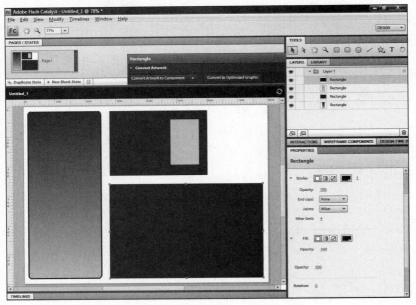

FIGURE 4.7

The Catalyst Color Picker

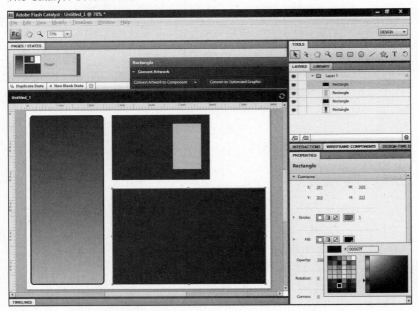

FIGURE 4.8

Creating a gradient stroke

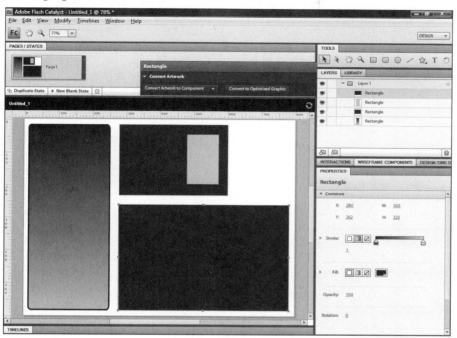

Additional settings for stroke are available by clicking the Stroke drop-down menu. From here, you can set the stroke's opacity, creating a transparent stroke on an otherwise opaque shape. The End caps settings have no effect on rectangles and are only used for lines. The Joints setting has three options:

- Round
- Bevel
- Miter

Round creates slightly rounded corners on the rectangle, in essence converting it to a rounded rectangle. Bevel creates hard diagonal corners, while Miter, the default, creates square corners. The Miter limit setting determines the appearance of a stroke at its joins. It will only be visible if you draw a star or triangle, set a very thick stroke, and then a very low miter limit. The setting primarily exists to allow you to alter a miter limit on artwork imported from Illustrator.

You can set fills in the same manner as strokes. You can use solid colors or gradients and create gradients using the same techniques as outlined previously for strokes. Only one additional setting is available when you click the triangle next to Fill: Opacity.

Below the Fill setting is another opacity property. Strokes and fills can have opacity set individually. If you want instead to have one opacity setting for the entire object, set it here (see Figure 4.9). Note that opacity settings are cumulative, so if you set stroke opacity and fill opacity individually and then modify the main-shape opacity, the fill and stroke become more transparent.

The Rotation setting, directly below Opacity, lets you rotate objects by scrubbing its value or typing a value of your own. Modifying the Corners property controls the roundedness of the corners of the rectangle.

Draw ellipses and circles

You can draw either ellipses or circles with the Ellipse tool. As with the rectangle tools, you click the Ellipse tool and then click and drag to draw the shape. Press and hold the Shift key to draw a perfect circle.

FIGURE 4.9

Semitransparent rectangles

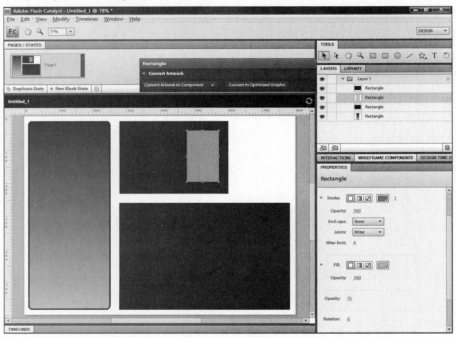

Tip

All shapes are surrounded by a rectangular bounding box. When you click and drag to draw any shape other than a rectangle, you are technically drawing the bounding box, which then contains the shape. Therefore, when drawing ellipses or circles, you need to imagine a spot outside the circle — the corner of the bounding box — as your starting point.

The Properties panel displays most of the same settings for ellipses and circles as it does for rectangles. Therefore, you can set solid or gradient strokes and fills, as shown in Figure 4.10.

While the End caps, Joint, and Miter limit settings are still available when drawing ellipses, they do not have any effect on the shape and can be ignored. As with rectangles, you can set opacity for strokes, fills, or the entire shape. You can also set a rotation for ellipses.

FIGURE 4.10

A circle and an ellipse, using various stroke, fill, and opacity settings

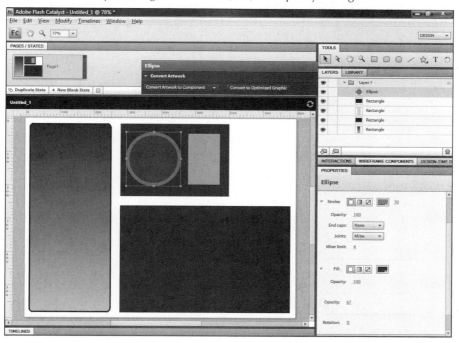

Drawing lines

You can draw lines using the Line tool. You can create lines at any angle, but holding the Shift key while you drag constrains the line to 45-degree increments.

Lines do not have fills, so you will notice that only the stroke settings are available. As with other shapes, the stroke can be a solid color or a gradient. The End caps setting changes the ends of the line to round or square (see Figure 4.11). Selecting None for the End caps removes them from the line, in effect making it slightly shorter. Neither the Joints nor Miter limit have any effect on lines.

FIGURE 4.11

A series of lines. The one on the left has its End caps set to rounded, while the one farthest to the right has been drawn while holding down Shift to ensure that it is perfectly horizontal.

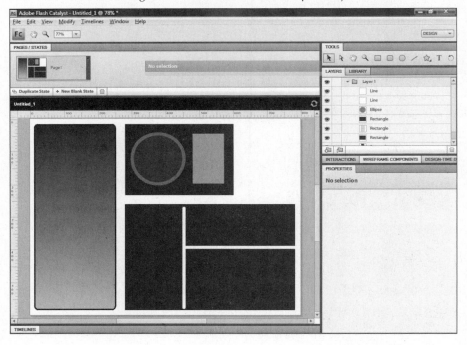

Drawing other shapes

The remaining shape tools share a space on the Tools panel to the right of the Line tool. The default tool is the Triangle, but you can click and hold your mouse on the tool to see a menu of other shapes such as Hexagon, Octagon, and Star (as shown in Figure 4.12). All four tools have the same setting options.

Like other shapes, you can set strokes and fills and adjust opacity. On the stroke, the End caps and Miter limit have no effect. Rounded joints round off the sharp edges on corners; you can further round the joints by adjusting the Corners setting.

FIGURE 4.12

Adding other shapes to the design

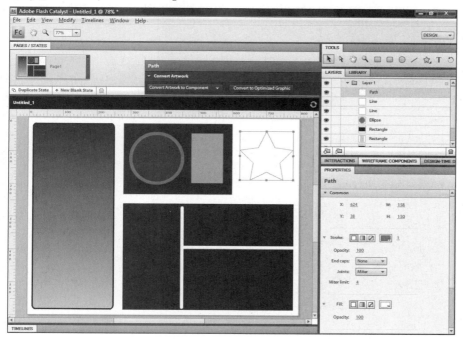

Adding text

Add text to your project with the Text tool. Click on the artboard and type to create a text box. After you finish typing, you can switch to the Selection tool and select the text frame to access the Properties panel for the text (see Figure 4.13).

From here, you can select a font, scrub, or type to set the font size, set a color, and make the text bold or italic. Note that Flash and Flex projects use embedded fonts. Therefore, you are free to select any font on your system to use in your project. At the bottom of the Properties panel are settings to add Strikethrough and underlining to your text.

In HTML, you should not underline text on your page, as this text will likely be confused with a hyperlink. The same theory should keep you from underlining text merely for emphasis in Catalyst. Hyperlinked text in Catalyst will not automatically become underlined; therefore, it can be useful to inform the user that a particular block of text is a hyperlink.

Note
The only unit of measurement available in the Flex framework to size fonts is pixels.

FIGURE 4.13

Text added to a project with the Text tool. Formatting has been applied with the Properties panel.

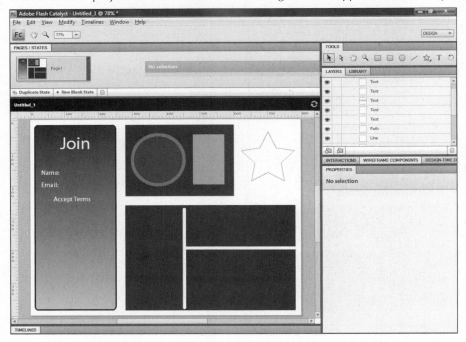

Caution

Inline formatting of text is not supported by the Flex framework and is therefore not possible in Catalyst. This explains why the text properties are only available when the entire text frame is selected and not available when you select a portion of the text using the Text tool.

Using the Transform Tool

The Transform tool allows you to rotate shapes. You can select a shape on the artboard and click and drag either directly on one of the corner handles or anywhere outside the shape to rotate it, as shown in Figure 4.14.

The point around which the shape rotates is by default its center. However, you can use the Transform tool to move this point to any other location on the artboard, even if that location is outside the shape, as shown in Figure 4.15. Rotating the shape after you have repositioned this point will cause it to rotate around the new axis.

FIGURE 4.14

Rotating a shape using the Transform tool

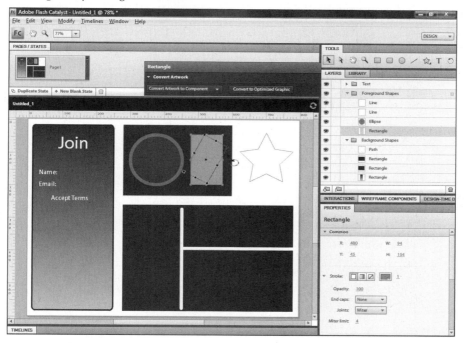

Understanding Layers

Like other design tools, Catalyst organizes the various objects on its artboard with layers. You can think of using layers as similar to drawing a picture using sheets of clear plastic, rather than drawing on a piece of paper. If you draw each piece of the picture on a new sheet of plastic, you can stack them together and view it as a single image or take the individual sheets and manipulate them without affecting the others. You can also rearrange the sheets, thus controlling which elements appear above or below other elements.

Catalyst layers most closely resemble those in Illustrator. In both programs, each layer is merely a container, with each item drawn on the layer placed into a new sublayer. Each time you draw a new object in Catalyst, it is automatically placed on a new sublayer within the currently selected layer. Each new object's sublayer is placed above the prior layer, so the most recent addition is on the topmost layer.

Note

The Rounded Rectangle tool is nothing more than the Rectangle tool with a preset value on the Corners property. Therefore, when you draw a rounded rectangle, the sublayer is still called Rectangle.

FIGURE 4.15

Moving the axis point

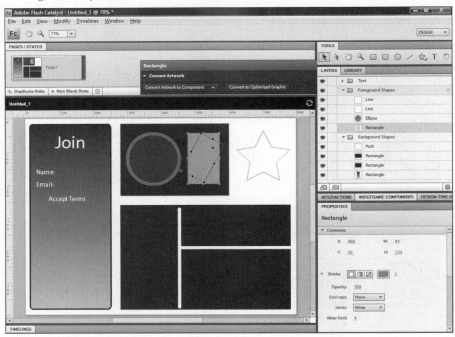

Sublayers are automatically named based on the shape you draw, so drawing a rectangle creates a sublayer called Rectangle, while drawing a circle creates a sublayer called Ellipse (see Figure 4.16).

This automatic naming of sublayers is in some ways nicer than the method employed by other design tools such as Photoshop, which simply names each layer Layer1, Layer 2, and so forth. You do need to note that in Catalyst you can have multiple sublayers with the same name, so if you draw two rectangles, the result is two Rectangle sublayers.

Because a normal project contains many, many layers and sublayers, you should get in the habit of renaming layers. Here again, the Catalyst team consciously mimicked the process from the other design tools. You can simply double-click the existing layer name and then type a new, more descriptive name.

FIGURE 4.16

The Layers panel in a Catalyst project. Layers have been logically named, and some of the sublayers are visible.

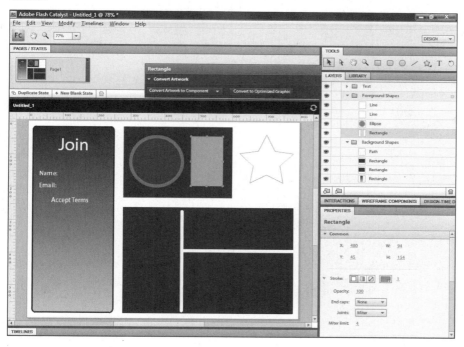

You can further help keep yourself organized by creating new layers, so that all of your objects do not end up in one massive layer. To create a new layer, follow these steps:

1. Click the layer above which you want to create a new layer.

2. Click the Create New Layer button at the bottom of the panel.

3. Double-click the new layer and rename it.

Note

Because layers hold zero or more sublayers, Catalyst depicts layers with a folder icon.

You can change the stacking order of layers and sublayers by simply dragging them up or down in the Layers panel, as shown in Figure 14.17.

Sublayers can be moved from one layer to another by dragging them below the desired layer, as shown in Figure 14.18.

FIGURE 4.17

Repositioning layers by dragging on the Layers panel

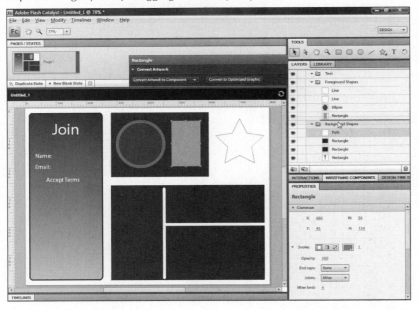

FIGURE 4.18

Moving a sublayer to a new layer

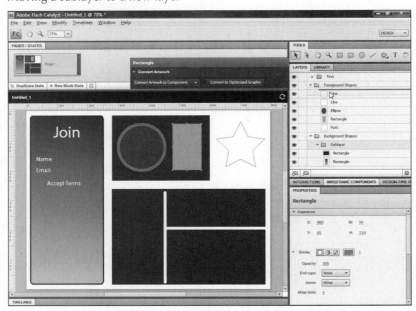

Working with Blend Modes

Blend modes allow you to control how pixels on one layer interact with those on the layer or layers below it. Blend modes are common throughout the Creative Suite. In addition to being available in Photoshop, Illustrator, and Fireworks, they are also present in Flash Professional, InDesign, Premiere Pro, After Effects, and now Catalyst. The exact list of blend modes varies from one product to the next.

Catalyst does not have nearly as many blend modes as Photoshop, but all of the most commonly used modes are available. Blend modes are available in a drop-down list on the Properties panel when a shape is selected. With almost all shapes, it is the last or next-to-last option on the panel.

When you have an object on a layer whose pixels overlap those of an object on a lower layer, the upper object normally obscures the lower. You can make the lower object appear by decreasing the opacity of the upper object, but this merely allows you to see through the top object. Many times, what you actually need is to blend the top pixels with the lower pixels (see Figure 4.19).

Tip

The blend modes available in Catalyst are the same as those found in Flash Professional, as those are the modes supported by Flash Player.

FIGURE 4.19

The shapes shown here have been blended. On the left, the top layer is using the Multiply blend mode, while Screen has been used on the right.

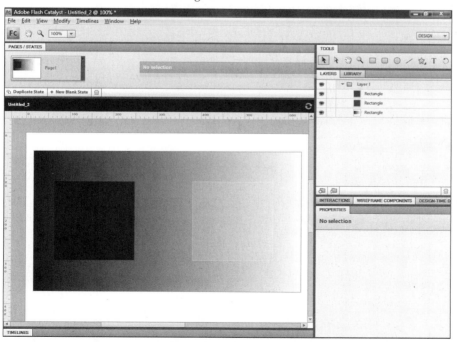

The most-used and most useful blend modes are Multiply and Screen. When you blend with Multiply, you are mixing the darkest pixels of the upper layer with the darkest pixels of the layers below. Therefore, if you take a black shape and attempt to blend with Multiply nothing appears to happen, as you have only very dark pixels.

Conversely, a white object will seem to disappear, as there are no dark pixels available, so only the dark pixels below — which would be any pixel, as everything is darker than white — will show through. However, take a shape with any other color fill, and you will see the blending. Multiply therefore makes the shapes darker through the blend.

Note

Color values on computers are expressed numerically. The Multiply blend mode is so named because you are performing multiplication: The color values of the top layer are multiplied by the values of the lower layers. The same is true with the Difference, Add, and Subtract modes: Each result in the mathematical operation is described by its name.

Screen is the opposite of Multiply. The lightest pixels of the top layer blend with the light pixels of the layer or layers below. Thus, a black shape blended with Screen seems to disappear as there are no light pixels, while nothing seems to happen with a white shape. Any colors in between will blend, with the result being something lighter than before.

Table 4.1 lists all of the blend modes available in Catalyst.

TABLE 4.1

The Catalyst Blend Modes

Mode	Result
Normal	No blending occurs.
Layer	No blending occurs; in practice, Normal and Layer do the same thing.
Multiply	Dark pixels from the layer being blended mix with the darker pixels in the lower layers. No part of the blended layers gets lighter when using Multiply.
Screen	Light pixels from the layer being blended mix with the lighter pixels in the lower layers. The mode actually multiplies the inverse values of the colors to result in a lightening of the image. No part of the blended layers will get darker when using Screen.
Darken	Each of the pixels with the blended layer is compared to the pixel directly beneath, and the darker of the two remains.
Lighten	The opposite of Darker; the lighter of each set of pixels is retained.
Difference	Difference divides the color values of the blended layer from those of the layers below. Large differences between the colors result in lighter colors, while small differences result in dark colors. Any pixels with the same value become black. The mode generally results in something that resembles a negative from film, although a true negative effect is available with the Invert mode (see below).

Mode	Result
Add	The color values of the pixels of the blending layer are added to those of the layers below. The effect is often very similar and at times indistinguishable from Lighten.
Subtract	The color values of the pixels are subtracted from one another. The result is usually similar to Difference, but some variations in the resulting colors are evident.
Invert	Each of the lower layer's pixels is inversed, resulting in a film negative effect.
Alpha	The blended layer's alpha value, which defines its transparency value, is used to determine its appearance. Flex developers using ActionScript 3 can use this blend mode to create interesting effects, but as you do not have direct access to ActionScript in Catalyst, it is of little use other than to preset it for the developer. The result in Catalyst will always be that the object being blended becomes invisible.
Erase	Like Alpha, this has little use in Catalyst. ActionScript 3 developers can use this blend mode to erase the pixels of the background layer, but in Catalyst it has the same effect as Alpha: the object being blended becomes transparent.
Overlay	Each pixel is adjusted based on the color value of the lower layer. If the lower layer is lighter than 50 percent gray, the pixels are screened. If the lower layer is darker than 50 percent gray, the pixels are multiplied.
Hard Light	Hard light multiplies the dark colors and screens the light colors, very much like Overlay.

Add Wireframe Components

When creating a Flex application, you have complete freedom to create buttons, lists, scrollbars, and other common application components to look how you want. For example, as you learn in later chapters, you can design your own scrollbars in Illustrator and make that scrollbar look any way that you want.

There are times that you may want to use standard components instead of drawing your own. You may have a client or boss who simply wants the application to look like those to which she is accustomed. The primary idea behind Catalyst is that you will begin your project in Photoshop or Illustrator, which implies that all of the design is done there and further implies that you are creating custom components. Neither Photoshop nor Illustrator contains any tools that allow you to add a standard browser button or scrollbar or other common component.

Note
The exception is Fireworks, which does contain a library of standard Web page and Flex components.

Fortunately, Catalyst contains these items. The Wireframe Components panel contains ten of the most common user interface components from the Flex framework, so adding them to your project is as simple as clicking and dragging.

Table 4.2 lists the Wireframe components included with Catalyst and briefly describes each.

TABLE 4.2

Wireframe Components

Component	Description
Button	Basic button to add interactivity to your project.
Checkbox	Check boxes are usually presented in groups to allow users to select zero or more options.
Data List	Data lists are basically the Flex equivalent of a table, although they provide a considerable amount of additional functionality, including hover and select effects, automatic sorting, and more.
Horizontal Scrollbar	A scrollbar for wide content.
Horizontal Slider	Slider controls allow users to modify a value by dragging the slider.
Radio Button	Radio buttons provide a set of mutually exclusive options.
Text Input	A single-line text input field to capture user-generated data.
Toggle Button	Toggle buttons function in the same way as regular buttons, but have a selected state to provide feedback as to whether or not they have been clicked.
Vertical Scrollbar	A scrollbar for tall content.
Vertical Slider	This provides the same functionality as the horizontal slider, but vertically.

As you add wireframe components to your application (see Figure 4.20), keep in mind that you are only building a design comp. Much of the functionality of these components is not designed to work directly out of Catalyst. You will be able to allow Buttons to go to external Web sites or change states within an application.

You can add sample data to a data grid, but you will add most of the functionality of the components later in Flash Builder.

Cross-Reference

Some of the components have customizable parts. For example, you can modify the appearance of the various pieces that make up a horizontal scrollbar. See Part IV for details on customizing component parts.

FIGURE 4.20

This project has had several wireframe components added to its layout, including text inputs, check boxes, radio buttons, a horizontal slider, a data grid, and a button.

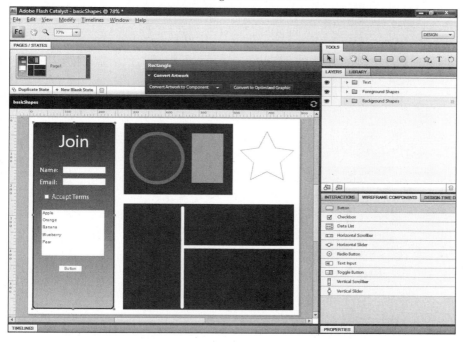

Run a Project

The design view in Catalyst shows you exactly what your final project will look like. Because your project will run in Flash Player, which also renders projects in exactly the same way regardless of the operating system or browser through with it is playing, you can be sure that the design you see in Catalyst is what your users will see.

Despite this, you will still want to run your project and view it in Flash Player in a browser. Primarily, this allows you to test interactive elements. Scrollbars, for example, don't work in the Catalyst design view; you must run the project in order to test them.

You can run a project by choosing File ⇨ Run Project (see Figure 4.21) or by pressing Ctrl+Enter (⌘+Enter). When you do so, Catalyst compiles the project, opens your computer's default browser, and launches the project (see Figure 4.22). Because it must compile the project before running, this process may take a few seconds to complete.

FIGURE 4.21

Choose File ⇨ Run Project to test your project.

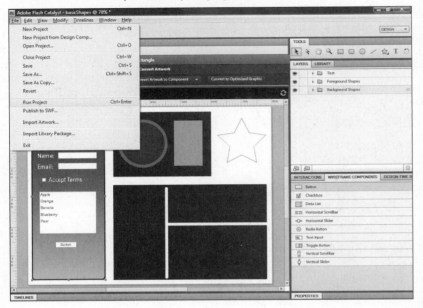

FIGURE 4.22

The project running in Flash Player in Internet Explorer

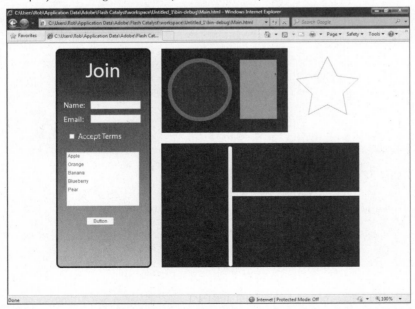

Note

Flash Professional users will be familiar with running or testing projects using the Ctrl+Enter (⌘+Enter) short-cut. Developers familiar with Flash Builder, or Flex Builder as it was called in earlier versions, may try to use its Run Project shortcut, Ctrl-F11. Unfortunately, this shortcut does nothing in Catalyst.

Tip

Catalyst doesn't provide a means by which users can control which browser is used to launch the project; it simply opens the computer's default browser. If you want to test your project in another browser, copy the project's URL from your default browser and paste it into a different browser, but keep in mind that as the project runs in Flash Player, there will not be any difference when viewing the page between browsers.

Caution

The minimum required version of Flash Player should have been installed when you installed Catalyst, but if for some reason it was not, you can download and install the latest version of the player from Adobe's Web site at www.adobe.com.

Saving a Project

As with any file on your computer, you should be in the habit of saving often. Catalyst does not have an auto save feature, so if your computer crashes or you experience a power outage, you will lose any work you have done so far.

You can save your project by choosing File ➪ Save As. Catalyst projects are saved as an FXP file. You can save your project anywhere on your computer, but be sure to save it in a location that you will remember later.

Cross-Reference

See Chapter 2 for details on FXP files.

Summary

Catalyst is not a graphics design tool. However, it does include a number of basic drawing tools that enable you to create basic page designs without the assistance of another product, such as Photoshop or Illustrator. Using Catalyst, you can draw rectangles, rounded rectangles, ellipses, lines, triangles, hexagons, octagons, and stars. You can also create solid or gradient strokes and fills and change the transparency of objects. Artwork in Catalyst is organized into layers, and graphics on one layer can be blended with those on other layers.

Catalyst also provides a set of wireframe components to which you can add common user interface elements such as scrollbars, sliders, data grids, and text input boxes.

Creating an Application Comp in Illustrator

For many designers, Flash Catalyst workflows begin in Adobe Illustrator. Illustrator provides a powerful set of drawing tools. These tools allow you to create a comp of your application design that you can later pull into Catalyst and convert into an RIA.

Create a New File in Illustrator

Like other Creative Suite tools, Illustrator displays a Start Screen when first launched (see Figure 5.1). The right side of this screen provides a set of options for new documents. The options provide default settings for your artwork.

Tip
For obvious reasons, designers creating work for Catalyst will usually want to select the Flash Catalyst Document option. There are no significant differences in the initial setup between a Web document and Flash Catalyst document.

You need to establish several basic parameters for your Illustrator document, discussed in the following sections, before you begin. All of these settings will be translated directly into Catalyst, so you need to think about what you want your final application to look like, even at this very early stage of development.

FIGURE 5.1

The Start Screen in Illustrator CS5

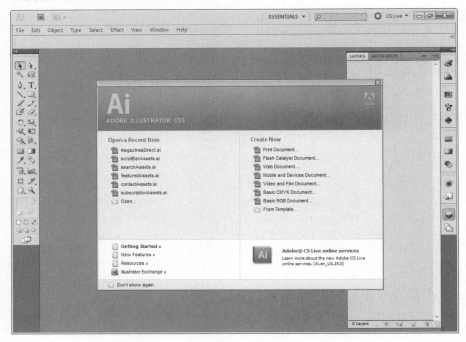

Choosing a print document or Flash Catalyst document

The main difference in Illustrator between selecting a new print document and a new Flash Catalyst document is the *color space*. Printers have long relied on a color space known as CMYK, so named after the primary colors used: cyan, yellow, magenta, and black.

Note
The K in CMYK is used for black to avoid it being confused with blue.

Computer monitors, like TV sets, color film, and the human eye, use a different model known as RGB, for red, green, and blue. Thus, when you select a new print document, Illustrator uses CMYK, while new Flash Catalyst documents will use RGB (see Figure 5.2).

In many projects, the decision about which color model to use can rely on many factors, but in a Catalyst project, it is quite easy; you are designing an application to be displayed on a computer screen and will thus always use RGB. Therefore, you would never want to click the option to create a new print document.

FIGURE 5.2

The New Document dialog box for a Flash Catalyst document

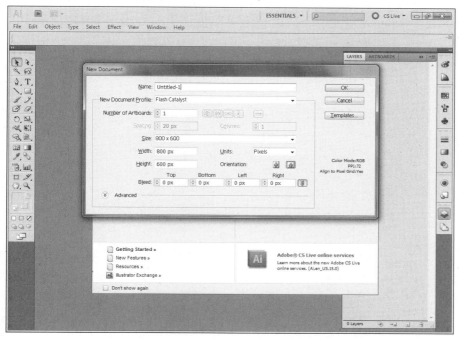

Choosing the file name and document size

The first option on the dialog box allows you to give the document a name. This name is ultimately used as the file name, so it should be descriptive of the file's purpose.

Next, you need to determine the document size in pixels. As this will translate into the size of your Catalyst project, and ultimately the size of your application, you should set this to whatever dimensions you have chosen for your project. There is no set correct size to use; every application is different and will have different size requirements.

You can either select one of the preset sizes from the drop-down list or type your own pixel dimensions. The units should be left at pixels, while the orientation will automatically change depending on the values input into the Width and Height fields.

Bleed is a term from the print world that allows designers to designate additional space around an artboard to eventually allow printing all the way to the edge of the document. It has no application in Web pages or RIAs, so you can always leave it at its default settings.

At the bottom of the dialog box, you will see an option to expand the dialog box to display advanced options (see Figure 5.3). These allow you to set the Color Mode, which you should always have as RGB.

The Raster Effects setting determines the resolution at which Illustrator rasterizes effects such as drop shadows. Make sure that this is always set to Screen (72ppi). Finally, set or leave the Preview Mode at Default.

FIGURE 5.3

Advanced options at the bottom of the New Document dialog box

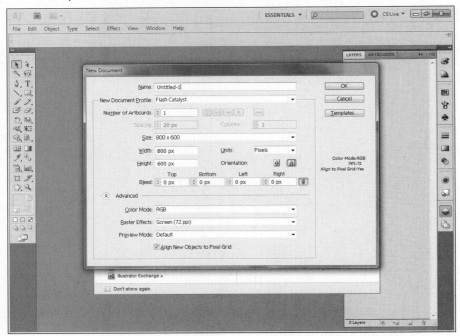

Drawing in Illustrator

As its name implies, the main idea behind Illustrator is drawing. It has a powerful set of tools that allow you to create vector-based artwork.

The Tools panel

Illustrator's Tools panel runs down the left edge of the screen (see Figure 5.4). Tools are organized into categories, grouping them together based on their main functions.

Note

Illustrator CS5 has close to 80 tools. A complete overview of each tool is beyond the scope of this book. What this section covers is a brief look at the primary tools that are likely to form the basis of most work in creating RIA comps.

FIGURE 5.4

The Tools panel

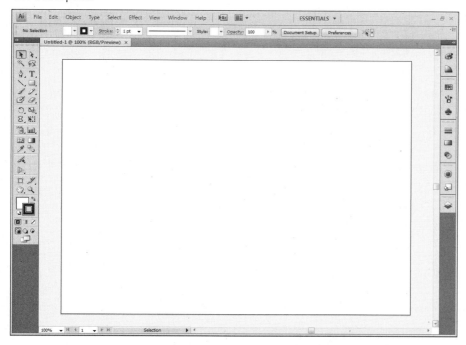

Selection tools

The top section of the Tools panel contains the selection tools. The black arrow represents the Selection tool. Any time you need to simply select an object on the artboard, whether to move it, delete it, group it with other objects, or change its properties, you can use the Selection tool.

The white arrow is the Direct Select tool. All objects drawn in Illustrator are made up of vectors. The Direct Select tool allows you to select portions of a vector drawing. For example, you can use the Direct Select tool to select a single line within a shape.

Cross-Reference

For more information on vector artwork, see Chapter 3.

Many of the tools on the Tools panel have a small arrow in the bottom-right corner that indicates that there are multiple tools grouped together. You can access the additional tools by pressing and holding your mouse down on the tool.

The Direct Select tool is the first example of this. Press and hold your mouse on the Direct Select tool to reveal the Group Selection tool. Despite its name, the Group Selection tool does not select groups of objects. Instead, it does the opposite: When you have a set of objects grouped together, the Group Selection tool allows you to select individual items within the group.

The Magic Wand tool, immediately below the Selection tool, allows you to select objects based on similar characteristics. For example, it can select all objects that have the same color fill or stroke.

To its right is the Lasso tool, which allows you to draw a free-form selection around an area of the stage. Any items that fall within the selection form, in whole or in part, are selected.

You will find that you need to use a combination of these tools frequently in any project. Taking some time to become familiar with these tools will pay dividends down the road.

Drawing tools

The bulk of Illustrator's tools are for drawing. Before you begin drawing in Illustrator, keep in mind that everything you draw is a vector. While Illustrator can import raster art, it does not create it.

Drawing in vectors can take some getting used to, as it often requires techniques that are different from drawing raster art. However, you will likely find that once you are familiar with the tools, you can generally draw much more precise shapes and lines with vectors than rasters.

The Pen tool

The primary tool used for drawing in Illustrator is the Pen tool (see Figure 5.5). All vector art is made up of anchor points that connect line segments or paths. When using the Pen tool, you are simply defining these anchor points, while allowing Illustrator to draw the connecting paths.

Drawing a straight line is fairly simple with the Pen tool. Simply click at a point where you want the line to begin, and then click again where the line should end. After you draw the second point, Illustrator draws the connecting line.

Tip

When using the Pen tool, you do not click and drag to trace the line you want to create. Remember, that you do not draw the lines themselves with the pen; instead, you define the points that make up the lines.

Creating a shape

Once you create the second anchor and have a line, any further clicks on the artboard create additional anchor points and new lines in the same shape (see Figure 5.6). If you eventually click back on your original point, you close the paths and create a single, closed shape that can then be filled.

FIGURE 5.5

Drawing a straight line with the Pen tool

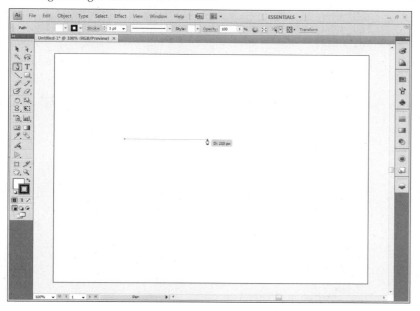

FIGURE 5.6

Creating a closed shape by clicking on the original point after creating a series of paths

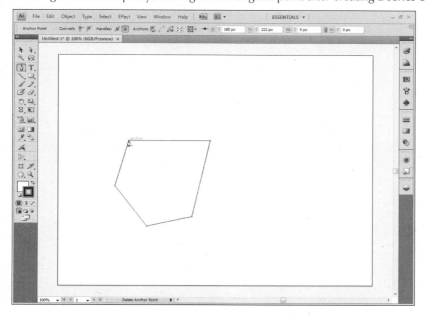

Tip

Pay attention to the indicator icon in the bottom right-corner of the Pen while moving around the art-board. An X indicates that you are about to start a new series of paths, while a closed circle indicates that you are over your original point and are about to close the path. Whenever you see the Pen tool with no icon in the corner, you are going to add to the existing shape.

If you want to start a new shape, you need to reset the Pen tool. Clicking on your original point to create a closed path accomplishes this.

However, if you want to leave a path open and simply start a new shape, you can simply click on the art board while holding down the Ctrl (⌘) key. Either way, you should now see a small X in the bottom-right corner of the tool, indicating that it has been reset and that your next click will begin a new shape.

Creating a curve

You can also use the Pen tool to create curves (see Figure 5.7).

FIGURE 5.7

Creating a curve path

Curves require that you click and drag with your mouse, but just as with straight paths, you are not tracing the actual curve you want to create. You still need to define anchor points, regardless of whether those points are defining curves or straight paths.

Straight path anchor points are only the anchor. Curves require both the anchor point, from which the curve originates, and a pair of *control handles*. The handles define the height and arc of the curve.

Therefore, when you define a *curve anchor point*, you click and drag to create one of these control handles. The other handle, which mirrors the first, is created for you. Your first control handle should be in the general direction you want your curve to go. If you want to create a curve that goes up from the point, drag up.

After you create the first control handle, release your mouse button and move to the point on the artboard where you want to place your second anchor point. This defines the end of the curve.

Here again, you click and drag to create your control handles. However, you need to drag in the opposite direction from your first control handle. If you dragged up for the first handle, you drag down for the second. The angle at which you drag determines the arc of the curve, while the distance you drag sets its height.

As with straight segments, you can continue creating additional curves on the path by clicking and dragging from new places. You can also return to your original point to close the shape.

Modifying paths

One of the nicest features of drawing vectors is that they remain editable at all times. If your first attempt at drawing a path is not exactly what you want, you can simply modify it until it looks the way you need it to.

The Direct Select tool is most often used to modify paths (see Figure 5.8). You can use it to move a straight line segment's anchor point to a new location, thus adjusting the path. You can also use it to modify curves. Moving the curved segment's anchor point adjusts it, but you can also move the control handles to further fine-tune the path.

Combining straight and curve segments

Straight segments and *curve segments* can be combined to create complex shapes (see Figure 5.9). The only difference between a straight segment's anchor point and a curved segment's anchor is the lack or presence of control handles.

Therefore, you can convert straight-segment anchors into curve anchors by adding handles, and you can change curves to straight anchors by removing them. These modifications can be done with the Pen tool and a modifier key on the keyboard or with specific tools.

FIGURE 5.8

Modifying a curve path with the Direct Select tool

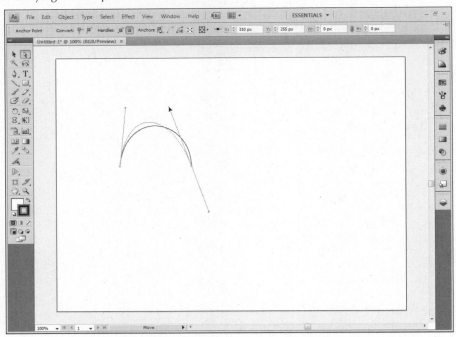

To create a path that combines straight lines and curves, follow these steps:

1. **Ctrl+click (⌘click) to reset the Pen tool.**

2. **Click on the artboard to create a straight-line anchor.**

3. **Click on another location to create a second straight anchor.**

4. **While pressing and holding the Alt (Option) key, click and drag from the anchor point created in Step 2 to add control handles to it.**

5. **Move your mouse to a new location.** Without holding any keys on the keyboard, click and drag to create a new curve anchor point.

6. **Press and hold the Alt (Option) key, and click on the anchor point created in Step 4.** The control handle that matches the direction of the curve remains, but its opposite handle is deleted.

7. **Click in a new location on the artboard to create a new straight anchor point.**

FIGURE 5.9

Combining straight and curve paths

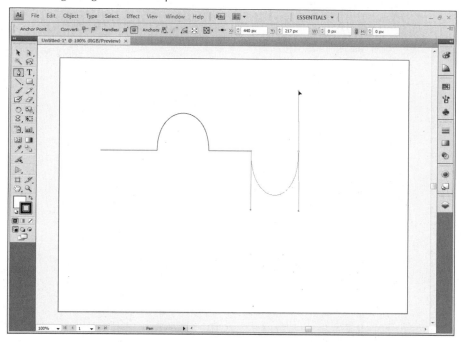

You can repeat these steps as often as needed to create complex artwork.

You can achieve the same technique by switching between the Pen tool and the Convert Anchor Point tool, which you can access by pressing and holding your mouse on the Pen tool in the Tools panel. However, it is much faster and easier to remember the keyboard modifier, rather than switching tools.

Changing the direction of curves

Sometimes, you need two consecutive curves that go in the same direction, creating a series of bumps. The problem is that when you click and drag to create the second anchor point, finishing your first curve, you are creating the first control handle for the next curve. Unfortunately, this handle is going in the wrong direction. This creates a series of flowing curves (see Figure 5.10) but does not allow you to have each curve mirror the prior curve.

FIGURE 5.10

A series of connected curves, each flowing from the last

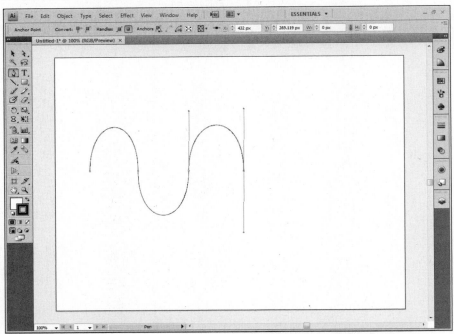

In order to get the second curve to match the first, you must change the direction of that second control handle after you draw it. You can do that using the same keyboard modifier you used to combine straight and curve line segments. To create a series of matching curves, as seen in Figure 5.11, follow these steps:

1. **Ctrl+click (⌘+click) to reset the Pen tool.**
2. **Click and drag on the art board to create an anchor point and control handles.**
3. **Click and drag in a new location to create a second anchor point, its control handles, and the curve path.**
4. **Press and hold the Alt (Option) key on your keyboard and position your mouse over the end of the second control handle.**
5. **While still holding down the key on the keyboard, drag the handle to a new location.**
6. **Release the key, move to a new location on the art board, and click and drag to create a new anchor point, control handles, and path.**

These steps can be repeated to create a series of matching curves. You can adjust and fine-tune the curves later with the Direct Select tool.

FIGURE 5.11

A series of matching curves

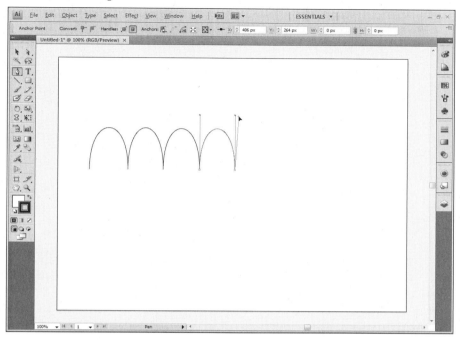

Draw shapes

While you can draw almost any complex shape manually using the Pen tool, Illustrator provides a set of shape tools to simplify the process of creating common shapes (see Table 5.1).

TABLE 5.1

Illustrator Shape Tools

Tool	Description	Notes
Rectangle	Draws a simple rectangle	Press and hold the Shift key while you draw to create a square.
Rounded Rectangle	Draws a rectangle with rounded corners	Hold the mouse while drawing a rounded rectangle. Press the Up and Down arrow keys to increase or decrease the amount of roundedness of the corners. As with the rectangle, holding the Shift key while you draw creates a rounded square.

continued

TABLE 5.1	*(continued)*	
Tool	**Description**	**Notes**
Ellipse	Draws ovals and circles	Press and hold the Shift key while you draw to create a perfect circle.
Polygon	Draws multisided shapes	While drawing, press the Up arrow key to increase the number of sides, and the Down arrow key to reduce the number of sides. You can rotate the shape by moving your mouse left or right while you draw or press and hold the Shift key while drawing to lock one corner at the top of the shape and prevent it from rotating.
Star	Draws stars	While drawing, press the Up and Down arrow keys to increase or decrease the number of points. You can rotate the star by moving your mouse left or right while you draw or press and hold the Shift key to lock the one point at the top of the star and prevent it from rotating.
Flare	Creates a flare or starburst effect	Drawing flares requires two steps. First, click and drag to create the center and halo part of the flare. Then click in another area of the art board to create additional rings radiating from the center point. While drawing the first part, use the Up and Down arrows keys to increase or decrease the number of rays. While drawing the second, use the Up and Down arrow keys to increase or decrease the number of additional rings. Press and hold the Shift key while drawing the first part to prevent it from rotating.

All of the tools are grouped together in one place on the Tools panel, so you need to click and hold your mouse on the Rectangle tool (see Figure 5.12) to access them.

Precise shapes

If you want to create a shape with precise dimensions, follow these steps:

1. **Select the Shape tool and click once on the artboard.** A dialog box appears.
2. **Enter the desired parameters.** The dialog box for rectangles and ellipses lets you set the width and height of:
   - Rounded rectangles, the width, height, and corner radius
   - Polygons, the radius and number of sides
   - Stars, the inner and outer radii and number of sides

Smart Guides and the Info tooltip

While you draw a shape, light green lines called Smart Guides appear on the artboard. Smart Guides help you align new shapes with existing objects on the artboard. By default, your new shape attempts to snap to these guides. You can disable Smart Guides by choosing View ⇨ Smart Guides.

FIGURE 5.12

The Rectangle tool dialog box

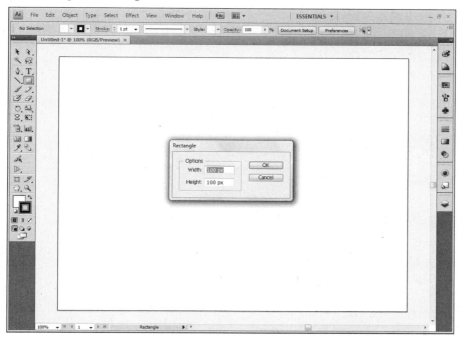

Similarly, a small tooltip appears in the bottom-right corner of your shape while you draw that displays the width and height of the shape, providing a reference to allow you to draw shapes at a given size (see Figure 5.13).

Painting

The Paintbrush tool allows you to draw on the artboard using more traditional techniques than those provided by the Pen tool. After you select the tool, the Control panel along the top of the screen updates to show the tool's properties. You can select the stroke color from the Color Picker. You are always painting strokes with the Paintbrush, so even though the Control panel displays Color Pickers for both the fill and stroke, only the stroke will have any effect.

Tip
Clicking on the Color Picker displays a list of the color swatches in Illustrator. You can also hold down the Shift key while you click to produce an alternate Color Picker interface that displays red, green, and blue sliders.

You can set the width of the stroke by either selecting a preset value from the Stroke drop-down list or typing a value in the text box. You can click directly on the Stroke label to display a panel that provides you with many additional stroke properties.

FIGURE 5.13

Drawing with Smart Guides and the tooltip

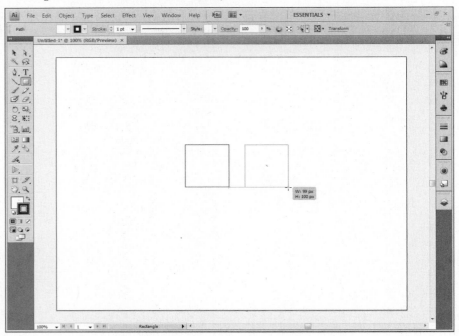

The drop-down list to the right of the Stroke settings allows you to pick a brush profile, which affects the appearance of the stroke around curves. To the right of the Stroke settings drop-down list is another list from which you can select one of several brush presets. At the bottom of this selection is a button that displays a menu of additional brush types. Finally, the style and opacity settings allow you to apply preset styles or change the transparency of the stroke.

Cross-Reference

See Illustrator CS5 Bible, by Ted Alspach, for more detailed information on brushes, presets, and styles.

Erasing drawings

The Eraser tool allows you to erase any objects you have drawn on the artboard. You can increase the size of the eraser by pressing the left square bracket key ([) or decrease it with the right square bracket key (]).

Note

Technically, the Eraser tool does not erase, but redraws the outlines of shapes into new compound shapes. Therefore, if you erase inside a shape that has a stroke, you will notice that its stroke appears around the edges of whatever area you erased. This also means that the erased area can be altered or basically redrawn using the Direct Select tool.

Modify Artwork

In addition to its drawing tools, Illustrator provides a set of tools that allows you to modify your artwork after you draw it.

Revisiting the Direct Select tool

The Direct Select tool's primary purpose is to modify vector art after it has been drawn (see Figure 5.14). Vector shapes are made up of paths connected to anchor points. You can adjust these anchor points with the Direct Select tool whenever you need to change the art.

FIGURE 5.14

Modifying a curve with the Direct Select tool

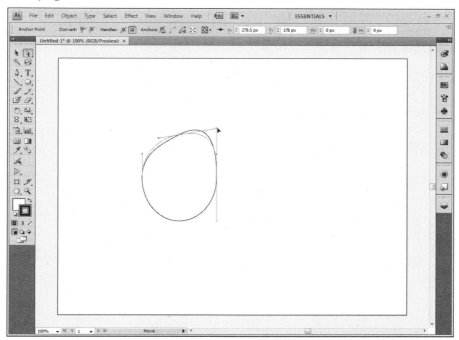

When you first click on an object with the tool, all of its anchor points become selected. If you then click on a single anchor, it remains selected while the rest are deselected. Selected anchor points display as solid, filled squares, while deselected anchors appear as open squares.

Anchor points are either for straight segments or curves. Straight anchor points do not have control handles. If you select one with the Direct Select tool, you can reposition it on the artboard, which causes the line segments attached to it to reposition as well. If you select a curve anchor point, you can reposition it, but you can also click and drag on either control handle to modify the curve.

Tip

Curve anchor points have two handles that are linked to one another, so moving one handle moves the other in the opposite direction. If you need to move only one handle, you can press and hold the Alt (Option) key while you drag. This breaks the connection between the handles and allows them to move independently. Once the link is been broken, you can continue to adjust either handle without holding down the modifier key.

You can also click and drag line segments with the Direct Select tool. Dragging a straight segment moves it and necessarily adjusts segments directly adjacent to the one being moved, but leaves the other anchor points on the shape in place. Dragging a curve segment has much the same effect as dragging its control handles.

Tip

You can select more than one anchor point by holding down the Shift key and then clicking additional points.

Work with color

Almost all objects in Illustrator are made up of two parts: a fill and a stroke. Each object can have its own color. The program provides several places to set these colors, but all have the same ultimate effect so you can use whichever one you prefer.

The Tools panel contains a fill and stroke color setting toward the bottom. These are two large squares, one filled and the other just an outline. The filled square represents the fill color, while the outline is the stroke. You can change the color of either by double-clicking it, which displays the Color Picker dialog box (see Figure 5.15).

You can also select colors for either the fill or the stroke using the Color, Color Guide, and Swatches panels. All are normally available from the panel sets on the right side of the screen, but if you don't see them, they can also be accessed from the Window menu.

The Color panel (see Figure 5.16) provides three sliders, one each for the red, green and blue in the color, along with a color spectrum along the bottom of the panel. You can select whether you are setting the fill or the stroke in the top-left corner of the panel.

FIGURE 5.15

The Color Picker dialog box

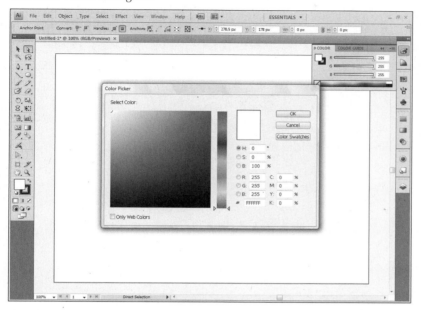

FIGURE 5.16

The Color panel

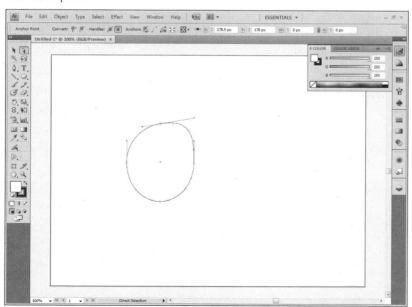

The Color Guide panel displays a set of color groups (see Figure 5.17). Once you select a group, you can choose from a variety of related tints. The panel does not provide an icon with which you can select whether you are creating a fill or stroke color. Instead, you need to click the appropriate button on the Tools panel.

FIGURE 5.17

The Color Guide panel

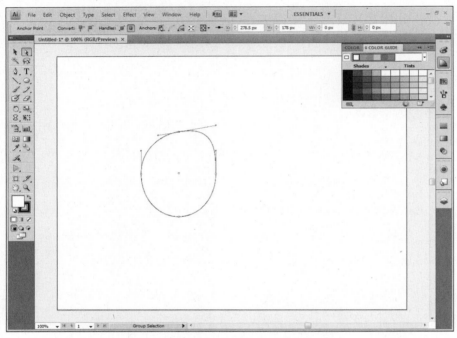

The small icon in the bottom-right corner of the Color Guide panel allows you to choose from a set of swatches upon which the guide's groups are based.

The Swatches panel provides a set of predefined colors (see Figure 5.18). Like the Color Guide panel, it doesn't have an icon to set whether you are applying the swatch to a fill or a stroke, so once again you need to use the Tools panel's button.

The Swatches panel also provides a menu in its bottom-left corner from which you can choose from a variety of additional panels, each of which opens as its own separate panel. You can add swatches from these individual panels to the main Swatches panel by simply dragging the swatch from the new panel to the Swatches panel.

The Swatches panel

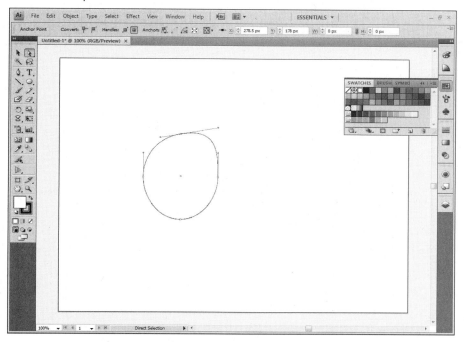

Caution

Most of the swatches in the additional panels use CMYK, so be aware that these colors may look different once they are applied to Catalyst and converted to RGB.

Once selected, you can use the current stroke color with any tool that draws strokes, such as the Pen or Paintbrush. Shapes use both the current fill and current stroke color.

Use gradients

Gradients are a gradual shift from one color to another over the course of a fill or stroke. Illustrator includes the ability to define custom gradients and use them as an object's fill or stroke.

Define a custom gradient

The Gradient panel allows you to create gradients (see Figure 5.19). Illustrator supports both linear and radial gradients. The Gradient panel displays a gradient ramp that shows the current gradient and allows you to define the colors to be used. Each color is called a color stop and is represented by a small box with an arrow just below the ramp.

FIGURE 5.19

A custom gradient created in the Gradient panel

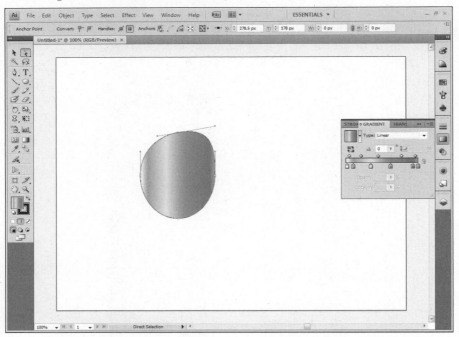

You can change the color of any color stop by simply double-clicking its box. This displays a pop-up panel that allows you to set any color you want by dragging sliders.

Note

The default gradient in Illustrator is a linear gradient from white to black. When you first attempt to modify the color stops, the Color Picker only displays a single slider for shades of black. You can either click the Swatches button in the top-left corner of the pop-up to use a swatch, or click on the panel menu — the button in the top-right corner — and switch from Grayscale to RGB.

You can add more color stops by clicking in the area immediately below the gradient ramp. Should you inadvertently add a color stop and decide you no longer need it, you can remove it by simply dragging it straight down, away from the ramp.

You can drag each color stop left or right to change its position within the gradient. Color stops can be duplicated by Alt (Option)-dragging them. You can reverse the entire gradient by Alt (Option)-dragging either the left-most or right-most stop to its opposite side.

You can save a custom gradient by placing it in the Swatches panel. To do this, simply drag it from the large Gradient Fill button at the top of the Gradient panel to the Swatches panel.

Tip

If you have your panels collapsed in iconic mode, you can still drag gradients to the Swatches panel. Simply drag the gradient from the Gradient Fill box onto the Swatches panel icon, pause for a second or two until the panel opens, and then complete the drag into the panel.

The Gradient tool

Once a gradient is applied to an object, you can use the Gradient tool to modify it. Clicking on an object on the artboard that contains a gradient displays a gradient ramp for that object. You can drag the circle at one end of the ramp to reposition the gradient within the object, or drag the square at the ramp's opposite end to resize it.

The ramp also displays each color stop, so you can adjust their positions within the gradient and even double-click them to change the colors. You can use the Gradient tool to redraw a gradient within a shape that already has the gradient applied by clicking and dragging inside the shape.

Transform objects

Illustrator's Transform tools allow you to rotate, reflect, scale, and shear objects.

The Rotate tool

The Rotate tool allows you to spin an object around an arbitrary anchor point. By default, the anchor will be in the center of the object, so you can simply click and drag to rotate the shape. You can also click with the tool to reset the anchor point — the point around which the object will rotate — at any time. The anchor point doesn't need to be within the object itself.

Note

In order to use the Rotate tool, you must first select the object you want to rotate with either the Selection or Direct Select tool.

The Reflect tool

The Reflect tool allows you to flip an object over an invisible axis. To use it, follow these steps:

1. Select the object, using either the Selection or Direct Select tools.
2. Select the Reflect tool.
3. Click on any point on the art board to define the first point in the invisible axis.
4. Click on a second point, defining the end of the axis.

Once you click on the second point, the object flips over the axis line. If you want to create a mirrored copy of the object, hold down the Alt (Option) key when you click on the second point.

Caution

If you use the Direct Select tool, be sure to select the entire object. If you only have some of the shape's anchor points selected, only those points will be reflected.

The Scale tool

The Scale tool allows you to resize objects. You can use it to click and drag over either an anchor point or a line segment on a selected object and resize that object. If you want to maintain the object's proportions, press and hold the Shift key while dragging.

The Shear tool

You can skew or shear an object along an axis using the Shear tool, which is grouped with the Scale tool. The object will be sheared relative to its axis point when you drag from either a path or anchor point. The axis point is represented by a small cross hair and by default in the center of the shape. You can drag this axis point to any other spot, inside or outside of the shape, to change this axis point.

The Free Transform tool

The Free Transform tool combines the functionality of the Rotate and Scale tools. When you click on an object with the Free Transform tool, you can click and drag just outside the object to rotate it or drag any of the white control handles around the selection outline to resize.

You can also drag anywhere inside the object to reposition it. Unlike the Rotate and Scale tools, the Free Transform tool does not allow you to change the axis around which the object rotates or from which it scales.

Organize Art Work on Layers

Illustrator allows you to organize your complex drawings into layers, sublayers, and groups. It might be easiest to think of drawing in Illustrator as analogous to drawing on clear sheets of plastic overlaid on one another. Each sheet is a sublayer in Illustrator. Each time you add a new object, Illustrator automatically creates a new sublayer on top of those that already exist.

You can see this represented on the artboard; when you draw an object that overlaps those you have already drawn, the new object appears on top of the others. All layers and sublayers are shown in the Layers panel (see Figure 5.20).

Layers and sublayers

Sublayers contain the actual artwork in your Illustrator drawing. You can group sublayers that contain similar or related artwork into layers for better organization.

When you first create an Illustrator file, the program automatically creates a single layer. Any objects you add to the file are placed on sublayers within this layer. However, in larger projects you will want to create additional layers, give them meaningful names, and place sublayers within them.

FIGURE 5.20

The Layers panel for a new document

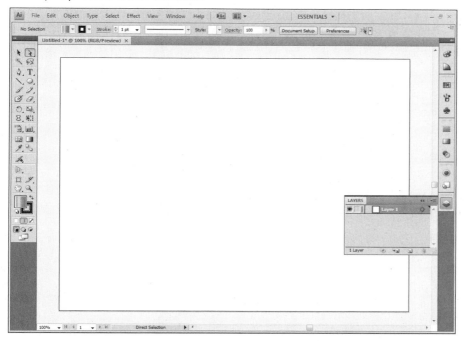

You can rename a layer by simply double-clicking its name in the Layers panel. This displays the Layer Options dialog box (see Figure 5.21). You should always give layers meaningful names based on their content.

The Layer Options dialog box also allows you to set a color for the layer. The selection box around objects on the layer is in this color, providing an easy way to tell which objects are on which layer.

Note
Layers are always made up of a set of sublayers.

FIGURE 5.21

The Layer Options dialog box

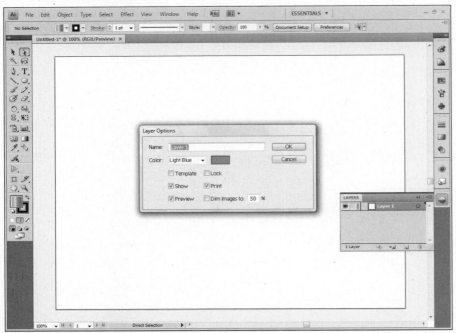

Click the small arrow to the left of the layer name to expand it and show its sublayers (see Figure 5.22). You can and often should rename sublayers. The procedure is the same:

1. **Double-click the sublayer's name.**
2. **Type a new name.** Any new objects are created as sublayers of the currently selected layer, so be careful to select the appropriate layer as you draw.

You can create new layers by clicking the New Layer button at the bottom of the Layers panel. If you want to rename the layer as you create it, press and hold the Alt (Option) key while you click the New Layer button to immediately display the Layer Options dialog box.

Click and drag a sublayer to move it from one layer to another. The order of the layers and sublayers in the Layers panel is the visual stacking order of objects on the artboard. Click and drag layers or sublayers to rearrange them to create a different stacking order.

The small circle to the right of the layer or sublayer name allows you to select the object or objects on the layer. This can be particularly helpful if you need to select an object that is visually behind other objects on the artboard. Simply click the circle for that layer or sublayer, and Illustrator selects the relevant objects on the artboard.

FIGURE 5.22

The Layers panel of a complex document, showing many named layers and sublayers

The eyeball icon to the left of the layer name allows you to show or hide the objects on the layer. Clicking the icon for a layer shows or hides all of its sublayers, but each sublayer has its own visibility icon as well.

The empty box to the right of the eye visibility icon allows you to lock a layer or sublayer. Once locked, the objects on the layer cannot be selected or modified in any way. As with visibility, you can lock a layer and thus lock all of its sublayers, or you can lock individual sublayers as needed.

Add Text to Your Designs

You can add text to enhance your artwork in Illustrator. The program includes a set of text tools for typing horizontal or vertical text, text within shapes, and text on a path.

Text tool

With the basic Text tool, you can click on the artboard and simply begin typing. The Control panel at the top of the screen displays common text properties, including font, style, size, and color.

You can click on the Character label in the Control panel to display the Character panel with additional text properties or the Paragraph label to display the Paragraph panel. Text, like other objects in Illustrator, can have both a fill and a stroke.

Area Text tool

The Area Text tool allows you to add text to an existing shape or object. Almost any path you create can be converted into a text box with this tool. Simply click on the path to add text. You will lose any strokes or fills you have applied to the shape.

Type on a Path tool

The Type on a Path tool allows you to type text that follows a path, most often one drawn with the Pen tool. Once typed, you can adjust the text's position along the path, as well as changing the path itself. The Vertical Text, Vertical Area Type, and Vertical Type on a Path tools all behave similarly to their horizontal counterparts.

Apply Effects

You can use effects to add more visual impact to your design. Illustrator contains a set of effects unique to it as well as Photoshop's Filters, providing you with a variety of effects to apply (see Figure 5.23).

All of the effects are in the Effects menu. You will need to select an object on the art board and then select the appropriate effect from the menu. Each effect displays a dialog box. Select the Preview check box to see the effect on the art board as you adjust its settings.

Once applied, effects can be modified using the Appearance panel. This panel can be opened by choosing Window ➪ Appearance. From here, you can click on the name of the effect, which reopens its settings dialog box.

Using Multiple Artboards

Beginning in Illustrator CS4, designers could divide their work across multiple artboards. A print designer might create a brochure and want to design the front cover, inner pages, and back cover in Illustrator, and so could put each page on a separate artboard.

Web applications rely on a similar multi-page construction. An e-commerce application, for instance, would have a page with a product list, another page with product details, and then several pages to display the shopping cart and checkout process. Almost every project you create for use in Catalyst is likely going to need more than one page. When creating the comp in Illustrator, you can either create the designs for these multiple pages as layers which can be turned on and off as needed, or you can create them on separate artboards. The advantage to the latter approach is that these artboards will be automatically converted into pages upon import into Catalyst.

FIGURE 5.23

Text with the 3D Extrude and Bevel effect applied

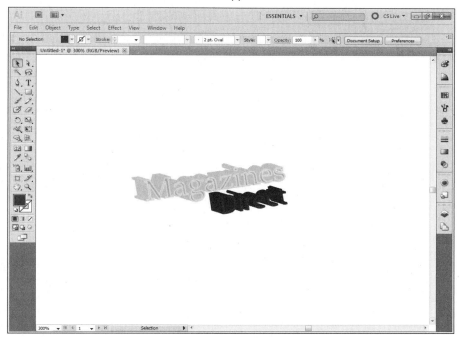

Cross-Reference

See Chapter 10 for more information on pages in Catalyst.

Best Practices when Using Illustrator with Catalyst

The preceding sections have served as a general overview of Illustrator. Much of the work you will do in Illustrator will be the same, regardless of whether you bring that artwork into Catalyst or are designing with something else in mind. There are, however, some things you need to take into account to make the transition to Catalyst easier.

Plan file structure

Illustrator files frequently contain dozens and sometimes hundreds of layers and sublayers. All of these layers and sublayers are imported into Catalyst and appear in its Layers panel. Therefore, taking the time as you design in Illustrator to ensure that your file's layers and sublayers are well organized will save time once you import the project into Catalyst.

Catalyst projects contain a series of application states. These are roughly the equivalent of pages in a traditional HTML-based Web site. For example, an e-commerce Web site will likely have a home page, catalog page, and shopping cart page. The same site as a Flex project will have a home state, catalog state, and shopping cart state.

Each of these states needs to be represented in your Illustrator project. You can simplify your work in Catalyst by grouping all of the assets for each state together in single layers, with shared components such as a logo or main navigation in its own layer.

Follow a naming convention

Every layer and sublayer in Illustrator should have a logical name describing its purpose in the application. Eventually, a Flex developer is likely to take on the task of finalizing the project, and the names you choose early on in Illustrator will be used by the developer in Flash Builder. Therefore, you need to follow a consistent naming convention. Adobe has yet to develop any guidelines on naming best practices for Catalyst comps, so you should instead discuss the issue with your Flex developer and decide on a convention that you can both use.

Do not link to external files

If you choose to import graphics into Illustrator to use as part of your design, you can choose to embed the graphics directly into your project or link to them as external resources. When designing in Illustrator for print, there are advantages to linking, but in Catalyst, linking to those files can be problematic. If you later pass on your project to a Flex developer, the Developer may be unable to access those files as the paths will have changed. Therefore, you should embed all assets.

Tip
If you import raster graphics, be sure to choose Object ⇨ Rasterize and set the resolution to 72dpi. Often, you will also want to set the background to transparent.

Designate duplicated assets

Typical designs will have many repeated assets. You may have a navigation bar that contains repeating backgrounds for buttons or a planned fillable form with repeated boxes representing the backgrounds of the form fields.

While standard practice in Illustrator is to simply copy these assets, Catalyst contains the ability to take an object, convert it to a component, and reuse that component as often as needed. In fact, you will want to avoid repeatedly defining components for artwork that is the same, as it needlessly bloats the file size of the final Flex project and makes updating and maintaining the application more difficult. Therefore, mark any assets that you are copying in Illustrator to make it clear that they do not need to be redefined.

One easy way to do this is to use a consistent name for these assets. For example, the initial box for a form field might be TextField_Background, while duplicates might be Dup_TextField_Background.

Create outlines for text that use filters and effects

A common practice among Illustrator designers is to convert text to outlines. This process changes the text from editable type into vector shapes and is often done when creating works that will be sent out to a commercial printer. If the printer doesn't have the font the designer used, the printer will be unable to produce the document, so converting to outlines removes that as a possibility.

Catalyst projects automatically embed fonts except for common system fonts such as Arial. Therefore, you don't generally need to worry about converting text to outlines. One exception is that Catalyst doesn't always correctly import text that has filters or effects, such as glows or drop shadows. Therefore, this text should be converted to outlines so that it looks correct in Catalyst. Keep in mind that this text will not be editable as text in Catalyst.

Create outlines for uncommon, rarely used fonts

The other time you should consider creating outlines for text is when you have small blocks of text that use an uncommon font. For example, if your organization's logo needs to be rendered in a particular typeface, and that font will only be used for that logo, then you can save file size on your final project by converting that text to outlines so that that font is not embedded into the project.

You might consider doing the same to other small blocks of text that will remain as static text in the final project, but keep in mind that you lose the ability to edit that text without going all the way back to Illustrator.

Use the Blob brush

Artwork drawn with Illustrator's Art and Pattern brushes will be converted into vector paths upon import into Catalyst. Each stroke drawn with these brushes becomes an individual path, which can result in hundreds or even thousands of paths, each of which needs to be treated as an separate object in Catalyst. Illustrator CS5's new Blob brush, however, automatically combines paths as you draw with it. In one example from the project created for this book, a line drawn with the Pattern brush was imported into Catalyst as forty paths; when redrawn with the Blob brush, it imported as a single path.

Rasterize Brushes

Any pieces of the artwork drawn with Illustrator's brush tools that will not need to be altered in Catalyst should be rasterized by selecting the object and clicking Object ➪ Rasterize. In the example project created for this book, the original artwork resulting in over 3000 objects in Catalyst. Rasterizing the artistic lines and silhouettes and then reimporting brought that number to less than 300, resulting in a noticeable performance improvement in Catalyst.

Summary

This chapter served as an introduction to Illustrator. For many designers, Illustrator will be the starting point for work in Catalyst. Most likely Catalyst will be the tool of choice for the creation of the initial design comp that is later converted into a Catalyst project.

You learned the following:

- How to create a new document in Illustrator
- How to use many of Illustrator's tools for drawing shapes and objects
- How to organize your artwork into layers
- How to use text in your designs
- How to apply filters and effects to layers
- Best practices to follow in your design

Creating Assets in Photoshop

Although you can create application comps in either Illustrator or Photoshop, it's likely that many designers will find Illustrator's drawing capabilities better suited to the task of creating the comp. Photoshop's strength, on the other hand, has never been in creating images but rather in modifying existing raster graphics.

Therefore, assets for your application, particularly photographic assets, will likely require a certain amount of work in Photoshop before they are ready to be brought into Catalyst.

Opening Files in Photoshop

It is possible to create images completely from scratch in Photoshop. There are, in fact, artists who create photo-realistic imagery entirely in the program. Most of the time, however, you will be opening pre-existing images, whether pulled from your company's image library, downloaded from a stock photo site, or taken by you on your digital camera.

Caution

Images are subject to copyright protection. Do not download an image off any Web site you do not own with the intent of using it in your application unless that site specifically states that such use is acceptable. If you have any doubt at all about whether or not you can use an image, it may be best to err on the side of caution and assume you cannot. Copyright laws vary from country to country and can be very complex, so when in doubt, seek competent legal counsel.

Tip

There are many extremely good royalty-free stock photo sites on the Web. A good list of many of the more popular sites can be found at www.smashingmagazine.com/2009/08/16/free-and-commercial-stock-photography-sites/.

Photoshop supports opening images in almost all of the most popular file formats, but images you download from stock photography sites will almost certainly be either JPEG or PNG images. Your company's image library may have them as TIFF or BMP files. This is only a small list of the formats supported by the program. Except for images saved in proprietary, application-specific formats, if you have an image on your computer, you can almost certainly open it in Photoshop.

You have a few options for opening images. You can click File ➪ Open, and navigate to the folder in which your images reside. If you do not currently have any files open, you can double-click on any blank, gray area of the Photoshop window to open the Open file dialog box.

Tip

The double-click shortcut to open files works over most of the screen in Windows. On a Mac, or on Windows if you have other files open, you can double-click in the darker gray area below the panels on the right or below the Tools panel on the left.

You can also open files from Adobe Bridge (see Figure 6.1). Bridge is a stand-alone application installed with any of the Creative Suite applications. You can access Bridge directly from the Start menu in Windows or the Dock on a Mac or by clicking File ➪ Browse in most Creative Suite products, including Photoshop. Photoshop also includes a button on its Application bar to launch Bridge.

Bridge allows you to organize and sort files with more freedom than is provided in either Windows Explorer or the Mac Finder. Bridge also allows you to rate images on a five-point scale and add keywords and other metadata, and then either search for files or filter file lists by the rating or keywords.

As long as your operating system's preferences are set to open the file type in Photoshop, double-clicking any image in Bridge opens it in Photoshop. Should you have a different program associated with the file, you can right-click (⌘+click) the file, then select Open With ➪ Photoshop CS5.

You can have multiple files open at the same time in Photoshop, and each one is represented by a tab along the top of the screen. You can switch to viewing another file by clicking its tab, or rearrange the order of the files by dragging the tabs. You can also drag a tab into the middle of the screen to detach it so that it floats in its own window.

To open multiple files at once, follow these steps:

1. **From Photoshop's Open dialog box, Ctrl+click (⌘+click) files to select them.**
2. **Either press Enter or click Open.**

FIGURE 6.1

Adobe Bridge

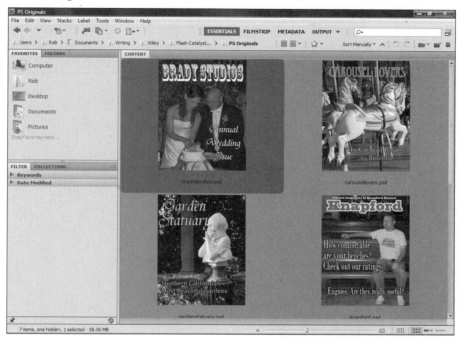

In Bridge, you can follow much the same procedure:

1. Ctrl+click (⌘+click) the files.
2. Either double-click any one of the files, or right-click (⌘-click) any of the files.
3. Select Open With ➪ Photoshop CS5.

Viewing Images

When you open an image in Photoshop, the program automatically opens the file at a level of magnification that allows you to see the entire image, which rarely is 100 percent. The Zoom tool allows you to increase or decrease the magnification to see more or less detail on the image.

Note

As with the chapter on Illustrator, this chapter on Photoshop does not attempt to cover every aspect of the program, or even every tool on the Tools panel. Instead, this chapter focuses on those tools, panels, and features most likely to be of use to the Catalyst designer. See Photoshop CS5 Bible, by Lisa DaNae Dayley and Brad Dayley, for a more thorough handling of the subject.

You can select the Zoom tool by clicking the magnifying glass toward the bottom of the Tools panel on the left edge of the screen (see Figure 6.2). Each time you click the image, you zoom in. When you need to zoom back out, press and hold the Alt (Option) key and click.

When you are busy using another tool, you can temporarily use various Zoom functions by checking out the shortcuts listed in Table 6.1.

You can quickly zoom in on a specific region of a page by using the Zoom tool to create a marquee selection. Click and drag the mouse with the Zoom tool to draw the marquee; when you release the mouse, Photoshop zooms you in so that the pixels within the marquee fill the screen.

FIGURE 6.2

Zooming in on an image using the Zoom tool

Note

Remember that Photoshop is primarily a raster-based editor, and all photographic images will be raster. Raster images are resolution-dependent, so how far you can zoom in and still maintain detail depends on the resolution of the image.

Once you have zoomed in on the image, you need to navigate to see other areas of the picture. You can of course use the scrollbars, but you can generally move more easily using the Hand tool. Once the tool is selected, click and drag to move to other areas of the image.

You may also use the Navigator panel, which you can open by clicking Window ⇨ Navigator. The panel shows a thumbnail of the image, with a red box outlining the portion of the image on-screen. Simply drag the red box to a different area of the screen to move there.

Tip

While using other tools, you can temporarily access the Hand tool by pressing and holding Shift and then clicking and dragging as normal.

TABLE 6.1	
Zoom Shortcuts	
Desired zoom	**Shortcut**
Access Zoomin tool	Press and hold Ctrl/⌘+spacebar
Access Zoom out tool	Press and hold Ctrl/⌘+Alt/Option+spacebar
Zoom in	Ctrl/⌘++
Zoom out	Ctrl/⌘+-
Zoom to 100 percent magnification	Ctrl/⌘+1
Zoom to 100 percent magnification when accessing the Zoom tool in the Tools panel	Ctrl/⌘+0 or double-click the Hand tool.

Selecting Images

Very often, you will want to work on a portion of an image and be sure to not affect other areas. For example, if a photograph had an overexposed background and a properly exposed foreground, you would want to darken the background without changing the foreground. To do this, you need to select the pixels in the background. When a region of pixels is selected, Photoshop's tools affect only the selection.

Rectangular and elliptical selections

Selecting geometric areas of an image is fairly easy with the Rectangle and Elliptical Marquee tools. Both share the same spot on the Tools panel, so you need to press and hold your mouse on one to select the other, just as you did in Illustrator.

With the tool active, click and drag on the image to create a selection marquee. You can press and hold Shift while you drag to create a perfect square or perfect circle (see Figure 6.3).

FIGURE 6.3

Creating a rectangular selection

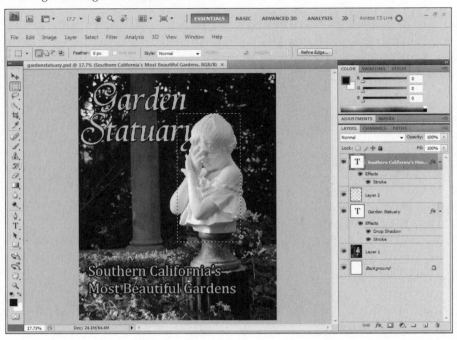

Tip

You can press and hold the Spacebar while you drag when using any selection tool to move the selection to a different location as you draw it. You can press and hold Alt (Option) while you drag with the Rectangle or Elliptical Marquee tools to draw the selection from the center, rather than the edge as is the default.

Lasso tool

When you need a freeform selection marquee, use the Lasso tool. Simply click and drag on the document. If you return to your original point before releasing the mouse, Photoshop creates a marquee selection in the shape you drew (see Figure 6.4).

If you release the mouse before returning to your original point, Photoshop draws a straight line between your release point and your starting point to complete the marquee.

The Lasso tool is not generally a good tool to use when you need precise selections. Unless you have either a graphics tablet or a very steady hand, you will likely have difficulty drawing the marquee with the Lasso tool.

FIGURE 6.4

Using the Lasso tool to create a rough selection marquee

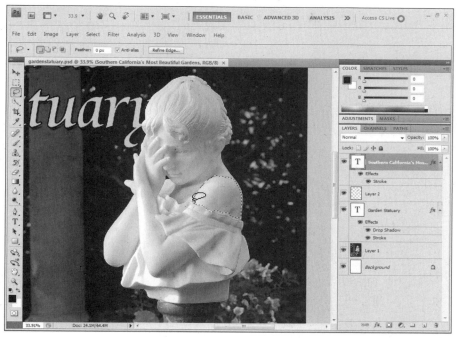

Therefore, it is best used when you need only a rough selection outline. Other selection tools, such as the Quick Select tool and the Magic Wand, give you better precision.

Polygon Lasso and Magnetic Lasso tools

Grouped with the Lasso tool are the Polygon and Magnetic Lasso tools. The Polygon Lasso allows you to draw a selection marquee in a shape with any number of straight sides.

Simply click on the image anywhere that you want to place a corner, and Photoshop draws a straight line for the marquee between that corner and the previous one. Click back on your starting point to complete the marquee and create the selection (see Figure 6.5).

The Magnetic Lasso allows you to follow lines in the image. If you have a portion of an image with high contrast and distinct outlines, such as the side of a dark building against a light sky, the Magnetic Lasso allows you to create a selection that follows that edge.

To use the Magnetic Lasso tool, follow these steps:

1. **Click a starting point on the edge and then drag along that edge.** You do not need to hold down the mouse button, but you will find that the tool is more precise if you drag very slowly.

2. **If the tool does not follow the edge, click to create points to lock in the side.** Keep in mind that the tool relies on high contrast, so it is unlikely to work on an image with indistinct edges.

FIGURE 6.5

Using the Magnetic Lasso tool to follow a distinct outline

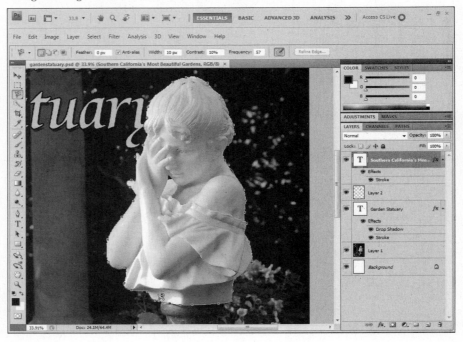

Smart Selection and Magic Wand tools

The Smart Selection tool allows you to very quickly create selections in areas with high contrast and distinct edges (see Figure 6.6).

To use the tool, simply click and drag within the area you want to select. As long as the area you are selecting has sufficient contrast with its background, the tool allows you to drag through the region and create the selection you want.

The circle you see while selecting is the brush size, which you can adjust before you begin selecting by using the left and right square bracket keys.

The Magic Wand tool selects areas based on similar colors. Simply click on a pixel in your image, and all contiguous pixels with the same or similar colors are selected. The Tool Options panel at the top of the screen includes a Threshold setting to determine how similar or dissimilar a color can be in order to get selected. High threshold numbers allow for a wider range of colors to get selected than lower thresholds.

Combining selection tools

You will encounter many occasions when one of the selection tools works for a portion of your image, but not other sections. Fortunately, Photoshop allows you to add to or subtract from selections, and even combine selection tools.

FIGURE 6.6

The Smart Selection tool

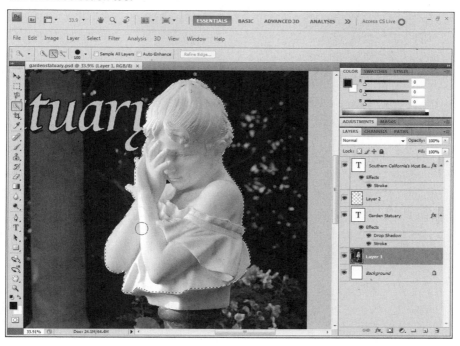

With any selection tool, you can press and hold Shift to add to your current selection (see Figure 6.7) or press and hold Alt (Option) to subtract from it.

Adding to an existing selection

You can do this with any tool, including a tool other than the one with which you made the initial selection. For example, if you wanted to select a single flower in an image, you might start with the Magic Wand, assuming that the flower was mostly a single color. Then, you could press and hold Shift and use the Smart Selection tool to add smaller petals or other details to the selection.

Conversely, if you began with the Smart Selection tool and ended up having a selection that included some areas that you did not want, you could press and hold Alt (Option) and drag over those extra areas to remove them from the selection.

Remove selections

You cannot do anything to any part of an image that is not selected. Therefore, once you are done manipulating a selected region, you need to deselect to continue working on other parts of the image. You can deselect by either clicking in an unselected area with a selection tool, or by clicking Select ➪ Deselect, or by using the keyboard shortcut Ctrl+D (⌘+D).

Saving selections

You may end up needing to spend a considerable amount of time creating a selection in Photoshop; you would not want to lose that selection by an inadvertent mouse-click.

There may also be times when you need to create a selection and manipulate a part of an image, and then later in your work return to that same selection. To help in both of these cases, Photoshop allows you to save selections. With an active selection, simply click Select ⇨ Save Selection.

The Save Selection dialog box allows you to name your selection and save it as a channel (see Figure 6.8). You can reload selections by following these steps:

1. Click Select ⇨ **Load Selection.**
2. **Choose the appropriate channel.**
3. **Click OK.**

FIGURE 6.8

The Save Selection dialog box

Introducing Color Channels

Channels store color information in Photoshop. An RGB image begins with four channels. one channel each for the red, green, and blue colors, and one composite channel with all three combined. Individual channels are displayed as grayscale images.

Pure white pixels represent pixels that contain that channel's color, whereas pure black pixels contain none of that color. In most images, each channel is mostly shades of gray because most pixels are some combination of the three.

When you create a selection, Photoshop creates a new channel. Pixels completely within the selection are white, pixels not selected black, and partially selected pixels a shade of gray. These selection channels are sometimes known as *alpha channels* because they can be used to store transparency information.

Sizing and Cropping Images

Photoshop allows you to resize and crop images. As rasters, images in Photoshop cannot be resized without affecting either their file size or their quality, and most often both. You can resize images by clicking Image ⇨ Image Size.

The dialog box shows the size of the image using two different but related methods (see Figure 6.9). The top section shows the pixel dimensions, and the bottom displays the document size, usually in inches.

Photoshop calculates this document size by multiplying the resolution of the image by the pixel dimensions. If you change the pixel dimensions, the document size changes while leaving the resolution alone. Conversely, changing the resolution changes the pixel dimensions according to the current document size.

Tip

The ideal resolution for images that you plan to display on Web pages is 72 pixels per inch. This ensures good quality images on most computer monitors while maximizing file savings. However, you generally want to work on images that are at least double the final resolution to give you a high-enough quality to do the edits you need. Therefore, you should try to work on images that are at least 150 pixels per inch, and plan to drop them to 72 when you are done editing.

You can almost always scale images down, making them smaller, without noticeable quality loss. The same is not true when scaling up because Photoshop needs to *resample* the image, filling data into what become new pixels in the image.

FIGURE 6.9

The Image Size dialog box

The bottom of the Image Size dialog box allows you to set the method that Photoshop uses for this resampling. For most images, the default method, Bicubic, works well, so you will rarely need to change it.

In addition to resizing images, Photoshop allows you to *crop* (see Figure 6.10). Cropping an image involves removing areas of the image you no longer want. You may choose to crop an image simply to make it smaller, but usually it is a more artistic decision. By cropping unwanted areas from the image, you can change the focus of an image.

Cropping an image. The image on the left is uncropped, showing the carousel; on the right, the same image has been cropped to draw attention to a single horse.

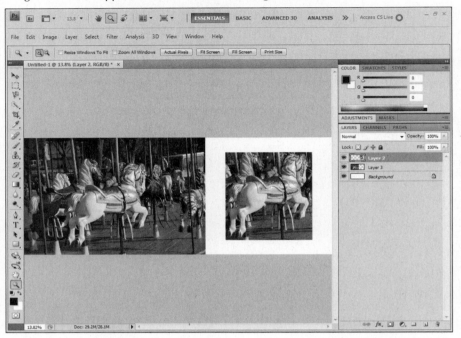

Work with Layers

Photoshop relies heavily on layers for organizing complex images, although its layers function slightly differently from Illustrator's. In Illustrator, every shape you draw is placed on its own sub-layer. Photoshop does not have sublayers; when you add multiple objects to the same layer in Photoshop, they simply overlap one another on that layer.

Because Photoshop does not automatically create sublayers as you work, you do need to be much more conscious about layers. Whenever you need to have a new portion of your work on a new layer, you need to be sure to create the new layer first. Two objects on the same layer merge into one another, so in order to maintain editability, you need to do almost everything on new layers.

Just as in Illustrator, Photoshop's Layers panel displays the layers in the image. The order in which the layers appear is their stacking order, bottom up. You can change this by simply dragging layers up or down as needed. The eye icon to the left of the layer thumbnail allows you to show or hide the layer.

Nondestructive Editing

A common phrase you will hear among Photoshop developers these days is *nondestructive editing*. The common practice as recently as a few years ago was to edit images directly on the image layer, thus permanently altering or destroying the original data.

Today, most Photoshop professionals recommend that all editing happen on new layers, which preserves the original data. This technique ensures that you can always go back and change aspects of the image.

You can create new layers in Photoshop by clicking the New Layer button in the bottom of the Layers panel. You should get in the habit early on of giving your layers meaningful names, which you can do by double-clicking the layer's current name.

Note
A checkerboard pattern on a layer's thumbnail represents transparent pixels on that layer.

Copy selections to new layers

Once you have an area of your image selected, you may want to copy that selection to a new layer. This allows you to further isolate the selection while working on it. With any range of pixel selection, you can click Layer ➪ New ➪ Layer via Copy. The selected pixels are placed on a new layer above the original.

Most of the time, it is better to copy pixels to the new layer, instead of choosing the Layer via Cut option. Copying the pixels gives you the new layer while preserving the original. If you later change your mind and decide you no longer need the new layer, you can delete it and return to your unaltered image.

Delete layers

You can delete layers at any time. Select the layer and click the small trashcan icon in the lower right corner of the Layers panel, or drag the layer onto the trashcan.

Selecting layers versus selecting layer contents

When you select a layer in the Layers panel, you are making that layer available for editing. Actions you perform apply to that layer. When you use a selection tool, it selects only the pixels on the currently active layer. However, selecting a layer does not automatically select any pixels on that layer. If you want to select all of the nontransparent pixels on a layer, you can Ctrl+click (⌘+click) the layer's thumbnail.

Layer opacity

Each layer has an opacity setting that allows you to make it semi and completely transparent. The property appears in the top right corner of the Layer panel. You can adjust the opacity by typing a percentage value in the text box, clicking the arrow and dragging the slider, or scrubbing the value by dragging left or right directly on the Opacity label.

Layer blend modes

You can blend the colors on layers with those below it by changing the layer's blend mode. Photoshop supports a long list of blend modes. The most commonly used blend modes are:

- Multiply
- Screen
- Overlay

Multiply blends the darkest pixels of the layer being blended with the dark pixels of the layers below it, resulting in a darker overall appearance.

Screen is the opposite of Multiply: The lightest pixels of the layer are blending with the light pixels below.

Overlay is somewhat in the middle, blending the midtones of the layers. There is no right or wrong when blending layers, and only experimentation reveals the blend mode that results in the effect you are trying to achieve.

Cross-Reference
Many of Photoshop's blend modes exist in Catalyst. See Chapter 4 for an overview of the Catalyst blend modes.

Cross-Reference
See Photoshop CS5 Bible, by Lisa DaNae Dayley and Brad Dayley, for a more detailed description of layer blend modes in Photoshop.

Image Retouching

One of the more common uses of Photoshop is *retouching* images. Images may need minor fixes such as removing blemishes on a model, correcting color, or major work such as fixing water stains on old prints.

Color correction

Many pictures, particularly those made with digital cameras, need to have their color corrected. Digital cameras contain a sensor that sets the white balance on the photo, which varies depending on the light source at the time the picture was taken. Some cameras are very good about automatically adjusting the white balance, but even the best sometimes get it wrong.

There may also be times when you simply want to change the white balance, and thus the overall coloring of the photo, for artistic reasons.

Several different techniques exist for correcting white balance in images in Photoshop, but one of the easiest is to use a Color Balance adjustment layer. Many easy-to-use adjustment presets exist in the Adjustments panel (see Figure 6.11). You can open the Adjustments layer by clicking Window⇨Adjustments. At the top of the panel, 15 icons, each represent a type of adjustment.

FIGURE 6.11

The Adjustments panel

The Color Balance is the icon that resembles a set of scales in the second row. Clicking the icon adds an adjustment layer to your image and presents you with three color sliders. The first adjusts the color between cyan and red, the second between magenta and green, and the third between yellow and blue. You can adjust your image's white balance by simply moving these sliders left or right until you get the desired effect (see Figure 6.12).

FIGURE 6.12

Changing the color balance on the adjustment panel

Note

When you use the Adjustments panel, Photoshop applies your changes through an adjustment layer. This is a special layer that allows you to perform nondestructive adjustments. Because all of the changes are made on a separate layer, you are not altering the actual image so you can always continue to fine-tune the adjustment by simply clicking on the layer. You can remove it altogether by deleting the layer.

Once you have made the desired adjustments, you can click the arrow in the bottom left corner of the panel to return to the main Adjustments menu. You can add as many adjustments as you want, but be aware that each is added on a new adjustment layer above the last so the adjustments are cumulative.

Fixing highlights and shadows

Another common issue with many photos is that they are either too bright or too dark. As with color balance, these problems can be fixed with an adjustment layer.

Several techniques exist to adjust the overall brightness of an image, but the easiest one to understand is Brightness/Contrast. This is the first of the icons on the Adjustments panel and simply presents two sliders (see Figure 6.13). The Brightness slider increases or decreases the level of the highlights in the image, whereas the Contrast slider does the same for the shadows.

FIGURE 6.13

The Brightness/Contrast adjustment

Removing blemishes

Photoshop contains several useful tools to alter the image itself. The Spot Healing Brush tool, Healing Brush tool, Patch tool, and Red Eye Removal tool are all grouped together.

Spot Healing Brush tool

The Spot Healing Brush tool allows you to paint over problem areas of your image (see Figure 6.14). It takes the painted pixels and blends them with those in the immediate vicinity. You can often correct small blemishes such as spots on a camera lens very quickly with this tool.

Tip

When using the Spot Healing Brush use short, small strokes. If you attempt to paint over too large an area at once, you get undesirable results.

Healing Brush tool

You can accomplish more precise work with the Healing Brush tool (see Figure 6.15). This tool creates the same basic effect as the Spot Healing Brush, but the Healing Brush allows you to define the spot from which the blending pixels are drawn.

FIGURE 6.14

Fixing blemishes with the Spot Healing Brush tool

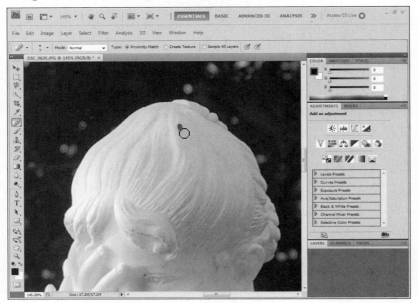

FIGURE 6.15

Fixing an image with the Healing Brush

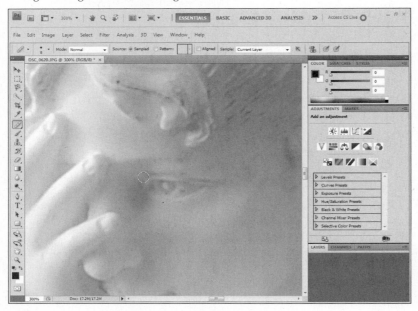

To use this tool, follow these steps:

1. **Define a source point from which to draw the pixels to be blended by Alt+clicking (Option+clicking) a spot on the image.** You generally want this to be a point fairly close to the area to be repaired.

2. **Click and drag over the area to be repaired.** Photoshop takes the pixels from the source point and blends them with the pixels over which you drag.

Patch tool

The Patch tool functions much as the Healing Brush tool does by allowing you to blend pixels from one area of the image with those from another (see Figure 6.16). However, with the Patch tool, you define the area to be fixed first and then drag it to the area with the pixels to be blended.

To use the Patch tool, follow these steps:

1. **Click and drag to draw a marquee around the area that you want to fix.**

2. **Position the cursor within the selected region, and click and drag it over the area with the good pixels.** Photoshop blends these pixels with those in the original region.

FIGURE 6.16

Using the Patch tool

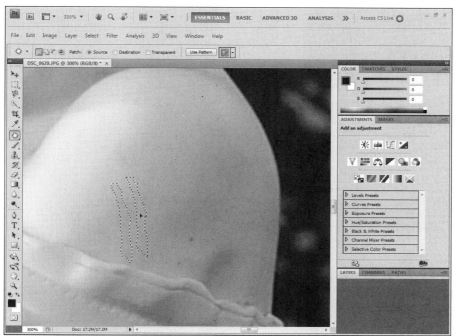

Tip

The Spot Healing Brush, Healing Brush, Patch, and Red Eye Removal tools must be used directly on the layer that contains the pixels to be fixed. Therefore, you should duplicate the layer that contains the image before you work. By doing so, you preserve the original image and follow the idea of doing only nondestructive editing. You can duplicate a layer by selecting it in the Layers panel, then clicking Layer ⇨ Duplicate Layer from the main menu.

Red-Eye Removal tool

The Red-Eye Removal tool is a somewhat unique tool in that it serves only one purpose, albeit an important one. Red-eye is a major issue on many photographs of people, particularly children. The tool makes it very easy to remove the red-eye. Simply click and drag to create a selection around the red part of the eye and Photoshop takes care of the rest.

Add Vector Shapes and Paths in Photoshop

Photoshop contains a set of vector-based drawing tools that allow you to create shapes and paths. While the program contains several tools for drawing vectors, the primary one is the Pen tool. You can draw paths using the Pen tool, relying on exactly the same techniques used in Illustrator (see Figure 6.17).

FIGURE 6.17

The Tools Options bar for the Pen tool, showing the three possible modes. These same options are available when using any vector tool.

Cross-Reference

See Chapter 5 for details on drawing paths with the Pen tool.

Whenever you draw vectors in Photoshop, you need to set the mode for your drawing. You can create shape layers, paths, or fill pixels.

Shape layers are special layers filled with a solid color that have a mask overlay in the shape you draw (see Figure 6.18). Shape layers appear as your desired shape on the document, but you can see the fill layer and mask in the Layers panel.

FIGURE 6.18

A shape layer. The shape appears as a solid shape on the document, but the fill layer and mask can be seen on the Layers panel.

If you select the Path option you can create paths, but they do not relate to pixels on the image. Paths drawn using this mode can be accessed via the Paths panel. The panel provides a set of buttons along the bottom that allow you to stroke or fill the path, both of which rasterize the path into pixels on the document, or convert the path into a selection (see Figure 6.19).

The final mode, Fill Pixels, simply allows you to use the control offered by the vector tools to create rasterized pixel-based drawings (see Figure 6.20).

FIGURE 6.19

A shape created by using the Paths panel to add a stroke to a path

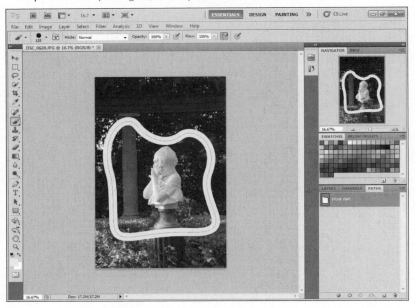

FIGURE 6.20

A shape drawn using the Fill Pixels mode

Note

The Fill Pixels option is not usable with the Pen tool. You can only use it with the shape tools.

In addition to the Pen tool, you can also draw vectors using the shape tools (see Figure 6.21). Photoshop includes a set of vector tools very similar to Illustrator; Rectangle, Rounded Rectangle, Ellipse, Polygon, and Line.

Photoshop also includes a Custom Shape tool. When selected, the Tools Options bar provides a Shape menu that allows you to choose from a set of included shapes.

Note

Just as with Illustrator, you can press and hold Shift when drawing with the Rectangle or Rounded Rectangle tools to draw perfect squares, or when drawing with the Ellipse to draw perfect circles. However, you cannot use the arrow keys to increase or decrease the radius of the corners when drawing Rounded Rectangles as in Illustrator, nor can you use those keys to change the number of sides of a polygon. Those options are instead located on the Tools Options bar.

FIGURE 6.21

The Shape menu

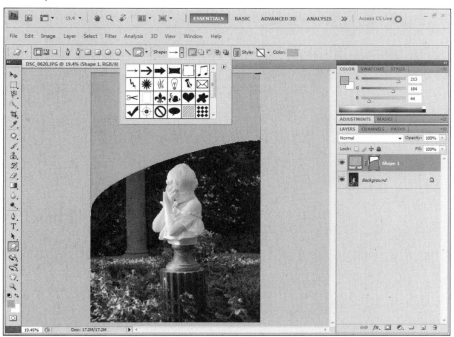

Add Layer Styles

Photoshop's layer styles allow you to add many special effects to your layers. Shape layers and layers with selections copied and pasted onto new layers can have effects applied to them.

Note

The default layer in any image opened in Photoshop is the Background layer. This is a special, protected layer. You can make selections on it and paint directly on it, but you cannot apply layer effects to it or move it up in the layer stacking order. You can convert it to a normal layer by double-clicking its name, which displays the Layer Properties dialog box. Simply type a new name and click OK.

You can add layer styles by selecting a layer and clicking the Add a layer style button in the bottom right corner of the Layers panel, then selecting the style to add (see Figure 6.22). This, in turn, displays the Layer Style dialog box, where you can modify the properties of the selected style or add additional styles.

FIGURE 6.22

The Add a new layer style menu

Tip

In the Layer Style dialog box, clicking the checkbox next to a style name adds that style to the current layer but does not display the style's properties. Clicking the style name both adds it to the layer and displays its properties.

Layer styles that have been applied to a layer are listed below the layer name in the Layers panel. Each has its own eye icon, allowing you to hide or show the layer as needed. At any point, you can change the style's properties by double-clicking its name in the panel.

Should you apply a layer style to a layer and then decide that you want it applied to a different layer, you can simply drag the style to the new layer. To copy a layer style, press and hold Alt (Option) while you drag the style to a different layer.

Add Text

The Text tool in Photoshop provides many powerful ways to add text to your image. When you select the Text tool the Tools Options bar changes to display basic text properties such as font, text styles, font size, alignment, and color. Many more options are available on the Character and Paragraph panels (see Figure 6.23).

The Character panel

All text is placed on its own layer. You can move it up or down in the Layers panel to change its position in the stacking order, turn it on or off by clicking its Show/Hide Layer icon, and apply layer styles to it.

Create embossed text

A common effect seen in many Photoshop images is text that appears to be embossed on top of an image (see Figure 6.24). You can achieve this effect through a combination of layer effects and masking.

To create this effect, perform the following steps:

1. **Duplicate the background layer by clicking Layer ⇨ Duplicate Layer.**
2. **Click the Text tool.**
3. **Type the text.**
4. **Set the font, size, and other properties of the text.** This effect works best on fonts with simple, straight lines.

FIGURE 6.24

The final embossed text effect

5. With the text layer selected, click Add a layer style ⇨ Bevel and Emboss from the bottom of the Layers panel.

6. Adjust the Bevel and Emboss settings as desired.

7. Move the text layer between the two image layers.

8. Select the top image layer.

9. Click Layer ⇨ Create Clipping Mask.

Create 3D Text

While Photoshop contains tools to work with 3D images, none are really appropriate for creating 3D text. Fortunately, you can create this effect fairly easily through a simple process of duplicating and moving layers. Figure 6.25 shows the completed 3D text effect.

FIGURE 6.25

The completed 3D text effect

To create this effect, perform the following steps:

1. **Create a new text layer by clicking the Text tool and typing the word or phrase you wish to use.**

2. **Set the font, color and size to any settings you wish.** This effect works best with large type.

3. **Click the Move tool.**

4. **On the Layers panel, be sure that your text layer is selected.**

5. **Click Ctrl-J (Cmd-J) to duplicate the layer.**

6. **On your keyboard, press the Up arrow once.**

7. **Press the Right arrow once.** This moves the new layer one pixel up and to the right.

8. **Duplicate the new layer by pressing Ctrl-J (Cmd-J).** Move the layer up and to the right by one pixel by pressing the appropriate arrow keys.

9. **Repeat step 8 as many times as desired until the text has the depth that you wish (see Figure 6.26.)**

FIGURE 6.26

The 3D text after duplicating and moving the layers

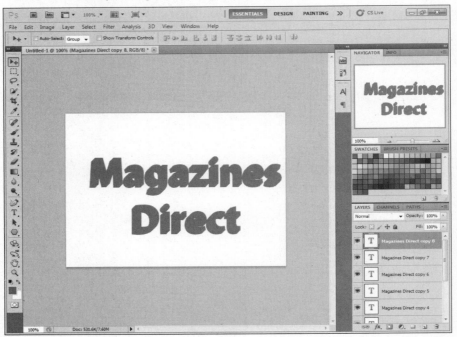

10. If you wish, make the text more visually interesting by applying a gradient fill to the top layer by ensuring that it is selected, then clicking the Layer Effects button at the bottom of the Layers panel and selecting Gradient Fill.

11. Select a gradient where either the beginning or ending color matches the color of the text you were using.

12. Click OK. (See Figure 6.27.)

FIGURE 6.27

Adding a Gradient Fill effect to the top 3D layer

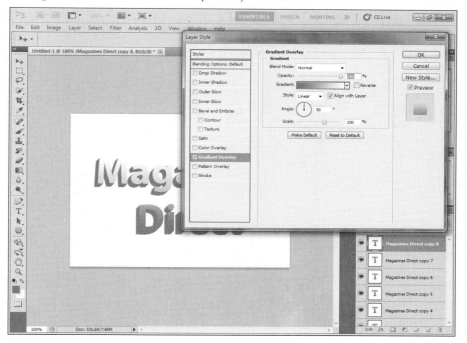

Summary

This chapter provided an overview of Adobe Photoshop, which you will likely use to modify photos and other raster-based assets for your Catalyst projects.

You learned how to:

- Open images in Photoshop
- View images by zooming in and out on them and moving them around on the screen

- Use Photoshop's selection tools
- Size and crop images
- Work with layers to organize your images
- Retouch images and fix image problems
- Use Photoshop's vector tools to add shapes and paths
- Create effects using layer styles
- Work with text

Using Fireworks with Flash Catalyst

While Adobe Illustrator excels at creating vector-based graphics and Photoshop remains an industry standard in raster or bitmap graphic editing, Adobe Fireworks nicely bridges the two.

Fireworks's real strength, however, is in working with graphics created specifically for the Web. While both Illustrator and Photoshop now contain tools for dealing with the specific demands of Web graphics, neither program was created for that purpose. Fireworks, however, was designed from the very beginning for Web graphics. Its mix of both vector and raster tools along with its superior Web optimization tools make it an ideal choice for creating images for your Web site.

With the release of Fireworks CS3, Adobe added features to the program to also make it a good tool for doing rapid prototyping of Web sites. Today, many professional Web designers begin the process of creating sites in Fireworks, which allows designers to create initial design comps to present to their clients.

Unfortunately, Fireworks does not, at this point, work seamlessly with Catalyst. In some ways the two products fill the same niche: Catalyst provides a means by which designers can create initial prototypes of Flex projects, whereas Fireworks provides the same tool for HTML-based sites.

That said, many designers still prefer Fireworks over Illustrator and Photoshop as their primary graphics tool. Adobe is not ignoring Fireworks in the Catalyst workflow, but a true round-trip workflow does not exist between Fireworks and Catalyst as it does with Illustrator.

IN THIS CHAPTER

Creating a new file in Fireworks

Fireworks tools

Working with color

Optimizing images

Exporting FXG files

Creating a New Fireworks File

As with other tools in the Creative Suite, Fireworks displays a Start screen on launch (see Figure 7.1). From here you will find a Create New category with a single option: Fireworks Document (PNG).

FIGURE 7.1

The Fireworks CS5 Start screen

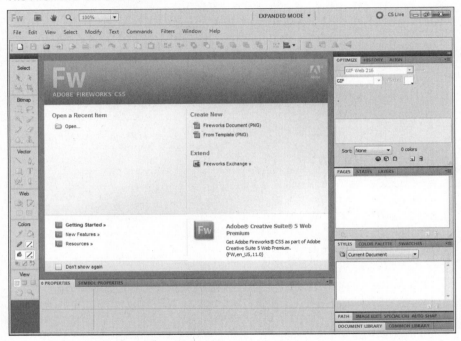

Clicking the option to create a new Fireworks PNG file displays the New Document dialog box (see Figure 7.2). From this dialog box, you can select the size, resolution, and canvas or background color.

Note

Fireworks's default file format is PNG. Most Web designers are already familiar with the PNG format due to its increasing popularity as a Web graphics format. PNG files often replace GIF and in some cases JPG files. However, Fireworks uses a specially modified version of the format that supports layers and other data needed by Fireworks. Therefore, a Fireworks PNG file cannot be placed directly on a Web page without first being converted to a traditional PNG.

Tip

When you create files for Catalyst keep in mind that you are still creating a file with the primary purpose of putting something online. Therefore, you should keep your resolution at 72 pixels per inch.

FIGURE 7.2

The New Document dialog box in Fireworks

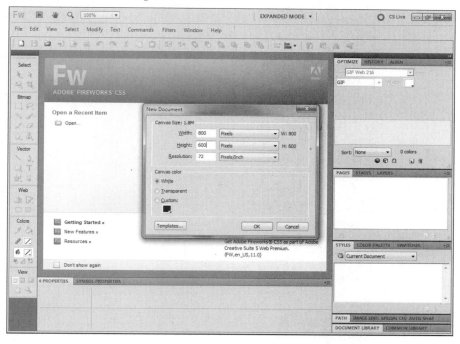

Fireworks Tools and Panels

As with other programs in the Creative Suite, Fireworks contains a set of tools and panels that allow you to interact with the application.

Tools

The Tools panel (see Figure 7.3), which by default displays on the left side of the screen, contains the main tools in the program. As with Illustrator and Photoshop, Fireworks groups its tools although it also displays headings for each group.

Like other graphics programs, Fireworks occasionally nests tools together requiring you to press and hold your mouse on one tool to display a menu of additional, related tools.

Part II: Designing the Application

FIGURE 7.3

The Fireworks Tools panel

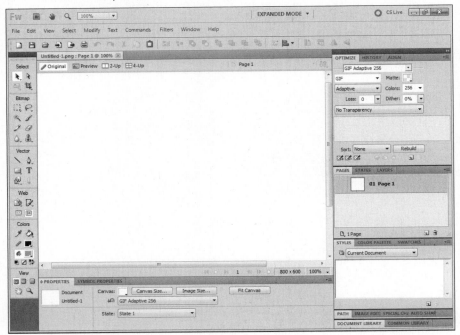

Table 7.1 lists all of the tools in Fireworks. Every tool can be selected by pressing an assigned key on the keyboard, as shown in the table. Those tools with multiple assigned keys can be selected with either key. Nested tools will often share the same key and can be selected by pressing the key repeatedly until the desired tool is chosen.

TABLE 7.1

Fireworks Tools

Tool	Description	Selection Key
Pointer	Used for selecting and moving objects on the screen.	V, 0 (zero)
Select Behind	Allows for selection of objects on lower layers without first locking or hiding the upper layer. The tool is nested with the Pointer tool.	V, 0 (zero)
Subselection	Allows for selecting paths or points on vectors.	A, 1
Scale	Used for scaling and rotating objects.	Q
Skew	Skewing shapes allows you to move specific points along a straight line relative to the side of the shape while keeping others locked in place. Nested with the Scale tool.	Q

154

Tool	Description	Selection Key
Distort	The Distort tool lets you move a specific point in any direction while keeping other points locked in place. Nested with the Scale tool.	Q
9-Slice Scaling	9-Slice scaling is a technique in which you divide the shape into 9 pieces, representing the top left, top center, top right, middle left, center, middle right, bottom right, bottom center, and bottom right sections. This allows you to scale only the center section, keeping the other portions intact. 9-slice scaling can be particularly helpful for scaling objects such as rounded rectangles, where you want to make the object bigger without distorting the rounded edges. It is nested with the Scale tool.	Q
Crop	Cropping allows you to cut off edges of an object.	C
Export Area	This tool lets you define a portion of an image to be exported as a PNG, GIF, JPG, or other format. Nested with the Crop tool.	C
Marquee	Creates a rectangular selection marquee.	M
Oval Marquee	Creates an oval or circular selection marquee. Nested with the Marquee tool.	M
Lasso	Allows you to draw a free-form selection marquee.	L
Polygon Lasso	Creates a selection marquee using defined points and straight lines. Nested with the Lasso.	L
Magic Wand	Selects all of the pixels with similar colors.	W
Brush	Paints bitmap shapes.	B
Pencil	Draws bitmap lines.	B
Eraser	Erases bitmap lines and shapes.	E
Blur	Applies a Gaussian blur to bitmaps.	R
Sharpen	Sharpens bitmap edges. Nested with the Blur tool.	R
Dodge	Lightens selected pixels in bitmaps. Nested with the Blur tool.	R
Burn	Darkens selected pixels in bitmaps. Nested with the Blur tool.	R
Smudge	Mixes adjacent selected pixels in bitmaps. Nested with the Blur tool.	R
Rubber Stamp	Copies pixels from a target area to the selected area in bitmaps.	S
Replace Color	Replaces a selected color with another chosen color in bitmaps. Nested with the Rubber Stamp tool.	S
Red Eye Removal	Removes red eye from photographs. Nested with the Rubber Stamp tool.	S
Line	Draws a vector line.	N
Pen	Draws vector points.	P
Vector Path	Draws free-form vector paths. Nested with the Pen tool.	P
Redraw Path	Allows you to re-create paths. Nested with the Pen tool.	P
Rectangle	Draws vector rectangles.	U

continued

TABLE 7.1	(continued)	
Tool	**Description**	**Selection Key**
Ellipse	Draws vector ellipses. Nested with the Rectangle tool.	U
Polygon	Draws vector polygons. Nested with the Rectangle tool.	U
Arrow	Draws vector arrow shapes. Nested with the Rectangle tool.	U
Arrow Line	Draws vector arrow lines. Nested with the Rectangle tool.	U
Beveled Rectangle	Draws vector beveled rectangles; in essence, octagons. Nested with the Rectangle tool.	U
Chamfer Rectangle	Draws vector chamfer rectangles. A chamfer rectangle is a rectangle with each corner recessed inward. Nested with the Rectangle tool.	U
Connector Line	Draws vector connector lines, such as those used in flow charts. Nested with the Rectangle tool.	U
Doughnut	Draws vector circles with empty center regions. Nested with the Rectangle tool.	U
L-Shape	Draws vector shapes that resemble a large L, or two joined rectangles. Nested with the Rectangle tool.	U
Measure	Allows you to measure the distance between two points. Nested with the Rectangle tool.	U
Pie	Draws vector pie charts. Nested with the Rectangle tool.	U
Rounded Rectangle	Draws vector rounded rectangles. Nested with the Rectangle tool.	U
Smart Polygon	Draws vector polygons that include shape hints that make it easy to change the number of sides after the shape is drawn. Nested with the Rectangle tool.	U
Spiral	Draws vector spiral shapes. Nested with the Rectangle tool.	U
Star	Draws vector stars. Nested with the Rectangle tool.	U
Text	Creates text areas.	T
Reshape Area	Allows you to click and drag on a shape to distort it.	O
Freeform	Similar to the Reshape Area, but the Freeform tools only distorts the edge of the shape. Nested with the Reshape Area tool.	O
Path Scrubber – Additive	Allows you to distort paths drawn with pressure-sensitive strokes. Nested with the Reshape Area tool.	O
Path Scrubber – Subtractive	Allows you to distort paths drawn with pressure-sensitive strokes. Nested with the Reshape Area tool.	O
Knife	Allows you to cut vector shapes into individual shapes.	Y
Rectangle Hotspot	Creates a rectangular area that can be converted into an HTML link in an image map.	J
Circle Hotspot	Creates a circular area that can be converted into an HTML link in an image map. Nested with the Rectangular Hotspot tool.	J
Polygon Hotspot	Creates a polygon area that can be converted into an HTML link in an image map. Nested with the Rectangular Hotspot tool.	J

Tool	Description	Selection Key
Slice	Allows you to create rectangular regions of images that can be individually optimized and exported as Web graphics.	K
Polygon Slice	Allows you to create polygonal regions of images that can be individually optimized and exported as Web graphics.	K
Hide Slices and Hotspots	Turns visibility of hotspot and slice indicators off.	2
Show Slices and Hotspots	Turns visibility of hotspot and slice indicators on.	2
Eyedropper	Picks up the color of the selected pixel and sets it as the foreground color.	I
Paint Bucket	Fills the selected region with the current foreground color.	G
Gradient	Fills the selected region with a gradient. Nested with the Paint Bucket.	G
Stroke Color	Sets the current stroke color.	N/A
Fill Color	Sets the current fill color.	N/A
Set Default Stroke/ Fill Colors	Sets the stroke to black and fill to white.	D
No Stroke or Fill	Sets either the stroke or fill to none.	N/A
Swap Stroke/Fill Colors	Sets the stroke color to the current value of the fill color, and vice versa.	X
Standard Screen mode	Displays the screen with all menus and toolbars showing. In Windows, the taskbar will be visible.	F
Full Screen with Menus mode	Displays the screen with all menus and toolbars. In Windows, the taskbar will be hidden.	F
Full Screen mode	Displays the canvas only with no menus, toolbars, or panels. In Windows, the taskbar will be hidden; on Macs, the Dock and desktop will be hidden. Unused screen displays as black.	F
Hand	Allows you to move your view to other parts of the screen without selecting or moving objects.	H
Zoom	Changes the magnification of the screen.	H

Panels

The panels in Fireworks provide an easy way to access common program interface components (see Figure 7.4). Panels are grouped around the right and bottom edges of the screen but are fully customizable and can be opened, moved, ungrouped, regrouped, and closed as desired.

A set of panels is known as a *workspace*. Fireworks ships with three workspaces. Unlike Illustrator or Photoshop, these workspaces merely show or collapse the panel groups along the right edge of the screen. If you prefer, you can create your own workspaces with your desired panel arrangements.

The default panel layout in Fireworks CS5

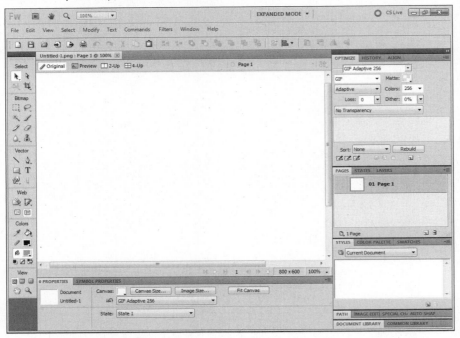

Table 7.2 outlines the panels available in Fireworks and provides a brief description of the purpose of each panel. You can open all panels via the Windows menu, and most panels can also be opened directly with a keyboard shortcut, as noted in the table.

The Fireworks Panels in the Default Workspace

Panel	Overview	Keyboard Shortcut
Optimize	Contains the tools used for optimizing Web graphics, a topic covered in more detail in this chapter.	F6
History	Shows the actions you have most recently performed in the program and allows you to step back through them to undo.	Shift+F10
Align	The tools on the Align panel let you line up objects by set axes. You can also distribute objects, equalize sizes, and space evenly.	None
Pages	Fireworks graphics can be organized into pages, which are roughly equivalent to using multiple art boards in Illustrator or creating multiple Web pages in Dreamweaver.	F5

Panel	Overview	Keyboard Shortcut
States	A state represents a particular grouping of layers. Each state can contain a different layer hierarchy from other states.	Shift+F2
Layers	Provides a container for a specific set of visual objects in Fireworks, so layers serve the same basic purpose in Fireworks as they do in Photoshop, Illustrator, Flash, or almost any other graphics tool.	F2
Styles	Allows you to save a set of visual attributes for an object, such as fill and stroke colors and applied filters, so that those same attributes can be easily applied to other objects.	Ctrl+F11
Color Palette	Displays a variety of different means by which you can work with color in your file.	None
Swatches	Save custom colors and then easily apply those colors to objects.	Ctrl+F9
Path	Displays a series of commands that allow you to manipulate vector paths.	None
Image Editing	Manipulate raster-based images such as photographs.	None
Special Characters	Presents a set of common special characters that can be easily inserted into text.	None
Shapes	Allows you to easily insert complex, premade shapes such as 3-D boxes or calendars.	None
Document Library	Stores symbols created in the current document.	F11
Common Library	Stores commonly used, precreated symbols.	F7
Properties	Displays properties or editable attributes for the currently selected object or tool.	Ctrl+F3

Table 7.3 describes each of the panels that are not visible in the default workspace. Panels are listed in the order in which they appear in the Windows menu.

TABLE 7.3

Other Fireworks Panels

Panel	Overview	Keyboard Shortcut
Access CS Live	This panel allows you to access CS Live, a new resource provided by Adobe that will offer a single point of entry to many of Adobe's online services. Note that CS Live is not unique to Fireworks and will be available from any Creative Suite product.	None
CS News and Resources	This panel provides a link to Adobe's Web site, from which you can access news on Creative Suite products, access downloads such as updates, view tutorials, and more. Like CS Live, this feature will be available from any Creative Suite product.	None

continued

Panel	Overview	Keyboard Shortcut
TABLE 7.3 *(continued)*		
Kuler	Adobe Kuler is a free, online resource for creating and sharing color palettes. The Kuler panel provides an interface to the Kuler Web site for use within Fireworks. The panel can be found in the Extensions submenu.	None
Search for Help	This panel provides an interface to the Adobe Help system for Fireworks.	None
URL	Fireworks allows you to create hotspots in an image that, when previewed in a Web browser, link to other files or Web sites. You can create a library of commonly used sites via the URL panel.	Alt+Shift+F10
Color Mixer	Yet another way to work with colors in Fireworks, the Color Mixer panel displays a color spectrum and includes boxes to enter values for Red, Green, and Blue.	Shift+F9
Info	This panel displays information about the current cursor location's Red, Green, Blue, and alpha values, and its x and y coordinates. While drawing shapes, the width and height and x and y scales are displayed.	Alt+Shift+F12
Behaviors	When creating HTML-based comps, the Behaviors panel can be used to add basic JavaScript actions such as rollover image effects.	Shift+F3
Find and Replace	This panel mimics the functionality of Find and Replace in other applications.	Ctrl+F
Symbol Properties	When using symbols, this panel allows you to tweak the settings of the selected symbol.	None

Working with Color

Fireworks provides a variety of tools and panels that enable you to work with color. The Color Palette and Swatches panels are the most commonly used. The Tools panel also provides a pair of color pickers, one each for the fill and stroke of shapes, as does the Properties panel when a shape is selected on the canvas.

Note

As with Illustrator and Photoshop, you can work in a variety of color modes in Fireworks. Keep in mind that Catalyst is a program devoted entirely to creating projects that will display on a computer screen. You will need to use RGB in your Fireworks projects that are destined for Catalyst.

Hexadecimal Colors

Hexadecimal is a method of counting using a base-16 model, rather than the base-10 with which you are generally familiar. In standard base-10 counting, you can count from 0-9 before needing to reuse digits with 10. In hexadecimal, you count from 0-15 before needing to reuse digits.

You still start by counting from 0-9, but then use the first six letters of the alphabet to count the next six digits, so after 9 comes A, then B, and so on through F. After F, you start reusing digits, so the next number is 10. 1A follows 19. 20 comes after 1F, and so forth on up to the highest two-digit number possible, which is FF. Its primary purpose in computers is to allow you to count from 0 to 255 using only two digits, rather than three.

Colors in the RGB model are each represented by a value from 0 to 255. Hexadecimal provides a convenient method for the expression of numbers as a six-digit hexadecimal value where the first two digits are the amount of red in the color, the second two the amount of green, and the final digits the amount of blue.

Thus, a Web page might express pure red as #FF0000, which would contain the maximum value of red, FF, and no green or blue. The pound sign is merely the character that HTML and CSS use to denote that the value is in hexadecimal.

The Color Palette panel

The primary panel for working with color in Fireworks is, appropriately, the Color Palette. The panel provides three methods of defining colors: Selector, Mixer, and Blender. You can switch among these modes using the buttons at the top of the panel.

All three modes have options at the top to determine whether your color will apply to the fill or stroke, as well as text boxes where you can type a hexadecimal color value.

Selector mode

Selector mode (see Figure 7.5) presents a fairly traditional set of tools from which you can define a color. A square displays the entire gamut of colors available in the selected color model, with a slider to the right to set the tint of the selected value.

Sliders are also available that you can drag to choose the desired amount of each color.

Mixer mode

The Mixer mode of the panel (see Figure 7.6) allows you to define five colors so that you can create and work with a consistent but limited color scheme in your document.

It contains a color wheel to help visualize related colors as well as a table of variations of the currently selected color. You can use the panel to export your schemes for use in other documents.

FIGURE 7.5

The Color Palette's Selector mode

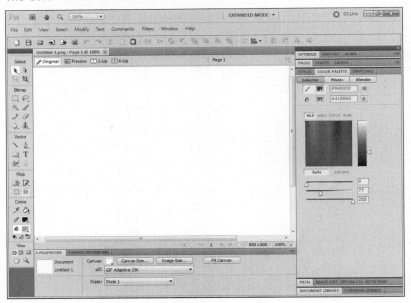

FIGURE 7.6

The Color Palette's Mixed mode

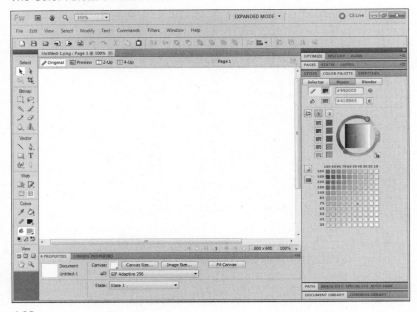

Blender mode

The panel's Blender mode (see Figure 7.7) primarily allows you to define two colors and then have the program calculate a set of gradations between those colors.

This panel can be helpful in setting up gradients or in using the gradations for color combinations in your document.

The Swatches panel

After you mix your colors, you can save them for reuse in the Swatches panel, shown in Figure 7.8. You must designate a color as either the fill or stroke color and then click in a blank area of the panel to add that color as a swatch. Swatches can be deleted by pressing Ctrl (⌘) and clicking the swatch.

Tip
The default set of swatches in Fireworks is the so-called Web safe palette. In the early days of the Web, many users had computers that could display a maximum of 256 colors. The palette was developed as a compromise between the colors that could display on Windows-based computers and those that would display on Macs. Today, there is no technical reason to limit yourself to the palette; Fireworks merely uses it as a convenient set of colors to display in the panel.

FIGURE 7.7

The Color Palette's Blender mode

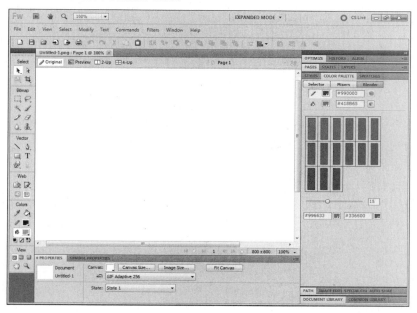

FIGURE 7.8

The Swatches panel

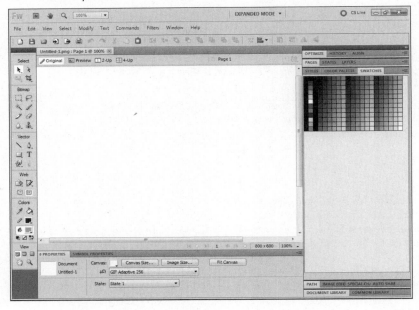

The Kuler panel

In late 2006, Adobe released the first public beta of a new Web-based application known as Kuler. Built with Flex, the application allows users to create color themes with a variety of tools. After a free registration process, you can save themes and share them with others.

Fireworks — along with Illustrator, Photoshop and several other Adobe products — includes a Kuler panel. In Fireworks, you can open the Kuler panel by choosing Window ➪ Extensions ➪ Kuler. If you have an active Internet connection, the panel connects to the Kuler application online and displays the publicly shared color themes. You can then select any theme and use it in your Fireworks drawings just like any other color.

Add Text

You can add text to your Fireworks document with the Text tool. The Properties panel (see Figure 7.9) displays options for formatting text whenever the Text tool is selected including character attributes such as font, font style, font size, font color, and paragraph attributes such as alignment and line spacing.

FIGURE 7.9

The Properties panel with the Text tool selected

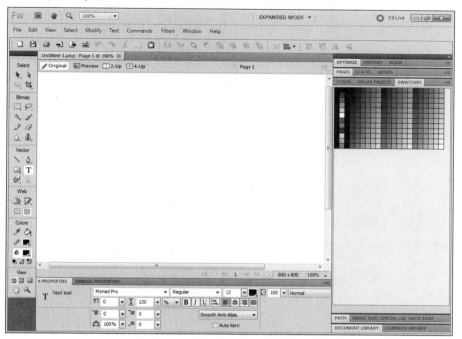

Faux Bold and Faux Italic

Fireworks provides a Font Style drop-down menu from which you can select regular, bold, semi-bold, italic, oblique or combinations such as bold italic. Below the Style drop-down menu are buttons to apply *faux bold* and *faux italic*.

When you install a font onto your system you will usually get a regular version of the font, but many fonts also include files for other styles such as bold or italic. These variants are drawn by the font artist and will generally result in bold and italic text that looks better.

The faux buttons are primarily designed to allow you to apply bold and italic styling to text when the actual font does not contain those variants; in this case, Fireworks simply makes the lines of the font thicker for bold and slanted for italic. The style drop-down applies these actual font faces, while the faux bold and faux italic buttons do not. Therefore, if the option to use the real typeface is available from the drop-down, you should select it; only use the faux buttons when the actual typeface is not available.

You can add type to a document by simply clicking on the canvas and typing. You can edit text that has been added by either clicking on the text box with the Text tool or double-clicking it with the Pointer tool.

You can change attributes of the text, such as the font face, for an entire block of text by selecting it with the Pointer tool and making the necessary adjustments on the Properties panel.

Importing Bitmaps

Fireworks contains a unique set of tools that allows it to work as well with bitmap or raster graphics as it does with vectors. While you can use the tools to create either type of image, you can also directly import bitmap graphics for manipulation (see Figure 7.10).

You can import bitmaps into an existing Fireworks image by following these steps:

1. **Choose File ⇨ Import.**

2. **Select the image to import.**

3. **Click Open.** Your cursor will appear as an angle bracket and represents the top-left corner of the image.

4. **Click the canvas at the point at which you want to place the image to finish the import process.**

You can also open bitmap images directly in Fireworks. The program supports opening most common graphics file formats. Standard formats such as GIF and JPEG will open as a single flat image. Photoshop images will open with all layers intact.

Working with Filters

Fireworks includes a set of filters to perform common manipulations on bitmap images. Filters are available either from the Filters menu on the main menu bar or from the Filters pop-up menu on the Properties inspector. You must have an image onto which filters can be applied, and the image must be selected to add a filter.

Filters Menu, Properties Panel: Destructive, Nondestructive

Although both the Filters menu and the Properties panel offer the same set of filters, results vary depending on how you insert them. Filters chosen from the menu are *destructive*; they can only be removed by selecting Edit ⇨ Undo before you do anything else, and the filters cannot be edited.

In contrast, the Properties panel applies Live Filters that at any point can be edited, deleted, and rearranged if more than one filter is applied.

FIGURE 7.10

A bitmap image imported into Fireworks

Table 7.4 describes the filters available in Fireworks.

TABLE 7.4

Fireworks Filters

Filter	Description	Submenu
Auto Levels	Adjusts highlights, shadows, and midtones based on pre-defined settings.	Adjust Color
Brightness/Contrast	Provides sliders to manually increase or decrease the brightness or contrast in the image.	Adjust Color
Color Fill	Fills the color with a solid color; a dialog box appears to allow you to set the color, blend mode, and opacity of the fill.	Adjust Color
Curves	Displays a dialog box allowing for adjustment of the lightness curves in the image, which allows you to lighten or darken the image.	Adjust Color

(continued)

TABLE 7.4 *(continued)*

Filter	Description	Submenu
Hue/Saturation	Displays a dialog box with sliders to adjust the hue, or overall color of the image, saturation, or amount of color, and lightness of the image.	Adjust Color
Invert	Reverses the colors in the image, creating a film negative effect.	Adjust Color
Levels	Displays a dialog box that allows you to adjust the highlights, shadows and midtones on the image via its histogram.	Adjust Color
Inner Bevel	Adds borders around the image to create a beveled appearance, where the image will appear to be depressed below the page.	Bevel and Emboss
Inset Emboss	Applies borders to two sides of the image to give the appearance that is has been embossed.	Bevel and Emboss
Outer Bevel	Applies the opposite effect as Inner Bevel, where the image will appear to be raised above the page.	Bevel and Emboss
Raised Emboss	Applies the opposite effect of Inset Emboss.	Bevel and Emboss
Blur	Slightly blurs the image.	Blur
Blur More	Applies a more pronounced blur to the image.	Blur
Gaussian Blur	Displays a dialog box with a slider allowing you to adjust the level of a smooth, uniform blur.	Blur
Motion Blur	Displays a dialog box allowing you to set the angle and distance of a single-direction blur.	Blur
Radial Blur	Displays a dialog with settings for the amount and quality of a blur emanating from the center of the image and radiating from there.	Blur
Zoom Blur	Displays a dialog box with settings for the amount and quality of a blur emanating from the center of the image and moving straight out.	Blur
Add Noise	Adds color noise to the image.	Noise
Convert to Alpha	Converts the image to a transparency based on its alpha properties.	Other
Find Edges	Creates a relief-like effect.	Other
Drop Shadow	Adds a shadow to the outside of image; the shadow's settings are configurable.	Shadow and Glow
Glow	Adds a configurable color glow around the outside of the image.	Shadow and Glow

Filter	Description	Submenu
Inner Shadow	Adds a configurable shadow effect to the inner edge of the image.	Shadow and Glow
Solid Shadow	Displays a dialog box with settings to configure a reflection of the image.	Shadow and Glow
Sharpen	Sharpens the edges of the image.	Sharpen
Sharpen More	Applies a more dramatic sharpening.	Sharpen
Unsharp Mask	Displays a dialog box with settings to configure the level of sharpening to be applied..	Sharpen
Photoshop Live Effects	Opens a dialog box identical to the Layer Effects dialog box in Photoshop, allowing you to apply any effect available in Photoshop to a Fireworks image.	None

Cross-Reference

See Fireworks CS5 Bible for more detailed information on filters.

Saving Artwork as Symbols

Fireworks provides the ability for objects drawn or imported on the canvas to be saved as *symbols*. Symbols are reusable objects; once something is saved as a symbol, you can drag it from the Document Library panel onto the canvas at any point.

You can convert an object to a symbol by choosing Modify ➪ Symbols ➪ Convert to Symbol or by pressing F8. A dialog box appears asking for the name of the symbol and the symbol type (see Figure 7.11).

Fireworks supports three symbol types:

- **Graphic.** Creates a static image that can be reused in the document
- **Animation.** Allows you to create an animated image by determining the number of states, movement, direction and other attributes
- **Button.** Automatically creates an HTML hotspot to which a behavior or URL can be attached.

Cross-Reference

See Fireworks CS5 Bible for more information on animation and button symbols. As neither applies to Catalyst projects, details on them are beyond the scope of this book.

Once an object is converted to a symbol it's available in the Document Library. By default, the Library is in the bottom-right corner of the screen. If the library is not visible, you can opt to display it by choosing Window ⇨ Document Library. You can add other instances of the symbol to the canvas by simply clicking and dragging them from the Library.

FIGURE 7.11

The Convert to Symbol dialog box

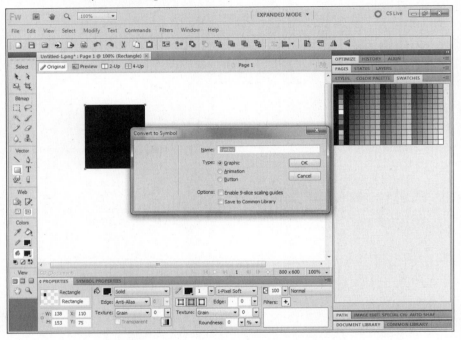

Instances of symbols retain a link back to the original. Therefore, if you edit a symbol, all instances are updated. You can edit symbols either by double-clicking the icon to the left of the symbol name in the Library or by right-clicking an instance and choosing Symbol ⇨ Edit Symbol.

Adding Prototype Objects

Adobe primarily markets Fireworks as a rapid prototyping tool. Adobe's intent is to position it not as a competitor to Photoshop or Illustrator as a graphics tool, but rather as a logical piece in a Web development workflow.

Fireworks is a tool that designers can use to quickly create comps of sites to present to clients for approval prior to beginning the actual design. With this in mind, Fireworks ships with a set of common interface components for HTML, Flex, and other application frameworks.

All of these prototyping objects are contained in the Common Library (see Figure 7.12). Symbols created within documents are stored in a Document Library that is unique to that document; symbols in the Common Library are available to every document in Fireworks.

Note
If you want to use a custom symbol in more than one document, simply select the check box in the Convert to Symbol dialog box to save the symbol to the Common Library rather than the Document Library.

When creating Catalyst projects, you may want to use the Flex Components objects to add representations of components that will eventually be used in the project.

Of particular use is the *ComboBox* component. ComboBoxes, or drop-down lists, are very common elements in many Web applications. Unfortunately, Catalyst CS5 does not include the ability to convert artwork to a ComboBox. Therefore, if you want to use a ComboBox in your application you may want to add the ComboBox symbol to a Fireworks document and import that into your Catalyst project.

You will not get the actual functionality of a ComboBox — the symbol is nothing more than a graphical representation of a ComboBox — however, you will have an effective placeholder in your design comp that your Flex developer can later replace with an actual ComboBox in Flash Builder.

Most of the components in the Common Library can be configured with the Symbol Properties panel. For example, the ComboBox component simply says *Text*. However, if you plan to use this in a Catalyst project you will likely want to change that text to better represent the purpose of the ComboBox in the project.

You can open the Symbol Properties panel by choosing Window ⇨ Symbol Properties (see Figure 7.13). The panel displays the properties of whichever symbol is selected on the canvas. Any properties represented on the panel can be edited directly.

FIGURE 7.12

The Common Library panel

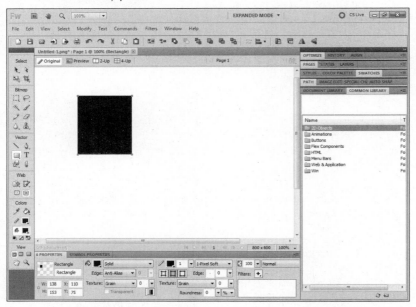

FIGURE 7.13

The Symbol Properties panel

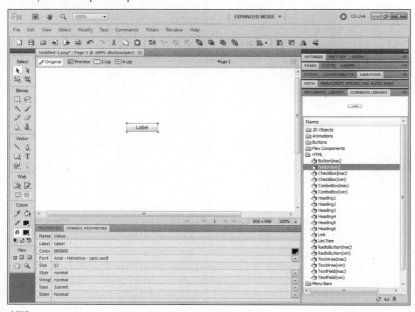

Exporting as FXG

You cannot import Fireworks documents directly into Catalyst. However, you can still use them as the basis for Catalyst projects, and you can import Fireworks images into Catalyst via the FXG format.

FXG is an XML-based format for describing Flash-based graphics. Its primary goal was to allow for other tools in the Adobe Creative Suite, such as Photoshop or even InDesign, to have a round-trip editing workflow with Flash.

Exporting your image is as easy as following these steps:

1. Choose File ⇨ Export.
2. In the Export dialog box, select FXG and images from the Export drop-down list.
3. Type a name for the file.
4. Click Save (see Figure 7.14).

FIGURE 7.14

The Export dialog box

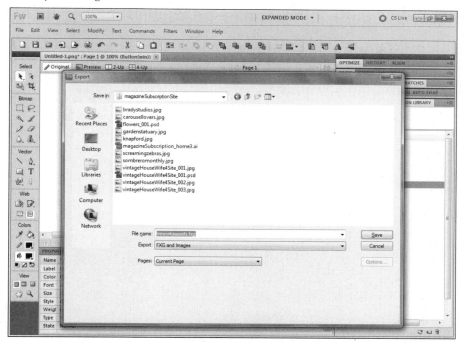

Summary

This chapter introduced the third primary graphic design tool in the Adobe Creative Suite: Fireworks. In it you have learned how to:

- Create a new Fireworks document
- Use the tools and panels in Fireworks
- Work with color
- Add and format text
- Import and work with bitmaps
- Save artwork as symbols
- Export graphics as FXG to use in Catalyst

Part III

Creating the Application in Catalyst

Converting Illustrator and Photoshop Artwork into Catalyst Projects

You can easily import Adobe Illustrator designs into Flash Catalyst and convert them into applications. Once imported, you can convert Illustrator graphics into components, the building blocks of Flex applications.

Create a New Project from an Illustrator Comp

The Catalyst Start Screen, which appears when you launch the program as shown in Figure 8.1, allows you to create new Catalyst projects from design files created in Illustrator Photoshop, and from FXG files.

Note

Although the Start Screen cannot be disabled, there may be times when you want to create a new project while you have another project open and therefore cannot see the Start Screen. In these situations, you can click File ⇨ New Project from Design Comp to create a new project from either Illustrator or Photoshop comps. File ⇨ New Project allows you to create a new wireframe project.

When you click the option to create a file from an Illustrator design file, a dialog box appears which allows you to select the AI design file. You can then select from a set of options to customize the project (see Figure 8.2).

Create a new project from an Illustrator file

Create a new project from a Photoshop file

Import graphics into an existing project

Round-trip editing with Illustrator

Create optimized graphics

FIGURE 8.1

The Catalyst Start Screen

FIGURE 8.2

Illustrator Import Options

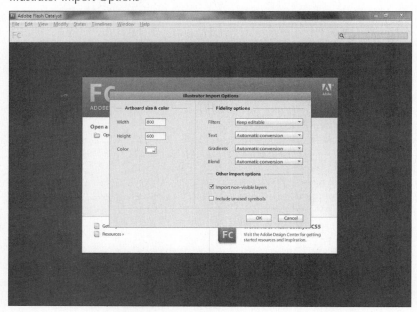

You can set the art board size and color, although Catalyst defaults these to match the Illustrator project (see Figure 8.3). You also have the ability to set Filters to Keep Editable, Expand, or Flatten. Keep Editable, the default, allows you to modify the filter directly in Catalyst. Expand converts the filter to a set of layers, while Flatten creates a bitmap image from the layer.

FIGURE 8.3

An Illustrator design file opened in Catalyst

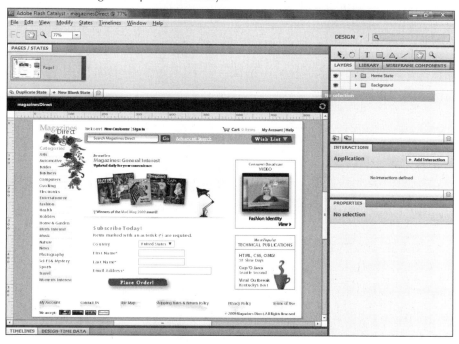

You can keep gradients in the Illustrator file either as *editable* objects or *flattened*, whereas text can be kept editable, converted to vector outlines, or flattened.

The Import Options dialog box allows you to import nonvisible layers, clip content to the art board, and include symbols that are in the Illustrator file but are not being used on the art board.

Once opened, the Layers panel in Catalyst displays the layers from the Illustrator file (see Figure 8.4). All of Illustrator's groups and layer names are preserved in Catalyst, so time you spend organizing the file in Illustrator saves time once the file is imported.

Just as in Illustrator, you can turn Catalyst layers on and off by clicking the small eye icon to the left of the layer name. You can click in the empty box between the eye icon and the name to lock a layer. You can rename layers by double-clicking their name in the panel.

FIGURE 8.4

The Layers panel in Catalyst, displaying layers imported from Illustrator

Should you discover that you need new layers or sublayers in your Catalyst project, you can add them by clicking the appropriate icons at the bottom of the panel.

Create a New Project from a Photoshop File

You can also create complete comps of projects in Photoshop. Often, the decision as to whether to use Photoshop or Illustrator is determined by your comfort level with each program.

But you will often find that comps that require a lot of custom drawings and artwork are easier to create in Illustrator, whereas comps that require more photos and other raster artwork are easier in Photoshop.

The Photoshop Import Options dialog box (see Figure 8.5) is very similar to the Illustrator Options. You can set the size of the project, although Catalyst automatically detects the size of the Photoshop file and sets the project to the same. You can set the art board color, and choose whether to keep image layers, shape layers, and text editable or flatten them.

Reducing File Sizes in Photoshop

Catalyst cannot open very large Photoshop files, so you may need to reduce the size of your file before opening it. Some methods for reducing the file size in Photoshop are:

- **Set the resolution to 72 dpi.** You can set the resolution of a file by clicking Image➪Image Size.

- **Set the pixel dimensions of the image to the size you need for your Catalyst project, rather than importing the full-size image and resizing in Catalyst.** You can change the size of an image by clicking Image➪Image Size.

- **Merge layers.** While merging layers reduces how much an image can be edited in the future, layers significantly increase file size.

Keep in mind that Catalyst projects are, by definition, designed for display on computer screens, not print, and therefore rarely have any need for a screen resolution higher than 72 pixels per inch. Layers and saved channels also dramatically increase file size. Removing channels or merging layers may help bring the file size down.

FIGURE 8.5

Photoshop Import Options

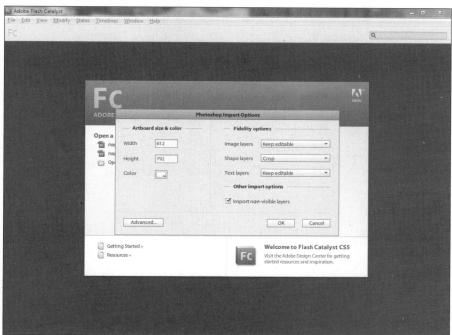

One important difference between importing from Photoshop and importing from Illustrator does exist. The Photoshop Import Options dialog box (see Figure 8.6) includes an Advanced button in the bottom-left corner.

The Import to Stage dialog box allows you to select individual layers and decide whether or not to import them. It also allows you to decide on a layer-by-layer basis whether to import layers as editable or flattened objects for your Catalyst project (see Figure 8.7).

FIGURE 8.6

The Import to Stage dialog box

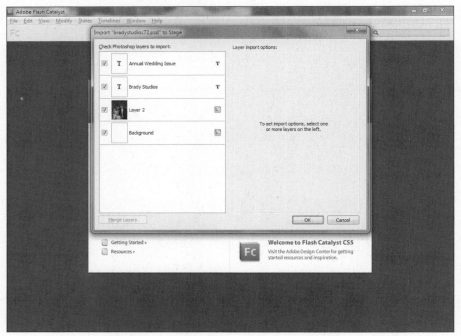

FIGURE 8.7

A Photoshop comp opened as a Catalyst project

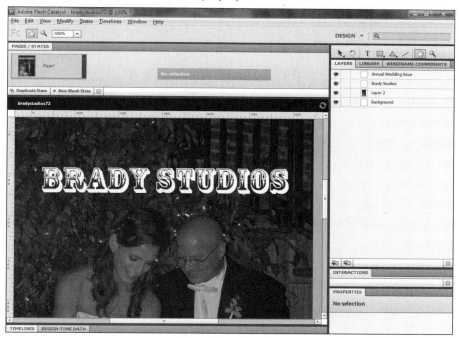

Import Graphics into an Existing Project

Whether you create a project from an Illustrator or Photoshop comp, you may need to import additional graphics as you work through the design process. For example, you may have a design created in Illustrator, but then want to import images that were retouched in Photoshop.

Import images to the artboard

You can import images directly onto the artboard by clicking File ➪ Import ➪ Adobe Photoshop File (.psd) (see Figure 8.8). The image you select is imported and placed on a new sublayer at the top of the currently selected layer.

Import Options

Catalyst's Import menu offers several options:

- Import ➪ Image allows you to select PNG, GIF, JPG or JPEG files.
- Import ➪ Adobe Illustrator File (.ai) allows you to import files created in Illustrator.
- Import ➪ Adobe Photoshop File (.psd) allows you to import Photoshop images.
- Import ➪ Abode FXG File (.fxg) allows for importing files created in Flash Builder or Catalyst.
- Import ➪ Video/Sound file allows you to select MP3, FLV, or F4V files.
- Import ➪ SWF File lets you select a SWF file, most likely created in Flash Professional.

FIGURE 8.8

Importing images to the artboard

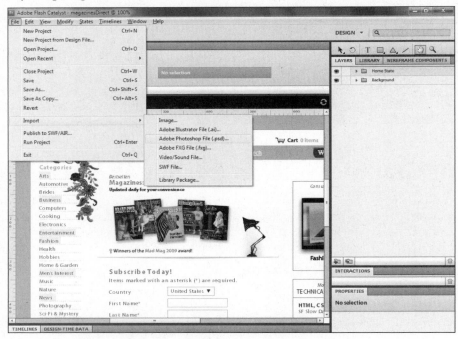

Importing multiple images

You can import multiple files at once into Catalyst by selecting more than one file in the Import dialog box (see Figure 8.9). Unfortunately, this only works when importing GIF, JPEG or PNG files. If you need to import multiple Photoshop or Illustrator files, you will need to import them one at a time.

You can select multiple contiguous images with these steps:

1. **Click the first image.**

2. **Press and hold Shift.**

3. **Click the last image in the sequence.** You can select noncontiguous images by pressing and holding Ctrl (⌘).

4. **Click Open.** Each of the selected images is imported into the library.

FIGURE 8.9

Importing multiple files

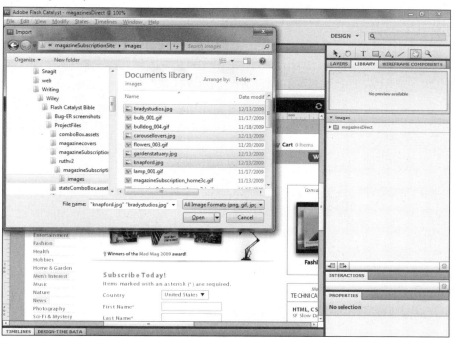

Using the Library panel

The Library panel in Catalyst (see Figure 8.10) provides a central storage location for all of your artwork. Any artwork you import to the artboard is automatically placed in the library and remains there even if you later delete the art from the artboard.

You can simply drag any image from the library to the artboard to insert it into your project. Before you drag, you should check to be sure that you have the correct layer selected, because the new image is added as the top sublayer to the currently active layer.

Tip

You can also copy and paste graphics directly between Illustrator, Photoshop, or Fireworks and Catalyst. Simply select the art in the graphics program, click Edit ⇨ Copy, then switch to Catalyst and click Edit ⇨ Paste.

FIGURE 8.10

The Library panel

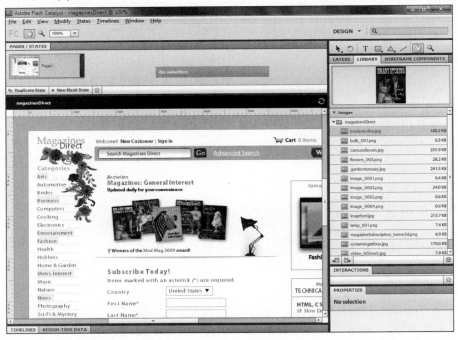

Round-Trip Editing with Illustrator

Catalyst supports *round-trip editing* with Illustrator, allowing you to select graphics in Catalyst (see Figure 8.11), edit them in Illustrator and then have Catalyst automatically accept the changes to the graphic.

FIGURE 8.11

Selecting a graphic for round-trip editing

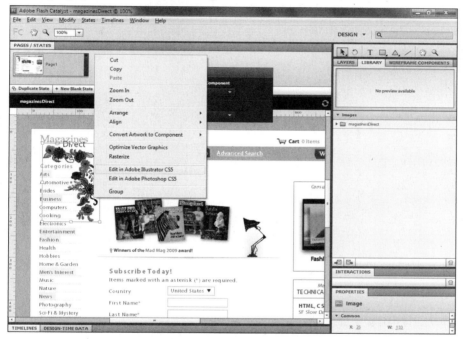

To edit a graphic in Illustrator (see Figure 8.12), simply follow these steps:

1. **Select it on the artboard.**

2. **Right-click (⌘+click).**

3. **Choose Edit in Adobe Illustrator CS5.** If Illustrator is not already open, it launches, and the graphic is opened in it.

4. **When you have completed the editing, save and close the Illustrator document.** Because this graphic is an FXG file, you are prompted by Illustrator to select FXG saving options.

5. **Once the FXG file has been saved, you can return to Catalyst.** You are asked if you want to accept the changed graphic.

6. **Click yes to accept the changes and return to working on the project.**

Tip

Graphics originally created in Illustrator are completely editable. Graphics created in other applications such as Photoshop or Fireworks may be only partially editable; there are likely to be limitations as to what can and cannot be altered in the graphic.

FIGURE 8.12

Editing a Catalyst graphic in Illustrator

Create Optimized Graphics

Graphics imported from applications such as Illustrator and Photoshop can, at times, be quite large and may end up causing the application to run slowly due to the overhead required to draw them in Flash Player. Therefore, anytime you have an imported graphic and there are no plans to have your application's final code modify the graphic programmatically, you should convert it to an optimized graphic.

Optimized graphics become components within the Catalyst project. A *component* is a reusable object, and as such it requires much less overhead for Flash Player. Optimized graphics are stored as separate FXG files within the project and are easier for your Flex developer to work with.

Cross-Reference
See Chapter 9 for more details on components.

You can convert artwork to an optimized graphic by selecting it on the artboard and then clicking the Convert to Optimized Graphic button on the HUD. A new graphic is added to the library, and the optimized graphic replaces the item on the artboard.

Optimized graphics, along with other components in your project, are stored in the Library. Be sure to rename components as they are created, because each new graphic you create is simply assigned a generic name. You can rename graphics by double-clicking their name in the Library and typing a new name.

Summary

This chapter discussed the various means by which you could convert Illustrator and Photoshop comps into Catalyst projects.

You learned how to:

- Import an Illustrator design into Catalyst
- Import a Photoshop design into Catalyst
- Import graphics into existing projects
- Organize graphics using the Library panel
- Convert imported graphics to optimized graphics

Converting Artwork to Components

When you create a project in Catalyst, you are creating the ground-work for a Flex project. Flex is a component-based application framework, and Flex developers working in Flash Builder or coding in some other environment create *modular applications*. That is, they avoid creating single, large files with all of the code for their application, and instead create a series of smaller files, each with a distinct purpose.

These individual modules are known to Flex developers as *components*. Almost everything a Flex developer works with is a component, from large application-specific modules such as a shopping cart down to individual user interface items like buttons and text fields.

In order for your Catalyst project to be easily imported into Flash Builder, you will want to define the contents of your artwork as components. Catalyst has the ability to convert artwork into a number of common Flex components, as well as custom, generic components.

Almost everything in your Catalyst project needs to be converted into a component before you hand the project over to your developer. Almost the only thing not converted to a component is the background of your application, and in certain situations, that is as well.

Tip
Static graphics should be converted to optimized graphics, but although they are given a different name in Catalyst, an optimized graphic is in fact a type of component.

Cross-Reference
See Chapter 8 for details on optimized graphics.

You can use the Heads Up Display (HUD) to convert any object or group on the art board to a component (see Figure 9.1).

You can convert selected artwork into one of several predefined common Flex components (see Table 9.1) or into a custom component.

FIGURE 9.1

The HUD

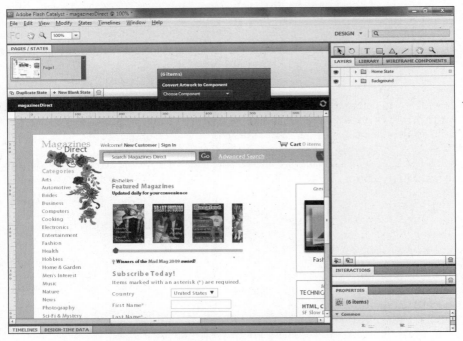

Note
You may need to use the Direct Select tool to select artwork in sublayers. The Selection tool generally selects only the layer. You can also select objects by clicking their appropriate layer or sublayer in the Layers panel.

Once artwork is selected, you convert it to a component by simply selecting the appropriate component from the drop-down list on the HUD. Once converted, the HUD changes to display any necessary settings for the component.

Tip
If you have turned the HUD off, you can convert selected artwork to a component by right-clicking (⌘+clicking).

TABLE 9.1

Available Components

Component	Description
Button	A clickable component, designed to respond to user interaction.
Checkbox	A selectable component for fillable forms. Normally, checkboxes are grouped into a set where the user can select one or more options.
Radio Button	A selectable form component, most often used within a mutually exclusive group.
Toggle Button	Similar to a button. Toggle buttons have a Selected state that remains active until the button is clicked again.
Text Input	A single-line form field for user-entered data.
Horizontal Slider and Vertical Slider	Sliders can be used to allow the user to select from a range of values.
Scroll Panel	A panel component is a container for other content. The panel contains a title area and can take Horizontal or Vertical Scrollbars.
Horizontal Scrollbar and Vertical Scrollbar	Scrollbars can be added to components to allow you to add more data than can fit.
Data List	A table-like structure for displaying rows and columns of data.
Custom/Generic Component	A component to use anytime your objects do not make sense as one of the other component types.

Convert Layers and Groups to Custom Components

The component types listed in the HUD represent common user interface components that appear in many applications. However, most of the interface of your application is unique to that application, and therefore converts to custom components.

With the exception of static items such as small blocks of text and images, you will want to convert almost everything into a component. Anything that does not logically make sense as one of the common component types should be converted to a *custom/generic component*.

The main portions of your application should also be converted to custom components. You will likely be planning on building multiple states or pages in your application, and all of the pieces that make up any particular state should be combined into a component. This not only makes it simpler for you to define the parts that make up states, because it is much easier to hide, move, and animate a single component than it is to do the same to a series of smaller pieces, but it also aids your Flex developer in working with the application in Flash Builder.

Editing components

You can edit any components at any time. You can edit a component by double-clicking it on the artboard (see Figure 9.2). This switches Catalyst to an Edit in Place mode, where you can select and manipulate the parts that make up the component. The remainder of your application will still be visible but grayed out.

Editing a component in place

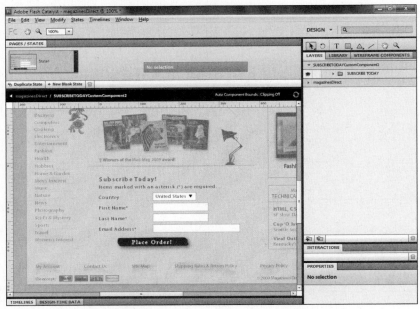

You can return to editing the entire application by clicking the small left-facing arrow on the left side of the black bar that runs just below the Pages/States panel or by double-clicking an area of the art board that does not contain a part of the component.

Nesting components

You can nest almost any component type within almost any other type (see Figure 9.3). For example, Scrollbar components can be nested within Scroll Panel or Data List components.

Any of the common user interface components will likely end up nested within your custom components: a series of Text Input, Radio Button, Checkbox, and Button components might, collectively, be combined into a single Form custom component. That form component might then itself be nested within a large component making up the overall page or state on which the form resides.

FIGURE 9.3

Editing a component nested within another component

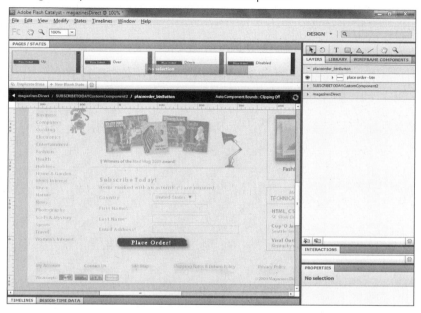

You can nest components by either selecting them as part of the set of objects that you convert when you create the component, or add nested components later by dragging them from the Library to the artboard while you are editing the component.

Naming components

You should get in the habit of immediately naming all components. Every time you create a component, it gets added to the Library. You can double-click the name of this component to rename it, ensuring that you give it a descriptive label that aids both you and your Flex developer later in referring to and using it in your application.

Names of components can contain only letters, numbers, and underscores, and need to begin with a letter. In addition, names are case-sensitive. Most Flex developers rely on a system known as *camel casing* for naming items, whereby multiple-word names are combined into a single word, with the first letter of the name in lowercase and the first letter of each additional word capitalized. For example, a name such as Home Address would be written homeAddress.

Reusing components

You can reuse any component; in fact, part of the reason why the Flex framework is built around components is to facilitate their reuse. Because all components are stored in the Library, you can simply drag a component onto the artboard at any time to create a new instance of it.

Creating Buttons

Buttons allow for interactivity with your user. You can convert any artwork into a button, so there is no limit as to the visual appearance of a button you create.

Buttons have four predefined states that allow you to define how the button looks initially:

- When the mouse is positioned over the button
- When the button is being clicked
- When the button is disabled

You can use separate artwork for each state, or simply modify the existing artwork.

Once a button is created, the HUD displays buttons of its own to allow you to access each of these states. Clicking any one of them, or double-clicking the button on the artboard, allows you to edit the states of the button directly (see Figure 9.4).

The Pages/States panel along the top of the screen shows you each of the button's states:

- **Up.** Defines the appearance of the button when the user is not interacting with it.
- **Over.** Defines its appearance when the user positions the mouse over the button.
- **Down.** How it will look when the user is pressing and holding the mouse button.
- **Disabled.** Shows what the button will look like when it is disabled, or unclickable.

Note

You cannot set a button to Disabled in Catalyst; you can merely define what the state looks like. Your Flex developer uses code to determine when the button is enabled or disabled.

Each of the component parts of the button can be edited in each state. You can change the colors of the fills or strokes (see Figure 9.5) or even replace the artwork with something else altogether.

To change the fill color of a button in different states, follow these steps:

1. **Double-click the button to edit its states.**
2. **Click the state you want to change.**
3. **Select the button's fill with either the Select or Direct Select tool.**
4. **Use the Properties panel to change the fill's color.**

Tip

You do not have to define the appearance for each state if you do not want to. Any state that you leave unchanged inherits its appearance from the state to its left, so if you define an appearance only for Up and Down, the Over state will look like Up, and Disabled like Down.

FIGURE 9.4

Editing a button's states

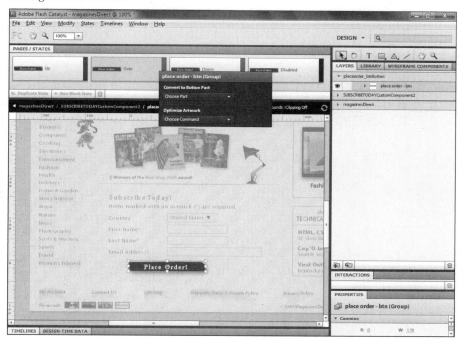

Cross-Reference

All components that contain multiple states can have animated transitions between those states. See Chapter 10 for details on defining these animations.

Once you have completed your work on the button, you can return to the main artboard by clicking the project's name on the black bar that runs across the screen, just below the Pages/States panel. You can return to editing the button at any time if further changes are necessary.

You cannot view the states of the button directly in Catalyst; instead, you need to run the project. Click File ⇨ Run Project to open it in Flash Player in a browser.

Cross-Reference

See Chapter 4 for more details on running a project.

FIGURE 9.5

Changing the stroke color in the Over state

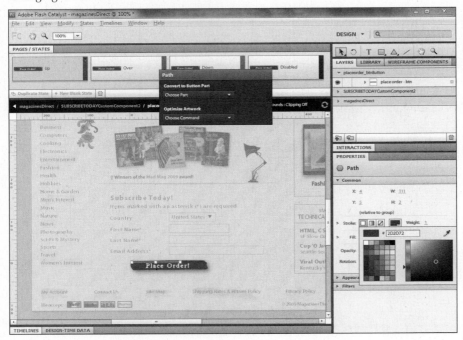

Convert Artwork to a Toggle Button

Toggle button components allow you to provide a visual clue when the button is selected (see Figure 9.6). Regular button components respond to mouse actions but do not have any selected states.

You can create a toggle button in the same way you create a normal button, except that you select Toggle Button from the HUD's Convert Artwork to Component drop-down.

Toggle buttons have all of the same properties as buttons. However, when you edit the button's states, you see that it contains the same four states as a button — Up, Down, Over, and Disabled — but also contains four additional states:

- Selected Up
- Selected Down
- Selected Over
- Selected Disabled

Edit these states to define the visual appearance of the toggle function of the button.

FIGURE 9.6

Toggle buttons

Convert Artwork to a Text Field

Many Web applications today require forms, whether to provide the ability to search the application, allow the user to register or log in to a site, or provide credit card information to purchase products.

When designing an application using Catalyst, you are free to design your forms as you want. Simply draw the elements needed for the form in your design comp in Illustrator or Photoshop, and then use Catalyst to convert the drawings to form fields.

The most basic and most common type of field is a *single-line text field*. Most often, these are represented in the design comp as a simple rectangle. As with buttons, you can select the rectangle and use the HUD to convert to a Text Input component. Once converted, click the Edit Parts button to configure the input component (see Figure 9.7).

FIGURE 9.7

Setting the text input properties

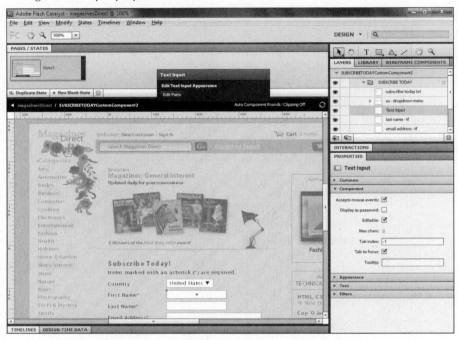

Text Input components contain two states:

- Normal
- Disabled

Most contain two parts:

- The Text Display
- The Rectangle or other shape defining the border of the field

The Text Display part provides the most options for editing on the Properties panel. There, you can set text to display in the field by default, select the font, and configure font properties such as size and color.

You can also set whether or not the field accepts mouse events or displays as a password, whether it contains user-editable text, and the maximum characters that can be entered into the field, and provide a tooltip that appears when the user mouses over the field. Options to add strikethrough and underlining to the text are also available.

Convert Artwork to Sliders

A *slider* is a component that allows your user to drag left and right, or up and down, to change a value (see Figure 9.8).

FIGURE 9.8

An example of a completed slider component

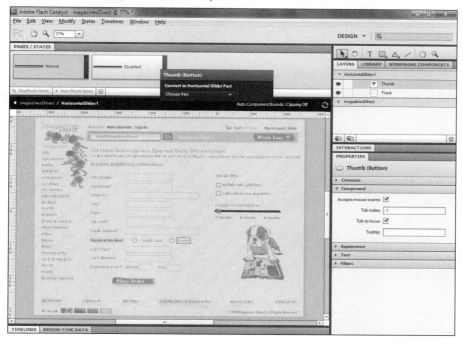

Sliders have two required parts:

- A thumb
- A track

The *thumb* is the part that the user drags to change the value, and the *track* defines the path along which the thumb slides. Therefore, you need to design your artwork in Illustrator to include these two pieces.

Caution
While designing the track, be aware that Catalyst supports only sliders that move along straight tracks.

To convert artwork to a slider, follow these steps:

1. Import your artwork into Catalyst, either as part of your design comp or as separate art.

2. Select both pieces of art.

3. On the HUD, click Convert Artwork to Component ⇨ Horizontal Slider or Convert Artwork to Component ⇨ Vertical Slider.

4. Select the resulting component.

5. Click Edit Parts on the HUD.

6. Select the thumb art.

7. On the HUD, click Convert Artwork to Horizontal Slider Part ⇨ Thumb (required) or Convert Artwork to Vertical Slider Part ⇨ Thumb (required).

8. Repeat steps 6 and 7 to define the track.

The slider contains a set of properties that can be configured on individual instances of the component (see Table 9.2).

TABLE 9.2

Slider Instance Properties

Property	Description
Accepts mouse events	Defines whether or not mouse events can be added by the Flex developer to this component.
Data tip while dragging	Adds a tooltip displaying the current position's data value while the user drags the thumb.
Maximum	The maximum data range for the slider.
Minimum	The minimum data range for the slider.
Snap interval	The amount by which the value changes as the user drags the slider.
Step size	Defines the space between steps on the slider or how far the user needs to drag to get to the next snap interval.
Tab index	An integer value defining the component's tab order in the application.
Tab to focus	Allows the user to set the focus on the slider with the Tab key.
Tooltip	Sets a tooltip to appear when the user mouses over the slider.

Note

Sliders are often attached to a text input field or some other component to accept their value. This association must be done in Flash Builder, not Catalyst.

Convert Artwork to Radio Buttons and Checkboxes

Radio button and *checkbox* components are common form elements that allow your user to select from a set of predetermined choices. A user can select only one radio button from amongst a group, whereas multiple checkboxes may be selected.

Both components are defined in much the same way and share almost all the same properties. Radio button and checkbox components share the same set of states as toggle buttons:

- Up
- Down
- Over
- Disabled
- Selected Up
- Selected Down
- Selected Over
- Selected Disabled

Use the selected states to provide visual clues to your users as they navigate over the buttons for the option or options they have chosen, and the others for the options they have not yet selected.

Tip

In almost every application, both on the Web and on the desktop, radio buttons provide circular selection areas, and checkboxes provide squares. You should consider maintaining this distinction when designing your buttons, because square radio buttons or circular checkboxes may confuse users.

The only difference between radio buttons and checkboxes is that you need to group sets of the former. Radio buttons allow users to choose one option within a set. You can define this set by clicking each radio button component and, from the Properties panel, enter a name in the Radio button group field.

Caution

Names for radio button groups need to follow the same rules as the names for components.

Convert Artwork to Scroll Panels and Data Lists

Catalyst provides two predefined components to use when you need to display a lot of data in a limited space:

- The scroll panel
- The data list

You can use the *scroll panel* for large blocks of text or similar content (see Figure 9.9), whereas the *data list* provides a table-like component for structured data (see Figure 9.10).

FIGURE 9.9

A completed scroll panel

Both components have a single required part: the data to be scrolled.

Scroll panels refer to this internal part as *scrolling data*, whereas data lists call it a *repeated item*. This scrolling information can be another component, text, or simple artwork. Often, it may end up being nothing more than placeholder information, with the plan that the final application will pull this information from a back-end server source such as a database.

For example, you might have a scrolling panel that will display the products your application is selling. When you do the initial design in Catalyst, you would likely represent those products with placeholders, but in the final application, the actual products would be pulled from a database.

Both components also need a *scrollbar*, which is a separate component that you create and define as such. The components can take a horizontal or vertical scrollbar or both.

Cross-Reference
See the next section of this chapter for information on creating scrollbars.

You can create a scroll panel or a data list by simply selecting the item to be repeated and choosing the appropriate component type from the HUD. Then, edit the component and define the scrolling data or repeated item.

FIGURE 9.10

A completed data list

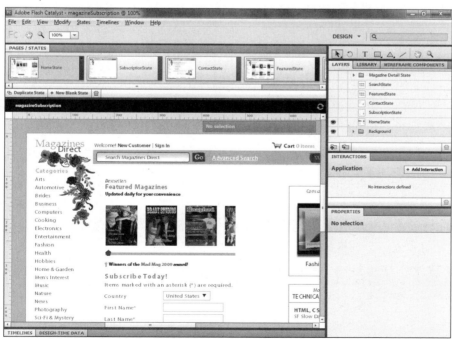

Data list properties

Data lists provide a few additional properties to set up the layout and spacing of the repeated item.

Once you define the item using the HUD, the component automatically populates itself with five copies of the item. Using the Properties panel, you can set the item to repeat vertically in a single column, repeat horizontally in a single row, or tile.

If you choose Tile, you can set the direction, specifying whether the data should go across a row before going down to the next column, or vice versa, going down a column before it repeats to a new row. You can set the alignment of the items within each column or row, and the vertical and horizontal spacing between each item.

Note
The alignment buttons for data list properties appear to do something only if the items in the list are different sizes.

Design-time Data

Most of the time, the actual data that populates the data list is from a server-side source and populated at run-time. This requires significant coding and is done by the Flex developer in Flash Builder.

Therefore, as a designer, you are most likely doing nothing more than adding placeholder information; you want to be able to see what the list will look like, even though you are not using the actual, live data.

Catalyst provides a Design-time Data panel (see Figure 9.11) that allows you to create a simple table of information to populate the data list. This way, you can have data that looks and feels like your real data, without having to worry about potentially complex coding.

If you define a set of objects that contain one or more individual elements as the repeating item of the list, the Design-time Data panel's table automatically populates with that information. If the table contains text data, you can simply click each item and type a new value.

You can swap images out with other images in your Library by double-clicking the image thumbnail in the panel. An Add Row button at the bottom of the panel allows you to insert additional data items.

Note
The Design-time Data panel does not automatically populate itself if you use a component as the repeating item in a data list. Instead, you need to double-click the component within the data list and then select the parts of the component you want to use as data and click the Add to Design-time Data button on the HUD.

FIGURE 9.11

The Design-time Data panel

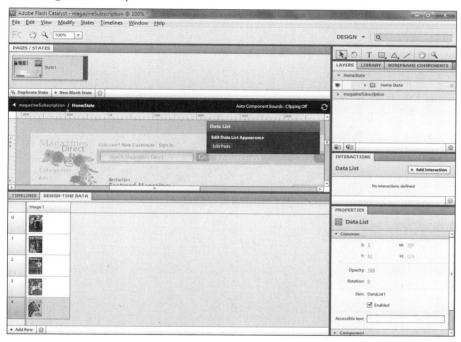

Convert Artwork to a Scrollbar

Many applications require areas that can contain more data than can fit in a limited space and thus require scrollable content. Although several Flex components include automatic scrollbars that look like those that are standard in the operating system, Catalyst provides the ability to completely customize scrollbars, using your own artwork (see Figure 9.12).

Scrollbars require a minimum of two parts:

- A thumb, which the user drags to scroll
- A track along which the thumb can be dragged

You can also add left and right buttons, but they are optional.

FIGURE 9.12

An example of a component with a custom scrollbar

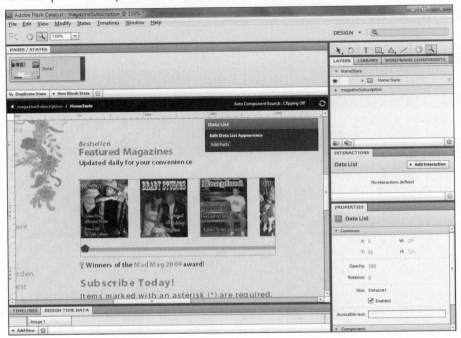

Create a scrollbar

You can create a scrollbar by following these steps:

1. Select at least two pieces of artwork.

2. Choose Convert Artwork to Component ⇨ Horizontal Scrollbar or Vertical Scrollbar.

3. Once the artwork is converted, either double-click the component on the artboard or click the Edit Parts button on the HUD to go into editing the component (see Figure 9.13).

Tip

The HUD displays a Component Issues message in its top-right corner anytime a component is selected that does not have required parts defined.

4. Once you are in the editing mode for the scrollbar, select the art to be used as the thumb.

5. Click the Convert Artwork to Scrollbar Part drop-down on the HUD.

FIGURE 9.13

Defining the parts of a scrollbar

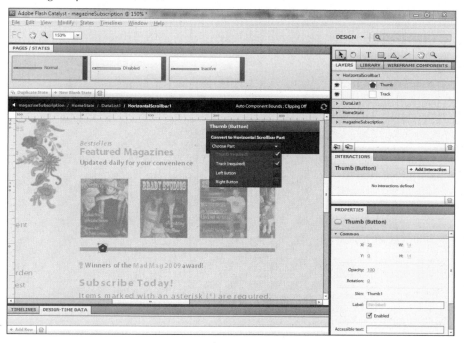

6. **Select Thumb (required).**

7. **Repeat this process for the track and, if desired, the right and left buttons.**

As with other components, scrollbars also contain states:

- Normal
- Disabled
- Inactive

Disabled is a state that can be selectively controlled through code when your Flex developer takes over the project. *Inactive* defines the scrollbar's appearance when it is visible on the screen in a component that does not contain enough data to require scrolling.

Associate a scrollbar with a scroll panel or data list

Scroll panel and data list components need a scrollbar in order to function properly. You can associate a scrollbar component with either of these by simply adding the scrollbar component to the scroll panel or data list.

You can do this before you create the component by following these steps:

1. **Place the scrollbar near the item you plan to use as the data.**
2. **Select both.**
3. **Convert the group to a Scroll Panel or Data List component.**

Alternately, you can add the scrollbar after the creation of the component: Double-click the scroll panel or data list to edit it; then drag an instance of the scrollbar from the Library.

Summary

In this chapter, you were introduced to the idea of using components as building blocks for your application. You learned what components are for and how to:

- Convert layers and groups to custom or generic objects
- Create buttons, toggle buttons, radio buttons, and checkboxes
- Covert artwork to text input fields, sliders, and scrollbars
- Create data lists and scroll panels

Creating View States

Traditional Web applications rely on a series of pages to display changing information. An e-commerce application, for example, would likely include one or more product pages, a shopping cart display page, one or more checkout pages, and an order summary page. Each of these would be individual, distinct documents.

In contrast, a Flex application is, once published, a single SWF document. The entire application is contained within this single document.

Individual pages are represented by *view states*. As a designer in Catalyst, you can define these view states, determine which assets appear on them, and set up interactions that allow users to move from one state to the next.

Note
To ease the transition to the Flex framework for designers, Catalyst refers to states as either view states or pages. For the purposes of working in Catalyst and for the purposes of this text either term is interchangeable. The Flex framework, however, only uses the term view states.

IN THIS CHAPTER

Creating new view states

Changing components in states

Triggering state changes with interactions

Setting up transitions

Using button states

Creating New View States

Every new Catalyst project contains a single state which by default is named Page1. Projects can, however, contain as many states as are needed. States are managed in the Pages/States panel at the top of the screen (see Figure 10.1).

You can create new states either from scratch or as a duplicate of an existing state. Most often, states contain assets and components from other existing states; therefore, you generally create them as duplicates of other states.

You can create duplicate states by following these steps:

1. **Click the Duplicate State button at the bottom of the Pages/States panel.** Alternately, you can right-click (⌘+Clicking) the state you want to duplicate.

2. **Selecting the Duplicate State option.**

FIGURE 10.1

The Pages/States panel in a new project

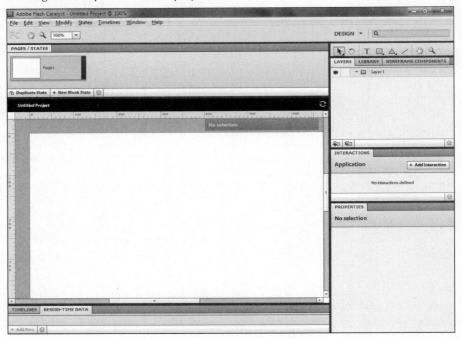

You can create blank states by following these steps:

1. **Click the New Blank State button.**

2. **Right-click (⌘+Clicking) an existing state.**

3. **Select New Blank State.** This can also be accomplished by right-clicking (⌘+Clicking) in a blank area of the Pages/States panel.

Once created, you should immediately rename the state (see Figure 10.2). State names can only be letters, numbers, and underscores. They must begin with either a letter or an underscore. State names are also case-sensitive, so you need to be consistent with your use of upper- and lowercase letters in the name. Most important, state names should be descriptive of the state's purpose.

Tip

If you attempt to type illegal characters for the state name, the name box turns red. When you press Enter to finish the name any name with illegal characters is ignored and the previous name restored.

Components can contain multiple states. You create states within a component by double-clicking it on the artboard to edit it and then using the Pages/States panel. Anything that can be done on the artboard with states can also be done within components.

FIGURE 10.2

Renaming states

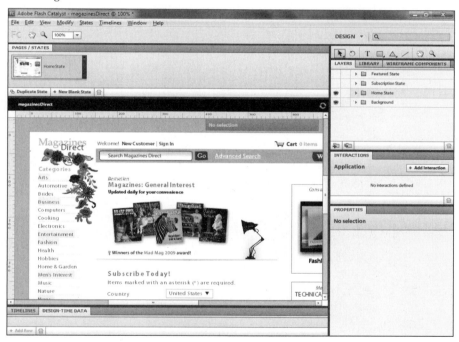

Changing Components in States

View states will contain differing components and assets. Components that exist on one state can be removed, hidden, or moved, and new components can be added to the state.

Any group of assets or artwork that you want to work with between states should be converted into a custom or generic component. While you can add, remove, move, or show and hide individual groups of artwork, it's far easier and more efficient to work with components.

Cross-Reference

See Chapter 9 for details on converting assets to custom or generic components.

Removing or hiding components

Components that are visible in one state but not visible in another can either be removed or hidden. To remove a component, simply select it on the art board and press Delete. You can also select Modify ⇨ Remove from State and then select the state from which you want to remove the component.

Once removed from a state, the component remains as part of the project and can be displayed on other components.

Rather than deleting components, you can choose to simply hide the component's layer on a state (see Figure 10.3). To do this, ensure that you have the correct state selected and click the Show/Hide Layer button on the Layers panel.

FIGURE 10.3

A layer hidden on a component

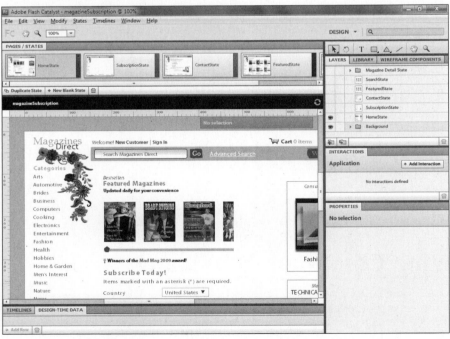

Delete Components or Hide Them?

When users run your application, they will have no way of telling whether you have deleted components between states or hidden them. Deleting components provides a performance boost, as Flash Player does not need to keep them in memory. Your application will also start up faster because Player doesn't have to load components until they are actually needed. As a general rule of thumb deleting components between states is preferable to hiding them.

If you want to animate the component's state change, you must hide it instead of deleting it. For example, if you want a component to appear to fade in as it appears during a state change, it must be hidden in the first state.

Caution

When working with components between view states, be careful to check that you have the current state selected in the Pages/States panel before you begin any modifications.

Caution

Layers are shared by all states. If you want to remove a component from a state, be sure to delete the component from the artboard and not the layer on which you want to place the component in another state.

Moving components

You can move components to new locations on the artboard between states (see Figure 10.4). This approach allows you to present the same basic information between states while changing the layout, perhaps to draw attention to one component while de-emphasizing another.

You can move components around on the artboard with the Selection tool or Direct Select tool. You may want to use the grid or add guides to help align components between states.

Cross-Reference

See Chapter 4 for details on adding guides or using the grids.

You can also place components to the left, right, above, or below the artboard. Placing components off the artboard allows you to animate them, moving the component onto the art board when the state changes.

Applying component changes to states

If you make a change such as resizing to a piece of art work in one state, you may want to apply that same change to all of the other states. Click States ⇨ Make Same in All Other States to apply this effect (see Figure 10.5).

FIGURE 10.4

Components moved to new locations in a state

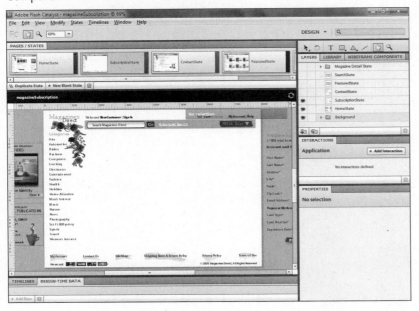

FIGURE 10.5

The Make Same in All Other States menu item

Sharing components between states

Often you will have assets in one state that you need to copy to another state. While any asset that exists in a state automatically copies to new states, assets added to a state after new states have been created will not automatically appear in the new state.

Catalyst provides a utility for sharing assets to states in the States menu (see Figure 10.6). You have the option to share selected assets to all states within the current component, share it to the currently selected state, or share it to a particular state.

The Share Assets menu

You can also remove assets from states using the Remove from State command, also located in the States menu.

Triggering State Changes with Interactions

You need to add interactions to your application in order to allow your users to change states. As is true throughout Catalyst, these interactions can be added to your application without the need to do any manual coding.

To add an interaction, follow these steps:

1. **Select the component that you want to use to trigger the interaction.** Most often, this will be a button, although almost any component can be used.

Note
If the component you want to use to trigger the interaction is nested within another component, you must double-click the parent component to go into its editing mode and select the trigger component.

2. **Click Add Interaction on the Interactions panel (see Figure 10.7).**

3. **Select the action you want to use.**

Each interaction is comprised of three parts:

- An event (see Table 10.1)
- An action (see Table 10.2)
- A target for the action

FIGURE 10.7

The Interactions panel

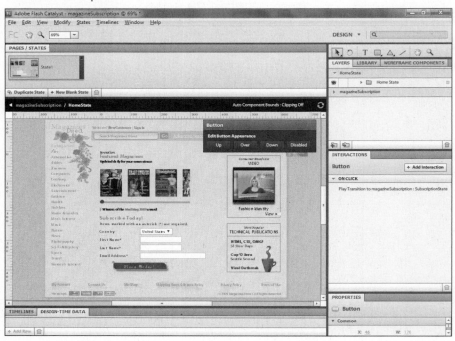

TABLE 10.1

Events

Action	Description
On Application Start	Interactions with onApplicationStart will happen automatically when the application is launched. This action is only available if no component is selected.
On Click	Occurs when the user clicks the mouse on the target component.
On Mouse Down	Occurs when the user is pressing the mouse button but has not yet released it.
On Mouse Up	Triggers when the user releases the mouse. Most often this is used in conjunction with On Mouse Down to create drag effects, where On Mouse Down initiates the drag and On Mouse Up releases it.
On Roll Out	Triggers when the user moves the mouse away from the target without having clicked.
On Roll Over	Occurs when the user moves the mouse over the component without clicking.

TABLE 10.2

Actions

Action	Description
Play Transition to State	Activates a state change.
Play Action Sequence	Plays a sequence of actions from the Timeline.
Go to URL	Navigates to a Web page.
Play Video	Starts a video player.
Pause Video	Pauses a video player.
Stop Video	Stops a video player.

Cross-Reference

See Chapter 14 for details on adding video to your projects.

The target of the action depends on the action you select. For example, Play Transition to State allows you to select a state; Play Action Sequence activates the Timeline to allow you to set up a sequence; Go to URL prompts you to type the path to the Web page to which you will navigate. You specify the video when you use any of the three video actions.

Note

When providing the path to a Web page for the Go to URL action, you can use either an absolute URL, such as `http://www.robhuddleston.com` or a URL relative to the location where the project's SWF file will eventually reside on the Web server, such as `products/product1.html`.

Cross-Reference
See Chapter 11 for details on creating action sequences.

You can test interactions and state changes by previewing the project in a Web browser. You can either choose File ➪ Run Project or press Ctrl+Enter (⌘+Enter).

Setting Up Transitions

When a project moves from one state to another, you can animate the change through a transition. *Transitions* are created on the Timeline (see Figure 10.8).

FIGURE 10.8

The Timeline

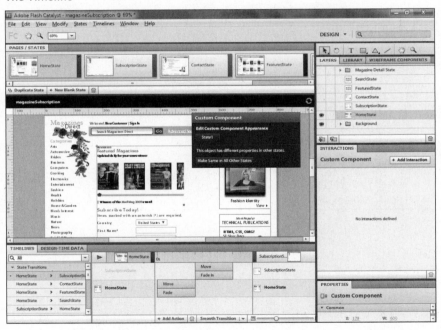

The left side of the Timeline displays any actions that currently exist in the project, organized into three categories:

- State Transitions
- Action Sequences
- SWF Asset on Click

Once you add an interaction to move from one state to another, that state change will be added to the Timeline.

Note

You do not need to be in the component that contains the asset being used to trigger the state change, nor do you need to be in either of the states to adjust the transition settings.

When you select a state transition from the left, the main section of the Timeline updates to display the states involved in the change. A default Fade Out transition is added for the layers that are hidden from the first state and a default Fade In for those that appear for the second. If you moved components between states, default Move actions are added for each.

You can increase the amount of time each action in the transaction will take by dragging its right edge. The timescale across the top of the Timeline shows how long, in seconds, each action will take. You can also move actions by dragging them left or right; so in a transition with multiple actions (see Figure 10.9), you can control the order in which they occur.

FIGURE 10.9

Multiple actions in a single transition. In this example, a crossfade effect has been created by lengthening the time for each fade and overlapping them.

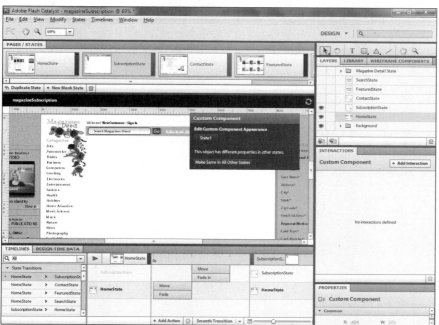

You can add other actions to the transition with the Actions menu (see Figure 10.10) at the bottom of the Timeline panel by following these steps:

1. **Click the menu.**

2. **Select an action**

3. **Adjust its timing just as you would the default actions.**

You can remove actions from the transition by selecting them and clicking the trashcan icon at the bottom of the panel.

FIGURE 10.10

Adding new actions to a transition using the Actions panel

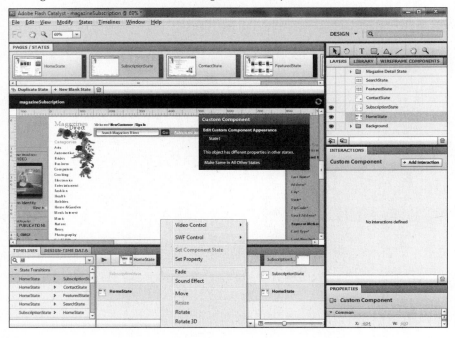

The Smooth Transition menu, located at the bottom of the Timelines panel as shown in Figure 10.11, allows you to more precisely control how the various actions in a transition play.

To use this feature, follow these steps:

1. **Click the small arrow to the right of Smooth Transition.**

2. **Select your desired settings.**

3. **Click Smooth Transition.**

Once complete, you can test your transition by previewing the project in a Web browser. You can either choose File ⇨ Run Project or press Ctrl+Enter (⌘+Enter).

FIGURE 10.11

The Smooth Transitions menu

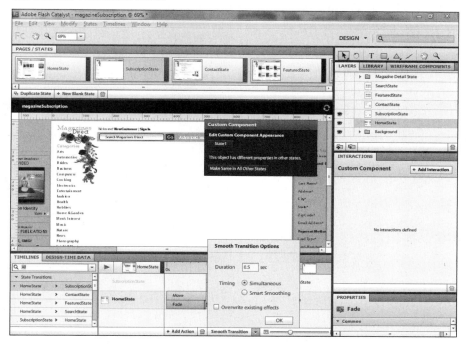

Using Button States

Buttons are a special type of component that automatically contain four states (see Figure 10.12):

- **Up.** Represents the appearance of the button when the user is not interacting with it.

- **Over.** Triggered when the user moves her mouse over the button.

- **Down.** Triggers when the user presses their mouse button to click the button.

- **Disabled.** Represents the appearance of the button when it has been programmatically disabled.

You can modify the appearance of the button in each of these states just as you would with any other component. While you generally only modify the general appearance of the button, such as the color, it is possible to show and hide layers, resize assets, or even replace assets altogether.

You do not need to add interactions in order for the button to trigger its state changes. The triggers for the state changes are built into the core of the button component, so they will occur automatically.

FIGURE 10.12

The states of a button

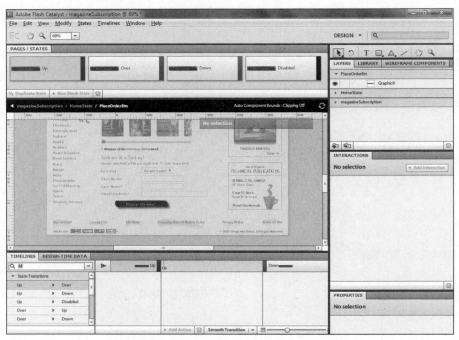

Summary

In this chapter, you were introduced to the concepts needed to create states in your application.

You learned:

- What states are and how they work in a project
- How to create new states
- How to change components in states
- How to trigger state changes with interactions and apply transitions to those changes

Adding Animation

Catalyst projects are ultimately compiled and published as SWF files to be run in Adobe Flash Player. While many advanced applications are being developed in tools such as Catalyst and Flash Builder, Flash is still best known as an animation platform. Because Flash Player is the eventual target for your project, you can apply animation effects to add more visual interest or interaction to your application.

You can use Actions to add animation directly within Catalyst, or you can create more complex, advanced animations in Adobe Flash Professional and import them into your project.

Creating an Action Sequence

You can add action sequences to any component. You begin creating an action sequence by following these steps:

1. Open the Interactions panel (see Figure 11.1).
2. From the Add Interaction menu, select the event that you want to use to trigger the sequence.
3. Select Play Action Sequence.

Once the sequence has been defined in the Interactions panel, it is added to the Timeline, where you can add actions and set their timings.

FIGURE 11.1

Creating an action sequence with the Interactions panel

Working with the Timeline

The primary panel used to work with animation in Catalyst is the *Timeline*, which is located along the bottom of the screen (see Figure 11.2).

The Timeline displays states, action sequences, and SWF controls. The left side of the panel displays any states or sequences you have created in your project and includes a filter text box along the top to help you find particular states or sequences.

The main portion of the panel displays the animation. The component to which you will be applying the animation appears on the left, while each action displays as a bar under the time scale.

Timing in Catalyst is measured in seconds. You can drag the slider at the bottom of the panel left to zoom out on the Timeline or right to zoom in.

FIGURE 11.2

The Timeline

Adding Actions

The Add Action menu at the bottom of the panel allows you to select an action to add to the sequence. You can add as many actions as you want (see Table 11.1 for available actions).

Cross-Reference

See Chapter 13 for more details on inserting and working with Flash SWF files in Catalyst projects. See Chapter 14 for details on inserting and working with video.

TABLE 11.1

Actions

Action	Description
Video Control ⇨ Play	Starts a video within a video player.
Video Control ⇨ Pause	Pauses a video in a video player.
Video Control ⇨ Stop	Stops a video in a video player.
SWF Control ⇨ Play – play()	Starts a SWF movie.
SWF Control ⇨ Stop – stop()	Stops a SWF.
SWF Control ⇨ Go to a Frame and Play – gotoAndPlay()	Moves the playhead in an embedded SWF to the specified frame and plays the movie.
SWF Control ⇨ Go to a Frame and Stop – gotoAndStop()	Pauses a SWF movie.
Set Component State	Sets the component to a specified state. Only available if the target component contains multiple states.
Set Property	Allows you to set a property of the component to a new value.
Fade	Fades the component out.
Sound Effect	Plays a sound.
Move	Moves the component down and to the right.
Resize	Resizes the component.
Rotate	Rotates the component 90 degrees to the right.
Rotate 3D	Rotates the object in 3-D.

Properties panel

After you add an action, you can configure it using the Properties panel (see Figure 11.3). Each action has distinct properties that can be configured. Each action has its own properties, which are outlined in the following sections.

Set Component State

The Set Component State action produces an effect similar to the Play State Transition interaction. The action, however, gives you more control over the state change by allowing you to set a delay.

The Properties panel allows you to set the component to which you want to change, and the delay, in seconds, before the state change occurs. This action can be particularly useful if you want to have the component change states following another action, such as a video playing.

Set Property

The Set Property action allows you to change either the Enabled or Alpha property of a component. If you set Enabled to False, your user cannot select or otherwise interact with the component. If the component is a button, you can design its Disabled state.

Cross-Reference

See Chapter 9 for details on designing the Disabled state of a button.

The Alpha property allows you to set the transparency of a component. You can set the property to a value between 0 and 100, with 0 completely transparent and 100 completely opaque. For either property, you can set a delay to determine how many seconds elapse before the property change takes effect.

FIGURE 11.3

The Properties panel showing the properties available for the Rotate3D action

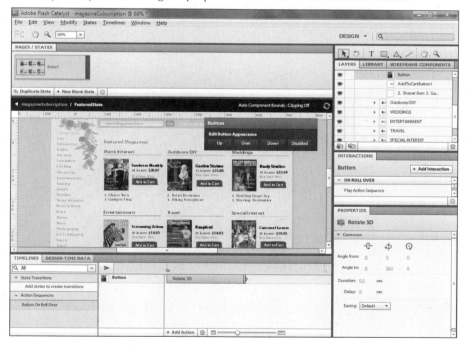

Fade

The Fade action functions much the same as Alpha but provides greater control. Using the Properties panel, you can control the starting and ending transparency of the object. You can also set the fade's duration and delay, and you can choose to have the effect repeat.

The Fade action also allows you to set up *easing*. Easing allows you finer control over the timing of the effect. Most of the time, components will fade in at a constant rate. Applying easing allows you to vary this rate, so that the component can for example begin fading in slowly and then gradually speed up. Table 11.2 outlines the easing values available.

Tip
Both the Fade and Set Property actions allow you to create semitransparent components. The difference between them is that the Set Property action happens instantly, while the Fade action animates the transparency.

TABLE 11.2

Easing Values

Value	Description
Linear	The effect begins slowly and then gradually speeds up, or vice versa; it can begin quickly before gradually slowing down.
Sine	The timing roughly follows a sine curve. Unlike Linear, Sine easing has no plateau the effect will always be either speeding up or slowing down.
Power	Power easing is very similar to Sine easing, only more pronounced.
Elastic	The effect will speed up, slow down, and speed up again. When used with Fade, the component will quickly disappear, reappear, and disappear again.
Bounce	Bounce is a similar effect to ease, but less pronounced. A Fade with Bounce easing applied will quickly fade out, then in, then out.

Sound Effect

The Sound Effect action allows you to play an imported sound. When you select this action, the Select Asset dialog box appears (even though you are not selecting anything visual), displaying the assets in your library.

Previously imported sounds will be in the Media folder. If you have not imported sounds, you can click the Import button to do so now.

Cross-Reference
See Chapter 15 for details on importing sounds into your project.

The Properties panel for sounds displays the source sound file. You can click the name of the sound in the panel to reopen the Select Asset dialog box if you wish to change to a different sound file. You can also set the duration that the sound will play and the delay.

Move

With the Move action, you can have a component travel from one location on your artboard to another.

The Properties allow you to set an X and Y coordinate for the end location of the move, and to determine whether those coordinates should be relative to the object's starting point or an absolute location on the artboard. The 0,0 point for the artboard is the top-left corner.

As with the Fade action, you can set a duration and delay, and apply easing, which provides the same settings outlined in Table 11.2.

Resize

The Resize action is unique among Catalyst's actions in that it can only be applied to assets within a component and not the component itself. Its options are the same as the Move action.

Rotate

The Rotate action spins the target component. Its properties allow you to set the angle of the rotation, either from its starting point or to a specific angle. As with Move, Resize, and Fade, you can also set the duration and delay, and apply easing as outlined in Table 11.2.

Rotate 3D

The Rotate 3D action leverages Flash Player 10's 3-D animation capabilities. You can set the Angle From and Angle To of each of three axes:

- Horizontal
- Vertical
- The imaginary third axis that allows for the 3D effect. You can see this as an imaginary line that passes perpendicularly through your monitor, both straight towards you and straight away from you. In reality, objects moving along this axis will be resized proportionally to create the illusion of moving closer to you or further away from you.

You can also set the duration and delay, and apply easing.

Set action timings

When you apply one or more actions you can control their timing on the Timeline. You can drag actions left or right to determine their starting and ending times; drag the right edge of the bar representing the action on the Timeline to increase or decrease its duration.

Tip

There is no difference between dragging an action on the Timeline and adjusting its delay in the Properties panel, nor is there any difference between dragging its right edge and adjusting the duration on the Properties panel. As Set Property actions cannot have durations, you cannot drag their right edges.

Summary

This chapter introduced several means by which you can add animation to your projects. In this chapter, you learned:

- How to create an action sequence using the Interactions panel
- How to work with the Timeline panel
- How to add actions to the sequence on the Timeline

Working with Design-time Data

A high percentage of modern Web applications rely on dynamic, server-generated data. In fact, a *Web application* is often distinguished from a *Web site* by the application's ability to access, create, or manipulate data at runtime, whereas a site will most often consist of static data.

The Adobe Flex platform provides code-based solutions for developers to retrieve data from a wide variety of server-side sources via an equally wide variety of server technologies. Whether your application's back end stores its information in a database or flat XML file, and whether you use Adobe ColdFusion, Microsoft ASP.NET, PHP, or Java to access that data, your Flex application can accept the data and work with it.

All of this coding and managing back-end systems, however, is the purview of the Flex developer, and requires significant coding. Flash Catalyst was not designed to replace this portion of the application development workflow.

You will likely have regions of your application that are intended to display information that, in the live project, will be populated by your database. Catalyst provides two key features to assist in this process:

- The data list
- Design-time data

IN THIS CHAPTER

Convert an asset to a data list

Add design-time data

Convert an Asset to a Data List

A *data list* is a special component type in Catalyst designed to allow you to easily create a block of repetitive information, such as that which would likely come from a database. The data can be represented in a table-like format or as a horizontal or vertical list.

Selecting the data list parts

A data list must contain at least two distinct parts:

- A repeating item
- A scrollbar (see Figure 12.1)

A repeating item and a scrollbar selected and ready to be converted to a data list

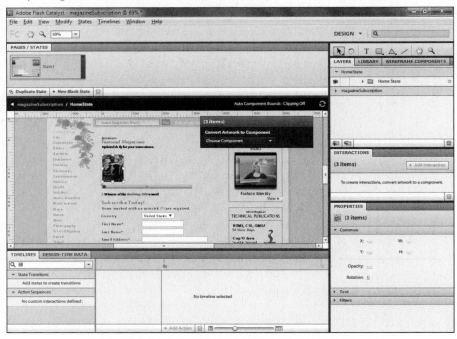

You need only one repeating item. If your design comp contained multiple items to initially repre-sent the data, you should delete all but one before converting it to a list.

Cross-Reference

See Chapter 9 for details on creating a scrollbar component.

Tip

If you have not yet created a scrollbar component, you can do so after you convert the repeating item to a data list, and then add the scrollbar back in. However, you will find that it is generally much easier to have the scrollbar created first.

Designating the parts

After you convert the item and scrollbar to a data list component, you need to designate which asset represents the repeating item. You can either click the Edit Parts button on the HUD or double-click the new data list component. Once inside the component, select the repeating item and choose Convert Artwork to Data List Part ⇨ Repeating Item (required).

After you designate the repeating item, Catalyst duplicates that item five times in a vertically tiled list. You can use the Layout category in the Properties panel to change this to a horizontal or tile list (see Figure 12.2). You can also adjust the spacing between items by scrubbing the value and adjusting the padding on each side.

FIGURE 12.2

The Properties panel for a data list

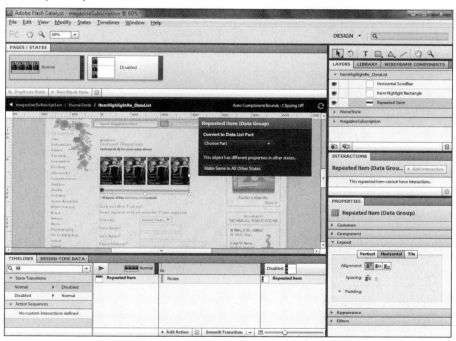

Add Design-time Data

In order to test your application or present it to your boss or client for approval, you will likely want to replace the single repeated item with multiple, different items that more closely match the actual data that will eventually be used to populate the application. The Design-time Data panel (see Figure 12.3) makes this possible.

FIGURE 12.3

The Design-time Data panel

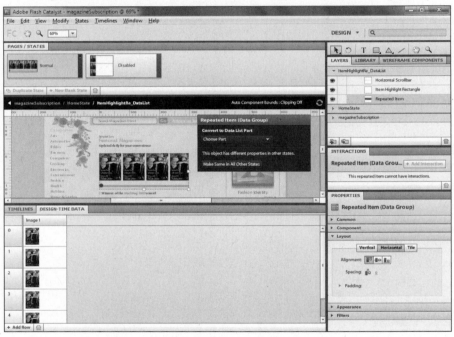

The panel automatically reads the pieces used in the repeating item and constructs a table of data from them. For example, if your repeating item contains a line of text such as a name or title and an image, the panel creates a two-column table with the names and images. If your repeating item contains only a single element such as an image, you will only see a single column in the panel.

You can change any text values by simply clicking them on the panel and typing a new value. You can change images by clicking and selecting a new image from the Library (Figure 12.4).

Note

You will need to import any of the images you plan to use in the Design-time Data panel into your Library.

You can add additional rows of data, and thus additional repeated items, by clicking the Add Row button at the bottom of the panel. You can in theory add as many rows as you want, but keep in mind that this is merely supposed to be a representative sample of the data. Your Flex developer will remove this sample information when she creates the code necessary to insert the real data from the server.

FIGURE 12.4

Changing the repeating elements in the Design-time panel

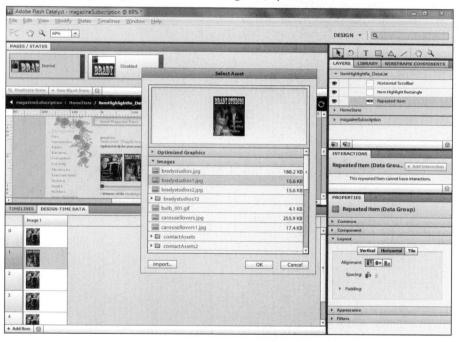

It is a good idea to add a few more data items than will fit in the data list's display. Add enough to show that it is scrollable, but do not spend a large amount of time on it.

Summary

In this chapter, you learned how to use the Data List component to represent repeating elements in your application. You also learned how to populate the list using the Design-time Data panel.

Adding Multimedia

IN THIS CHAPTER

Adding SWF files to your project

Importing video

Controlling a video player

Importing and playing sound

Catalyst projects are imported into Flash Builder 4, where you or a Flex developer add the necessary coding to create connections to back-end services, add additional ActionScript, and otherwise finalize the project.

The finalized project is compiled into an SWF for viewing in Flash Player. You may already be familiar with SWF files, as it is the same file type that results from publishing a movie in Flash Professional. A Catalyst or Flex project is really nothing more than a Flash movie, and just like Flash movies created in Flash Professional, these projects can contain multimedia assets.

Adding SWFs to Your Project

While no direct round-trip editing capabilities exist between Flash Catalyst and Flash Professional, any SWF created in Flash Professional can be imported into Catalyst (see Figure 13.1).

Note

The Flex framework only supports ActionScript 3.0, the most current version of the language. Flash Professional supports the creation of projects that use ActionScript 2.0, as well as ActionScript 3.0. ActionScript 2.0 projects may be imported into Catalyst, but you will be unable to control them from your Catalyst project. Therefore, it is recommended that any movie from Flash Professional that you plan to use in a Catalyst or Flex project be created using ActionScript 3.0.

FIGURE 13.1

A Catalyst project with an imported SWF movie

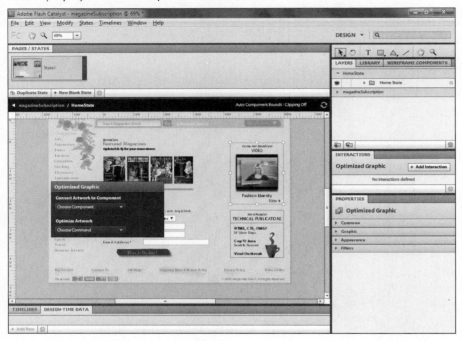

FLA versus SWF

Flash Professional relies on two primary file types:

- FLA
- SWF

FLA files are editable and are the files you use while you work in Flash Professional to create the movie or project. *SWF files*, on the other hand, are the final product and are not editable.

This distinction exists in Catalyst as well. The project file you work on during production is an FXG; when the project is finalized for publishing, either Catalyst or Flash Builder will create an SWF.

You may only import SWF files, not FLAs, from Flash Professional into Catalyst. Therefore, you must publish your movie in Flash Professional before attempting to import it into Catalyst. As noted previously, there are currently no round-trip editing capability between Catalyst and Flash Professional. Therefore, if the Flash Professional movie needs to be edited after import, you need to return to Flash Professional, edit the FLA, and republish the SWF.

Note

It is perhaps a slight misnomer to refer to the process of including SWFs in a Catalyst project as importing, as this might be taken to imply that the SWF becomes a part of the Catalyst project. In fact, Catalyst merely links to the SWF. Therefore, if the SWF is changed from within Flash Professional, there is no need to reimport it into Catalyst since Catalyst automatically detects the changes from the linked file.

Importing an SWF

To import an SWF into Catalyst, follow these steps:

1. Choose File ➪ Import ➪ SWF File.
2. Navigate to the folder that contains the SWF file to be imported (see Figure 13.2).
3. Click Open.

The imported file is placed in the upper-left corner of the art board. In addition, it will be placed in the Media folder of your project Library.

FIGURE 13.2

The Import SWF dialog box

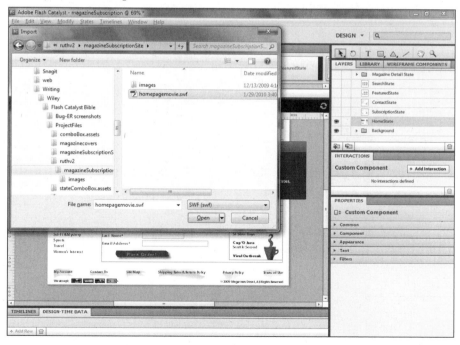

Controlling an SWF through action sequences

You can control ActionScript 3.0-based SWFs through action sequences. You can allow your user to start, stop, or pause the SWF's animation and jump to specific spots in the animation when they interact with it. Follow these steps to add an action sequence:

1. Select the SWF on the artboard.

2. Use the Interactions panel to create a Play Action Sequence interaction.

3. On the Timeline, use the Actions menu (see Figure 13.3) to add Play, Go to Frame and Play, Pause, or Stop actions from the SWF Control submenu.

Note

At this time, it is not possible to have other components, such as buttons, control an SWF.

FIGURE 13.3

The SWF Control Actions menu

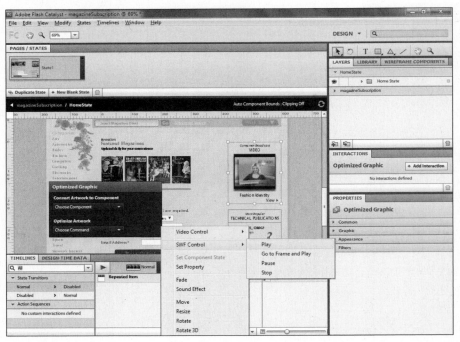

242

Importing Video

One of the most important innovations in the Flash Platform was the introduction of Flash Video.

Because of its huge install base, Flash Player quickly became the video player of choice for many Web sites, including YouTube. Flash Video files tend to be small, they support streaming for seamless playback, and the Flash platform allows designers complete freedom to add playback controls and other visual elements on and around the video itself.

Converting video to FLV

Catalyst supports two formats for imported video: FLV and F4V. Both are Flash video formats; F4V is simply a later version of the format.

FLV and F4V, like SWF, are not editable formats. Therefore, you would begin the process of creating a video component by shooting the video and editing it in any one of the hundreds of available video-editing tools.

The video-editing software you use will almost certainly generate video in one of a few common formats, such as the following:

- AVI
- MPEG
- MOV

Once the video file is created, you need to convert it to FLV using Adobe Media Encoder (see Figure 13.4). Media Encoder is a stand-alone application included with any of the Creative Suite bundles, as well as stand-alone installations of Flash Professional or any of Adobe's video-editing tools.

Media Encoder is, fortunately, also included with the installation of Flash Catalyst. Therefore, if the person responsible for creating the video doesn't have Media Encoder, you can still convert the file.

To encode your video in the FLV format, follow these steps:

1. **Launch Adobe Media Encoder.** On Windows, it will most likely be in the Start Menu folder that contains the rest of your Adobe programs. On Mac OS X, you will find it in the Dock or the Applications folder.
2. **Click Add.**
3. **Navigate to the folder that contains your video file.**
4. **Click Open.**
5. **Choose Format ⇨ FLV/F4V.**
6. **From the Preset menu, select the preset you wish to use for your video.**

7. If necessary, click the Output File link and navigate to the folder into which you want your FLV file to be saved.

8. Click Start Queue.

FIGURE 13.4

Adobe Media Encoder converting an MOV movie to FLV

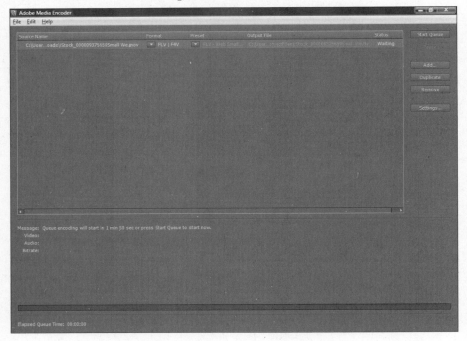

Note

Depending on the size of the video file, the conversion process may take quite some time.

Importing video into Catalyst

Once converted, you can import your FLV file into your Catalyst project by following these steps:

1. Choose File ➪ Import ➪ Video/Sound file.

2. Navigate to the FLV.

3. **Click Open.** Catalyst automatically creates a video player component and link to the FLV (see Figure 13.5).

FIGURE 13.5

An imported video

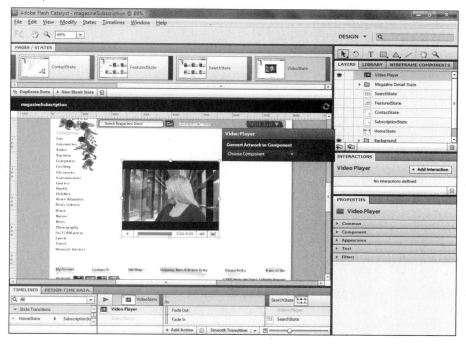

Controlling a Video Player

An instance of the video player component is automatically created for each video you import into your project. The component contains two unique interactions and provides the ability for the video to be controlled by other components.

Video player interactions

The video player has two unique interactions:

- On Video Play Complete
- On Video Load Complete

The first allows you to set up interactions that occur once the video is done playing. The second gives you control over the video as soon as it loads in the project.

With either interaction, you have the same set of actions as you do with other components:

- Play a transition to a state
- Play an action sequence
- Go to a URL
- Play a video
- Stop a video
- Pause a video

You can apply the final three options to the current video player or to any other video player in your project; you can set up your project so that a second video plays as soon as the first finishes.

Playback controls

The video player component includes a default *skin* that provides playback controls along the bottom of the component (see Figure 13.6). This skin has buttons to play or pause the video; scrub forward or backward while the video is playing; mute the video's audio; and switch the video to full screen.

FIGURE 13.6

The default playback controls on the video component

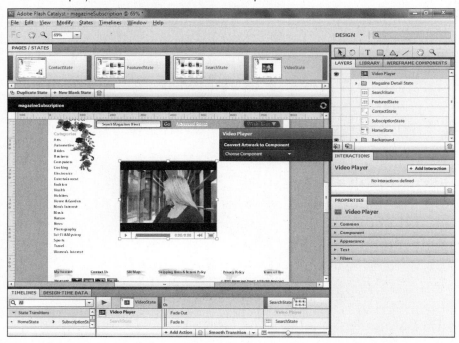

The skin has two default appearances:

- Wireframe
- Standard

The buttons on both are the same. The difference is that the Wireframe's buttons have a blue background, while the Standard is white (see Figure 13.7). You can switch between them using the Video controls drop-down list in the Common category on the Properties panel.

FIGURE 13.7

The playback controls set to Standard appearance

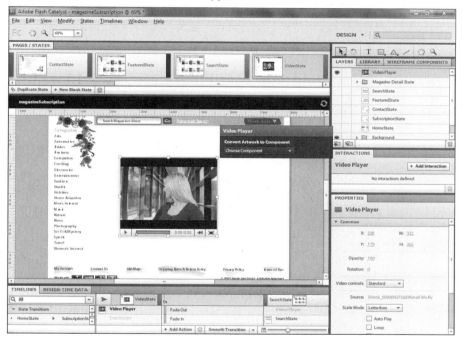

You can create your own controls for the video if you want. When providing your own controls, first turn off the default skin by selecting None from the Video controls drop-down list in the Common category on the Properties panel. Then add your own custom button components, which are created just as you would any other button component in the project (see Figure 13.8), using these steps:

1. **Select the button.**
2. **Choose the appropriate trigger from the Interactions panel, such as On Click.**

3. Select Play, Stop, or Pause from the Interactions drop-down list.

4. Select the appropriate video player from the Choose Video drop-down list.

Cross-Reference

See Chapter 9 for details on creating buttons.

Video component properties

The Properties panel provides a set of controls for your video. From the Common category, you can set the video to play automatically, loop so that it plays back repeatedly and have its audio muted by default.

The Component category contains a set of controls shared by all components: Accepts mouse events, Tab to focus, and Tooltip. It also contains a control unique to the video component, Volume. Volume allows you to set the default volume for the video's audio. The Appearance and Filters categories are the same as for other components.

Cross-Reference

See Chapter 9 for details on Appearance and Filters settings.

FIGURE 13.8

Custom video playback controls

Importing and Playing Sound

Sound, if used appropriately, can enhance your projects. You can add sound effects to buttons or other components and trigger them via action sequences.

Importing sound

You can import a sound by following these steps:

1. Choose File ➪ Import ➪ Video/Sound File.
2. Select the appropriate sound.
3. **Click Open.** Unlike other imported assets, sound files cannot be placed directly on the artboard, so your imported sound is placed in the Media folder of your Library.

Note

The only sound file format supported by Catalyst is MP3. Many applications exist that you can use to convert other formats to MP3, including many freeware applications that can be downloaded from the Internet.

Caution

Be sure that you have the legal right to use any sound files you plan to import into your project. You can download royalty-free sounds from www.istockphoto.com/audio.php, www.shockwave-sound.com, and many other online sites.

Playing sound

Sounds can be played in your project through an action sequence. To associate a sound with a button click, follow these steps:

1. Select the button.
2. From the Interactions panel, click Add Interaction.
3. Select On Click.
4. Select Play Action Sequence.
5. Click OK.
6. On the Timelines panel, click Add Action.
7. Click Sound Effect.
8. From the Select a Visual Asset dialog box, choose the sound file you want to use.
9. Click OK.
10. From the Properties panel, set the duration for the sound, the delay before the sound begins, and whether to repeat once the sound is finished.

Summary

In this chapter, you learned how to add multimedia assets to your project. You learned how to:

- Import SWF files created in Flash Professional
- Control imported SWFs
- Encode video files to the FLV format
- Import and control FLV videos
- Import and play sounds

Part IV

Exporting Projects into Flash Builder 4

Flash Builder 4 and the Flex Framework

F lash Catalyst CS5 is designed to provide an easy way to create the *front-end* or *user interface* for Rich Internet Applications (RIAs). It is not designed as a solution for creating complete applications, however. Most applications require a significant amount of programming to add advanced interactions and connect to server-side resources. The task of finishing the project will need to be handled with programming in the Flex Framework, most often via Flash Builder 4.

The Flex Framework

Flex is an open-source framework for creating RIAs that will run in Flash Player or on the desktop via the Adobe Integrated Runtime (AIR). Flex applications are created using a combination of two languages:

- MXML
- ActionScript

MXML

MXML is an XML-based markup language. Flex applications use it primarily to define the visual aspects of the project. Most of the coding created by Catalyst is MXML.

The Meaning of MXML

Officially, MXML does not stand for anything. It was created by Macromedia at a time when it was using MX as a descriptor for most of its products. Macromedia had a Studio MX release that included Flash MX, Dreamweaver MX, and Fireworks MX, which was followed by Studio MX2004. ColdFusion held onto the moniker through two versions as well. MX was merely a catchy name, likely developed by a marketing company.

As an XML-based language, MXML follows XML's very specific syntax rules:

- **All tags must be closed.** You must always have a matching closing tag for every opening tag. Tags that do not contain content can either have an explicit closing tag or must contain a slash before the closing angle bracket.

- **Everything is case sensitive.** Element names, attribute names, and attribute values must all use the correct case. Most element names in MXML begin with capital letters. Attributes and most attribute values use the *camel casing method*. Elements named using camel case begin with a lowercase letter. The first letter of any subsequent words in the name is capitalized (for example, camelCase).

- **Elements must be properly nested.** You must close tags in the opposite order from which you opened them.

- **Documents must have a single root element.** The first element on the page must contain all other elements in the document.

- **All attribute values must be enclosed in quotation marks.** You can use either double or single quotation marks.

If you have prior experience using XML, these rules will be familiar to you. If you are a Web designer who has been using XHTML, MXML rules will seem familiar because XHTML, like MXML, is an XML language.

ActionScript 3.0

All Flex applications are written in ActionScript 3.0. MXML is, in fact, nothing more than a simplified way of writing ActionScript. When you compile and run the application, the Flex compiler first rewrites all of your MXML into ActionScript. Therefore, it is possible to write a Flex project in nothing but ActionScript. There is an ActionScript equivalent to every MXML element, although the reverse is not true; there are many things that can only be done in ActionScript and not MXML.

ActionScript was originally developed as a rather simplistic scripting language for Flash. Originally, it did little more than allow designers to enable buttons in their Flash movies. Alternatively, ActionScript 3.0 is an object-oriented programming language. While many designers still use it to perform simple `gotoAndPlay` actions on buttons in Flash, today it can be used to create complete applications.

Members of the Flash design community are still somewhat split on which ActionScript version they prefer, with some designers continuing to rely on ActionScript 2.0 and its simpler syntax. This is because of Flash Professional's continued support for the older version of the language. No such division exists within the Flex community, however, as Flex projects can only be written using ActionScript 3.0.

Note

As ActionScript 3.0 is the only version usable in Flex, the remainder of this book will simply refer to it as ActionScript, omitting the version number.

Object-oriented programming 101

To many nonprogrammers, the thought of learning *object-oriented programming* (OOP) is as daunting as learning advanced calculus. However, most people actually find that once they learn a few key terms and concepts, OOP is not that difficult.

Classes

OOP relies on the idea of modeling real-world objects in code. For example, grocery stores rely on customers placing products in shopping carts; e-commerce applications follow these conventions by allowing users to place products in shopping carts as well. While the grocery store products and carts are real, physical things, the e-commerce application models products and carts using programmatic objects.

The first part of this modeling is a *class*, which is a definition of an object. You cannot use a class in your application; it simply serves as the descriptor for the object. It can help to think of OOP development in terms of building a housing community. A class is then analogous to the blueprints used for the homes: You cannot live in a blueprint; instead, you use it as the basis from which you will build the home.

Objects

An *object* is an instance of a class. While you cannot use a class, you can use objects. In the housing community example, the class is the blueprint, whereas the actual houses are the objects. An e-commerce application would define a shopping cart as a class. Subsequently, as each customer begins shopping, an instance of the class is created as an object. This allows customers to place products in their carts.

Using Pascal Case

ActionScript is completely case sensitive. Every class in the language uses what is known as *Pascal case*; multiple word class names are combined into a single word, with the first letter of each word capitalized, including the first letter of the name itself. Therefore, you have classes such as TextInput and FormItem. As you begin creating your own classes in your project, you should follow this same technique to avoid confusion.

Tip

In ActionScript, the terms instance and object are interchangeable.

Properties

Properties define characteristics of objects. Think of properties as the nouns of the object. A house is defined by its square footage, the number of bedrooms and baths it contains, its address, the color of its paint; all of these are properties of the house. Likewise, a virtual shopping cart contains properties. The most important properties are likely the list of products it contains. Visual objects, such as a text field, have properties that define its location on the screen and its width and height.

Objects often contain properties that are shared by all instances of the class, as well as other properties that are unique to each instance. For example, a check box shares certain characteristics with other check boxes, such as the shape of the box and appearance of the check mark. The check box also has unique properties, including its location on the screen and whether it is checked or unchecked.

Tip

Properties are nothing more than variables defined within a class. All properties in predefined classes in ActionScript use camel casing, where multiple word names are combined into a single word, with the first letter of each word except the first capitalized. The first letter is always lowercase. As you create your own variables and properties, you should follow this naming convention to maintain consistency.

Methods

If properties are the nouns of the object, *methods* are its verbs. Methods define the things the object does. A house would have methods such as enter, exit, sleep, eat dinner, and watch TV. Virtual shopping carts would, at a minimum, have methods to add products to the cart, delete products from the cart, and initiate the checkout process.

Tip

Methods are defined in classes as functions. As with properties, all methods in ActionScript use camel casing. Functions, whether defined as a method in a class or simply defined within a file, are called by using the function name followed by a set of parentheses, such as addEventListener().

Packages

ActionScript classes are nothing more than text files with the necessary ActionScript code to define the class. *Class files* are stored in folders on your computer, just as any other file would be. A group of related classes should be stored together in a folder. You can then group folders further into organizational units by placing them in higher-level folders. In OOP terminology, the folders in which classes are saved are known as *packages*.

Tip
Package names in ActionScript use camel casing, although most package names are single words and are lowercase.

Dot notation

OOP uses a technique known as *dot notation* to denote relationships between packages and classes and between objects, properties, and methods. You can refer to classes by their *fully qualified name*, which denotes the class and the packages in which it resides from some known starting point. Thus, the ActionScript Alert class' fully qualified name is `mx.controls.Alert`, meaning that the `Alert.as` file is in a folder called `controls`, which is in turn in an `mx` folder.

Properties and methods of the class are likewise referenced via dot notation. For example, the `Alert` class contains a `show` method, which is thus referenced as `Alert.show()`.

Flash Builder 4

You can develop Flex projects entirely for free because the Flex framework is open source. However, Adobe has created Flash Builder 4 as an integrated development environment (IDE) for Flex projects. While it is a commercial product that must be purchased from Adobe, the time saved in developing projects using Flash Builder versus other tools generally makes the cost worthwhile.

Flash Builder, like Catalyst, is built on Eclipse, an open-source editor used primarily by Java developers. Unlike Catalyst, Flash Builder can be installed using one of two methods:

- Install Flash Builder as a stand-alone application.
- Install Flash Builder as a plug-in to an existing copy of Eclipse that you already use.

Flex Builder or Flash Builder?

Prior versions of the Flex IDE were known as Flex Builder, not Flash Builder. Adobe decided to change the name in large part to bring all of its tools for Flash development under the same name. So we now have Flash Professional, Flash Builder, and Flash Catalyst, all of which create projects to be run in Flash Player. There are no plans at this time to change the name of the framework.

You can use Flash Builder to create projects using the Flex framework, which was another reason behind the name change; the new name will help distinguish the commercial product — Flash Builder — from the open source framework — Flex. While this might seem odd, it in fact follows the convention of other frameworks. For example, Microsoft .NET developers primarily use Visual Studio to create their projects, while Java developers use Eclipse or some other tool. Flex was actually the odd one in having an IDE and framework that shared a name.

Both installations cost the same; the one you use depends entirely on whether you already use Eclipse for other development.

Note
All of the screenshots used in this book are from the stand-alone version of Flash Builder.

Interface

While the Flash Builder interface (see Figure 14.1) is similar in many ways to the interface used in other Adobe tools, its terminology is different; the names of elements in the interface are adopted from Eclipse.

The primary Flash Builder interface is called a *workbench*. A workbench is a combination of views and editors. *Views* are the panels around the side of the screen, while each open document is an *editor*.

FIGURE 14.1

The Flash Builder interface. The Package Explorer and Outline views are visible to the left, while a single editor is open showing a Flex application file.

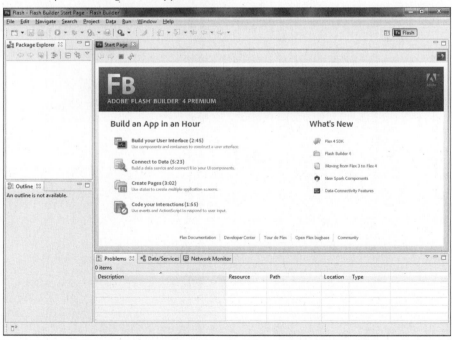

Design and Source modes

Flash Builder contains both a Design and a Source mode. The Design mode (see Figure 14.2) provides a what-you-see-is-what-you-get (WYSIWYG) visual environment. The WYSIWYG environment allows you to design elements in your application by dragging and dropping components from the Components view and then setting parameters with the Properties view.

You can switch between Design and Source modes at any time by clicking the button in the top-left corner of the editor.

FIGURE 14.2

A Flex project open in Design mode

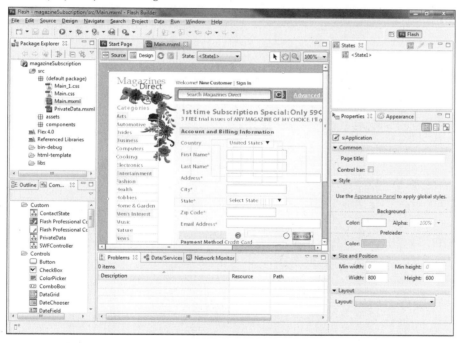

Source mode provides a code editor. The majority of your work in developing your project will be in Source mode (see Figure 14.3).

Source mode

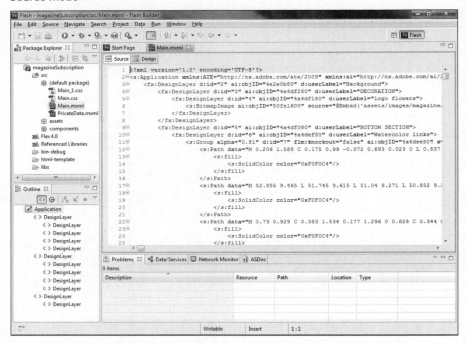

Creating a Flex Project

In order to create a Flex application, you need to first create a project.

Flex projects are made up of a series of files organized into folders. In order to create a new Flex project, follow these steps:

1. **Choose File ➪ New ➪ Flex Project (see Figure 14.4).**

2. **Type a name for the project (see Figure 14.5).** This name can be anything, but it should be descriptive of the project's purpose.

3. **Save the project in Flash Builder's default location within your user profile.** Alternatively, you can deselect the Use default location check mark and specify a different location on your computer to store the project's files.

4. **Choose whether you want to create an application for the Web or AIR.** The default is a Web application.

Cross-Reference
See Chapter 18 for details on working with AIR.

5. **Select which version of Flex you want to use.** The default is Flex 4.

Note
If you plan to write the project yourself from scratch, you can use either Flex 3 or 4; however, Catalyst only supports Flex 4.

FIGURE 14.4

The New project menu

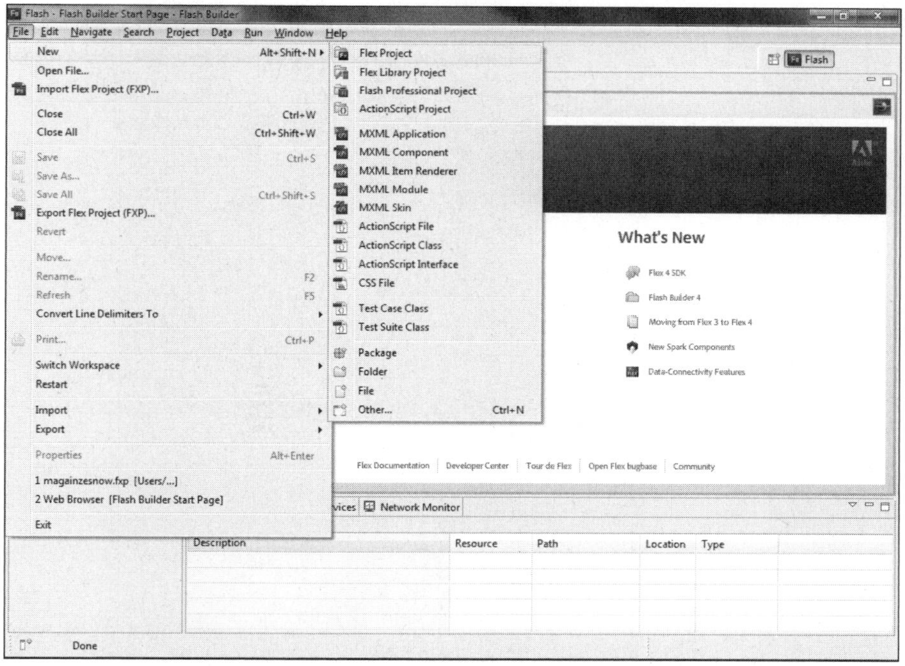

6. **If you will be using a server-side technology — for example, to get data from a data-base — select the appropriate option from the drop-down menu.** The default is none.

7. **Click Next.**

The first screen of the New Project wizard, in which you name the project and establish basic parameters for the application such as the project type and Flex version

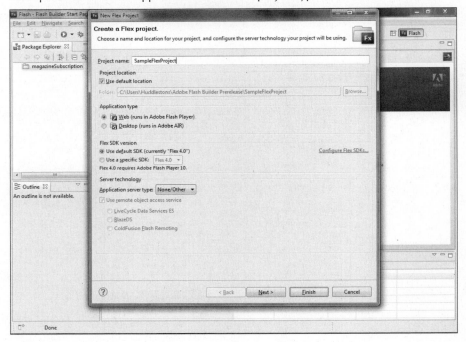

8. **Select the output folder for your project.** The default, `bin-debug`, is used by most developers (see Figure 14.6).

9. **Click Next.**

10. **Enter a source folder, into which all of your project files will be saved.** Most developers use the default, `src`.

11. **Enter the name of the main application file (see Figure 14.7).**

12. **Click Finish.**

Once created, your project will be displayed in the Package Explorer view in the top-left corner of the screen (see Figure 14.8).

FIGURE 14.6

Setting the output folder for the project

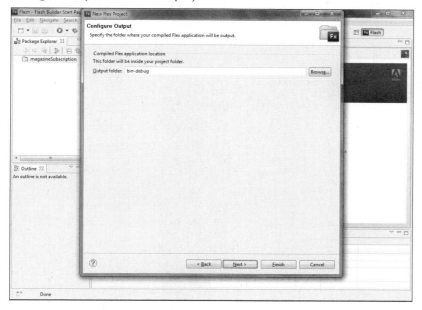

FIGURE 14.7

Finalizing the new project setup by setting the source folder and naming the main application file

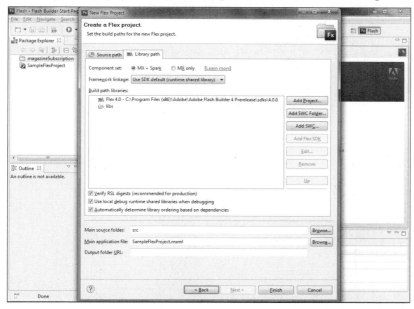

FIGURE 14.8

The new project in Flash Builder

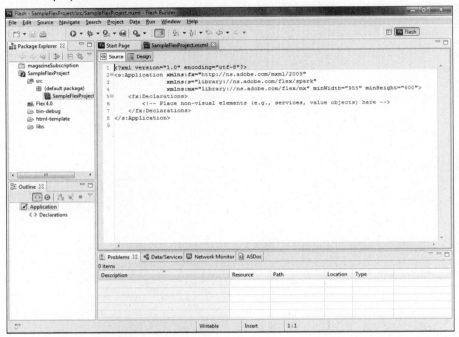

Project folders

A project created by Flash Builder automatically adds several folders to the project. The `src` folder contains all of your project's files. Most developers place the main application file in the `src` folder directly and then create subfolders for other files and components. This structure is not required. The only thing that matters is that the project's structure makes sense to you or other developers who might work on it.

The `bin-debug` folder is the folder into which the project will be compiled and run while you develop and test the project. The project's SWF file, the HTML page that will contain the SWF, and several helper files will be in this folder.

The `html-template` folder contains the HTML file that will hold the project's SWF. By default, this page is essentially blank; it only contains the code necessary to display the SWF. However, it is possible to modify this file to add additional HTML elements if you choose.

Cross-Reference

David Gassner's excellent Flex 4 Bible contains a detailed description of how to edit the HTML template for your project.

> The libs folder, which will initially be empty, can contain libraries of SWC files. SWCs are pre-compiled components that can be used across multiple Flex projects.

Cross-Reference

A detailed explanation of SWCs and component libraries is beyond the scope of this book. See the Flex 4 Bible for more details.

Understanding Flex 4

Flex 4 represents a significant upgrade to the Flex framework. Even experienced Flex developers are going to discover that they have much to learn about the new methodologies presented in Flex 4.

According to Adobe's open source wiki, less than half of all Flex-based applications are *drastically skinned*. Put simply, this means that most Flex applications look like most other Flex applications. Companies would obviously prefer that their applications carry the corporate branding. While this was certainly possible in Flex 3, many developers failed to do it. Catalyst was ultimately introduced to solve this problem, but addressing the issue forced Adobe to rethink many other aspects of the framework.

Cross-Reference

This chapter is intended to provide a high-level overview of the new features of Flex 4. It is not intended to be a complete tutorial or reference to the framework. For more information, see the Flex 4 Bible.

Main application file

All Flex projects must have a *main application file*. This file contains the primary code base for the application. It also instantiates the main components that make up the application. When you create a new project in Flex, a main application file is created for you.

The application file must have an Application tag as its root. Each Flex application can only contain one file that uses the Application root tag; all other MXML files must be components that use some other element as their root.

Flex 4 is based around a component architecture known as Spark; Flex 3 used the Halo architecture. Spark represents a significant shift in the way in which you build Flex applications. Spark was created to make the process of working on the visual aspects of the project more intuitive, primarily by separating the visual portions of the project such as the appearance of elements from their programming logic; in many ways, Spark was created to enable designers to use a tool like Catalyst to define that appearance without having to deal with the programmatic side of the application,

Note

The names of both Halo and Spark are references to the Halo video game, a favorite of many members of the Flex development team.

Namespaces

An important concept in XML is that of *namespaces*.

There is no predetermined set of tags in XML. Instead, each developer invents the tags he wants to use in the document. It's possible, and in fact likely, that two developers working independently on similar projects might use the same element names for tags, albeit for slightly different purposes. Should these developers later come together and attempt to combine their document structures, conflicts would occur in those cases where the same name was used with a different meaning.

Namespaces exist to solve this problem. By defining one set of elements as being from one namespace and the other from a different namespace, conflicts will not occur. The program responsible for parsing the XML will know to differentiate between them.

Namespaces are defined with an xmlns attribute, most often in the root tag of the document. The attribute includes a prefix, which will be added to the beginning of each element used from the namespace. The attribute's value is set to the location of the document that defines the elements from the namespace.

The model used in Flex 3 defined a single namespace for MXML in the root element of each document. Thus, the root of the main application looked like this:

```
<mx:Application xmlns:mx="http://www.adobe.com/2006/mxml" />
```

Early in the development of Flex 4, Adobe realized that it needed to greatly expand the capabilities of MXML, particularly in its ability to define and draw graphics. This realization was driven in large part by the needs of Catalyst to take complex vector graphics from Illustrator and render them in MXML.

A wholesale rewriting of MXML, however, would have created compatibility problems, and Adobe did not want Flex 4 projects to be incompatible with existing Flex 3 components. Thus, Adobe simply leveraged the power of XML namespaces. Flex 4 applications rely on four namespaces:

- **MXML 2006.** The legacy MXML namespace, used by Flex 3 components, but fully compatible with Flex 4. It uses the default mx namespace prefix, and its definition is still http://www.adobe.com/2006/mxml to ensure backwards compatibility.

- **MXML 2009.** Unlike MXML 2006, this new Flex 4 namespace is used purely for built-in language elements and does not include components. It uses the fx prefix to avoid conflicts with MXML 2006 and points to http://ns.adobe.com/mxml/2009 for its definition.

- **Spark.** The Spark namespace is used for all of the new Spark components in conjunction with the MXML 2009 namespace. By default, it uses the s prefix and is defined at http://ns.adobe.com/flex/spark.

- **MX.** You can use this namespace for using Halo components when using those components with MXML 2009. It uses mx for its prefix and is defined at `http://ns.adobe.com/flex/halo`.

Therefore, a Flex 4 project's main application page would begin with the following `Application` tag, in which the three new namespaces are declared:

```
<s:Application xmlns:fx="http://ns.adobe.com/mxml/2009"
    xmlns:s="library://ns.adobe.com/flex/spark" xmlns:mx="library://
    ns.adobe.com/flex/halo">
```

Note that the `Application` tag itself is from the s namespace. Components such as a `Label` or `TextInput` are still from the mx namespace, but use the new definitions provided by Halo.

Components

Catalyst bases much of its design paradigm around the idea of *components*. Almost every graphic in a Catalyst project ends up being either a component by itself or a part of a component.

Cross-Reference
See Chapter 9 for more details on Catalyst components.

Flex projects are also based around the idea of creating and working with components. The framework includes a large set of components to enable developers to quickly build an application. These include user interface components such as text input fields and labels, buttons, and layout components such as canvases and panels. These interface components control the placement and navigation of other components such as button bars and tab bars. Flex developers can also create their own components. In Catalyst, you should take any set of objects that needs to function together as a unit and define it as a component. Flex works the same way. For example, if you have a long form that you want your user to fill out, you would likely define the form as a separate component rather than placing its code in the application file.

Tip
Components are in fact nothing more than classes defined via MXML. As with every class in the framework, all built-in Flex components have names that begin with a capital letter. To maintain consistency, any component that you create whether in Flex or Catalyst should follow this naming convention.

Components can be created in Flash Builder by choosing File ➪ New ➪ MXML Component (see Figure 14.9).

Unlike in Flex 3, where custom components were defined as being based on practically any element in MXML, most Flex 4 custom components are based instead on a single element, `Group`. This follows the general idea behind much of what it being done in Flex 4 to separate the design of the application from its implementation. Many Flex 3 components would rely on a root element that did not necessarily make sense for the component simply because it needed a root, which tended to add unnecessary overhead to the component.

Group adds no additional overhead; it is simply an element that, as its name implies, groups other elements. The component will contain, as the group's children, those elements necessary to implement the purpose of the component, along with new tags to define the layout and graphical skinning or appearance of those child elements.

Components are instantiated in MXML by first declaring a new namespace. As with the default namespaces, you use the xmlns attribute in the document's root tag with a namespace prefix. The prefix is arbitrary and can be anything you prefer. The value of the attribute will be the path to the component being instantiated, relative to the root of the project. You can use an asterisk (*) to have the namespace make available all of the components within a directory.

FIGURE 14.9

The New MXML Component dialog box in Flash Builder 4

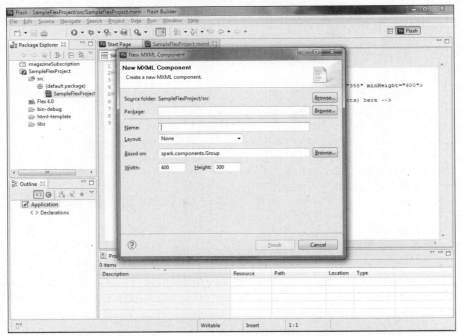

Components are often grouped in a folder within the project, and most developers will use the folder name for the namespace prefix. For example, a project might contain a login form component (Login.MXML) stored in a folder called forms. If you want to instantiate the component in the main application, you can add a new namespace declaration to the Application:

```
<s:Application xmlns:fx="http://ns.adobe.com/mxml/2009"
    xmlns:s="library://ns.adobe.com/flex/spark" xmlns:mx="library://
    ns.adobe.com/flex/halo"
Xmlns:forms="forms.*">
```

The component can then be called as a tag with the component's filename as the element name, using the namespace prefix:

```
<forms:Login />
```

Flash Builder provides context-sensitive code hinting to assist in this process. Once a namespace is declared, components available within that namespace appear in the code hinting (see Figure 14.10).

FIGURE 14.10

Code hinting a custom component in Flash Builder 4

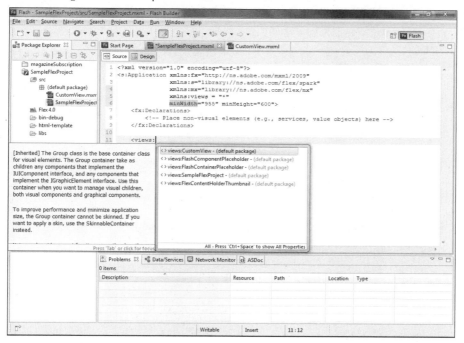

Running Projects

Throughout the development process, you will want to run your Flex project to ensure that you do not have any errors and ensure that it looks and functions as you planned.

You can run an application by clicking the Run button in the Flash Builder toolbar, clicking Run (*projectname*) in the Run menu, or by pressing Ctrl+(⌘+)F11.

If you have unsaved changes in any files within the project, Flash Builder prompts you to save those changes. It then runs the Flex compiler to compile your application, assemble the HTML container, launch a Web browser, and display the resulting page (see Figure 14.11).

FIGURE 14.11

A project opened in a browser

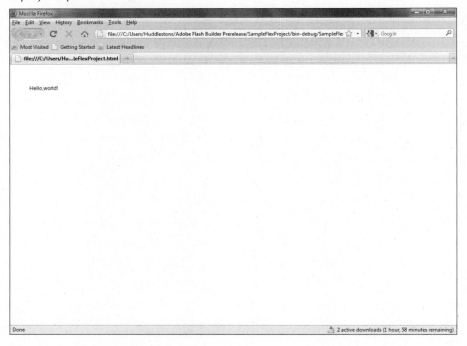

Tip

By default, the project always opens in whichever Web browser you defined as the default for your operating system. If you would like Flash Builder to use a different browser, you can change this setting by choosing Window ➪ Preferences ➪ General ➪ Web Browser.

Debugging

Debugging is an unfortunate but necessary part of any programming process. Fortunately, Flash Builder provides a very powerful set of debugging tools so that when an error occurs, you should be able to track it down quickly.

In any program, there are three general types of errors you are likely to encounter:

- **Syntax error.** A syntax error occurs when you have incorrect code. A common source of syntax errors in Flex is capitalization. As all component names, attributes, and attribute values are case sensitive, you should be careful to always use the correct case.

- **Logical error.** Logical errors occur when your syntax is correct but the application fails to run the way you expect. For instance, you might have a conditional statement that executes one block of code if a variable is equal to a certain value and another if it is no equal. You may think that the variable has the value to make the statement true, but something in your code is causing it to have a different value. Therefore, even though your code is syntactically correct, your application will not run the way you expect.

- **Runtime error.** Runtime errors are those that occur when the application is running in real-world scenarios. Most often, runtime errors are caused by a user who performs unanticipated actions. These types of errors are common in traditional HTML-based Web applications when a programmer expects that a page will always be accessed from a certain other page and forgets to account for a user who manually enters an address or follows a bookmark, thus circumventing the expected navigation.

  A similar situation can occur in a Flex application if a user jumps directly to a state without having followed the path through the application that you expect. Runtime errors can also be caused by temporary factors such as a network outage that prevents the application from accessing back-end components such as databases.

Of the three, syntax errors are far and away the easiest to fix. Syntax errors are almost always caught by the compiler when you attempt to run the project, and a dialog box appears informing you that errors were encountered. Details of the error appear in the Problems view at the bottom of the screen (see Figure 14.12).

Caution

The nature of a Flex project is that you will have multiple files working together to create your application. However, you can only run the application file itself — individual components cannot be run directly. Do not assume that the error message you see in the Problems view is a reference to code in the application. Instead, be sure to look at the Resource column in the Problems view, which indicates the file in which the error exists.

Logical errors are much more difficult to track down. Often, a logical error will occur when a variable is set to a value other than what you expect it to be. This can cause other elements of the code to behave in unexpected ways. You can tell that a logical error is occurring because your application doesn't work correctly as you test it as there is nothing syntactically wrong with your code; neither Flash Builder nor Flash Player will display any error messages.

FIGURE 14.12

The Problems view displaying an error

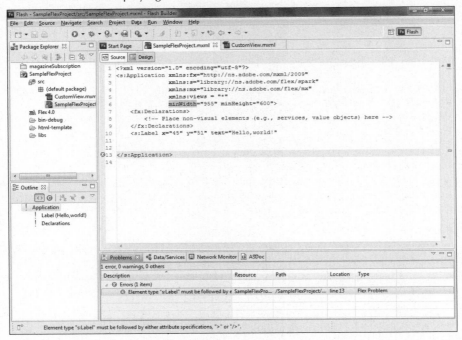

Flash Builder's Debugging Perspective is a useful tool for tracking down logical errors. You can force the application to stop at a given point in its processing and then examine the value of any variables created at that point. From there, you can often determine which values are incorrect and then track back through the application to figure out when and why the incorrect value appeared.

Setting a breakpoint allows you to stop the applications flow. Breakpoints can be set by simply double-clicking in the margin next to the line number at the point at which you want the breakpoint. Code up to that line will execute; however, as soon as Flash Player encounters the line with the breakpoint it stops processing and sends the application back to Flash Builder.

Caution

You can only set breakpoints on lines of code that contain ActionScript. Lines that are purely MXML cannot contain breakpoints.

Caution

You must have the debug version of Flash Player in order to work with debugging in Flash Builder. The debug version is automatically installed on your system when you install Flash Builder. Be aware that if you later upgrade to a newer release of Flash Player you will lose the debug version and will need to manually reinstall it from www.adobe.com/support/flashplayer/downloads.html.

The Debugging Perspective (see Figure 14.13) displays a set of views that provide you with information while you debug. Perhaps the most useful of these is the Variables in the top-right corner, which displays the values of any variables created up to the breakpoint.

Caution

You can only have one debugging session open at a time. Once you are finished debugging, be sure to click the Terminate button — the red square in the Debug view — to end the session.

You can switch between the development and debugging perspectives in Flash Builder using the buttons in the top-right corner of the screen (see Figure 14.14).

FIGURE 14.13

The Debugging Perspective in Flash Builder

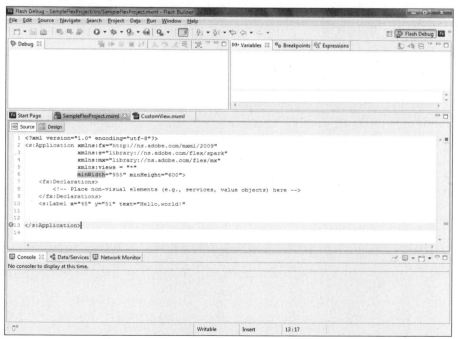

Switching perspectives in Flash Builder

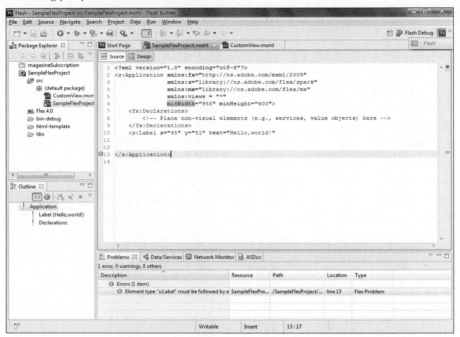

Summary

The Flex framework is the basis for projects you create in Catalyst. Flash Builder provides a powerful development environment in which you can work with Flex. In this chapter, you:

- Gained a basic understanding of the Flex framework and object-oriented programming
- Learned the basics of Flash Builder
- Learned how to create a new Flex project, run it in a browser, and debug it

Exporting a Flash Catalyst Project to Flash Builder

F lash Catalyst is not designed to create complete projects. At some point, almost all projects will need to be exported to Flash Builder where a Flex developer can finish creating the interactive aspects of the application and add server-side connections for live data. Fortunately, the process of moving your project from Flash Catalyst to Flash Builder is fairly easy.

View the Project's Code

Flash Catalyst is designed for designers, not programmers. Everything that you do in Catalyst results in MXML and ActionScript code being generated, but all of the coding is happening in the background. Catalyst allows you to view the code that it creates for your project, but the view is read-only; you cannot edit the code directly in any way from within Catalyst. Any and all code editing must happen in Flash Builder.

To view the code from your project choose Window ⇨ Code Workspace, or click the workspace drop-down list in the top-right corner of the screen and select Code. The Code workspace (see Figure 15.1) is divided into three sections. The main section displays the MXML and ActionScript that has been generated by Catalyst for your project. Below that is the Problems panel, which displays any errors in your project. The Project Navigator on the right side of the screen displays the files in your project.

Note

The only time you should see errors in the Problems panel is when you have components with required parts that have not been defined.

FIGURE 15.1

The Code workspace in Flash Catalyst

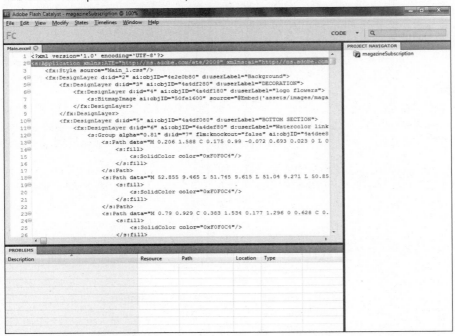

The Code workspace (see Figure 15.2) will initially only display the code for the main application file. It will not display the code for the components you have defined, as they are separate files.

If you expand the project's main folder in the Project Navigator by clicking the small arrow to the left of the folder, and then expand the src folder, you will see the main application file. That same folder should also contain a components folder, which in turn contains the files for each of the components in your project. You can double-click any of these files to view their code.

In general, MXML is used to create the visual aspects of the project while ActionScript handles the programming logic. Thus, most of what you create in Catalyst will be MXML. There may be small blocks of ActionScript in your code, such as that needed for action sequences, and video and SWF control; therefore, if your project contains any of these things you will see ActionScript code in your project.

FIGURE 15.2

A component open in the Code workspace

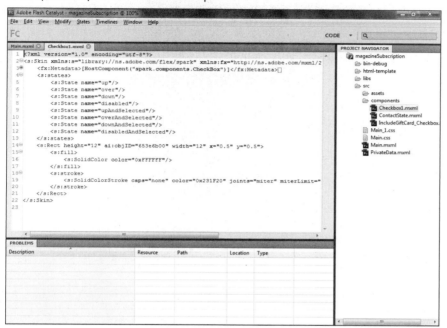

Import the Project into Flash Builder

You do not need to do anything special to export your project from Catalyst before using it in Flash Builder. Catalyst saves projects as an FXP file. The FXP format is in fact a zipped file that contains the project's assets. All of the files and folders you see displayed in the Project Navigator panel in Catalyst are contained within the FXP. The only thing you need to do to prepare a file for export is save it in Catalyst.

Importing a project in Flash Builder is likewise a simple process. You simply choose File ➪ Import Flex Project (FXP) to open the Import Flex Project dialog box (see Figure 15.3). Click the Browse button next to the text field labeled File to select the Catalyst project. Then select a path into which you want to have the file extracted; this will be the folder in which the Flex project resides on your hard drive. Click Finish and your project will be imported (see Figure 15.4).

The Package Explorer view in Flash Builder displays the folder structure of the project. The basic structure will match what you saw in Catalyst, but Flash Builder will have added references to the Flex 4 and Referenced Libraries folders from which it can draw additional assets you may need as you work on the project.

FIGURE 15.3

The Import Flex Project dialog box

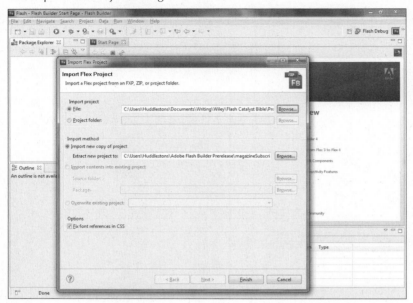

FIGURE 15.4

The Catalyst project imported into Flash Builder

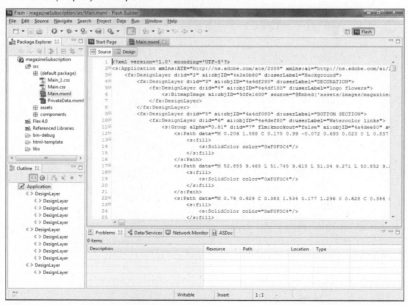

Also, the `src` folder will display its contents as packages, so whereas in Catalyst the main application file is directly in the folder, it now resides in the `(default package)`. The components and assets are also shown with package icons, but their functionality is the same as folders.

Cross-Reference

See Chapter 14 for a discussion of packages.

Tip

If your project opens in Design mode (where it looks as it did in Catalyst) rather than in code, click the Source button in the top-right corner of the document window. Design mode is discussed later in this chapter.

Run the Project from Flash Builder

After you import the project into Flash Builder you can run it just as you would any other Flex project. Choose Run ➪ Run (*projectname*), click the Run button on the toolbar or press Ctrl+(⌘+) F11. Flash Builder will compile the project into a SWF and open it in your default Web browser (see Figure 15.5).

FIGURE 15.5

The project running in a browser

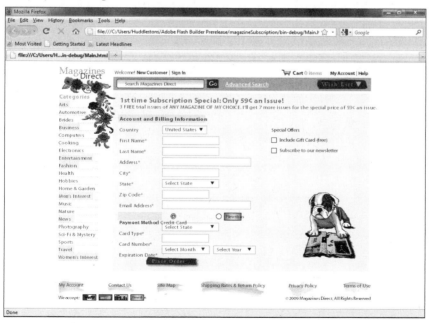

Viewing Help on the Code

The code required to render a Catalyst project in MXML can be daunting, whether you are new to the Flex framework or new to Flex 4's graphical capabilities. Fortunately, Flash Builder provides context-sensitive help that allows you to quickly view detailed information about any code in the page.

For most tags a simple description can be displayed by simply moving your mouse over the element (see Figure 15.6). A tooltip will appear describing the component. The same help is available for attributes of tags, function calls, and most other language elements.

FIGURE 15.6

Help tooltip when moving your mouse over an element

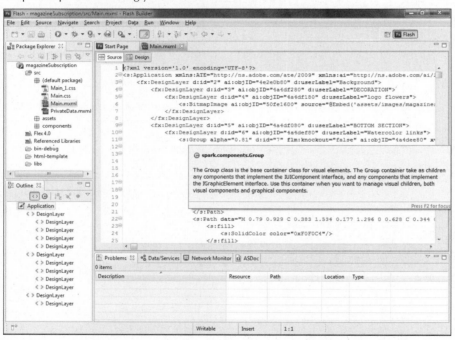

Additional information is provided in the Help view, which can be opened by choosing Help ➪ Dynamic Help. The Dynamic Help view displays a list of relevant help links for any element you click on (see Figure 15.7).

The Dynamic Help view links to the Adobe help files for a selected item. Clicking a link opens help in a new window directly within Flash Builder's internal Web browser (see Figure 15.8).

FIGURE 15.7

Dynamic help displaying links based on the selected element on the page

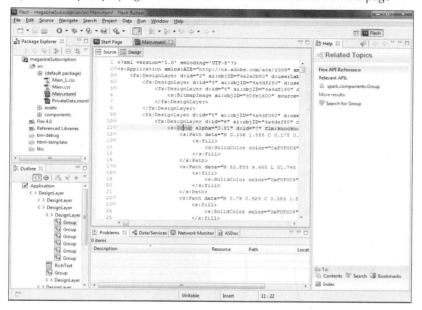

FIGURE 15.8

Help displayed in Flash Builder's internal Web browser

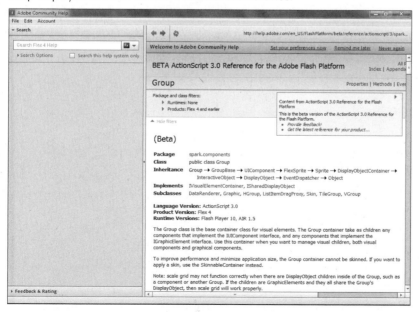

Viewing the Project in the Design Mode

Flash Builder features a design mode that allows you to see what the project will look like when it runs in Flash Player. The design mode is, in some ways, similar to the view you have of the project in Catalyst. However, whereas Catalyst features an editable design view and a read-only code view, Flash Builder's design mode allows you to edit the project.

To switch between the code or source view and design view in Flash Builder, click the button in the top-left corner of the document window (see Figure 15.9).

FIGURE 15.9

The project open in Flash Builder's design mode

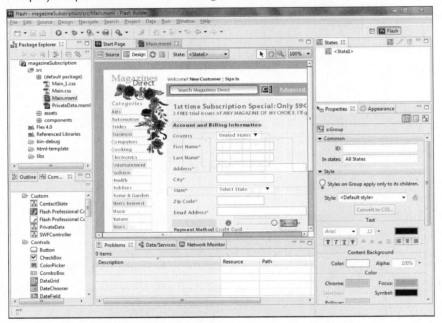

User-interface Components in Catalyst and Builder

The Eclipse toolset uses a different set of names for its user-interface components than Adobe. With Catalyst, Adobe renamed these components to match the names used in other Creative Suite products. Alternatively, with Flash Builder it has retained the Eclipse names. Thus, open documents are called *editors* and panels are known as *views*. A set of views and editors, which other Adobe products would call a workspace, is known in Flash Builder as a *perspective*. Somewhat confusingly, Flash Builder also recognizes workspaces, but a workspace in Flash Builder is a set of open projects.

The design mode in Flash Builder features a stage area that displays the project with a set of views surrounding it for editing. Just as in Source mode, the top-left view is the Package Explorer, while the Outline view remains in the bottom-left corner.

Likewise, the Problems, Data/Services, Network Monitor, and ASDocs views will remain visible along the bottom edge of the screen. However, a set of new views, all particularly useful for working on the project in Design mode, will now also be open. Table 15.1 briefly describes each of these views.

TABLE 15.1

The Default Views in Flash Builder's Design Mode

View	Default Location	Description
Components	Bottom left, grouped with Outline	The Components view provides drag-and-drop access to the components in the Flex framework. They are grouped into three folders: Custom, which contains any components created by you or your Flex developer; Controls, which contains the common user interface components such as buttons and text inputs; and Navigators, which contains the components in the framework designed specifically for navigational use.
States	Top right	Displays the states in the project. The selected state will be displayed in the design window.
Properties	Bottom right, grouped with Appearance	Displays the common properties of the component currently selected on the stage.
Appearance	Bottom right, grouped with Properties	This panel contains tools that allow you to modify the overall look and feel of the application.

Connecting a Project to Live Data

Flash Catalyst allows you to create areas of your application that can be used to display dynamic data. It cannot, however, actually assist you in bringing that data into the project, a step that must instead be completed in Flash Builder.

Flex applications run entirely *at the client*. In other words, they are applications that run locally in your user's browser and not on a server. Therefore, they cannot connect directly to back-end resources such as databases any more than an HTML-based Web front end can. Instead, just as in HTML-based applications, your Flex application will need to connect to a program on the server that can in turn access back-end databases or other resources.

You can write this server-side script in almost any Web programming language, such as Adobe ColdFusion, PHP, or Microsoft ASP.NET. You can also access scripts written in Java. Regardless of the language, the script will need to be written as a Web service in order for your Flex application to have access to it.

A detailed description of writing such a script is well beyond the scope of this book. If you want to connect to your own data source, you will need to consult a reference on the language of your choosing.

Note

Strictly speaking, Flex applications can connect directly to server-side Java and ColdFusion resources, even if they are not Web services, via the Adobe LiveCycle DS or Breeze DS servers. Discussion of these alternatives is beyond the scope of this book; David Gassner's Flex 4 Bible goes into detail on these methods.

Cross-Reference

So that you can experiment with server-side data, several files are available on the book's Web site (www. wiley.com/go/flashcatalystbible) to allow you to work through this process. Detailed setup instructions for these files are included on the site.

Once the server-side script has been written and properly deployed on the server, Flash Builder mostly automates the task of connecting your application to the script and consuming the data returned from it. The Data/Services view, which by default appears along the bottom of the screen, allows you to launch a set of wizards to get started using server-side data (see Figure 15.10).

FIGURE 15.10

The Data/Services view

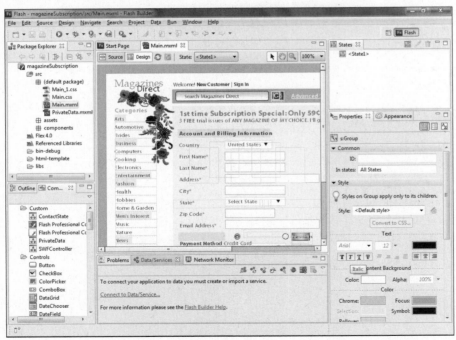

To begin using server-side date, follow these steps:

1. **Click the Connect to Data/Service link on the panel.** This launches the first step of the wizard. A default installation of Flash Builder includes wizards for six types of services:

   - **Blaze DS.** An Adobe application server for the Flex framework.
   - **ColdFusion.** Adobe's server-side scripting environment.
   - **HTTPService.** Allows you to connect directly to files on the server that return properly formatted date, most often using XML.
   - **LCDS.** Short for LiveCycle Data Services, this is another Adobe application server for Flex.
   - **PHP.** An open-source alternative to ColdFusion.
   - **WebService.** Lets you connect to other resources such as those created using ASP. NET.

2. **Select the type of service you want to use.** Flash Builder now needs to modify your project to work with the server. When you import a project from Catalyst, Flash Builder creates a generic project.

3. **Once the project is created, you need to configure the project to use the server-side resources.** A dialog box warning you that this change is necessary appears when you select the service.

4. **Click Yes on the dialog box.** The Server Settings dialog box opens.

5. **Complete this dialog box by selecting the appropriate application server type and specifying the path to the server** (see Figure 15.11). The wizard will resume with the New Flex Service dialog box.

Cross-Reference

See the Flash Builder help files or the Flex 4 Bible for detailed instructions on configuring the server-side settings. The figures in this chapter display the settings necessary to connect to a ColdFusion script.

6. **If you are using ColdFusion, you can have Flash Builder generate a ColdFusion Component (CFC) to provide you with basic functionality.** Alternatively, you can select Import CFC to use a prebuilt ColdFusion component for your project. Flash Builder will introspect the imported CFC file and return a list of the functions, or methods, available from the CFC (see Figure 15.12).

7. **Use one of more of the methods on the returned list to retrieve the data for your project.**

8. **Select the method you want to use (see Figure 15.13).**

FIGURE 15.11

The Server Settings dialog box, showing the settings for setting up a connection to a locally installed instance of ColdFusion 9.

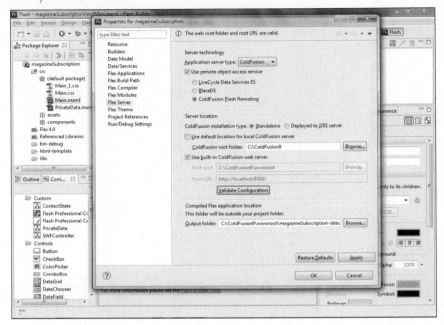

9. **Click Finish.** Flash Builder generates a number of ActionScript files to implement the necessary functionality to receive the data from the server so that it can be used by Flex.

10. **Configure the type of data that will be returned.** You can accomplish this by either of the following methods:

    - Clicking the Configure Return Type button on the panel.
    - Right-clicking (⌘+clicking) the method (see Figure 15.14).

    Either way, the Configure Return Type dialog box appears (see Figure 15.15). Most of the time, you will want to create your own custom data type with a name that represents the kind of information being returned.

Tip

A data type lets a computer program know how it should interpret information and places restrictions on how that information is used. Common data types include strings, which represent text and other nonnumeric characters; numbers; and Boolean or true and false values. Data types in ActionScript are defined through the use of classes. This makes it possible for developers to define their own data types through the creation of custom classes. When you select the option in the Configure Return Type dialog box to use a custom data type Flash Builder writes the code needed to define this type as a new class.

Chapter 15: Exporting a Flash Catalyst Project to Flash Builder

FIGURE 15.12

The New Flex Service dialog box for ColdFusion services

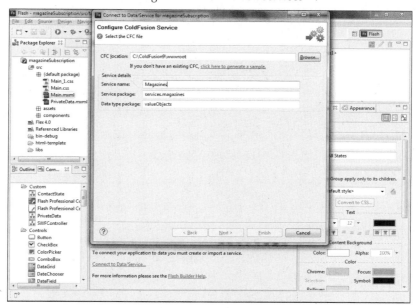

FIGURE 15.13

The Service Operations screen of the New Flex Service dialog box

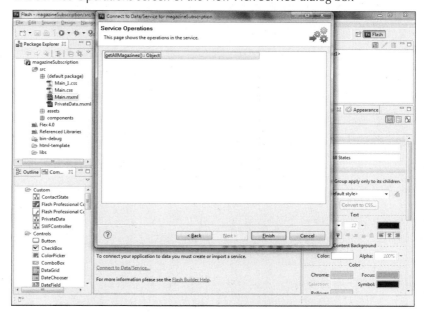

FIGURE 15.14

The Data/Services panel after setting up the service. The return type can be configured by clicking the Configure Return Type button from the panel's toolbar or by right-clicking the method.

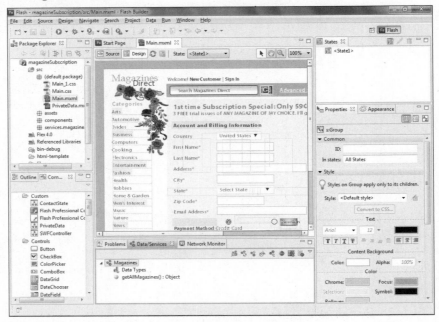

11. Once the return type has been defined, determine which method of the service will be called and provide any necessary arguments to it (see Figure 15.16).

Note

Arguments are pieces of data that need to be passed to a service. For example, a Web service that displays the local weather would need an argument informing it of the user's location, such as a ZIP code.

Tip

You need to specify the data type of the argument, which must match the type expected by the service. You need to look at the service's documentation or contact its developer to determine what this type should be.

The final step of the wizard displays after Flash Builder invokes the service's method. It displays the information being returned and the data type of each piece.

12. Review the information displayed after the Flash Builder invokes the service's method to ensure that it is correct.

13. Click Finish.

FIGURE 15.15

The Configure Return Type dialog box

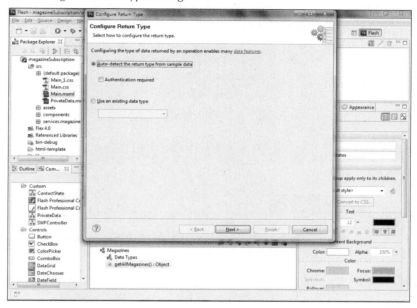

FIGURE 15.16

The Configure Return Types dialog with the data type name

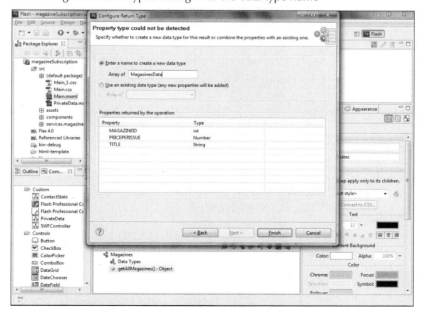

Now that the service has been configured, you can use a process known as *data binding* to associate the data with a control in your project. This process can be completed in Design mode and requires no code be written by you. Follow these steps to bind data:

1. **Select the control to which you wish to bind the data.**

2. **Click the Bind control to data button in the Data/Services view.** Alternately, you can drag the icon that represents the data from the view onto the control or right-click (⌘+click) the control and select Bind to data.

   When you designed the control in Catalyst, you likely added placeholder data to show what the control might look like. Flash Builder will detect that the control already contains data.

3. **Confirm that you want to replace this dummy data with the live data coming from the service.** The Bind to Data dialog box appears (see Figure 15.17).

FIGURE 15.17

The final step of the wizard

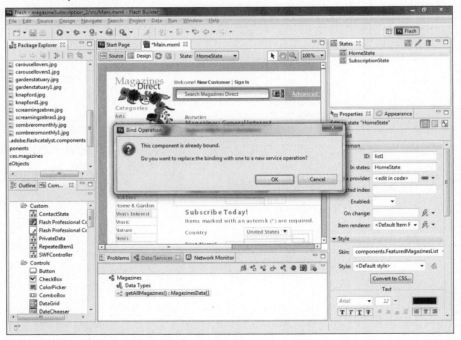

4. Determine the service being called and the type of data to be used (see Figure 15.18).

Cross-Reference

See Chapter 12 for details on adding design-time or placeholder data in Catalyst.

FIGURE 15.18

The Bind to Data dialog box

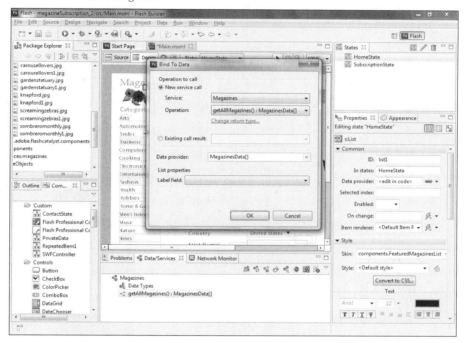

5. **Click OK on the Bind to Data dialog box.** Flash Builder switches to Source view and displays an event handler function that it has created. This function is invoked by the application as soon as it finishes building the list control that will display the data and is responsible for populating the control with the data. You need not make any modifications to this code (see Figure 15.19).

6. **Click File ⇨ Save, then click the Run button on the toolbar to see the results.**

FIGURE 15.19

The event handler function in Source view

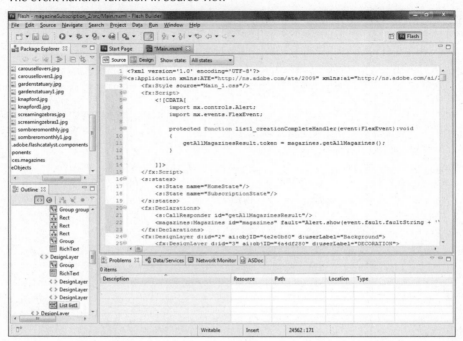

Summary

In this chapter, you imported a project from Flash Catalyst to Flash Builder. You learned how to:

- Create a new Flex project in Flash Builder from an FXP file
- Run the project
- View help information on the code generated by Catalyst
- Populate a control with live data

Returning a Project to Flash Catalyst

A fter you import your Catalyst project into Flash Builder, development of the project should be done entirely in Builder. Full round-trip editing between Catalyst and Builder is not available.

However, in real-world environments, there may be situations where some updating or editing of the project will be easier in Catalyst than in Builder. For example, if your client decides to change some aspect of the look and feel of the project, such as deciding that a button should be a different shape or color, you may want to make the necessary modifications in Catalyst.

While no direct path exists to open a project in Catalyst, it is nonetheless possible to work between the two applications.

Flash Builder Projects in Flash Catalyst

Once a project has been modified in Flash Builder it's no longer possible to open and edit that file in Catalyst. Attempting to do so will result in an error. Even though Flash Builder contains a menu item to export the project as an FXP, Catalyst will not be able to open the project.

The reason for this limitation is based on the differences in the workflow between Flash Builder and Catalyst. A Flex developer working exclusively in Flash Builder might begin by working in Design mode to create the basic interface of the application, but will likely very quickly switch to working in code. Ultimately, many of the changes the developer makes in code will result in Design mode being unable to display the project any longer.

In Catalyst, all you have to work with is Design mode, so once the project reaches the stage where it cannot be rendered in Design mode, it's no longer logical to work within Catalyst. There are too many variables to consider as to when a project might reach this point, so the Catalyst team decided it would be best not to allow projects that have been edited in Flash Builder to be opened in Catalyst.

Note

Many of the Catalyst developers at Adobe have stated in a variety of public forums that they are working on solutions to this issue and hope to resolve it in a future version of Catalyst.

Merging Projects

Because projects cannot be directly opened by Catalyst once they have been edited in Flash Builder, it's necessary instead for the designer to maintain a copy of the original FXP file created in Catalyst. That way, if the design of the project needs to be changed after it has been handed off to the developer, the designer will have access to a file that can be opened and modified in Catalyst.

Once the designer completes the changes in Catalyst, the developer can merge the file back into Flash Builder and continue working on the project (see Figure 16.1). The developer will use the same menu option to import this file as he would have when importing a new project: File ➪ Import Flex Project (FXP). This time, however, he selects the Import new copy of project option. This will result in a new project being opened in Flash Builder; the process of merging the changes is a manual process.

Flash Builder includes a merge tool to assist the developer in identifying changes and merging these changes into the project without disturbing the work already done in Flash Builder. The developer can right-click (⌘+click) the new project and choose Compare with *name of the original project*. Flash Builder will examine each of the files in both projects and display a list of those files in which it detects differences.

Ideally, the developer will not be making modifications to the skins or other visual aspects of the project within Flash Builder. Any changes identified in Flash Builder to those files should represent changes made in Catalyst that the developer can accept simply by clicking the appropriate button to copy the changed code from the new project into the old one. At that point, the developer can delete or ignore the new project and continue work on the original.

Importing changes into Flash Builder

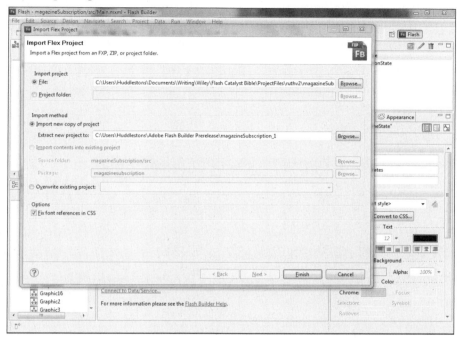

Using a Flash Catalyst Library Package to Manage Changes

An alternative approach to managing the designer/developer workflow in Catalyst and Flash Builder is to use an alternate file type recognized by Catalyst: FXPL or Library Package file. Unlike a more traditional FXP file, which contains both the visual assets of the project as well as a main application file to manage those assets, the FXPL file contains only the visual assets:

- Component skins
- Item renderers
- Custom components

In order to use FXPL files, you need to maintain your main application file and other supporting MXML and ActionScript files in a separate Flex project. This could be a project designed using the wireframe components in Catalyst or one created from scratch in Flash Builder.

Cross-Referencce

See Chapter 4 for details on creating a wireframe application.

Create an FXPL file

The FXPL file can be created in Catalyst by right-clicking (⌘+clicking) anywhere in the Library panel. Select the Export Library option (see Figure 16.2) and choose a location in which to save the file.

FIGURE 16.2

Exporting an FXPL file in Catalyst

Import an FXPL into Flash Builder

You can import an FXPL file into a Flash Builder project (see Figure 16.3) by choosing File ⇨ Import Project (FXP). This results in the creation of a Flex Library project.

Once imported, your library project can be associated with any Flex project. In fact, a single library file can be associated with any number of Flex projects.

FIGURE 16.3

Importing an FXPL file into Flash Builder

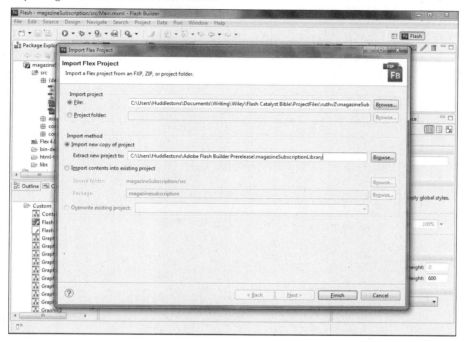

This association is done by defining the library project's location as part of a Flex project's build path. You can add the project to the build path by following these steps:

1. **Modify the project's properties by choosing Project ⇨ Properties or by right-clicking (⌘+clicking) the project in the Package Explorer and selecting Properties.**

2. **In the Properties dialog box, click Flex Build Path.**

3. **Make sure you are on the Library Path tab (see Figure 16.4).**

4. **Click Add Project.**

5. **Select the library project from the list that appears.**

Changing library items in Catalyst

As changes are needed in the project's visual assets, the designer can simply reopen the project file in Catalyst and make the needed changes. Then the designer can reexport the library project, replacing the original library project with the new one. These changes are available automatically in the Flex project.

FIGURE 16.4

The Flex Build Path tab of the Project Properties

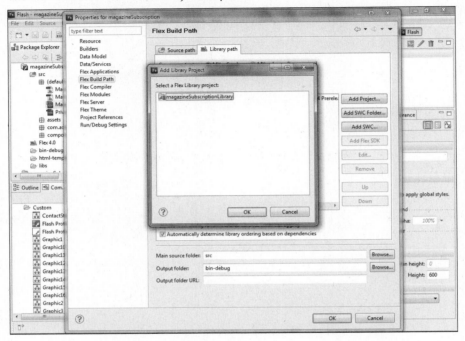

Caution

For this workflow between designer and developer to work, the developer must be sure not to edit the code in the library files directly within Flash Builder. Doing so will result in the changes being lost the next time the designer modifies the assets and overwrites the library package. Instead, all changes need to be made in Catalyst.

Summary

This chapter discussed the workflow between Flash Builder and Catalyst. In it, you learned:

- Why Flash Builder projects cannot be directly opened in Catalyst
- How to merge changes between projects in Flash Builder
- How to create and use Catalyst library projects

Exporting Catalyst Projects Directly to Flash Player

C atalyst is primarily intended to be *middleware* (that is, a program that exists as a sort of bridge between design programs such as Illustrator and development applications such as Flash Builder). It is not intended to be a tool that you can use to design completed projects.

However, in certain specific scenarios, you can export the completed project to run directly in Flash Player. In particular, projects that do not require server-side data connections or complex actions may be created completely in Catalyst.

Exporting a Project as a SWF

Catalyst projects are saved as FXP files, but Flash Player can only work with SWFs. Thus, you will need to specifically publish the project as a SWF in order to run it directly. Choose File ➪ Publish as SWF to display a dialog box that will allow you to select the location in which the project will be saved (see Figure 17.1).

You can also choose to make the project accessible, build deployable and redistributable versions, an AIR version, and embed fonts.

Cross-Reference

See Chapter 18 for more details on working with AIR. Other options for deployable and redistributable projects and on embedding fonts are covered later in this chapter.

FIGURE 17.1

The Publish as SWF dialog box

When you select the Publish as SWF option in Catalyst, it creates a folder at the specified location on your computer, using the project name as the folder name. Assuming that both the Build deployable version and Build redistributable version options were selected in the Export dialog box, this folder will contain two folders: `deploy-to-web` and `run-local`. Both folders contain a similar set of files, as described in Table 17.1.

Flash Content Accessibility

A common myth is that content in Flash is inaccessible to users with disabilities, particularly those with visual impairments. While this was true at one time, it is no longer the case. Modern versions of Flash player can expose its content to screen readers, the software used by blind or very-low-vision users.

Turning this feature on by selecting the relevant check box in the Publish to SWF dialog box adds to the size of your SWF. Not doing so, however, means turning away a portion of your potential customer base and potentially exposing yourself or your clients to legal penalties. It is recommended that you always leave the Publish to SWF option selected.

TABLE 17.1

Files and Folders Created When Publishing to SWF

File or folder	Description
`assets`	This folder contains links to multimedia files from the project, such as music or video.
`history`	This folder contains several files to implement history management; that is, to get the browser's Back and Next buttons to work for the user as would be expected when navigating the project.
`Main.css`	A Cascading Style Sheets document that describes the visual layout of the HTML page into which the SWF will be embedded.
`Main.html`	The HTML file into which the SWF is embedded.
`Main.swf`	The actual SWF file of the project.
`playerProduct Install.swf`	Catalyst projects require Flash Player 10 or later to run. The SWFObject JavaScript library includes player version detection and uses this SWF to prompt the user to upgrade his version of Flash Player if needed.
`swfobject.js`	All Adobe products that embed Flash movies into Web pages use the open-source SWFObject JavaScript library to handle the embedding of the SWF, overcome browser differences, and manage Flash Player version detection. All of the necessary JavaScript code to implement SWFObject is contained in this file.

All of the files referenced in Table 17.1 are available in both the `deploy-to-web` and `run-local` folders. The deploy-to-web folder contains a few additional files:

- `framework_4.0.0.10485.swz, rpc_4.0.0.10485.swz`
- `spark_4.0.0.10485.swz`
- `textLayout_4.0.0.10485.swz.`

Each of these files contains Flex runtime shared libraries.

In order to keep the overall size of Flash Player small, not all of the classes for the entire Flex framework are included in Flash Player. Rather, these class definitions are embedded and installed into each Flex application. While this helps to keep Flash Player small, it also increases the size of each Flex application.

Runtime shared libraries are the recommended solution to this issue. These libraries contain commonly used Flex classes that can possibly be used by more than one application. A user can download these libraries the first time he encounters a project that needs them. Flash Player then stores the libraries locally, and subsequent projects that rely on the same libraries can simply use the local version.

Every SWF created by Catalyst will contain these libraries. All projects created by the program, including those created by other developers, will be able to use these libraries from local copies. The difference these libraries make can be seen by comparing the file size of the `Main.swf` file in the `deploy-to-web` folder and the `run-local` folder. The former uses the libraries and will be considerably smaller than the later which does not.

Font Embedding

Font handling has long been one of the weakest links in Web development. HTML pages generally rely on *device fonts*, meaning that the HTML or CSS document can specify that a particular font be used on a page. However, the font will only be rendered if the user has that font installed on his or her system.

While this limitation is slowly changing for HTML, the tools in the Flash platform (including Flash Professional, Flex, and now Catalyst) have never used device fonts by default and have instead always relied on *embedded fonts*. Therefore, while traditional HTML designers may be limited to three or four common fonts, Flash platform designers are able to use any font they want in their projects.

Unfortunately, the freedom to use any font in your design comes at a price; embedded fonts increase the size of the final SWF file. The designer should carefully consider whether to embed the fonts or if limiting typographical choices to a few common fonts such as Arial and Times New Roman is okay, thus saving space. By default, Catalyst will not embed fonts. Instead, you must select the option in the Publish to SWF dialog box.

Deploying the Project to the Web

Once you have published the project, you need to upload it to the Web for others to access it. To do this, you need to transfer the files created by Catalyst to a Web server using an FTP program. If you are an experienced Web designer, you should have no issues with this process as the steps are identical to what you would normally do.

In order to put your project online, follow these steps:

1. **Set up an account with a Web host.** There are thousands of hosts available online, with prices ranging from free to hundreds or even thousands of dollars per month. By definition, if you are publishing your project directly from Catalyst and not exporting it to Flash Builder, your project will not require any server-side programming. Therefore, most basic, and thus free or very inexpensive, hosting plans will be sufficient for your needs.

2. **Select an FTP application to do the actual uploading of the files.** Both Windows and Macintosh have basic FTP applications built in, but many other applications exist on the market as well. If you have purchased Flash Catalyst as part of one of the Creative Suite

packages, you will also have Adobe Dreamweaver, which includes FTP functionality (see Figure 17.2). While the specifics of uploading files via FTP vary from one application to the next, in general they all follow the same basic idea.

3. **Establish a connection to the FTP's server, using credentials provided by your hosting company.** Once connected, most FTP programs display the files and folders on the server in one half of the window and files on your local machine in the other half (see Figure 17.3).

4. **You can generally simply drag files from the local side to the server side to upload.**

The Server settings dialog box in Adobe Dreamweaver. While the interfaces vary, most other FTP programs have a similar screens asking for similar information.

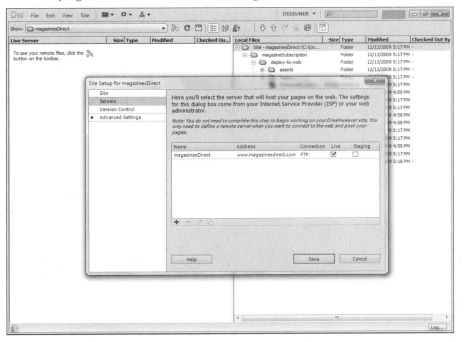

5. **Upload all of the files and folders in the `deploy-to-web` folder, although likely not the folder itself.** The files can be uploaded into any directory under your server's Web root.

6. **Make sure that you keep all of the path directories the similar to one another.** In other words, make sure that the files `Main.css`, `Main.html`, `Main.swf`, and `swfobject.js` along with the assets and history folders remain in a single directory with one another.

FIGURE 17.3

The FTP window in Adobe Dreamweaver, showing the local files on the right and the server files on the left.

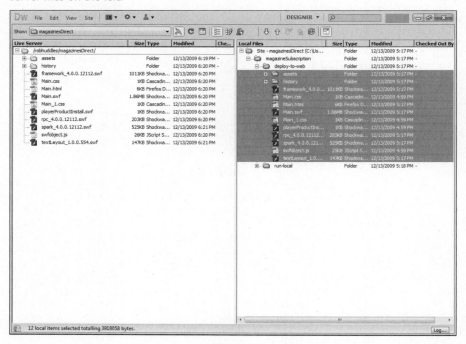

Summary

This chapter discussed the means by which projects can be exported directly from Catalyst for publication to the Web. You learned:

- How to export a project as a SWF
- Embed fonts
- Deploy the project to the Web via FTP

Creating a Project for AIR

I n the spring of 2007, Adobe released a public preview of a new technology code-named Apollo. About a year later in February 2008, Adobe released the final version, which had been renamed *Adobe Integrated Runtime* (AIR).

AIR, put simply, allows Web designers and developers to leverage their existing skill sets in Flex and Flash, or even HTML, CSS, and JavaScript to develop applications for the desktop.

Prior to AIR's release, desktop application development was done solely by high-end programmers using languages such as Java or C# that required years of training.

Currently, anyone with knowledge of HTML, CSS, and JavaScript or anyone designing or developing in the Flash platform can create an application that users can install on their computers and run without a browser. Better yet, they can now develop applications that will run on any desktop, regardless of the operating system.

Understanding AIR

AIR works by providing a universal runtime. That is, AIR is an application that must be installed by users before they can install your application.

Most of the complexity of building traditional desktop applications had to do with the challenges of interfacing with operating systems and hardware; drastic differences between the ways in which operating systems work further complicated matters.

AIR, however, masks those difficulties. By providing a layer between your application and the operating system and hardware, AIR allows you to develop in much the same way that you develop Web applications. AIR is available free from Adobe's Web site (www.adobe.com). According to the company, it has been downloaded and installed more than 100 million times.

Note

The idea of a universal runtime that provides a layer between the application and the operating system is neither new nor radical. Sun Microsystems, the manufacturer of very high-end computer systems and the company responsible for Java, released the first version of the Java Runtime Environment (JRE) long before Adobe developed the idea for AIR. What makes AIR unique is the ease with which applications can be developed.

AIR contains a Web browser built on the open-source *Webkit engine*, the same browser engine that runs Apple's Safari browser and Google's Chrome browser. It includes an SQLLite database engine for local data storage, as well as Flash Player and Adobe Reader for playing SWFs and reading PDF files.

AIR applications can either be:

- Disconnected
- Completely self-contained and able to run without an Internet connection
- Connected and thus require an active link to the Internet to access information
- Semiconnected, going online to collect information when a connection is available but functioning off-line when the computer is disconnected

Flash movies that run in a browser have many of the same capabilities as an AIR application. However, Flash Player, when run in the browser, has a set of key limitations imposed for security purposes. For example, it cannot directly read and write files on the local user's computer, nor does it have hardware access.

Alternately, an AIR application runs at the same level of security as any other installed application, giving it file system and hardware access. AIR 2.0, a beta that was released in the fall of 2009, even includes hardware detection. This feature detects and responds to events such as a USB drive being plugged into the computer.

Popular AIR Applications

Hundreds of AIR applications have been developed over the last several years. Twitter fans can download one of dozens of desktop Twitter applications built on AIR, including the extremely popular Tweetdeck and Seesmic applications. *The New York Times* has a *Times* Reader available, an AIR application that provides a nicer environment for reading the paper than what you get on its Web site. eBay has an AIR application for tracking auctions, while Pizza Hut has developed an AIR application that lets users order pizzas for delivery.

If you are interested in learning more about Flex, you can download Tour de Flex from www.flex.org. Tour de Flex is an AIR application that provides a complete overview of the Flex framework, including live examples of the components and code samples.

Converting a Project to AIR

Flex-based AIR projects require slightly different code than Web-based projects. Thus, when you create a project in Flash Builder, you must designate from the beginning whether you will be creating a project for the Web or for AIR. Catalyst does not have a method for designating a project to be deployed for AIR instead of the browser. Therefore, you will not need to do anything special in Catalyst when you design a project that is intended for AIR.

Once you import the project into Flash Builder, you must convert it to an AIR project before commencing any other work. To do so, follow these steps:

1. **Right-click (⌘+click) the project in the Package Explorer.**

2. **Choose Add/Change Project Type ➪ Convert to Flex Desktop Project.** Flash Builder displays a dialog box informing you that the project will be converted (see Figure 18.1).

FIGURE 18.1

The Convert to Desktop/Adobe AIR Project menu

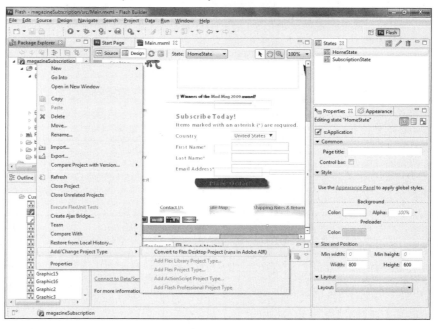

3. **You can have Flash Builder make the necessary change to the root element of your main file from Application to WindowedApplication.** Should you choose to not have the conversion done automatically, you need to do so manually before your project can be exported to AIR.

Completing an AIR Project

You can do a significant amount of work within Flash Builder to have your project take advantage of AIR's unique capabilities. However, this additional work may not be necessary, depending on the requirements of the project. It is possible to take a project from Catalyst once the project conversion is complete and simply publish directly to AIR. Flash Builder includes a wizard that steps you through the process of finalizing the project for AIR:

1. **Choose Project ➪ Export Release build to launch the wizard (see Figure 18.2).**

2. **Confirm that the correct project and application file are selected.**

3. **Enable the option to allow users to view the project's source code.**

4. **Select the name of the project's AIR file, which will be the file that the user selects to install the application.**

5. **Attach a digital certificate to the project at the wizard's prompt (see Figure 18.3).** Certificates assure users that the application was actually delivered from the company they expect, rather than a malicious user merely posing as a company.

FIGURE 18.2

The Export Release Build Wizard's first page

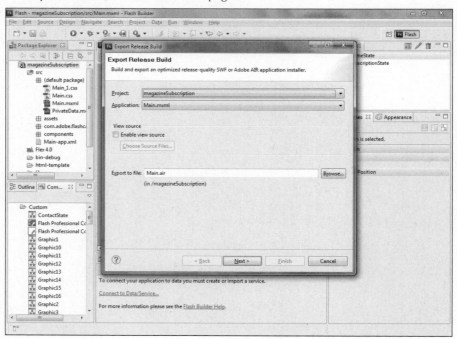

Hiding or Showing Your Source Code

Web designers are accustomed to allowing users to view their source code, but for application designers, the same is not true. By default, the source MXML and ActionScript code behind a Flex project is hidden.

However, in certain situations you may decide that you want users to view your code from the completed project. If enabled when exporting the build, users can right-click (⌘+click) the project and select View Source, just as they would on an HTML page. All of the project's MXML and ActionScript code will then be visible. Care should be taken to ensure this option is not used when viewing the source could compromise the project's security.

FIGURE 18.3

The Digital Signature page of the Export Release Build Wizard

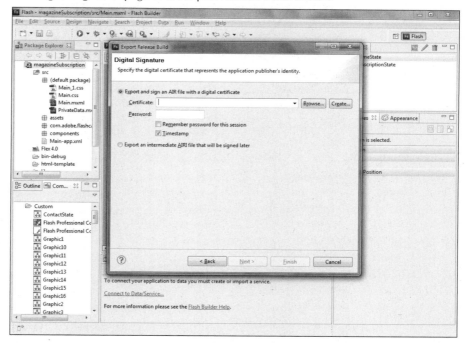

For example, anyone could claim that an application was developed by Adobe. However, only Adobe has access to its digital certificate, so only applications signed by Adobe are guaranteed as coming from Adobe.

If you are developing a project that will only be distributed within a closed network environment, use a certificate issued by your network administrator from the network's own servers. Applications that will be distributed publicly via the Internet can only be trusted if the certificate is issued by a trusted third party, such as VeriSign. VeriSign and its competitors thoroughly investigate individuals and companies before issuing a certificate. The companies offer a variety of certificate products covering a range of prices.

6. **If you do not have a certificate, you can create your own.** Ideally, this would only be used for local testing of the project; any application distributed with a self-signed certificate is not likely to be trusted or installed as much as one with a verified certificate. The process of creating a certificate is simple: Click Create and follow the steps outlined in the dialog boxes.

   You can also create an intermediate AIR project that is not signed, but will be later. You will not be able to install this project until it is signed. However, this will allow you to publish the project if you are waiting for approval of a certificate from VeriSign.

7. **Ensure that all required files are going to be included in the AIR package.** There may be rare occasions when files within the project are not needed by the AIR application. If this is the case, you can deselect them to minimize the project's file size.

8. **Click Finish (see Figure 18.4).** The AIR project is exported and ready to install.

FIGURE 18.4

The final page of the Export Release Build Wizard

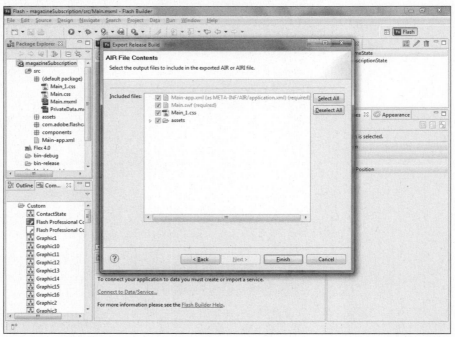

Cross-Reference

For details on additional options for AIR applications, including customizing the application icon, controlling its install directory and leveraging unique AIR capabilities like local file system access, see the Adobe AIR Bible.

Installing an AIR Application

Once you export the project, you can install the AIR application to test and ensure that it works properly. AIR applications are installed in much the same way as any other application:

1. **Double-click the project file, either from within the operating system or directly from the Package Explorer in Flash Builder.** The installer will launch beginning with a screen that provides details about the project and its certificate.

2. **Click Install (see Figure 18.5).** The project will install onto your computer.

FIGURE 18.5

The AIR application installer

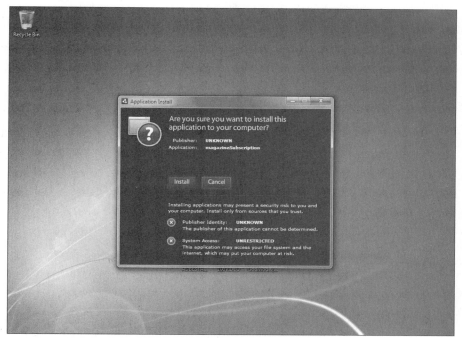

3. **Launch the application by selecting it in the All Programs directory in the Windows Start menu or from the Applications folder in Finder on a Mac.** When launched, the program should behave just as any other locally installed program, including display of an icon on the Windows taskbar (see Figure 18.6).

FIGURE 18.6

An AIR application running in Windows

Deploying to AIR Directly from Catalyst

If no modifications need to be made to the project in Flash Builder, it is possible to deploy an AIR application directly from Catalyst. The Publish as SWF command in the Catalyst File menu includes the option to create an AIR application (see Figure 18.7).

FIGURE 18.7

The Publish to SWF dialog box in Catalyst with the option to export to AIR selected

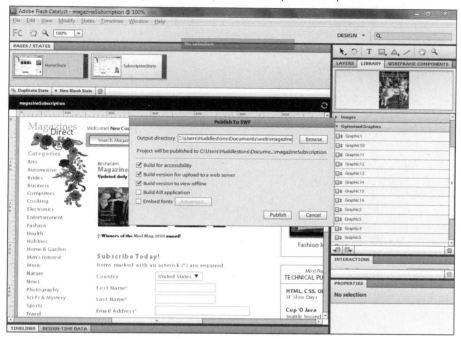

Cross-Reference

See Chapter 17 for more details on the Publish to SWF dialog box and a discussion of its other options.

Selecting the AIR option in the dialog box creates an AIR package along with the Web-specific packages normally produced.

In the folder specified in the dialog box, you will find an AIR folder which in turn includes the AIR file. You can double-click this file to launch the installer (see Figure 18.8), which follows the same steps as an AIR file created in Flash Builder.

Note

Catalyst does not provide a means by which AIR applications can be digitally signed. If you have a digital certificate and want to use it to sign your application, thus avoiding the warning screen at the start of the installation process, you need to import the project into Flash Builder and package it for AIR from there.

FIGURE 18.8

Installing an AIR application created directly from Catalyst

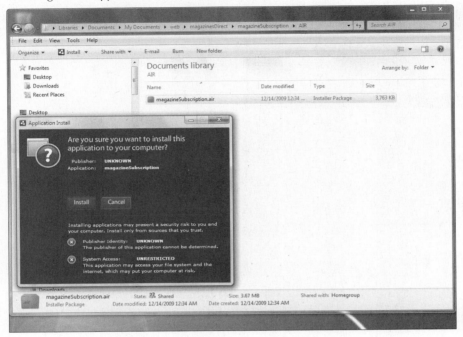

Summary

In this chapter you explored the Adobe Integrated Runtime (AIR). You learned:

- The basic concepts of AIR
- How to convert a project to AIR and publish from Flash Builder
- How to install and run an AIR application
- How to publish a project to AIR directly from Catalyst.

Part V

Build a Complete Project

Creating a Design Comp in Illustrator

The remaining chapters in this book assist you in pulling together the primary lessons learned through the earlier chapters by providing step-by-step tutorials that guide you through the process of creating an application using Flash Catalyst.

This tutorial is by no means designed to cover every aspect of any of the programs listed, nor detail the steps required for every workflow in Catalyst. Instead, it follows the primary workflow for which Catalyst is designed: taking an Illustrator design comp through Catalyst to Flash Builder.

Identifying the Design Requirements

Good design does not happen by accident. Instead, you should always undertake a process of careful planning to determine the requirements of the application and expectations of the client before attempting to begin the design work.

In the hypothetical scenario detailed here, you have been tasked with creating an online presence for a magazine subscription service. The client has stated his needs as follows:

1. Present a modern, Web 2.0 look and feel for the application.

2. Provide an intuitive user interface focused on driving the user to purchase subscriptions.

3. Allow the company to organize magazines by category, price, and other criteria as needed.

4. Provide search functionality for users to look up magazines.

5. Include an area for featured titles that the company can populate as needed.

6. Incorporate the company's existing color schemes, logo, and other branding to ensure that the Web site feels like an extension of existing marketing materials.

In discussions with the client, you have decided that a Flex-driven application can meet its needs. The inherent animation capabilities will satisfy requirement No. 1, while the relative ease with which server-side data can be used in an application makes Flex an obvious solution given requirements 3, 4, and 5. Given requirements 2 and 6, it seems easiest to design the application using Illustrator and use Catalyst to convert the design into a front end for the Flex application.

You have located a developer well versed in the Flex framework and ColdFusion to handle the details of creating the back-end services needed for the data aspects of the application. Thus, you feel ready to begin the design process in Illustrator.

Design the Application in Illustrator

You begin the process of designing the application by creating a file in Illustrator. To do this, begin with a new, blank file in the program and begin drawing the visual assets of the project.

Note

All of the screenshots used and steps outlined in this tutorial use Illustrator CS5. However, none of the features of the program being used was introduced specifically in CS5, so older versions will work.

Create a new file

The first steps in the design process involve opening Illustrator and creating a new file.

On the Web

The book's accompanying Web site (www.wiley.com/go/flashcatalystbible)includes all of the files needed to complete the design comp. Download the Chapter19.zip file and extract it to a location on your hard drive.

1. **Open Illustrator.** In Windows, you are likely to find Illustrator in Start ⇨ All Programs, then the folder corresponding to whichever version of Creative Suite you purchased. Macintosh users should launch Illustrator from the Applications folder, just as they would any other application on their computer.

Note

All of the screenshots through these tutorials were taken on a Windows-based machine, but the interfaces of Illustrator, Catalyst, and Flash Builder are the same on both platforms, so Macintosh users should have no problems following along.

2. **From the Illustrator Start screen, click Flash Catalyst Document under the Create New category (see Figure 19.1).**

FIGURE 19.1

The Illustrator CS5 Start screen

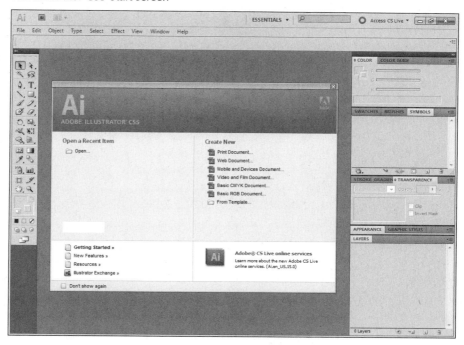

3. **From the New Document dialog box, type a name, width, and height for your project (see Figure 19.2).** Keep in mind that in this first version Catalyst can only create applications with fixed dimensions. While it is impossible to accurately predict the size of your user's browser window, most average computer users today set their monitors to 1024 × 768.

   While this number is rapidly changing and becoming much less predictable thanks to the proliferation of wide-screen monitors, 1024 × 768 still provides as good a starting point as any.

4. **Account for the additional space lost by the browser's toolbars, scroll bar, and status bar.** If you want your application to fit nicely on most screens without needing to scroll down, designing for around 800 × 600 makes sense.

5. **Click OK.** The document is created and Illustrator opens a blank artboard.

6. **On the Layers panel, double-click Layer 1 to open the Layer Options dialog box.**

7. **Use the dialog box to rename Layer 1 to Background (see Figure 19.3).** It is easier to rename layers and maintain organization within the application if you rename layers in Illustrator rather than waiting to rename them in Catalyst.

FIGURE 19.2

The New Document dialog box

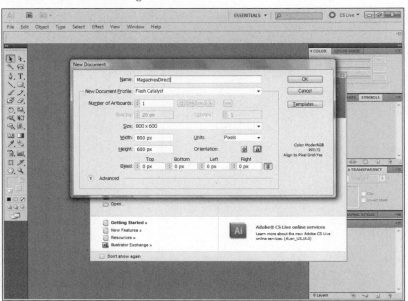

FIGURE 19.3

Renaming Layer 1

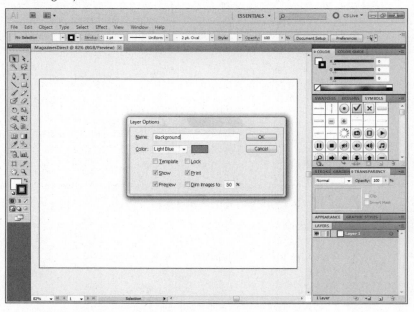

8. If necessary, choose View ⇨ Rulers ⇨ Show Rulers.

9. **Press and hold your mouse down on the vertical ruler on the left side of the screen and drag to create a guide that will define the application's left margin.** Margins are not required in your project as assets can go all the way to the edge of the application window; many projects, however, will be more visually appealing with margins.

10. Repeat Step 9 to create a guide defining the right margin (see Figure 19.4).

FIGURE 19.4

Creating guides

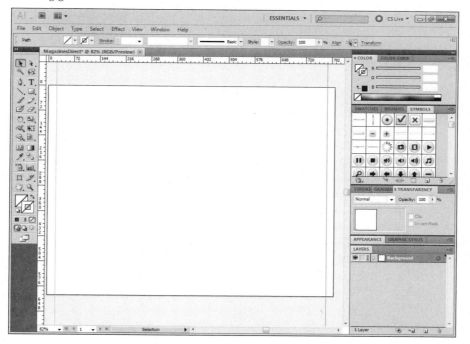

11. If desired, press and hold your mouse over the ruler along the top of the screen and drag down to create guides defining the application's top and bottom margins.

12. Save the file by choosing File ⇨ Save As.

13. Type a name for the file and click Save. The design file is now created and saved on your computer.

Tip

Just as with any other task on your computer, you should get in the habit of frequently saving your work in Illustrator.

Create the logo

The logo in this case is simple: merely two lines of text using the client's desired font, color, and size. While many clients would likely provide a logo in some electronic form, possibly even as an Illustrator file, in this case re-creating the logo in the project is easy enough.

1. **Click the Type tool.**

2. **From the Control panel, select a type face, font size, and color for the main logo type.** In this example, the first line of the logo, Magazines, is in 23-point Book Antiqua, with a 1-point stroke color of #CBC92B and a black fill.

3. **Type Magazines.**

4. **Click the Appearance panel.**

5. **Set the opacity to 40 percent (see Figure 19.5).**

FIGURE 19.5

Using the Appearance panel to set the opacity of the text

Tip

You may want to zoom in while you work. You can click the Zoom tool at the bottom of the toolbox and then click the artboard until you reach the magnification you want.

6. Ctrl+click (⌘+click) a blank area of the artboard to reset the Type tool.

7. From the Control panel, set the font to 21-point Myriad Pro.

8. Use the Appearance panel to set no stroke and a black fill.

9. Type Direct.

10. Click the Selection tool.

11. Move Direct so that it partially overlaps the lower portion of Magazines (see Figure 19.6). You have finished designing the logo.

FIGURE 19.6

The completed logo

Organize the logo's layers

Throughout this tutorial, the importance of maintaining layer organization in the Illustrator file will be stressed repeatedly.

1. On the artboard, click the Magazines text.

2. Shift+click the Direct text.

3. Choose Object ⇨ Group to combine the logo elements into a layer group.

4. Rename the group Logo by double-clicking it in the Layers panel and typing the new name (see Figure 19.7). The logos layers are now organized.

Renaming the grouped layer

Position the logo

Another advantage to grouping the layers, beyond organization, is that grouped layers can be repositioned together.

1. **Click the Target icon for the Logo layer group in the Layers panel.** It is the small circle to the right of the layer name. Clicking the target icon selects the layer or group's content.

2. **With the Selection tool, drag the logo to the top-left intersection of the left-most and upper-most guides.** This positions the logo in the top left corner of the application.

Create the category list

The design requirements for the project specified that the client wanted an easy way to maintain the list of categories and change it as needed. The final project needs this list to be generated from a database table of possible categories.

In the design comp stage, you just need to add placeholder text that will eventually be replaced by live data.

1. **Click the Type tool.** Use the Control panel to set the font to 15-point Myriad Pro Bold, with a fill color of #CBC92B, the same color used in the logo, and no stroke.

2. **Click the word Character on the Control panel to open the Character panel.** You can also choose Window ➪ Type ➪ Character.

3. **Set the leading to 19 points.** *Leading* defines the space between lines.

4. **In the document, type Categories.**

5. **Press Enter.**

6. **Use the Control panel to change the font to 12-point Myriad Pro Regular, with a black fill and no stroke.**

7. **Check the Character panel to be sure that the leading remains at 19 points.**

8. **Type Arts.**

9. **Press Enter.**

10. **Type Automotive.**

11. **Repeat Step 6 to add between 15 and 20 categories.** Keep in mind that these are merely placeholders for the live data that will eventually be used to populate the list, so the actual values are not important.

12. **Rename the layers involved appropriately (see Figure 19.8).** The category list is created and its layers renamed and organized appropriately.

Add the floral element

A clip art image of flowers is going to be used to set off the category list from the logo and the rest of the page.

1. **Choose File ➪ Place.**

2. **Navigate to the folder that contains the image of the flowers.**

3. **Click Place.**

4. **Click near the logo and top of the category list.** The flower image is placed on the artboard.

5. **Use the Selection tool to position the flowers.**

6. **Rename the layers involved appropriately (see Figure 19.9).** Finishing the floral element completes the left sidebar area of the comp.

325

Part V: Build a Complete Project

FIGURE 19.8

The completed category list

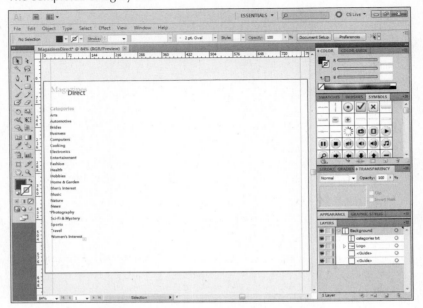

FIGURE 19.9

The finished sidebar with the logo, category list, and flowers in place

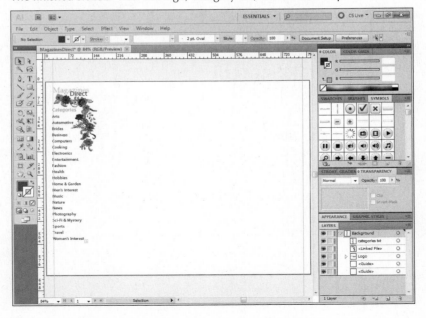

Create the top navigation

The top of the screen contains a line of basic navigation, whereby the user can see a welcome message.

The message will be personalized if a user is logged in; links next to the message take users to forms where they can sign up with the company or log in if they are already signed up. To the right, aligned with the message, are links to the shopping cart, the user's account, and the home page.

1. Click the Type tool.

2. Use the Control panel to set the font to Black 12-point Myriad Pro Regular.

3. Type Welcome.

4. Set the font style to Bold and the color to #282A73.

5. Type New Customer | Sign In.

6. Ctrl+click (⌘+click) a blank area of the artboard to reset the Type tool.

7. Toward the right edge of the screen, click on the artboard and then type Cart 0 Items.

8. Click and drag to select 0 Items.

9. Change the color to #CBC92B.

10. Ctrl+click (⌘+click) a blank area of the artboard to reset the Type tool.

11. Change the color back to black.

12. Click and type My Account | Help.

13. Align the three blocks of text as desired.

14. Rename the layers involved appropriately (see Figure 19.10). The top navigation is complete.

Create the Search and Wish List boxes

The design requirements call for a search function. In further discussions with your client, he also expressed a desire to have a wish list function similar to the one found on sites like Amazon.com.

To that end, you have decided to combine both into a single area of the screen, offset in a rectangular shape.

1. **Click the Rounded Rectangle tool.** You may need to press and hold your mouse on the Rectangle tool to see the Rounded Rectangle tool.

2. **Click once on the artboard.** Most of the time, you click and drag to create shapes, but when you make a shape with precise dimensions, it may be easier to click once on the artboard and use the dialog box to set the size of the shape.

3. Type a width of 627 pixels and a height of 33 pixels.

4. Set the Corner Radius to 2.

5. With the Selection tool, click the rectangle.

FIGURE 19.10

The top navigation bar

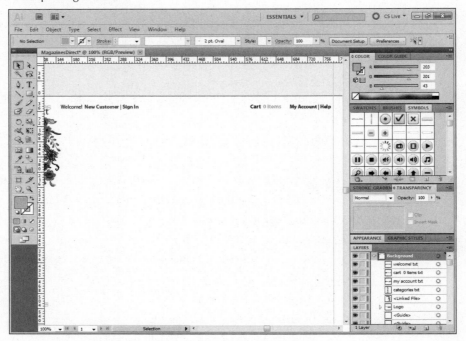

6. Use the Appearance panel to change the fill color to #8A854E and the opacity to 64 percent.

7. Click the Rounded Rectangle tool.

8. Click on the artboard again.

9. Set the width to 212 pixels and the height to 22 pixels, with a corner radius of 5.

10. Use the Selection tool to position this new rectangle within the one created in Step 2.

11. Use the Appearance panel to set the fill to white and add a 1-pixel black stroke.

12. Use the Type tool to type Search Magazines Direct in 12-point black Myriad Pro in the smaller rounded rectangle.

13. Use the Rectangle tool to create a 30-×-22-pixel rectangle with a fill of #282A73.

14. Type Go in this newest rectangle in white 14-point Myriad Pro Regular.

15. Type Advanced Search in white 14-point Myriad Pro Regular.

16. Create a rectangle 125 pixels wide × 22 pixels tall with a fill of #282A73, the same fill used in Step 9.

17. Type Wish List in 14-point Myriad Pro Bold.

18. Arrange the Search and Wish List bar so that the elements all fit within the large brown rectangle.

19. **Rename and organize the layers as needed (see Figure 19.11).** The search and wish list bar are now done.

FIGURE 19.11

The search and wish list bar

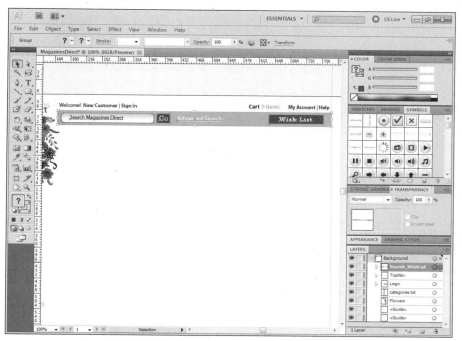

Create the bottom navigation

The page will provide a set of site-wide links along the bottom of the screen, along with copyright information and an indication of what credit cards are accepted.

1. **Using the Type tool, type each of the necessary blocks of text to represent the bottom navigation bar.**

2. **Choose File ⇨ Place to insert the credit card images.**

3. **Position the elements as desired, using the guides if you want.**

4. **Rename and organize the layers involved appropriately (see Figure 19.12).** You have now added the credit card images to the bottom navigation.

FIGURE 19.12

The bottom text elements

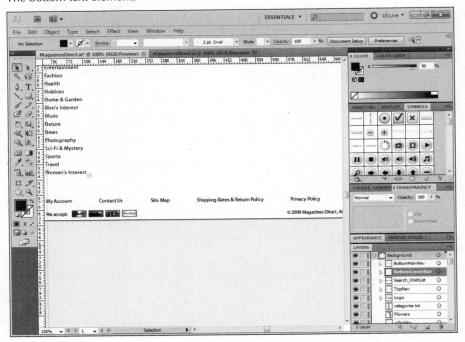

Create the backgrounds for the bottom navigation

Each link in the bottom navigation contains a stylistic brush stroke as a background. Illustrator contains a set of specialized brushes that make creating effects like this simple.

1. Click the Brush tool.

2. Click the Brush Definition drop-down list on the Control bar (see Figure 19.13).

3. Click the drop-down menu button in its top right corner (see Figure 19.14).

4. If no check box appears next to the Show Art Brushes option, select it.

5. Scroll through the list of brushes in the drop-down list and select Watercolor Stroke 3.

6. Click the Stroke color box on the toolbox to open the Swatches panel.

7. **Select the color you want to use for the stroke.** In this example, you will use the grape green color.

FIGURE 19.13

The Brush Definition drop-down list

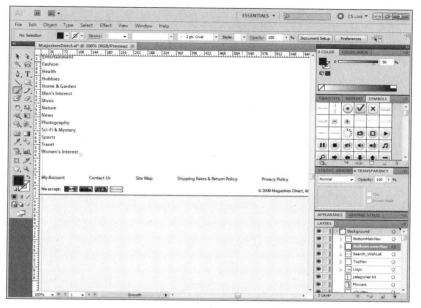

FIGURE 19.14

The drop-down menu

On the Web

The color swatches for this file are available as part of the download for this chapter. To access them, click the Swatches Panel menu and select Open Swatch Library ⇨ Other Library. Navigate to swatches.ai in the files you downloaded.

8. Press and hold the Shift key.

9. Click and drag to draw a straight line the same length as the text (see Figure 19.15).

10. Repeat Steps 8 and 9 to add a brush stroke for each navigation element.

11. Select all of the brush strokes and choose Object ⇨ Group.

12. From the Layers panel, rename this group Watercolors.

13. Drag the group below the group containing the links (see Figure 19.16). The bottom navigation bar, with its links and credit card images, is complete.

FIGURE 19.15

Drawing the background stroke

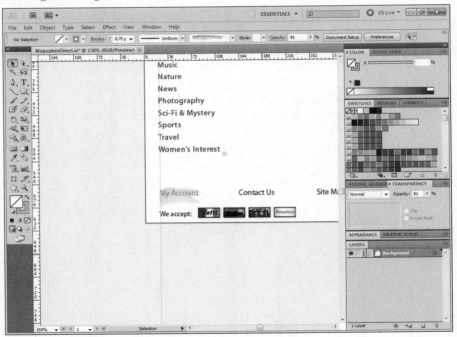

FIGURE 19.16

Grouping the brush strokes in a layer

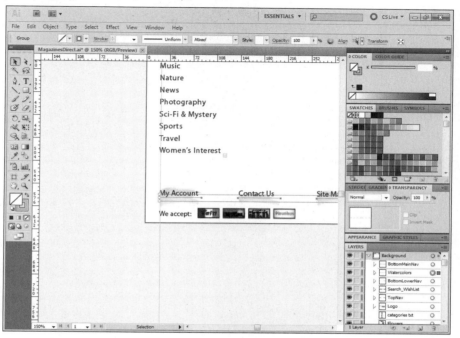

Create the main content area for the Home state

Now that the common areas of the application are complete, you can move to creating the content area for each state of the application.

First, you will create the Home state, or the content users see when they first launch the application. This state is comprised of three main sections:

- A list of the magazines currently being featured
- A form to collect basic information for the user to subscribe to a magazine
- A sidebar

The featured magazine section is fairly straightforward, as it only contains some text and placed images.

Create the featured section heading

You begin the featured section by creating the three text blocks that make up its heading.

1. On the Layers panel, click the New Layer button.

2. Rename this layer Home.

3. Select the Type tool.

4. Use the Control panel to set the font to Myriad Pro, the style to Italic, the size at 11pt, and the color to black.

5. Type Bestsellers (see Figure 19.17).

FIGURE 19.17

Typing the Bestsellers text block

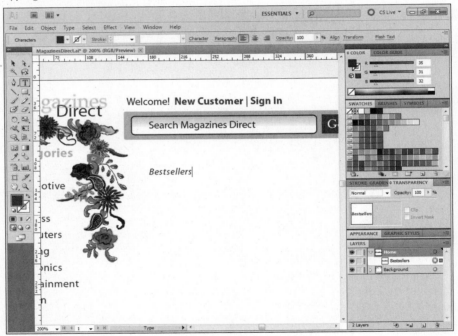

6. **Ctrl+click (⌘+click) a blank area of the artboard.** This deselects the piece of text you just typed so that you can enter different text properties and create a new text block.

7. Use the Control panel to change the font style to bold, the size to 16pt, and the color to the HeadingColor swatch (see Figure 19.18).

8. **Click just below the text you typed in Step 3 and type** Magazines: General Interest (see Figure 19.19).

FIGURE 19.18

Setting the main heading color

FIGURE 19.19

The second line of the heading

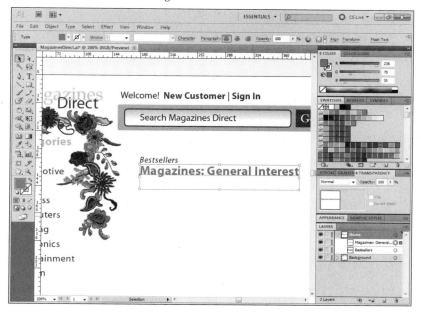

9. Ctrl+click (⌘+click) the artboard to again deselect the text block.

10. Set the font style to Semibold, the size to 11pt, and the color to black.

11. Type Updated daily for your convenience.

12. On the toolbox, click the Selection tool.

13. **Reposition the text to create the featured section heading (see Figure 19.20). The featured section heading is complete.**

The completed heading

You can now place the five magazine images that will serve as placeholders for the featured magazines.

1. **Choose File ⇨ Place.**

2. **Navigate to the folder into which you downloaded and unzipped the cover images.**

3. **Click on one of the covers.** The exact order in which you place the covers is unimportant.

4. **Click Place.**

5. Repeat Steps 1 through 4 to place the remaining covers.

6. From the toolbox, click the Selection tool.

7. Below the heading, position the cover that will be the farthest to the left so that it aligns with the left edge of the heading text.

8. **Position the cover that will be farthest to the right so that it is far enough over to allow room for the other covers.** Do not worry about getting the other three covers distributed evenly or about getting any of the covers lined up exactly (see Figure 19.21).

FIGURE 19.21

Placing and positioning the covers

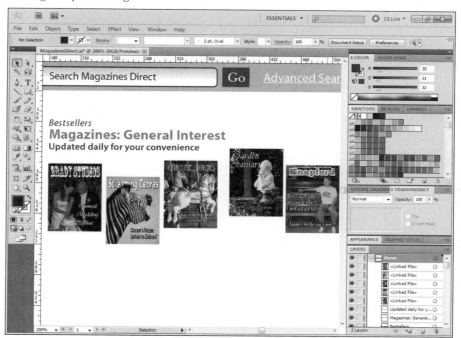

9. Choose Window ➪ Align to open the Align panel.

10. With the Selection tool, click one of the covers.

11. While holding the Shift key, click on each of the other covers until all five are selected.

12. On the Align panel, click Align Vertical Center and then click Horizontal Distribute Center (see Figure 19.22).

13. **With all five covers still selected, move them as a group up or down as desired to place them where you want them.** You have added the magazine covers to the design.

FIGURE 19.22

Aligning and distributing the covers

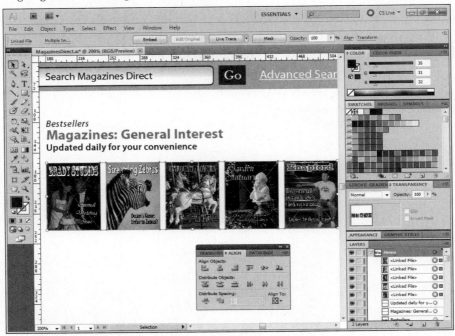

You will finish off the featured magazine section by adding the remaining text and images and adding the separator line.

1. From the toolbox, click the Type tool.

2. Use the Control box to set the font style to Semibold, the size to 11pt, and the color to black.

3. Type Winners of the Mad Mag 2009 award!

4. Click and drag to select the words Mad Mag 2009.

5. From the Control bar, change the color to the Heading Color swatch (see Figure 19.23).

6. Click the Selection tool.

7. Choose File ⇨ Place.

8. Select the bulb_001.gif image.

9. Position the image just to the left of the text (see Figure 19.24).

FIGURE 19.23

Adding the text

FIGURE 19.24

Placing the light bulb image

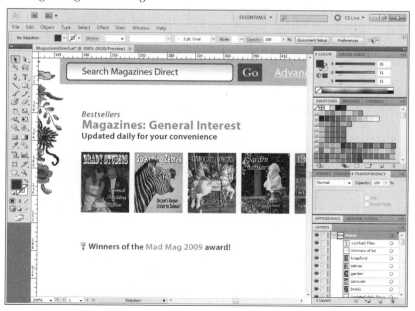

10. Choose File ⇨ Place.

11. Select `lamp_001.gif` and click Place.

12. Position the lamp image to the right of the magazine covers (see Figure 19.25).

Placing the lamp image

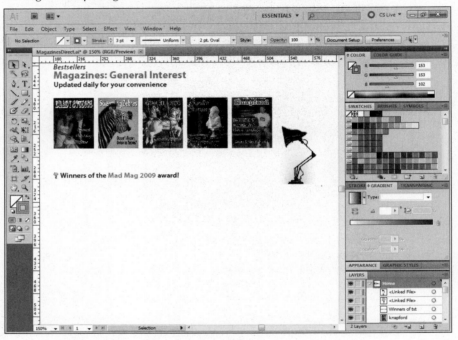

13. Click the Brush tool.

14. Set the stroke color to #999966.

15. Press and hold the Shift key.

16. Click and drag to draw a line under the text and lamp.

17. Click the Selection tool in the toolbox.

18. Click the line.

19. Use the Control bar to adjust the thickness of the line as desired.

20. Move the line so that it just touches the bottom of the lamp graphic (see Figure 19.26). The visual elements of the featured section is now complete.

FIGURE 19.26

Drawing the dividing line

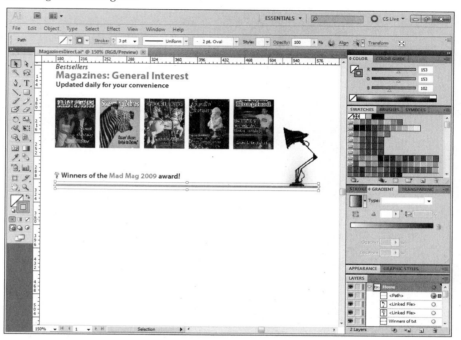

The final step to complete the featured magazines section is organizing its layers.

1. On the Layers panel, click the New Sublayer button.

2. Rename the layer as Best Sellers.

3. Drag the layers for the elements of the section into this layer (see Figure 19.27). With its layers organized, you are now done with this section of the design.

FIGURE 19.27

Organizing the layers

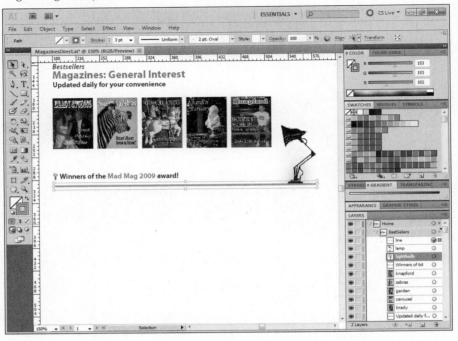

Create the subscription form section

Below the featured magazines is a simple form that users can fill out to begin the process of sub-scribing to a magazine. Begin by creating a sublayer to hold the new elements.

1. **On the Layers panel, click the New Sublayer button.**
2. **Double-click the new layer and name it** SubscribeToday **(see Figure 19.28).** This cre-ates the layer for this section of the design.

Now, you add the text elements for the form.

1. **Click the Type tool.**
2. **Use the Control panel to set the font to 16pt Bold Myriad Pro.**
3. **Set the color to Heading Color.**
4. **Type** Subscribe Today! **(see Figure 19.29).**

FIGURE 19.28

Creating the sublayer

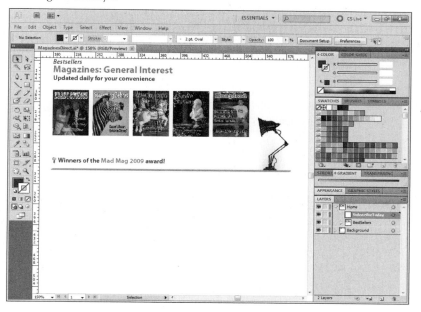

FIGURE 19.29

Adding the heading

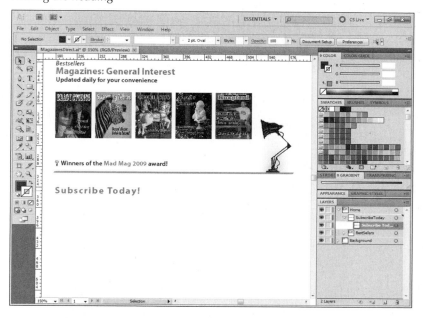

5. Ctrl+click (⌘+click) the artboard.

6. Use the Control panel to change the font style to Regular, the size to 12pt, and the color to black.

7. **Type** Items marked with an asterisk (*) are required **(see Figure 19.30).**

FIGURE 19.30

Adding the subheading

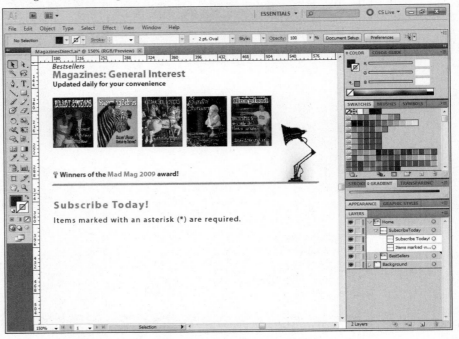

8. Ctrl+click (⌘+click) the artboard.

9. **Type** Country.

10. Ctrl+click (⌘+click) the artboard.

11. **Type** United States.

12. **Type** First Name*.

13. Ctrl+click (⌘+click) the artboard.

14. **Type** Last Name*.

15. Ctrl+click (⌘+click) the artboard.

16. Type Email Address*.

17. Click the Selection tool.

18. Position the text as needed (see Figure 19.31).

FIGURE 19.31

Adding the form's labels

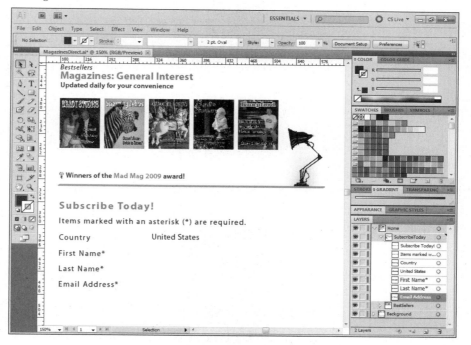

19. Click the Rectangle tool.

20. Set the stroke color to a light gray and the fill color to None.

21. Click and drag to create a rectangle over the words United States. Make the rectangle about a quarter of an inch wider than the text.

22. Click and drag to create a rectangle to the right of the First Name label.

23. Double-click each of the new layers and rename them appropriately (see Figure 19.32).

FIGURE 19.32

Adding the Country and First Name text field representations

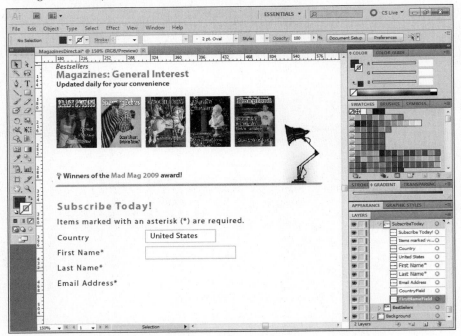

24. Click the Selection tool.

25. Press and hold the Alt (Option) key.

26. Click and drag the rectangle you created in Step 22 to create a copy immediately below it.

27. Rename the new layer (see Figure 19.33).

28. Repeat Steps 25, 26 and 27 to create a second duplicate.

29. Click and drag the control handle on the right edge of this second field to make it wider (see Figure 19.34).

FIGURE 19.33

Creating the Last Name field

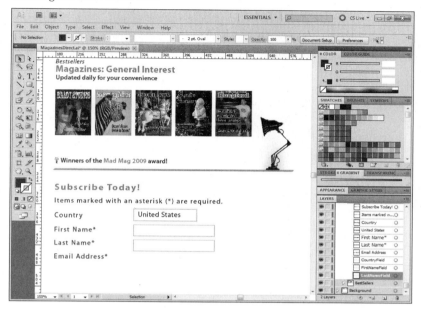

FIGURE 19.34

Creating the e-mail field

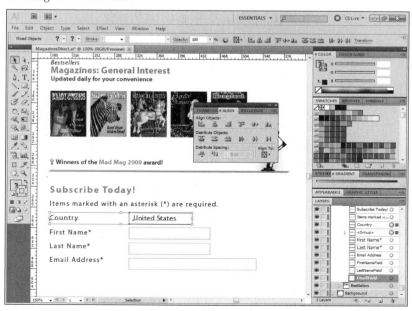

30. If the Align panel is not open, choose Window ⇨ Align.

31. Shift+click the United States text and the rectangle around it.

32. Choose Object ⇨ Group.

33. Shift+click the group and the Country text.

34. Click Vertical Align Center on the Align panel (see Figure 19.35).

FIGURE 19.35

Aligning the Country text and field

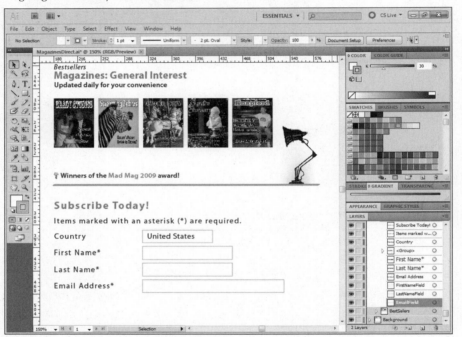

35. Shift+click the First Name text and the rectangle to its right.

36. Click Vertical Align Center on the Align panel.

37. Repeat Steps 33 and 34 for the remaining text and fields (see Figure 19.36).

FIGURE 19.36

Aligning the fields and labels

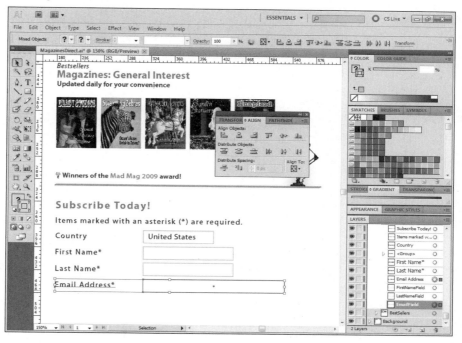

38. Click the Polygon tool.

39. Set the stroke to None and the fill to Black.

40. Click and drag to begin drawing a polygon.

41. While still holding your mouse button, press the Down-arrow key repeatedly until you have a triangle.

42. Rotate the shape as you finish drawing so that its top line is horizontal.

43. Make the triangle small enough to fit in the rectangle next to the United States text block.

44. Click the Selection tool, and move the triangle into the rectangle and to the right of United States (see Figure 19.37).

FIGURE 19.37

Creating the drop-down arrow

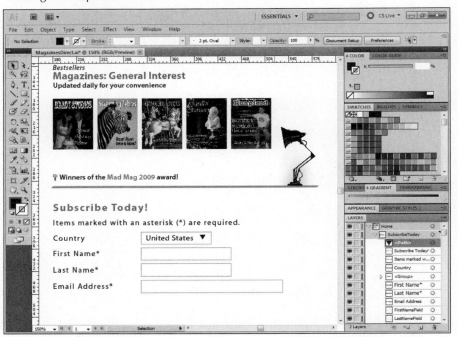

45. On the Layers panel, drag the triangle into the group containing the United States text and the rectangle.

46. Rename the triangle's layer and the group (see Figure 19.38).

47. Use the Rectangle tool to create a 185-x-25-pixel rectangle with a fill of #282A73.

48. Type Place Order in this newest rectangle in white 14-point Myriad Pro Regular (see Figure 19.39).

FIGURE 19.38

Organizing the drop-down element's layers

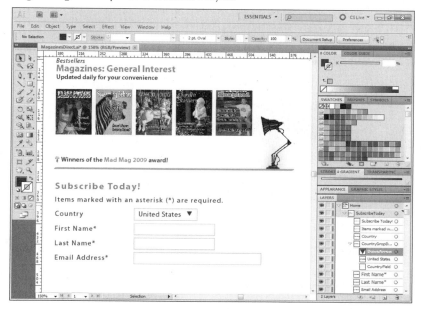

FIGURE 19.39

Adding the button

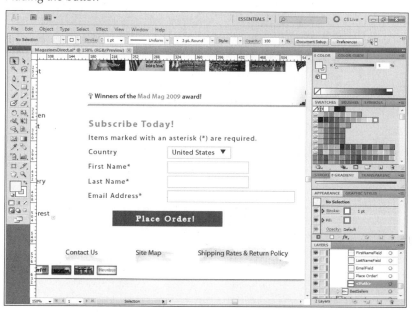

49. Select the button's rectangle and text.

50. Choose Object ⇨ Group.

51. Rename the button elements as needed (see Figure 19.40). The subscription section of the design is complete.

Organizing the button's layers

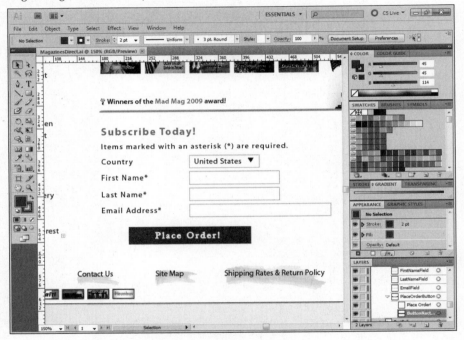

Add the first sidebar

The sidebars are final element of the main content. The top sidebar will contain an image of the video player and some descriptive text.

1. Click the New Sublayer button on the Layers panel.

2. Rename the sublayer Sidebar.

3. From the toolbox, select the Rectangle tool.

4. Set the fill to None and the stroke to Warm Gray.

5. Click and drag to create a rectangle approximately 177 pixels wide and 210 pixels tall on the right edge of the artboard.

6. Line the top of the rectangle up with the Magazines: General Interest heading.

7. Rename the layer SidebarTopRectangle (see Figure 19.41).

FIGURE 19.41

Creating the first sidebar rectangle

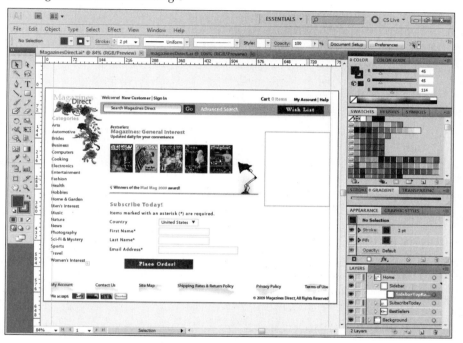

8. Click the Type tool.

9. Set the font to Italic, black, 11pt, Myriad Pro. Type Consumer Broadcast.

10. Ctrl+click (⌘+click) the artboard.

11. Set the font to 14pt Regular Myriad Pro and type VIDEO.

12. Use the Selection tool or Align Panel to position the text (see Figure 19.42).

13. Choose File ⇨ Place.

14. Select videoplaceholder.jpg and click Place.

15. Position the image below the text (see Figure 19.43).

FIGURE 19.42

Adding the sidebar text

FIGURE 19.43

Placing the video placeholder image

16. Click the Type tool.

17. Set the font to 14pt Regular Myriad Pro.

18. Set the color to the Sidebar Text swatch.

19. Type Fashion Identity.

20. **Change the font to the Italic style.** Leave the other settings as is.

21. Type View.

22. **Click the Selection tool and position the text below the image (see Figure 19.44).** You are now done with the first sidebar.

FIGURE 19.44

Finishing the first sidebar

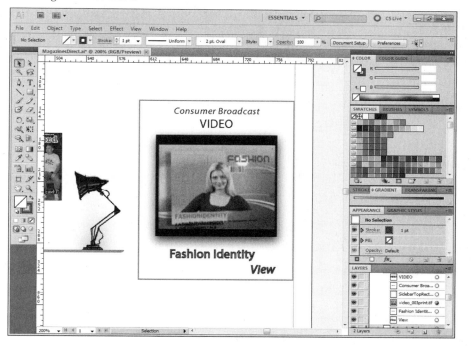

Create the second sidebar

The second sidebar is made up of a rectangle, text blocks, and a placed image.

1. From the toolbox, select the Rectangle tool.

2. Set the fill to None and the stroke to Warm Gray.

3. Click and drag to create a rectangle approximately 177 pixels wide and 164 pixels tall on the right edge of the artboard.

4. Position the rectangle below the first and rename the layer as SidebarBtmRectangle (see Figure 19.45).

Creating the bottom rectangle

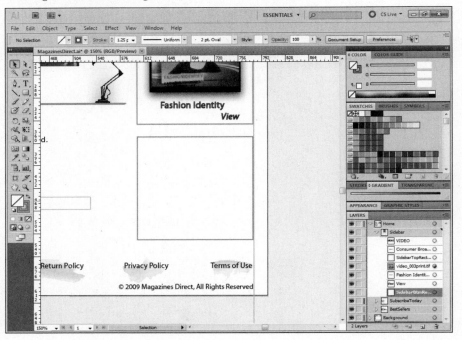

5. Click the Type tool.

6. Set the font to Italic, black, 11pt Myriad Pro.

7. Type Most Popular.

8. Ctrl+click (⌘+click) the artboard.

9. Set the font to 14pt Regular Myriad Pro and type TECHNICAL PUBLICATIONS.

10. Use the Selection tool or Align Panel to position the text (see Figure 19.46).

FIGURE 19.46

Adding the first text blocks

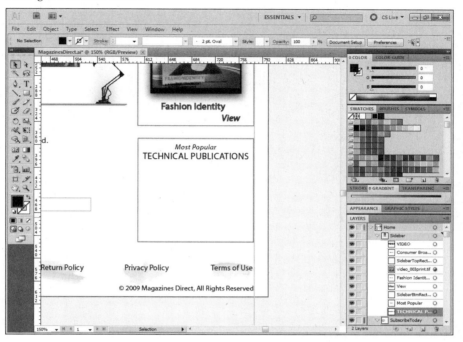

11. Click the Type tool.

12. Set the font to 14pt Regular Myriad Pro.

13. Set the color to the SidebarText swatch.

14. Type HTML, CSS, OMG!

15. Ctrl+click (⌘+click) the artboard.

16. Change the font size to 12pt and the color to black.

17. Type SF Slow Days.

18. Position both text blocks in the sidebar (see Figure 19.47).

Adding additional text

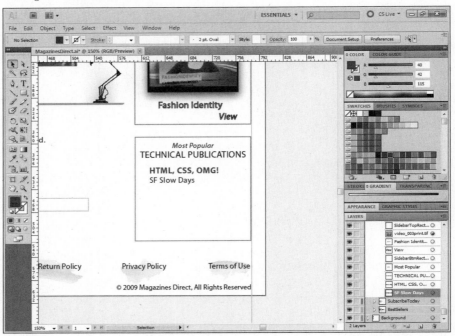

19. Ctrl+click (⌘+click) the artboard.

20. Reset the font size to 14pt and the color to SidebarText.

21. Type Cup O' Java.

22. Ctrl+click (⌘+click) the artboard.

23. Type Viral Outbreak.

24. Ctrl+click (⌘+click) the artboard.

25. Set the font size to 12pt and the color to black.

26. Type Seattle Second.

27. Ctrl+click (⌘+click) the artboard.

28. Type Kentucky's Best.

29. Position the text in the sidebar (see Figure 19.48).

30. Choose File ⇨ Place.

31. Select cupofcoffee.gif and click Place.

32. Position the image in the bottom-right corner of the sidebar (see Figure 19.49). Both sidebars are now done.

FIGURE 19.48

Adding the remaining sidebar text

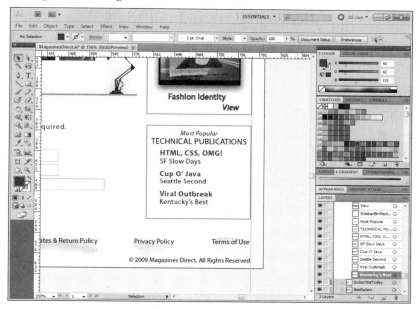

FIGURE 19.49

Adding the image

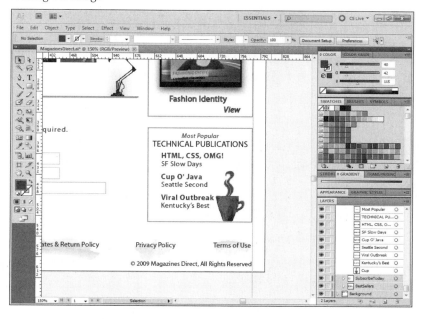

Draw the shopping cart

Although it is part of the heading, the shopping cart icon is one of the more difficult items to create, as it is very small yet intricate and contains many individual pieces. However, now that you are more comfortable with Illustrator from completing the other exercises, it will be easier to understand the steps required.

1. On the Layers panel, click the Background layer.
2. Click the New Sublayer button.
3. Rename the new layer ShoppingCart.
4. Position the new sublayer just below the TopNav sublayer (see Figure 19.50).

FIGURE 19.50

Adding the cart sublayer

5. Use the Zoom tool to zoom in very tight on the area just to the left of the word Cart (see Figure 19.51).
6. Click the Brush tool.
7. Use the Control bar to set the stroke color to black and weight to 1pt.
8. Set the brush definition to Pencil – Thin (see Figure 19.52).

FIGURE 19.51

Zooming in to draw the cart

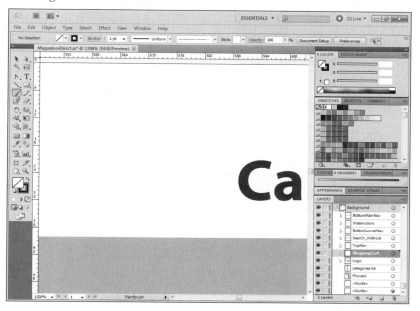

FIGURE 19.52

Setting the brush properties

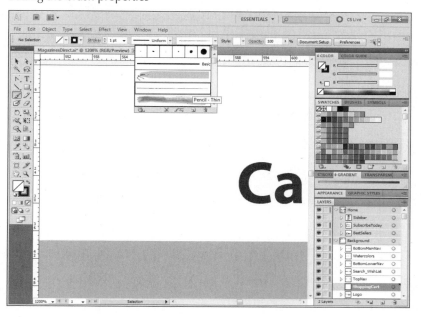

9. **Draw the basic outline of the cart (see Figure 19.53).** You can draw it either in a series of strokes or as a single stroke. If you do not like the results, choose Edit ➪ Undo and try again.

10. **Using the same brush properties, draw the wheels of the cart (see Figure 19.53).**

FIGURE 19.53

Drawing the cart outline and wheels

11. Set the fill color to #CBC92B and the stroke color to None.

12. Click the Ellipse tool.

13. Click on the artboard.

14. Set both the width and height at 2 px.

15. Position the ellipse in the shopping cart (Figure 19.54).

FIGURE 19.54

Drawing the first shopping cart ellipse.

16. Select the ellipse.

17. Choose Edit ➪ Copy.

18. Choose Edit ➪ Paste.

19. Move the new ellipse to a new position in the shopping cart.

20. Repeat Steps 18 and 19 to add more ellipses until the cart appears to be filled (see Figure 19.55). This completes the shopping cart.

Tip

You may need to disable the Smart Guides by choosing View ➪ Smart Guides as they may prevent you from freely positioning the ellipses.

Note

There is no need to name the layers involved in the shopping cart, as you will end up rasterizing it into a single image in the next section.

FIGURE 19.55

Adding the other ellipses

Optimizing the Project

With the design complete, you can analyze the project and determine what parts of it can be optimized. Your main goal is to reduce the number of vector paths in the project, as importing a project into Catalyst that contains a large number of paths may cause Catalyst to suffer from performance problems.

The best method for optimizing vectors is to rasterize them, which converts the vector paths into a single raster image. Not every graphic in your project should be rasterized, however, as the process flattens all of the layers, reducing or potentially eliminating your ability to make additional changes to it in Illustrator. Also, because Catalyst is a vector tool you won't be able to make changes to the rasterized image in it, either.

Rasterize the shopping cart

The shopping cart icon you just completed contains a large number of vector paths. If you were to import the project as is, each of these paths would be converted into an object in Catalyst, which would likely slow the program down. As there is no need for the cart to change as the project runs, it is a good candidate for rasterizing.

1. **If necessary, zoom in on the shopping cart icon.**

2. **With the Selection tool, click and drag to draw a selection box around the cart.**
   Make sure that the selection box completely encapsulates the cart, but does not touch any other object on the page (see Figure 19.56).

Selecting the cart

3. **Choose Object ➪ Rasterize.**

4. **Set the color model to RGB, the resolution to 72 ppi, and the background to Transparent (see Figure 19.57).**

5. **Click OK.**

6. **On the Layers panel, rename the layer to** ShoppingCart.

FIGURE 19.57

The Rasterize dialog box

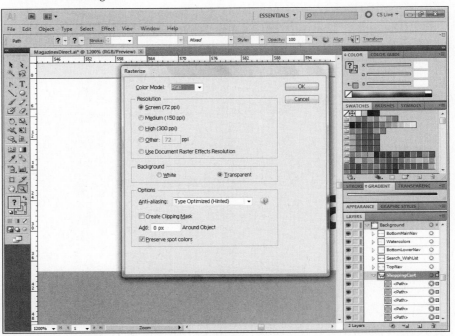

The image will be rasterized. If you are zoomed in very tight on the cart, it may appear to have lost all definition (see Figure 19.58). However, remember that your users will not be able to zoom in on your project when it is running, and once you zoom back out to 100 percent, the cart will be so small that you will not be able to make out the details anyway.

All of the images that were imported or placed on the page are already rasters, so you don't need to do anything to optimize them unless they were high-resolution print graphics. In that case, you would want to rasterize them to reduce their resolution to 72 ppi.

One remaining vector path that you might want to rasterize is the line that separates the Bestseller and Subscribe Now sections, since they do not need to remain editable in Catalyst. Catalyst contains tools to add interactivity to non-rasterized design elements.

The blue rectangles that make up the Place Order, Go and Wish List buttons should not be rasterized as you will want them to be editable in Catalyst so that you can change their color when the user mouses over them.

FIGURE 19.58

The cart after rasterization, viewed at 1200 percent. The details that have been lost in the process are not noticeable at 100 percent.

Embed linked artwork

While the imported artwork does not need rasterization, it's likely that it's all linked as this is the default setting in Illustrator. When you complete your work in Catalyst and hand the project off to the Flex developer, these linked graphics might not be available to the developer. Therefore, embed the graphics instead.

You can embed the graphic when you first import it by deselecting the Link check box in the Place dialog box. However, if you don't do this, you can embed the images as you finish the project.

1. **Choose Window ⇨ Links.** This panel displays all of the images you placed in the project, along with the shopping cart and any other vectors you created in Illustrator and then rasterized. These are designated by a small icon of a triangle and rectangle.

2. **Click the top graphic in the list.**

3. **Press and hold Ctrl (⌘) and click any additional images.** Make sure to not select rasterized vectors such as the shopping cart.

4. **Click the Links panel's menu button in the top-right corner of the panel.**

5. **Select Embed Image (see Figure 19.59).** If this option is grayed out, you have selected rasterized images, so you need to go back to the panel and deselect them.

   If a dialog box appears allowing you to set TIFF import options, select Flatten Layers to a Single Image and click OK.

FIGURE 19.59

The Embed Image menu command

Your project is now ready to be imported into Catalyst.

Summary

In this chapter, you created the Illustrator file that will be used as the design comp for the Catalyst project. You learned how to:

- Identify the design requirements for the project
- Create a new Flash Catalyst file in Illustrator
- Create the logo

- Organize Illustrator's layers
- Import images
- Add and format text
- Use Illustrator's drawing tools
- Optimize the project to prepare it for import into Catalyst

Importing the Design into Catalyst

Once your design comp is complete in Illustrator, you will be able to import it into Catalyst and begin the process of converting it to an application. This chapter shows you how to perform this import step by step. Make sure that your layers are properly organized, and convert objects into optimized graphics to reduce the final project's file size.

Creating a Catalyst Project from a Design Comp

To begin the process of bringing a comp over from Illustrator, you need to create a new Catalyst project from your design comp. This is a fairly straightforward process, although it might be slow depending on the size and complexity of the design and your computer's resources.

1. **Open Flash Catalyst.** On Windows, this will likely be in Start ⇨ All Programs, then either the Adobe folder or, if you purchased Catalyst as a part of one of the Creative Suite bundles, the folder for that bundle.

2. **From the Start Screen (see Figure 20.1), click From Adobe Illustrator .AI File under the Create New Project from Design File heading.**

3. **Navigate to the folder that contains the AI file you wish to import.**

4. **Click the file.**

IN THIS CHAPTER

Importing an Illustrator design into Catalyst

Organizing artwork

Resizing and moving artwork

Converting objects to optimized art

FIGURE 20.1

The Catalyst Start Screen, showing the Create New Project from Design File options

5. **Click Open.** Catalyst displays the Importing Adobe Illustrator File dialog box (see Figure 20.2) and shows a progress bar as it opens the Illustrator file, analyzes it, and prepares it for import. Once complete, the Illustrator Import Options dialog box appears (see Figure 20.3).

On the Web

If you have not created a design file to use, you can download `chapter20_start.ai` from the book's Web site (`www.wiley.com/go/flashcatalystbible`).

6. **Double-check that the artboard size and background color options are correct.** The importer should have detected the correct size and background color from the artboard.

7. **Set the Fidelity options and Other import options as desired.** For this example, we will keep all of the defaults.

FIGURE 20.2

The Importing Adobe Illustrator File dialog box and progress bar

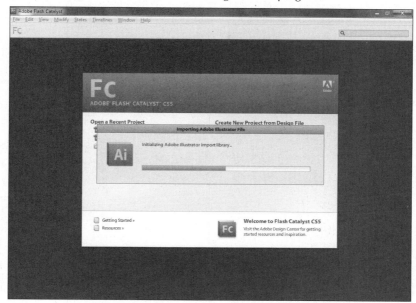

FIGURE 20.3

The Illustrator Import Options dialog box

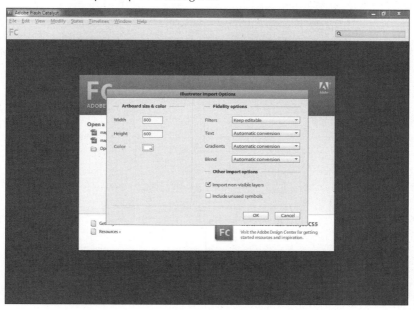

Cross-Reference
See Chapter 5 for a detailed discussion on the Fidelity and other options in the dialog box.

8. **Click OK.** The Importing Adobe Illustrator File dialog box appears with a progress bar. Once complete, the design should open in Catalyst (see Figure 20.4).

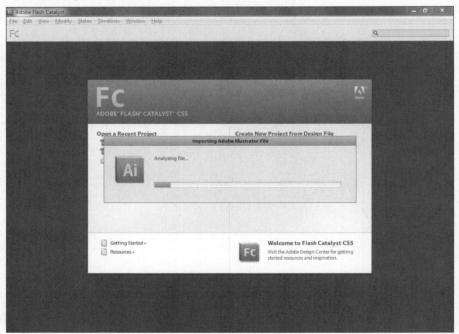

FIGURE 20.4

The Importing Adobe Illustrator File dialog box and progress bar

Catalyst cannot import extremely large or complex Illustrator files. If you get an error message during the import that tells you the file has too many objects to be imported, you will need to return to Illustrator and break the file into smaller, separate files that can be imported (see Figure 20.5).

Cross-Reference
See Chapter 19 for details on breaking a design into smaller files to allow for import.

FIGURE 20.5

The error message displayed if an Illustrator design is too complex

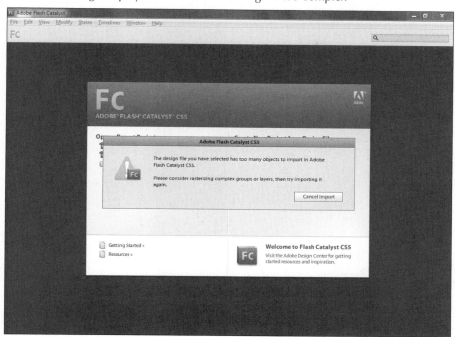

The Importing Adobe Illustrator File dialogbox may update during import informing you that your artwork contains a large number of bitmap or vector graphics and that you may want to consider optimizing them (see Figure 20.6). This process is discussed later in this chapter. In addition, a dialog box may appear when you complete the import process informing you of problems that occurred (Figure 20.7).

Often, this occurs when your Illustrator design uses Illustrator features such as Live Paint or Live Trace, or when text could not be preserved as editable objects. These issues will rarely affect your work as you build the project in Catalyst. If this dialog box appears, simply click OK.

FIGURE 20.6

The Optimized Graphics dialog box

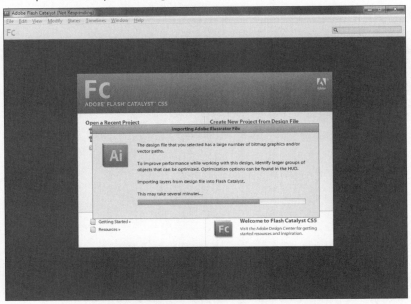

FIGURE 20.7

A dialog box after your import informs you problems have occurred

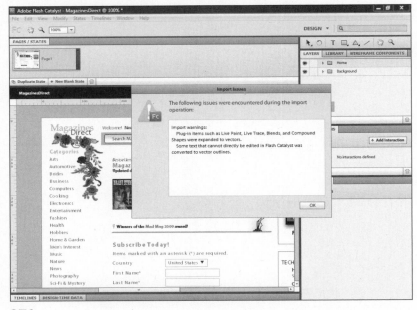

Organizing Artwork

Once your file is imported into Catalyst, you will want to check the Layers panel and ensure that the artwork is organized the way you want. Ideally, this will be done in Illustrator, but in dealing with large or complex files, it can be easy to forget to rename layers or organize them into groups, so you will likely need to do at least some of that work in Catalyst.

Rename layers

Layers and layer groups will be imported from directly from Illustrator. Just as in Illustrator, you can double-click a layer name to rename it (see Figure 20.8).

1. Click the small arrow to the left of a layer group to expand it and examine its sublayers.

2. Double-click a layer you want to rename.

3. Type a new name and press Enter.

FIGURE 20.8

Renaming a layer in Catalyst

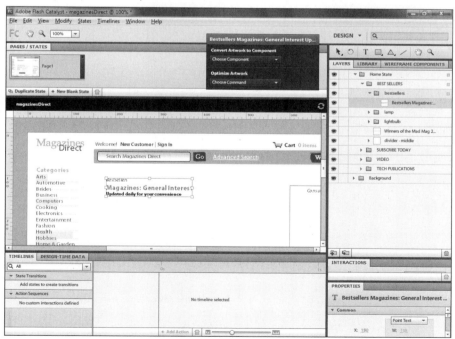

Note

Renaming a layer in Catalyst has no effect on the layer's name in Illustrator, as the files are not linked.

Create new layers

You can create new layers in Catalyst if you discover the need for a group that was not created in Illustrator.

1. **Click the Create New Layer button at the bottom of the Layers panel.** This creates a new layer at the top of the layers panel (see Figure 20.9).

A newly created layer

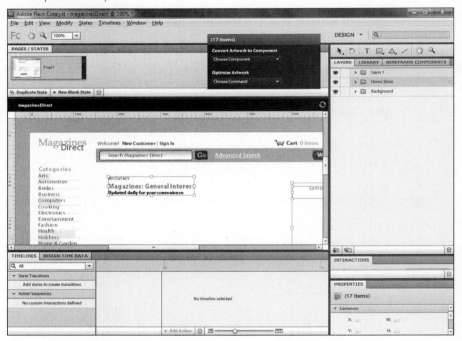

Note

New layers are always added at the top of the Layers panel, regardless of the layer you currently have selected.

2. Double-click the new layer and type a new name.

3. Drag existing layers or groups onto the new layer to move those elements into the layer (see Figure 20.10).

FIGURE 20.10

Adding content to a new layer

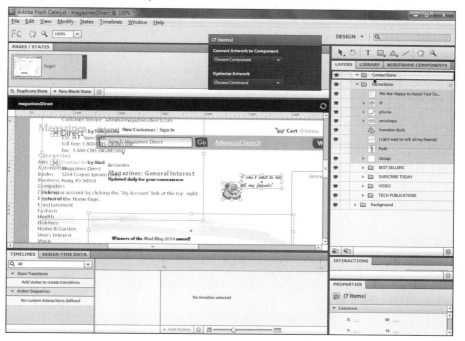

Creating new sublayers

Layers in Catalyst are top-level items and are placed at the top of the layer stack. If you want to create a new layer within an existing layer, you need to use the Create New Sublayer button.

1. Click the layer into which you want to add a sublayer.

2. Click the Create New Sublayer button. A new sublayer appears (see Figure 20.11).

3. Drag existing layers or layer groups onto the new layer to place them in the new sublayer (see Figure 20.12).

FIGURE 20.11

A newly created sublayer

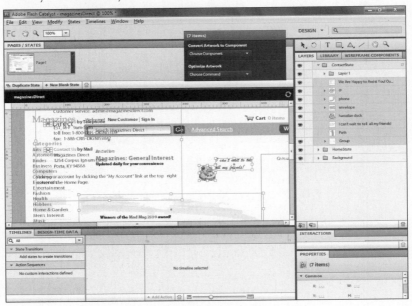

FIGURE 20.12

Adding existing elements to the layer

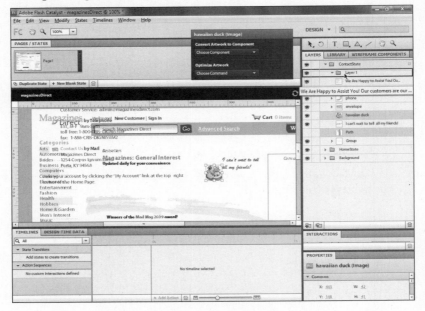

Deleting layers

Occasionally, you may encounter situations where Illustrator creates layers that add unnecessary complexity to your project. These layers can be deleted.

1. Drag a sublayer's content to another sublayer.
2. Click the sublayer.
3. Click the Delete button in the bottom of the layer panel (see Figure 20.13).

FIGURE 20.13

Deleting a layer

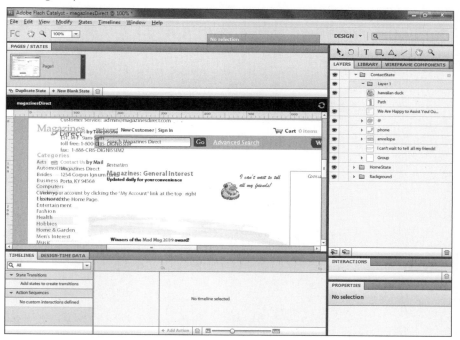

Removing unneeded groups

Almost all artwork from Illustrator will be in a group, which can, like unneeded layers, add complexity to your project. If you remove all of a group's contents, the group is deleted automatically (see Figure 20.14).

FIGURE 20.14

Removing a group by moving its contents to a different sublayer

Moving, Rotating, and Resizing Artwork

Should you change your mind about the size or location of artwork once you have imported a design into Catalyst, you can use its drawing tools to make the needed changes without having to go back to Illustrator.

Moving artwork

You may need to reposition artwork as the design of the project undergoes changes. In this case, the design initially had the featured magazines artistically placed at angles in a group, but the client has now requested that they be displayed in a linear fashion. This will allow you to convert them to a data list and eventually populate the list with data from a database.

1. **Click the Select tool.**
2. **Click the item to be moved and drag it to a new location (see Figure 20.15).**
3. **Repeat Step 2 for any additional items to be moved.**

FIGURE 20.15

Moving the magazines into their new positions

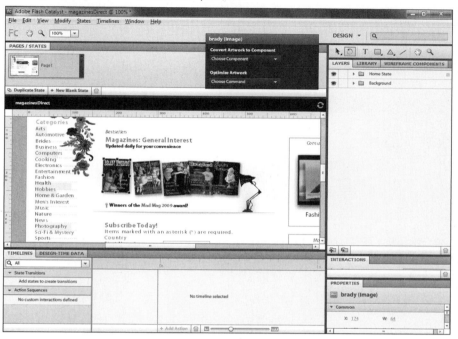

Rotating artwork

The magazines now need to be rotated so that they are straight.

1. Click the Select tool.

2. Click the object you want to rotate (see Figure 20.16).

3. Click the Rotate tool.

4. Click and drag near a corner of the object until you reach the desired rotation.

5. Repeat Steps 1 through 4 to rotate any additional objects.

FIGURE 20.16

Rotating the magazines

Resizing artwork

You can resize the artwork using either the Select or Direct Select tools in Catalyst. Prior to converting artwork to components or optimized graphics, the two tools will work the same.

1. **Click the Select tool.**

2. **Click the object you want to resize.**

3. **Click and drag one of the control handles — the white squares along the edge of the object — to resize (see Figure 20.17).** You can resize while maintaining the shape's proportions by holding the Shift key while you drag one of the corner handles.

FIGURE 20.17

Resizing an object in Catalyst

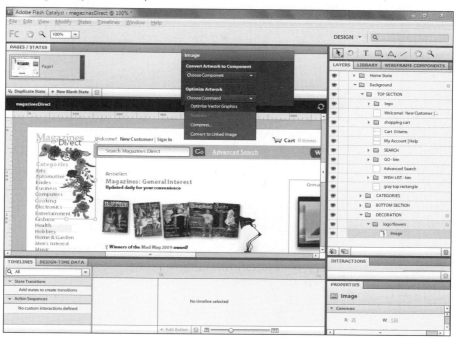

Convert Artwork to Optimized Graphics

Most artwork that will not be converted to components should be converted to an *optimized graphic*. Complex artwork, particularly vector art created in Illustrator, requires significant overhead when rendered in Flash Player. Optimizing the graphic allows Catalyst to define it in such a way as to minimize this overhead.

Tip

Catalyst is generating code for every object it creates. MXML in Flex 4 provides the ability to define even extremely complex shapes through code. When you convert a shape to an optimized graphic, Catalyst removes its corresponding code from the main project file and places it in a separate file that is then referenced in the main code. This process allows Catalyst to keep the size of the main file smaller, allowing it to run more efficiently.

Caution

Do not optimize graphics that you will need to alter dynamically at runtime, as optimized graphics will become static artwork in your application.

1. **Click the Select tool.**

2. **Click the artwork on the artboard that you want to convert.** You can press and hold the Shift key to select multiple items to convert as a group, such as an item with a drop shadow.

3. **On the HUD, click Choose Comment ⇨ Optimize Vector Graphics under the Optimize Artwork heading (see Figure 20.18).** The graphic is converted.

FIGURE 20.18

Converting artwork to an optimized graphic

Once converted, optimized graphics are stored in your project's library. Therefore, if you want to reuse the graphic elsewhere in your application, you can simply drag it from the library to the artboard as needed.

Summary

In this chapter, you continued building the Magazines Direct Web application. You saw how to:

- Import Illustrator artwork into Catalyst
- Organize the artwork in layers
- Move, rotate, and resize artwork
- Optimize complex graphics in Catalyst

Importing Additional Artwork from Illustrator and Photoshop

Often, you will be unable to import your entire project as a single design comp from Illustrator. In the case of the Magazines Direct application, the original design comp was too complex to be imported into Catalyst and had to be broken into smaller individual files that could be imported.

You may also on occasion have additional assets that will, for a variety of reasons, be created in separate Illustrator files or at later times. In the Magazines Direct example, the design requirements were changed after the initial design, so that the featured magazines are now displayed in a scrollable data list.

Changing the magazines to be displayed in a linear list was done easily enough in Catalyst, but the project now requires a scroll bar, which will need to be imported separately.

Cross-Reference
Refer to chapters 19 and 20 to start the Magazines Direct application from the beginning.

Not all design work needs to be done in Illustrator. Illustrator is a fantastic tool for creating and manipulating vector artwork, but raster artwork is better handled by Photoshop.

Therefore, you may have assets such as photographs in Photoshop that need to be imported into your design. While these could have been imported into Illustrator in the initial design phase, they can also be brought directly into Catalyst.

Importing Additional Artwork from Illustrator

Artwork that is not part of the initial design in Illustrator can be imported into Catalyst at any time. Artwork in a distinct file can be imported from the File menu.

On the Web

If you did not create the new asset files in Chapter 19, you can download them from the book's Web site (www.wiley.com/go/flashcatalystbible).

1. **Click the New Layer button.** Creating a new layer for the imported assets will ensure that you know where they will be placed.

2. **Name the new layer.**

Cross-Reference

See Chapter 20 for information on renaming layers.

3. **With the new layer selected, click File ⇨ Import ⇨ Adobe Illustrator (AI) File (see Figure 21.1).**

FIGURE 21.1

The Import menu

4. Navigate to the folder that contains the Illustrator file.

5. Select the file to be imported and click Open (see Figure 21.2).

FIGURE 21.2

Selecting the file to be imported

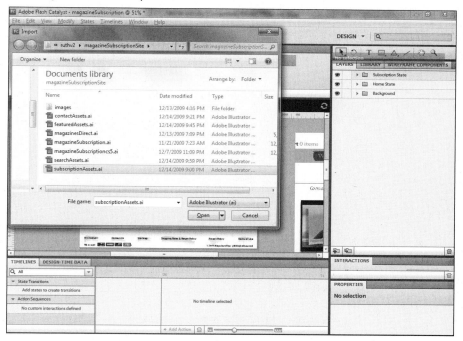

Just as when you created the project from an Illustrator file, the process of importing artwork begins with the import progress display on the Import Illustrator File dialog box. The Illustrator Import Options dialog box appears (see Figure 21.3) and contains many of the same controls as the dialog box you saw when you created the file, minus the size options.

6. Select the options for importing the artwork. In this example, the default selections are ideal.

7. Click OK. The artwork is imported into the layer you created in Step 1 (see Figure 21.4). You may want to click the eyeball icon next to any existing layers to hide them so that you can see your new artwork.

If desired, you can hide the new layer by clicking the eyeball icon to the left of the layer name. The artwork being imported in this example is intended to be a new view state, so it is best to hide it until needed.

FIGURE 21.3

The Illustrator Import Options dialog box

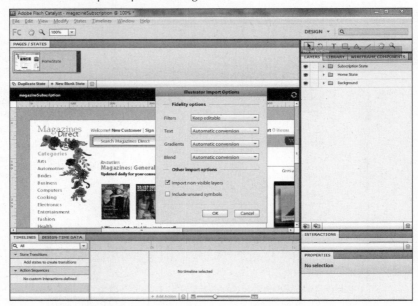

FIGURE 21.4

The imported artwork, placed on its own layer. The Home State layer has been hidden.

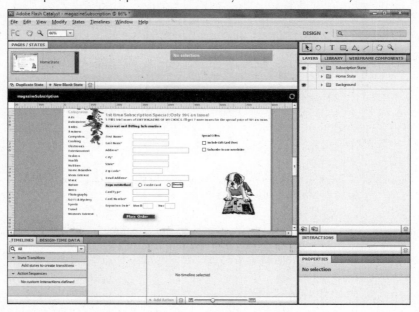

8. Optimize the graphics on the new layer as needed.

Cross-Reference

See Chapter 20 for step-by-step instructions for optimizing images.

9. **Repeat Steps 1 through 7 to import additional files from Illustrator as needed.** Each planned view state is a separate file (see Figure 21.5), so you will need to import each in order to complete the steps in Chapter 23.

FIGURE 21.5

The project after importing the assets for each of the planned view states. Currently, only the last layer with imported assets, Search State, has its visibility turned on.

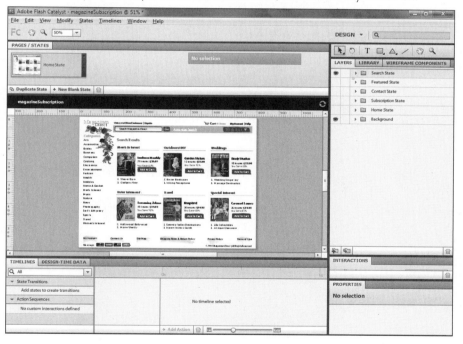

Importing Bitmap Artwork from Photoshop

Photoshop is the industry standard graphics tool for working with bitmap or raster-based graphics such as photographs, and its import process is similar to Illustrator's. In the Magazines Direct application, you need to import an additional magazine cover.

On the Web

The magazine cover being imported in these steps can be downloaded from the book's Web site (www.wiley.com/go/flashcatalystbible).

1. **Click the New Layer button.** As with importing Illustrator graphics, creating a new layer for the imported assets ensures that you know where they will be placed.

2. Name the new layer.

Cross-Reference

See Chapter 20 for more information on renaming layers.

3. With the new layer selected, choose File ➪ Import ➪ Adobe Photoshop (PSD) File (see Figure 21.6).

FIGURE 21.6

The Import menu for Photoshop files

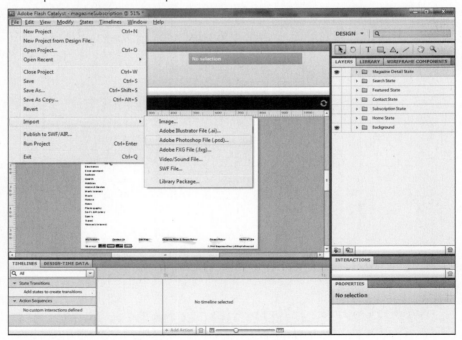

4. Navigate to the folder that contains the Photoshop PSD file.
5. Select the file to be imported (see Figure 21.7) and click Open.

FIGURE 21.7

Selecting the file to be imported

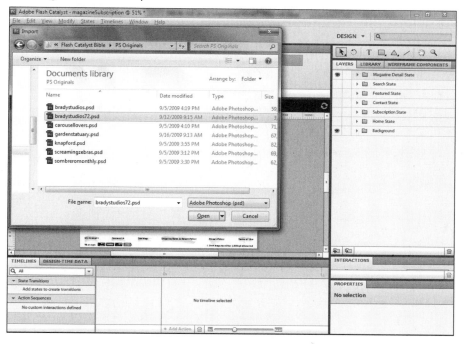

Importing Photoshop files follows the same basic procedure as importing Illustrator files, beginning with the import progress on the Import Photoshop File dialog box (see Figure 21.8). You will then be presented with the Photoshop Import Options dialog.

Cross-Reference

See Chapter 8 for a detailed discussion of the options on the Import Photoshop File dialog box.

6. **Select the options for importing the file.** In this example, select Flatten for all three Fidelity options. We will not need to perform any editing on this image, so flattening each option will reduce the file size and improve performance within Catalyst. Note that this will not flatten the entire file into a single image, as the image, text and shape layers will still be independent of one another.

7. **Click OK.** The artwork is imported into the layer you created in step 1 (see Figure 21.9).

FIGURE 21.8

The Photoshop import options dialog

FIGURE 21.9

The imported artwork, placed on its own layer

8. **Because you do not need to edit the parts of the image individually, navigate to Choose Command ➪ Rasterize from the HUD's Optimize Artwork menu (see Figure 21.10).** This will flatten the Photoshop file into a single image.

FIGURE 21.10

The HUD's Optimize Artwork menu

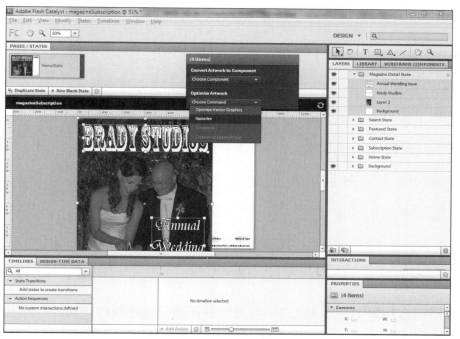

If desired, you can hide the new layer by clicking the eyeball icon to the left of the layer name. As the artwork being imported in this example is intended to be a new view state, it is best to hide it until needed.

9. **Using the Select tool, resize the image to fit within the artboard.** You can see the imported project in Figure 21.11.

FIGURE 21.11

The project after importing the new PSD file

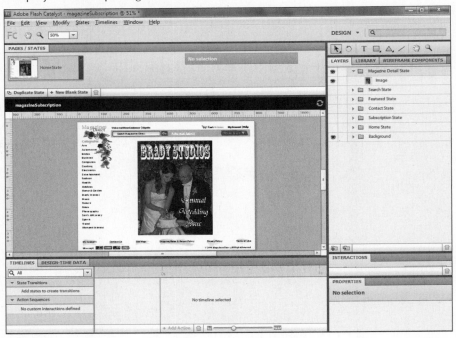

Using Copy and Paste to Import Assets from Illustrator and Photoshop

The Import command allows you to easily import Illustrator and Photoshop files, but you are importing the entire file. Often, you only need a portion of the file. In our example, the newly required scrollbar has been added to the original Illustrator file.

While it could have been designed in its own individual file, building it in the original Illustrator file made it easier to create the scrollbar and maintain the same color scheme as the rest of the application. Therefore, the easiest means by which the scrollbar can be imported is via copy and paste.

On the Web

You can download a copy of the Illustrator design comp that contains the scrollbar from the book's Web site (www.wiley.com/go/flashcatalystbible).

1. **In Illustrator, select the assets to be copied using the Pointer tool (see Figure 21.12).** You can press and hold the Shift key to select multiple assets. You can also select items by clicking the target icon in the Layers panel. If the artwork is in a distinct section of the artboard, you can click and drag a marquee selection around it to select.

FIGURE 21.12

Selecting the scrollbar assets in Illustrator

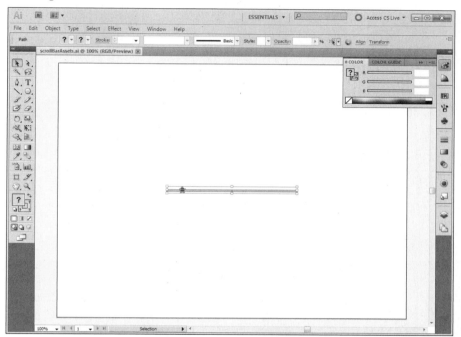

2. **Click Edit ➪ Copy (see Figure 21.13).**
3. **In Catalyst, select the layer into which you want to paste the artwork.** Alternately, you can create a new layer or sublayer for the art. If you create a new layer or sublayer, be sure to name it. In this example, the artwork will be placed on the Home State layer.
4. **Choose Edit ➪ Paste (see Figure 21.14).**

FIGURE 21.13

The Edit ➪ Copy command in Illustrator

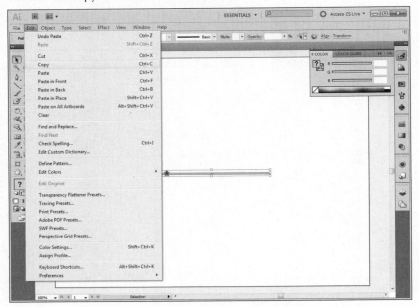

FIGURE 21.14

Pasting Illustrator artwork into Catalyst

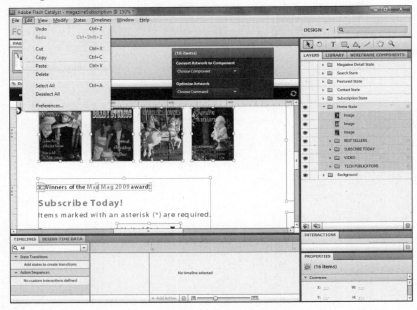

5. **On the Illustrator Import Options dialog box (see Figure 21.15), make any selections you deem necessary.** In this case, the defaults will work.

FIGURE 21.15

The Illustrator Import Options dialog box when pasting artwork

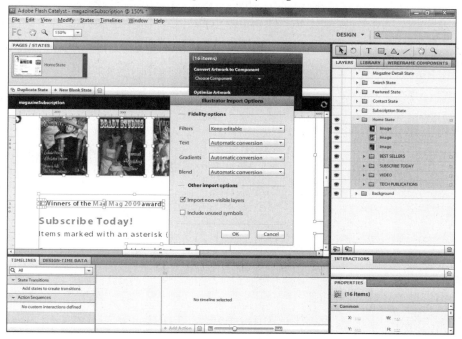

6. **Click OK.** Once imported, the new artwork can be treated and manipulated just like any other art (see Figure 21.16). The scrollbar imported in these steps will be converted into an actual scrollbar in Chapter 22.

FIGURE 21.16

The artwork imported into Catalyst by copy and paste

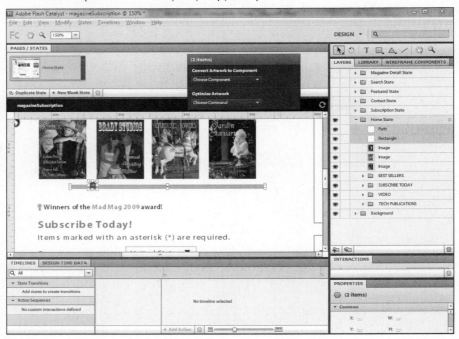

Edit an Asset in Illustrator with Round-trip Editing

If you discover that an asset needs to be modified after import from Illustrator, you can use the Catalyst–Illustrator round-trip editing workflow to edit it and ensure that Catalyst immediately updates with the changes.

While the following steps detail the process with Illustrator, a similar process exists with Photoshop.

1. **In Catalyst, click the Select tool.**
2. **Click the artwork you want to edit in Illustrator (see Figure 21.17).**

FIGURE 21.17

The asset to be modified in Illustrator has been selected on the artboard

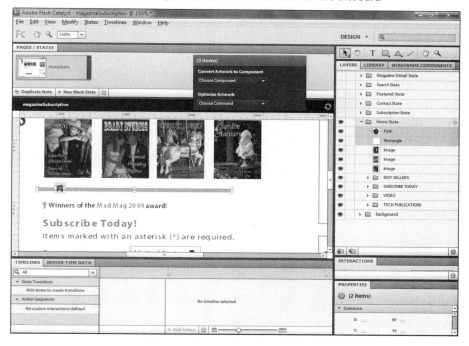

3. **Choose Modify ➪ Edit in Illustrator CS5.** You can also right-click (⌘+click) the item and select Edit in Illustrator CS5.

   Illustrator launches, and the selected asset is displayed on the artboard. You can now perform whatever modifications you want on the asset. In this example, the color of the scrollbar's thumbnail will be changed.

Note

Round-trip editing is only designed to work with the CS5 versions of Illustrator and Photoshop.

4. Click the thumbnail of the scrollbar.
5. Choose Window ➪ Appearance (see Figure 21.18).
6. In the Fill section, select a new color.

FIGURE 21.18

Updating the scrollbar's appearance in Illustrator

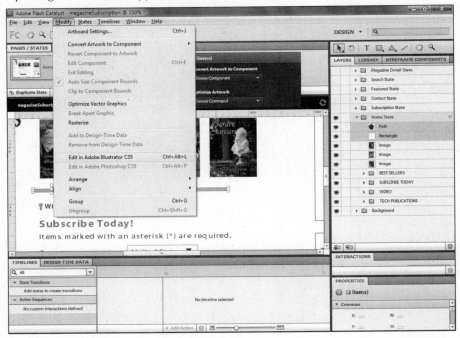

7. **Click Save.** The file is saved, and Catalyst is updated.

8. **Close Illustrator or switch back to Catalyst.** The updated asset will be available immediately (see Figure 21.19).

FIGURE 21.19

The updated scrollbar in Catalyst

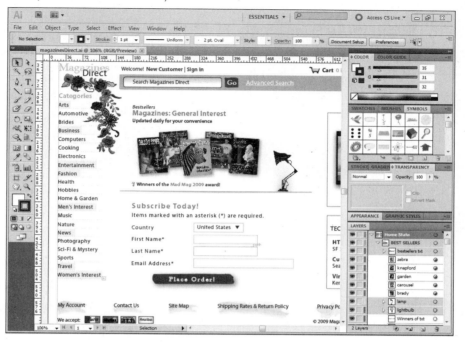

Summary

This chapter detailed the process of importing additional assets from Illustrator and Photoshop. It showed you how to:

- Import Illustrator files into an existing project
- Import Photoshop files into an existing project
- Use copy and paste to import portions of Illustrator and Photoshop files
- Use round-trip editing with Illustrator to modify graphics

Converting Artwork to Components in Your Projects

F lex applications are constructed as a collection of components. Each component fulfills a specific function, be it displaying a particular aspect of the visual interface of the application or performing some specific programming task.

You can use Catalyst to convert your primary interface elements into components.

Creating Custom Components

Catalyst includes the ability to convert artwork into one of 11 common Flex user interface components. They are:

- Button
- Checkbox
- Radio Button
- Toggle Button
- Text Input
- Horizontal Slider
- Vertical Slider
- Scroll Panel
- Horizontal Scrollbar
- Vertical Scrollbar
- Data List

IN THIS CHAPTER

Convert layers to custom components

Nesting components

Convert artwork to a button

Create check boxes and radio buttons

Convert artwork to a text input field

Convert artwork to a scroll bar

While those provide important building blocks for your application, most of your assets will in fact end up becoming custom components. Any element, or more often, any group of elements, that does not fit into one of the 11 existing component types will become a *custom component*.

More frequently, you will simply want to convert any group of related assets as a component. For example, the collection of elements that is designed to make up a view state should be converted to a custom component.

Convert artwork to a custom component

You can create a custom component by selecting the assets you want to convert, then use the heads-up display (HUD) to convert to a custom/generic component.

On the Web
If you have not completed the exercises in the prior chapters, you can download a version of the application for this chapter from the book's Web site (www.wiley.com/go/flashcatalystbible)**.**

1. **Click the Select tool.**
2. **Select all of the assets that will be converted to a custom component.** You can press and hold the Shift key to select multiple items. If all of the assets to be converted are in the same layer, you can simply select the layer in the Layers panel to select all of the items on that layer. In this case, click the Home State layer (see Figure 22.1).

Selecting the Home State assets by clicking the layer

3. **From the HUD, choose Convert Artwork to Component ⇨ Custom/Generic Component.** The artwork will be converted (see Figure 22.2).

Caution

Do not confuse the layer name and the component name. When you convert a layer to a component, its icon in the Layers panel changes to indicate that its only content is a component. While there is no particular harm in renaming the layer, be aware that renaming the layer will not rename the component. You must use the Library panel to rename the component.

Converting the art using the HUD

4. **Once the artwork is converted, name your component.** Components can be found in the Library under the Custom Components category. If you convert a layer to a component, Catalyst automatically names the component by appending CustomComponent to the layer name. Spaces are not allowed in component names, so they are removed. For example, the Contact State layer will become HomeStateCustomComponent.

   If you do not like this potentially cumbersome name, you can change it by double-clicking the component in the Library panel and typing a new name. Component names should be reflective of their purpose.

5. **Repeat Steps 1through 3 to convert the contents of each state layer to a custom component.** When complete, go to the Library panel, double-click each component, and rename it (see Figure 22.3).

Tip

All existing components in the Flex framework begin with a capital letter, and capitalize the first letter of each additional word in the name. Examples include TextInput and DataGrid. Because both MXML and ActionScript (the two languages in which Flex applications are written) are case sensitive, you should maintain consistency with this existing format for component names; thus, you should name the component created above something like ContactState or ContactStateComponent. The actual name is not terribly important, so long as it continues to reflect the purpose of the component.

FIGURE 22.3

The Library panel after completing Step 3

Edit a custom component

Custom components function in a way like symbols in Flash Professional, Illustrator, or Fireworks. Just as with those other programs, Catalyst stores a single copy of the component as a part of the application and allows as many instances of it to be placed on the artboard as you want. Certain properties, such as the width, height, and position, can be changed for each instance, but most properties of the component are stored in the component itself and are only changeable by editing the component.

You can edit a component by double-clicking an instance of it on the artboard. The view will change to display the component itself. The Pages/States panel will display the states defined within the component. The Layers panel will update to show the layers contained within the component. While the rest of the application is still visible, any elements on the page that are not a part of the component will be grayed out. The individual artwork and assets that make up the component will be individually selectable and editable.

Caution

Any changes you make to a component while editing it will affect every instance of the component throughout the application.

1. Click the Select tool.
2. Double-click the component instance on the artboard (Figure 22.4).

FIGURE 22.4

Editing a component on the artboard

3. Make any desired changes to the component's elements.

4. Use the navigation bar below the Pages/States panel to return to the application (Figure 22.5).

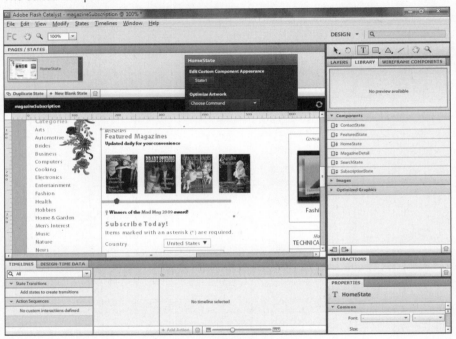

FIGURE 22.5

The edited component

Nest Components within Components

Most components can be nested within most other components, which allows you to maximize their reusability. Almost any aspect of your application that you need to reuse can be made into a component, and then you can nest it within any other component in which it needs to appear.

User interface components such as buttons, radio buttons, check boxes, and scroll bars will likely be nested within custom components. In the remaining exercises in this chapter, you will nest user-interface components within custom ones.

You can nest them by simply ensuring that you are editing a component when you create a new one. For example, a button will be created within a custom component if you edit that custom component when you create the button. The navigation bar just under the Pages/States panel displays the name of the component you are currently editing.

You can also nest components by copying and pasting their instances into other components or by dragging them from the library while in the editing mode of another component.

Convert Artwork to a Button

One of the most commonly used interface components in an application is a button. Whether it submits a form, takes a user to another state, or even another Web site, buttons provide core functionality that few applications can do without.

The standard Flex button is a simple gray rectangle with a label. Prior versions of the Flex framework allowed users to *skin* or change the appearance of buttons, but it was a fairly complex process.

Catalyst simplifies this process by enabling you to take any set of artwork from Illustrator and convert it to a button. In this way, your application's buttons can look like almost anything you want.

Create the button

On the Web

The following exercises modify the Subscription custom component of the application. If you have not completed the exercises in Chapter 21 for importing this into the project, you can download a version that has this component from the book's Web site (www.wiley.com/go/flashcatalystbible).

1. If necessary, double-click the HomeState custom component to ensure that the button will be nested within the custom component.

2. Click the Select tool.

3. Click the artwork that will make up the button (see Figure 22.6). You can hold the Shift key to select multiple pieces of artwork. Alternately, you can Shift+click the layers that contain the artwork.

Note

While the examples presented here all include buttons with text labels, your buttons are not required to contain text. Obviously, they need something to make their purpose clear to the user, but carefully designed icons can be as useful as labels.

4. On the HUD, choose Convert Artwork to Component ➪ Button (see Figure 22.7).

FIGURE 22.6

Selecting the artwork for a button

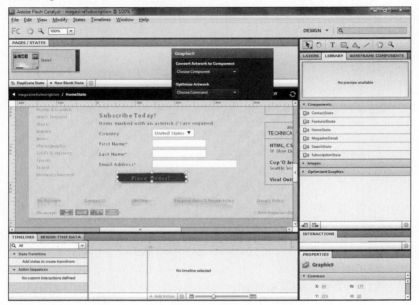

FIGURE 22.7

Using the HUD to convert to a button

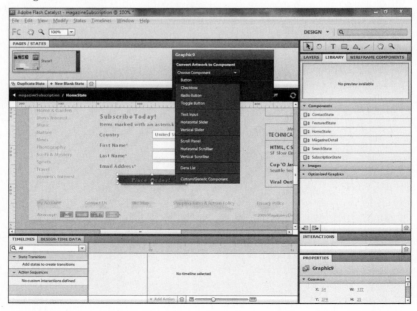

Rename the button

As with custom components, you will likely want to give the button a more logical and memorable name than the one automatically generated by Catalyst. Renaming a button follows the same procedure as renaming custom components.

1. **Click Library.**

2. **If necessary, expand the Custom Components section.**

3. **Double-click the button's name.**

4. **Type a new name (see Figure 22.8).**

FIGURE 22.8

Renaming a button

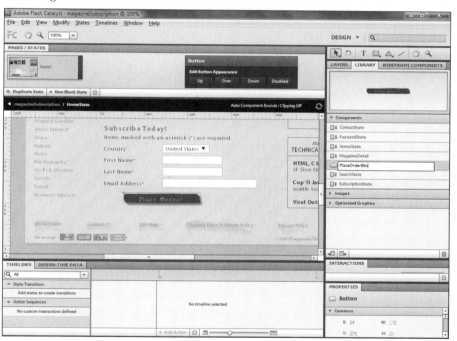

Create Check Boxes and Radio Buttons

Check boxes and radio buttons allow users to select from a group of options. Check boxes are most often used when you want your user to select zero or more options from a set of choices, while radio buttons present a set of mutually exclusive options. For example, an e-commerce site might present a set of special offers as additional purchases, and you will likely want your user to be able to select more than one of these offers, so you would present them with check boxes. Conversely, the customer can only logically select a single credit card type, so you would use radio buttons for that.

Create check boxes

On the Web

The following exercises modify the Subscription custom component of the application. If you have not completed the exercises in Chapter 21 for importing this into the project, you can download a version that has it from the book's Web site (www.wiley.com/go/flashcatalystbible).

1. If necessary, show the SubscritionState layer and double-click its custom component.
2. Click the first small square that represents a check box on the form.
3. Shift+click the text next to the check box (see Figure 22.9).

FIGURE 22.9

Selecting the check box assets

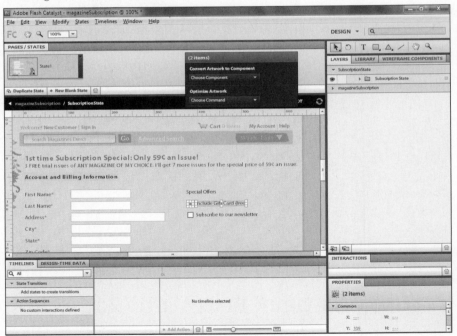

4. On the HUD, choose Convert Artwork to Component ➪ Checkbox, as shown in Figure 22.10).

Converting the assets to a check box using the HUD

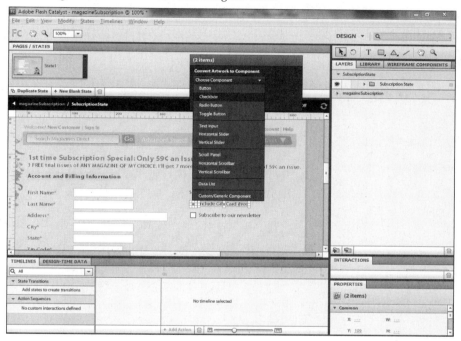

5. Repeat Steps 1 through 4 to convert any additional check boxes.

Create radio buttons

Radio buttons provide a set of mutually exclusive options. An order form will likely use radio buttons to allow the user to select which type of credit card he will use or to select the length of a subscription.

On the Web

The following exercises modify the Subscription custom component of the application. If you have not completed the exercises in Chapter 21 for importing this into the project, you can download a version that has it from the book's Web site (www.wiley.com/go/flashcatalystbible).

1. If necessary, double-click the `Subscription` custom component.
2. With the Select tool, click the circle that will represent the radio button.
3. Shift+click the label next to the button (see Figure 22.11).

Selecting the radio button's assets

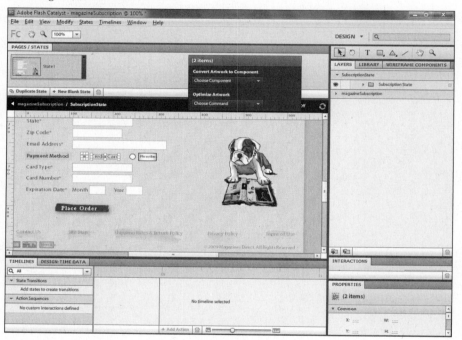

4. On the HUD, choose Convert Artwork to Component ⇨ Radio Button, as shown in Figure 22.12.
5. Repeat Steps 1 through 4 to create any additional radio buttons.

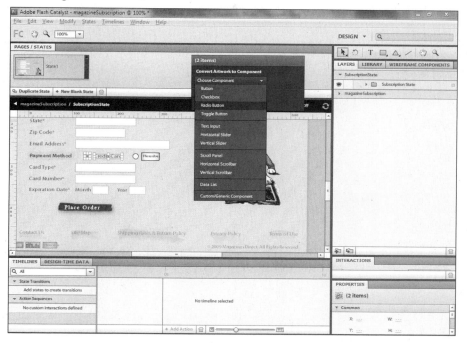

FIGURE 22.12

Converting the radio button

Defining a radio button group

You must combine radio buttons into groups so that Flash Player, when running the application, knows which sets of buttons should be handled together and limited to a single selection.

You can define a group by typing a group name in the Properties panel (any radio buttons with the same name are treated as a group). Catalyst assigns a default group name for buttons, but you should change it to something more descriptive of the group's purpose and to ensure that buttons are properly grouped.

1. **Click one of the radio button components.**
2. **From the Properties panel, expand the Component section.**
3. **Change the Radio Button Group name (see Figure 22.13).**

FIGURE 22.13

Creating a group name for a radio button

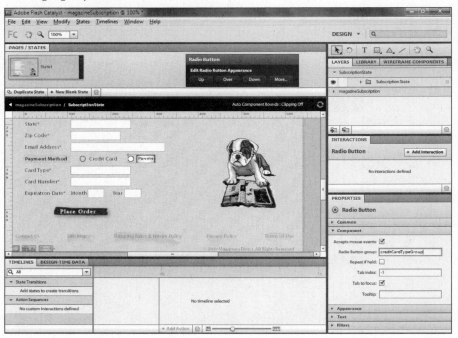

Note

Radio button group names must begin with a letter and can contain only letters, numbers, and underscore characters. Do not use spaces. It is recommended, but not required, that you use a lowercase letter for the first character and capitalize the first letter of any additional words in the group name. For example, a group of buttons for selecting the type of credit card might be named creditCardType.

4. **Repeat Steps 1 through 3 for the remaining radio buttons.** Be sure that the names of grouped buttons match exactly, including case (see Figure 22.14).

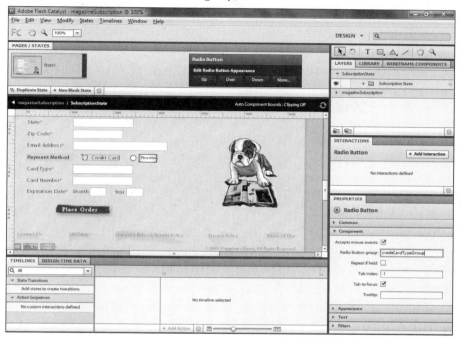

FIGURE 22.14

Giving another radio button the same group name

Convert Artwork to a Text Input Field

Forms, where your users can provide information such as their name, address, and e-mail address, are likely going to be made up primarily of text fields. Text fields are likely to be drawn in Illustrator as simple rectangles, although you can actually use any shape.

On the Web

The following exercises modify the Subscription custom component of the application. If you have not completed the exercises in Chapter 21 for importing this into the project, you can download a version that has it from the book's Web site (www.wiley.com/go/flashcatalystbible)**.**

1. If necessary, double-click the Subscription custom component.

2. Select the artwork you want to use for the text input field.

3. From the HUD, choose Convert Artwork to Component ⇨ Text Input (see Figure 22.15).

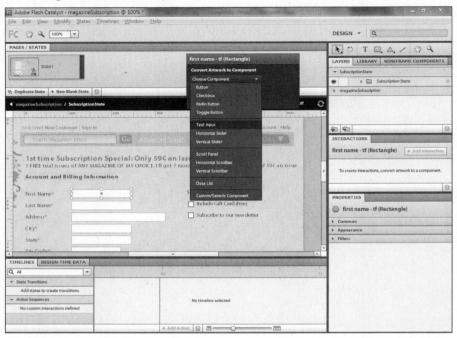

FIGURE 22.15

Converting artwork to a text input field

Configure the component

Once you've created the text input component, you can configure it. Of particular interest is the ability to configure the font properties so that you can control the appearance of the text as your user types in the field.

1. **Select a text input component.**
2. **On the HUD, choose Edit Parts (see Figure 22.16).**
3. **Click (Text).**
4. **On the Properties panel, select the desired font settings, as shown in Figure 22.17.**
5. **Click the name of the project to return to the main editing view.** In this example, you will click magazineSubscription (see Figure 22.18).

FIGURE 22.16

Selecting a Text Input component

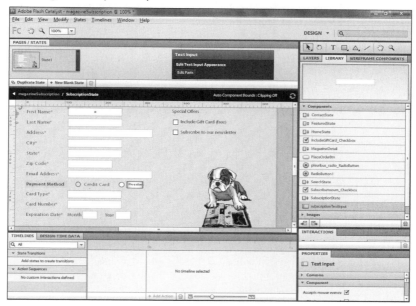

FIGURE 22.17

Changing the font settings on a text input component

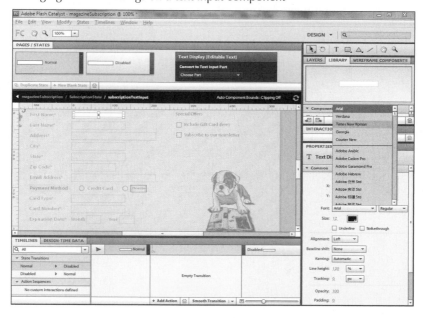

FIGURE 22.18

Returning to the main project

Reuse components

One of the primary advantages of creating components is that you can reuse them. A form, for example, does not need individual components to be defined for each field. Instead, all of the text fields can and should be instances of the same text input component.

To reuse a component, delete the artwork that represents the duplicate instances. Drag the component from the Library to the artboard.

1. **In the Library, rename the text input component to something more generic.**
2. **Select the artwork representing each duplicate text input field (see Figure 22.19).**
3. **Press Delete on your keyboard.**
4. **Click Library.**
5. **Drag the TextInput component to the artboard.** Position it as needed.
6. **Repeat Steps 3 and 4 to re-create the remaining text fields (see Figure 22.20).**

FIGURE 22.19

Selecting the text input artwork for deletion

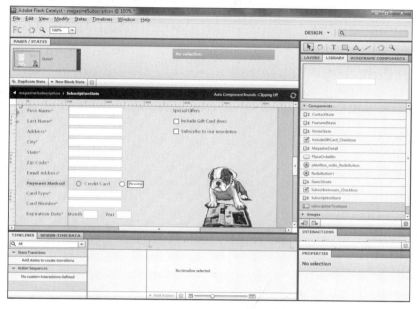

FIGURE 22.20

Reusing the TextInput component

Convert Artwork to a Scrollbar

You can add scrollbars to any component that will require that the user scroll to see more content; most often, however, you will add them to data lists. As with other components, scrollbars can be created based on any artwork.

Create the scroll bar

Scrollbars require at least two pieces:

- **Thumb.** Represents the piece that the user will click and drag to scroll.
- **Track.** The path along which the thumb travels.

Optionally, you can add two additional pieces, arrows that exist at the ends of the scroll bar that the user can click to scroll. You can create scroll bars to be either horizontal or vertical.

Note
Unlike the other exercises in this chapter, the following steps are not done within the Subscription custom component.

1. **If necessary, click the name of the project from the navigation bar to return to the main project.** Show or hide layers as necessary to view the HomeState assets. Double-click the component on that layer.

2. **Select the art that will represent the thumb.**

3. **Shift+click the art that will represent the track (see Figure 22.21).** If you have artwork representing left and right or top and bottom arrows, Shift+click that artwork as well.

4. **On the HUD, choose Convert Artwork to Component ⇨ VerticalScrollbar or Convert Artwork to Component ⇨ Horizontal Scrollbar.** In this example, the horizontal scroll bar option is selected, as shown in Figure 22.22.

FIGURE 22.21

Selecting the artwork that will make up the scroll bar

FIGURE 22.22

Converting the scroll bar

Configure the scroll bar

Many components will be ready to use as soon as you convert the artwork. Scrollbars, however, require an additional configuration step: You must specify which piece of artwork represents which part of the component.

1. **Click the new scroll bar component.**
2. **On the HUD, click Edit Parts (see Figure 22.23).**

The HUD with a scroll bar selected, showing the warning that component parts must be specified. Clicking Edit Parts allows you to fix this issue.

3. **Select the artwork that represents the thumb.** You can use Shift+clicking if the thumb will actually be comprised of more than one asset.
4. **On the HUD, choose Choose Part ⇨ Thumb (see Figure 22.24).**
5. **Select the artwork that will make up the track.** You can Shift+click to select multiple pieces of artwork if necessary.
6. **On the HUD, choose Choose Part ⇨ Track (see Figure 22.25).**

FIGURE 22.24

Designating the thumb

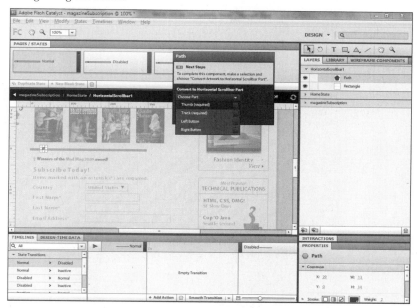

FIGURE 22.25

Designating the track

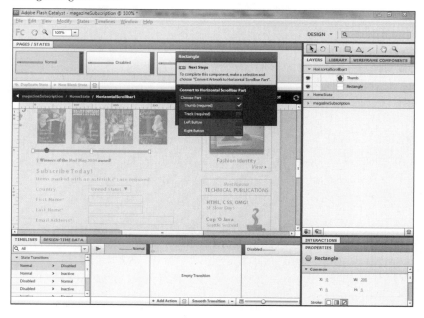

7. **Click the name of the project to return to the main editing window.** The thumb automatically moves to the far-left side of the track, as shown in Figure 22.26.

The completed scroll bar

If you have artwork for the left, right, top, or bottom button, you can select it, click Choose Part, select the appropriate option for the button, and then repeat for the other button.

Summary

In this chapter, you completed the process of converting the primary pieces of the application into components. You learned how to:

- Convert artwork into a custom component
- Create buttons, check boxes, and radio buttons
- Convert artwork to text input fields and configure the fields' font properties
- Create and configure a scroll bar

Creating View States in Your Project

View states in a Flex application are roughly equivalent to pages in a traditional Web application. Anytime you need to change the appearance of either your entire application, or just a portion of it, you can use view states. Setting up view states in the application requires nothing more than creating a new state and then modifying its contents.

Components can contain states as well; custom components have states created in the same manner as the application, while many user interface components come with a set of pre-defined view states.

Creating States in the Main Application

The Pages/States panel in Catalyst allows you to create and manage view states. A new application will have a single state, but the panel allows you to create as many additional states as you want. States can either be created as duplicates of an existing state or as new blank states.

Catalyst gives each state a default name of Page1, Page2, and so forth. You should give each state a logical name descriptive of its contents or purpose in the application. State names can contain only letters, numbers and underscores; you cannot use spaces.

On the Web

The exercises in this chapter build on the application as of the end of Chapter 22. If you have not yet completed that chapter, you can download a version of the project that you can use for this chapter from the book's Web site (www. wiley.com/go/flashcatalystbible).

1. On the Pages/States panel, double-click Page1.

2. Type HomeState, **as shown in Figure 23.1.**

FIGURE 23.1

Renaming the initial state

3. **Click Duplicate State.**

4. **Double-click Page2.**

5. Type SubscriptionState, **as shown in Figure 23.2.**

6. **Repeat Steps 3 through 5 to add any additional states (see Figure 23.3).** In this example, you will want a total of five states:

   - HomeState

   - SubscriptionState

   - ContactState

   - FeaturedState

   - SearchState

   Each state should be a duplicate of the prior state.

FIGURE 23.2

Adding and renaming a new state

Note

The order in which you create states is for the most part irrelevant. In the example in this chapter, each state is a duplicate of the last, so they are all the same at this point and their order does not matter. Catalyst does not have a means by which states can be reordered in the Pages/States panel, so if you prefer to have them in a particular order for organizational purposes, make sure you create them in that order.

Note

Duplicate states copy everything from the current state. Duplicating states is useful in applications like this one that have common elements such as headers, navigation and footers. Blank states are just that: a completely empty artboard from which you can build a new state from scratch.

FIGURE 23.3

The application with all of the new states added

Modify the Contents of a State

Each state's contents can be modified at will without affecting other states. Often, modifications to states will simply involve either deleting components that you do not want in a state or hiding their layers and then either adding new components from the library or showing their layers.

Cross-Reference

See Chapter 22 for details on creating components, and Chapter 9 for a discussion on the differences between hiding layers and deleting components in states. The following example hides the layer to enable animation, rather than deleting its assets which is covered later in this chapter.

On the Web

The exercises in this chapter build on the application as of the end of Chapter 22. If you have not yet completed that chapter, you can download a version of the project that you can use for this chapter from the book's Web site (www.wiley.com/go/flashcatalystbible).

1. On the Pages/States panel, click the SubscriptionState (see Figure 23.4).

FIGURE 23.4

Selecting the state to edit

2. On the Layers panel, hide the HomeState component's layer (see Figure 23.5).

3. **Click the eyeball icon next to the layer that contains the assets you wish to display on the state.** This will display the subscription assets on the state, so that the home state and subscription state show different information (see Figure 23.6).

FIGURE 23.5

Hiding unwanted assets from a state

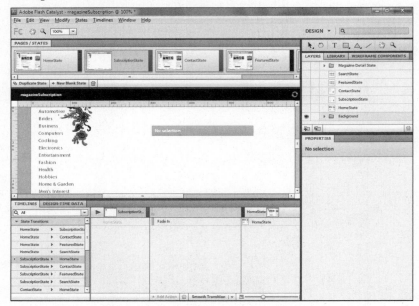

FIGURE 23.6

Showing a layer for the state's assets

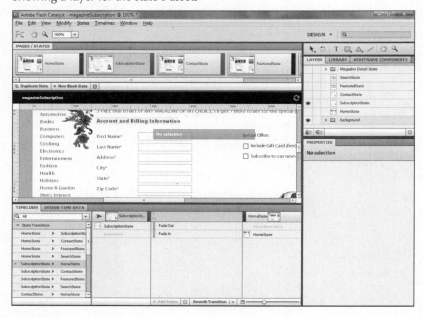

4. **Repeat Step 3 for each additional state (see Figure 23.7).** You will want to hide the assets currently on the state and then show the assets for the new state.

Finishing setting up the main application's states

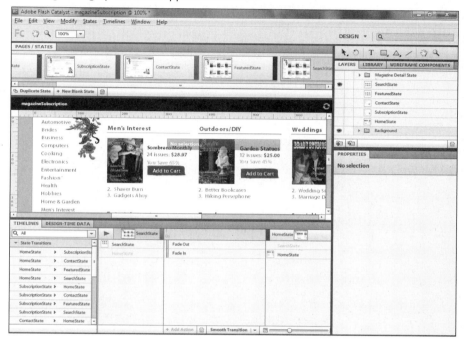

The application will now contain a set of states that display the appropriate assets for the state. Later in this chapter, you will learn how to add interactions so that your user can move between the states.

Create New States within a Component

Just as the main application can contain multiple states to represent different aspects of it, components can likewise contain multiple states. For example, if you have a subscription or order form that spans multiple pages, you would likely encapsulate the form in a custom component, and then have the component contain multiple states to represent the pages of the application.

Cross-Reference

See Chapter 22 for a step-by-step tutorial on creating custom components.

On the Web

The exercises in this chapter build on the application as of the end of Chapter 22. If you have not yet completed that chapter, you can download a version of the project that you can use for this chapter from the book's Web site (www.wiley.com/go/flashcatalystbible).

1. On the Pages/States panel, select the SubscriptionState.

2. Double-click the SubscriptionState component on the artboard (see Figure 23.8).

Editing the custom component

3. Rename Page1 as SubscriptionForm.

4. Click Duplicate State.

5. Rename the new state SubscriptionConfirm (see Figure 23.9).

6. On the Layers panel, hide the layers that contain the form elements.

7. Create a new sublayer named ConfirmedStateAssets (see Figure 23.10).

FIGURE 23.9

Creating a new state in a custom component

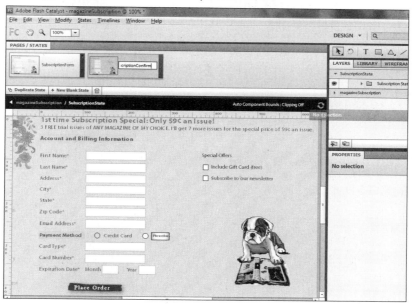

FIGURE 23.10

Setting up the layers for the component's new state

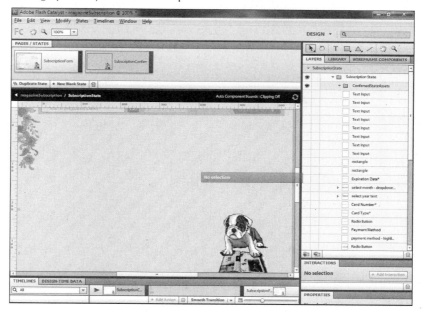

8. On the Library panel, drag the ConfirmedComponent to the artboard (see Figure 23.11).

FIGURE 23.11

Adding assets to the new state.

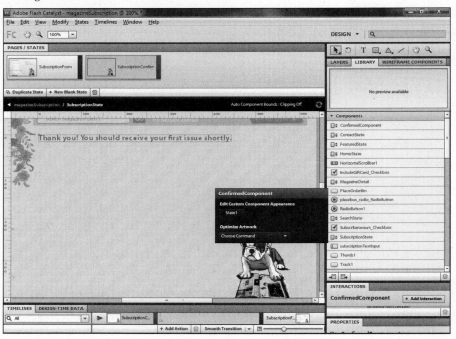

On the Web

If your application does not have a ConfirmedComponent, you can download it from the book's Web site (www.wiley.com/go/flashcatalystbible)**.**

9. Click the main application's name on the navigation bar to exit editing the component.

You have now created a state within a component. States within components serve the same purpose as states in the main application, allowing you to display different information to your users based on their actions.

Components with Built-in View States

Many of the standard user interface components have default view states. Buttons, for example, have the following states:

- Up
- Over
- Down
- Disabled

Radio buttons have these states:

- Up
- Over
- Down
- Disabled
- Selected Up
- Selected Over
- Selected Down
- Selected Disabled.

These states define the appearance of the component during various expected user interactions. View state changes within these components are automatic; you need not specifically add the ability for a button to change from the Up to the Over state when the user interacts with it.

1. **Click a button component.**
2. **From the HUD, click either Up, Over, Down, or Disabled.** Regardless of which button you click, you will switch to editing mode for the component. The state that is initially selected depends on which button in the HUD you click, but you can always simply select a different state in the Pages/States panel (see Figure 23.12).
3. **Edit the appearance of the button as desired.** In this example, a drop shadow is being added to the button in the Over state (see Figure 23.13).

FIGURE 23.12

Using the HUD to go into editing mode on a button

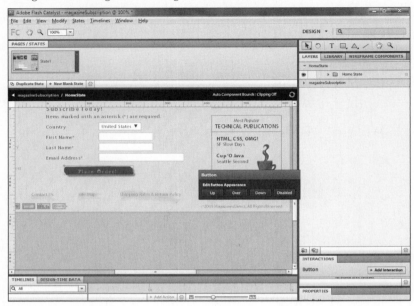

FIGURE 23.13

Changing the appearance of a button in the Over state

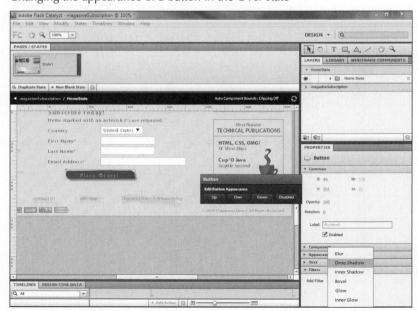

4. Click the name of the application in the navigation bar to exit editing mode on the button.

You now have a button component that provides visual clues to the user during interaction, an important aspect of usability. If you wish, you can test the project at this point by pressing Ctrl-Enter on your keyboard. While the button will not actually do anything, you will be able to see that its appearance changes when you mouse over it.

Trigger View State Changes with Buttons

In order to allow your user to move from one state to the next, you need to add an interaction to an element in the application. Almost any component can be used for this interaction, but the most commonly used one will be a button.

Create the interaction

Creating the interaction on a button is very straight-forward, as buttons are designed for interaction. In the following steps, you will add the ability for the user to click the Place Order button in the Home State to be taken to the Subscription State.

1. In the main application's HomeState, double click the component on the page and then click the Place Order button (see Figure 23.14).

FIGURE 23.14

Selecting the Place Order button

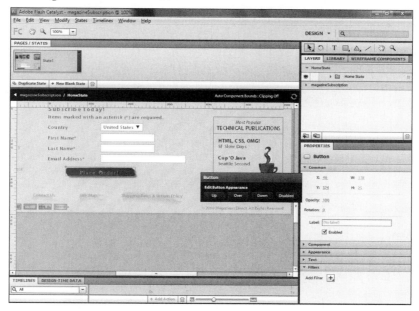

---

2. If necessary, expand the Interactions panel by double-clicking its tab (see Figure 23.15).

FIGURE 23.15

The Interactions panel

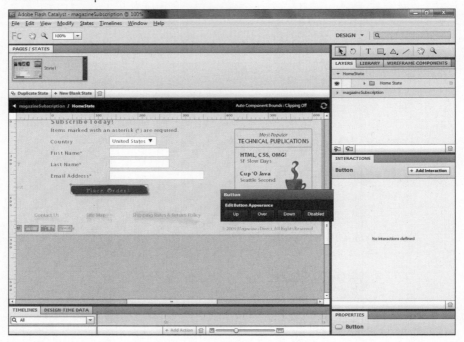

3. Click Add Interaction.

4. Ensure that the first drop-down list is set to On Click, and the second to Play Transition to State.

5. From the Choose State menu, select SubscriptionState (see Figure 23.16).

6. **Click OK.** The interaction has now been added to the button (see Figure 23.17). When run through Flash Player, the application will allow users to click the button and trigger the state change.

FIGURE 23.16

Creating an interaction to transition to another state

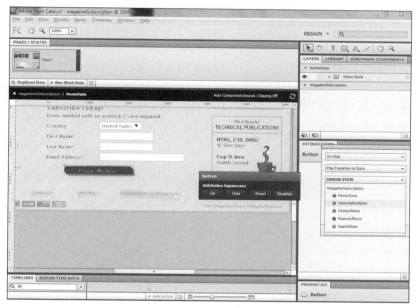

FIGURE 23.17

The completed interaction

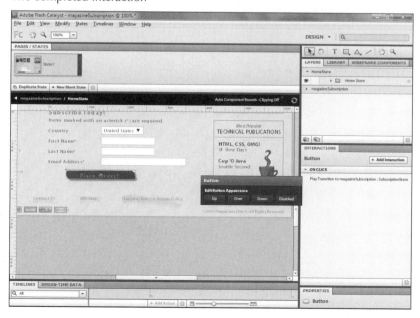

Test the interaction

After you create an interaction to trigger a state change, you can test it by running the project. Follow these steps:

1. **Choose File ⇨ Save.** It is not required that you save the project before running it, but it is highly recommended.

2. **Click File ⇨ Run Project (see Figure 23.18).** Catalyst will build the project — which may take a minute or so, depending on the speed of your computer — and then open it in Flash Player.

3. **Click the Purchase Now button.** The project will change to show the Subscription state. The transition to the state will be instantaneous.

Later in this chapter, I will discuss adding animation to the state change. Also, keep in mind that there is nothing in this application to validate that the form on the home page be filled out before moving to the subscription state.

In a real application, you would want to add the necessary code to implement validation. You would need to add this code in Flash Builder; however, that is not something currently supported by Catalyst.

FIGURE 23.18

Running the project from the File menu

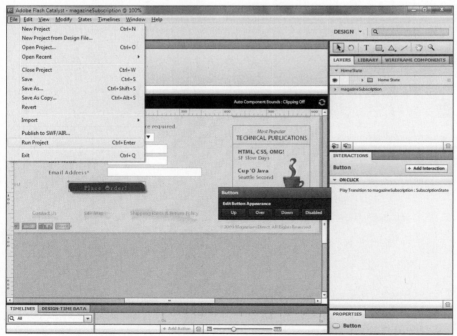

Animating State Change Transitions

Transitions between states can be animated. Catalyst includes a set of pre-built animation effects that can be used in transitions. After you add an interaction to trigger a state change, the effected states appear on the Timelines panel. You can increase or decrease the time each transition takes and choose the effect to be played.

Changing the timing of effects

By default, most effects trigger instantly, which generally prevents users from seeing animation. Using the Timeline panel, you can adjust this timing to create smoother effects.

Note

Consider what types of animation effects you want to apply to components when you set up your view states. If you want to have components animate in or out of a state, you need to be sure to merely hide that component's layer, rather than deleting the component altogether.

1. **If necessary, expand the Timeline panel by double-clicking its tab.** The Timelines panel is at the bottom of the screen, as shown in Figure 23.19. If you are still editing a component, you will want to click the name of the application in the navigation bar.

FIGURE 23.19

The Timeline panel in the application

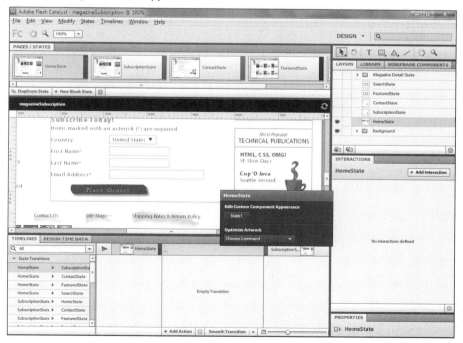

2. On the Pages/States panel, click SubscriptionState.

3. **On the Layers panel, click the eyeball icon to show the HomeState's assets, and the eyeball to hide the SubscriptionState's assets.** You want each to slide in on the transition, so you need to show the HomeState's assets to move them off the artboard.

4. **Double-click the Hand tool to zoom out to see the entire application (see Figure 23.20).**

Showing the appropriate assets

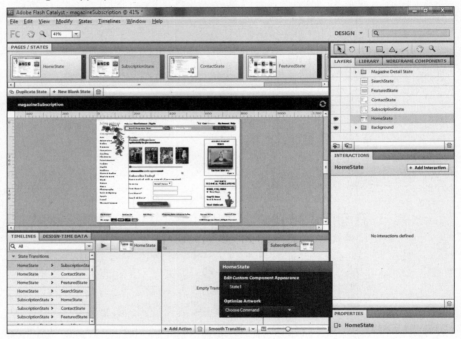

5. **Click the Select tool.** While pressing and holding the Shift key, drag the HomeState's component so that it is completely off the left edge of the artboard (see Figure 23.21).

6. **On the Library panel, click the eyeball icon to show the SubscriptionState's assets.**

7. **While pressing and holding the Shift key, drag the SubscriptionState's assets off the right edge of the artboard (see Figure 23.22).**

FIGURE 23.21

Moving the components

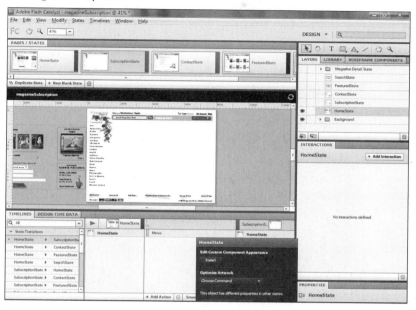

FIGURE 23.22

Moving the other assets

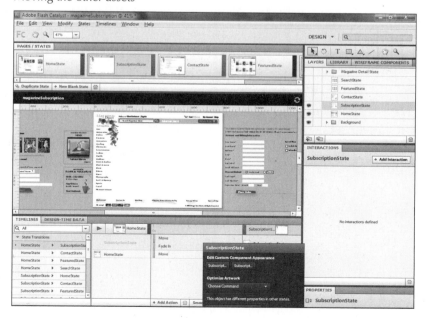

8. **On the right side of the Timeline panel, choose the first transition, HomeState ⇨ Subscription State.** The timeline updates to show the HomeState on the left, and the SubscriptionState on the right (see Figure 23.23).

Selecting the transition from the HomeState to the SubscriptionState

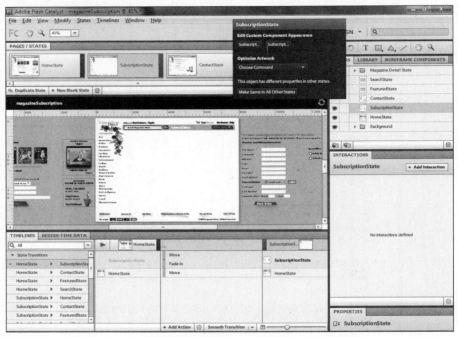

9. **Mouse over the bar representing the HomeState.** A small half-circle appears at the edge of the bar.

10. **Drag this half-circle to the right to expand the time over which the component appears (see Figure 23.24).**

Note

The timeline is measured in fractions of seconds. A slider along the bottom of the panel allows you to zoom in or out on the timeline.

11. Repeat Step 3 for the SubscriptionState's Move action.

12. Set it to the same amount of time as the other state.

13. Set the Fade In action to the same timing (see Figure 23.25).

FIGURE 23.24

Expanding a component's transition time

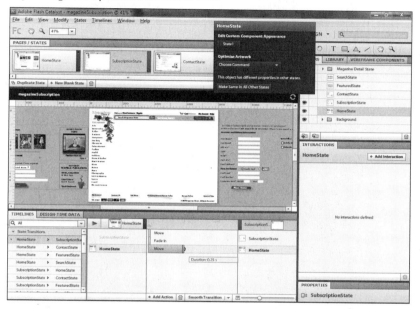

FIGURE 23.25

Setting the timing on the second state

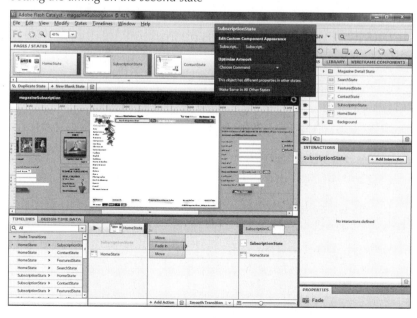

14. Drag both the FadeIn and Move effects for the Subscription state so that they begin when the HomeState's transition ends (see Figure 23.26).

FIGURE 23.26

Changing the timing of the transition

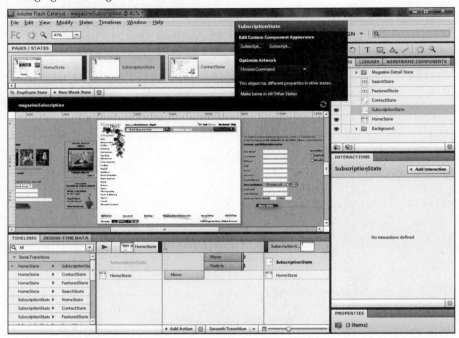

Now that you have established the timing of the effects, users will see the Home State's assets slide off to the left, to be replaced by the Subscription State's assets sliding in from the right while also fading in.

Applying other effects

Catalyst automatically adds a Fade In effect to components being added to a state. If you reposition a component, a Move action will be applied. You can, however, add additional effects. In the following steps, a FadeOut effect isadded to the HomeState.

1. On the Timeline, click HomeState.
2. Click Add Action.
3. Click Fade (see Figure 23.27).
4. Adjust the timing of the new effect as needed (see Figure 23.28).

FIGURE 23.27

Selecting the Fade effect for the HomeState

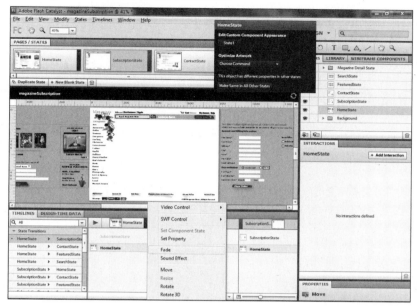

FIGURE 23.28

Adjusting the timing of the added effect

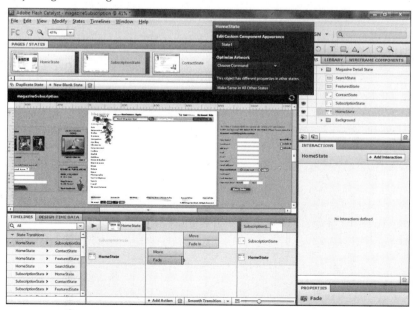

The animation of the Home State now matches that of the Subscription State, as both fade while they move.

Summary

This chapter demonstrated the process of creating and working with states. In it, you learned:

- How to create new view states in the main application and within components
- Modify components in states
- Use the built-in states of certain components
- Use buttons to trigger state changes
- Apply animation to state transitions

Adding Data Lists

Many applications will have sections that require dynamic data from server-side resources. Whether product lists, employee directories, items in a shopping cart or photo galleries, these kinds of data lists will likely be an important element in your application. In many cases, Flex's ability to pull in server-side data and display it graphically will be one of the key factors in deciding to build the application in Flex.

Catalyst cannot connect your application to server-side resources nor display live data; both of those must be done by a Flex developer in Flash Builder. However, it is possible to include a representation of the data in your application through data lists and design-time data.

Convert Artwork to a Data List

Data lists are one of the default component types in Catalyst. Converting artwork to a data list requires the same procedure as converting any other artwork: You select the elements that make up the data list and then use the heads-up display (HUD) to convert to the component.

While the process of converting to a data list is the same as any other component, there are a few important caveats to consider before you convert. First, if your application is going to pull in enough data to require that the data list be scrollable, you need to create a scrollbar component and be sure to include it in the elements that you select to convert to the data list.

Cross-Reference

See Chapter 23 for details on converting artwork to a scrollbar.

The second item to consider is the artwork that will represent the data. Often, this will be made up of multiple items, such as an image and text. The individual items might be components.

For example, you could convert the image you want to use to a button and then utilize its state to provide interaction when the user selects the item. You cannot, however, combine all of the elements of the planned data item into a single component. Catalyst can only populate the design-time data panel, which gives you the ability to have multiple, different items in the data list, if the repeated item is made up of individual pieces. Therefore, be careful that you do not create a single component out of the items for the list.

On the Web

The following exercises assume that you have completed the steps outlined in Chapter 23. If you have not yet done that, you can download a version of the application ready for this chapter from the book's Web site (www.wiley.com/go/flashcatalystbible).

1. **With the Select tool, click on an item that you plan to use for the data list.** In this example, the magazines in the Featured Magazine section on the HomeState are used for the data list, so you will need to double-click the HomeState component and then click the first magazine.

Caution

Do not select all of the magazines. Instead, only select the first. You will end up deleting the rest and re-inserting them via the design-time data panel.

2. **Press and hold the Shift key and click any additional items to be included in the data list (see Figure 24.1).** Be sure to select the scrollbar component.

3. **From the HUD, click Convert Artwork to Component ⇨ Data List (see Figure 24.2).**

The art work has now been converted to the data list. In the following sections, you will learn how to customize the new list.

FIGURE 24.1

Selecting the items for the data list

FIGURE 24.2

Converting the artwork to a data list with the HUD

Configuring the Data List's Parts

Once you convert the artwork to a data list, the HUD displays a warning message that you need to configure its parts. At a minimum, you need to specify which piece or pieces of the artwork will be used as the repeating item — the item that represents the actual data. If you have included a scroll-bar, you also need to designate it.

1. **If necessary, select the Data list.**
2. **On the HUD, choose Edit Parts (see Figure 24.3).**

The Edit Parts button the HUD

3. **Using the Select tool, click on the artwork that will make up the repeating item (see Figure 24.4).**
4. **On the HUD, navigate to Choose Part ⇨ Repeating Item (see Figure 24.5).**

FIGURE 24.4

Selecting the artwork for the repeating item

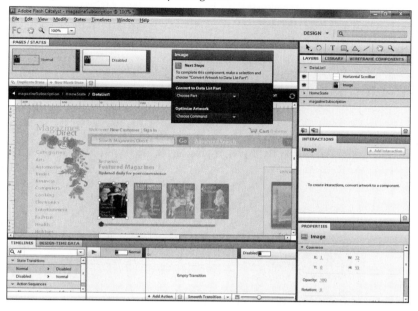

FIGURE 24.5

Designating the repeating item with the HUD

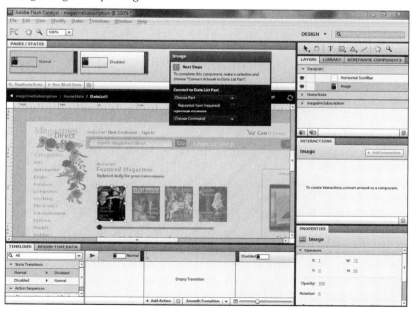

The data list has now been configured to recognize the image as the repeating item. The next section details how to change the alignment and spacing of the instances of the item.

Configuring the Repeating Item's Appearance

When you designate the repeating item in the data list, Catalyst automatically adds five instances of it in a vertical list. The Properties panel makes it easy to change this to a horizontal or tile list and set the spacing between items. Follow these steps:

1. **Before changing the list to a horizontal list as required by the design, remove the other sample magazines from the design (see Figure 24.6).** If necessary, click HomeState on the navigation bar to return to the main application. Then, click on the magazines that you did not include in the data list and press the Delete key to remove them.

FIGURE 24.6

Removing the extra sample magazines

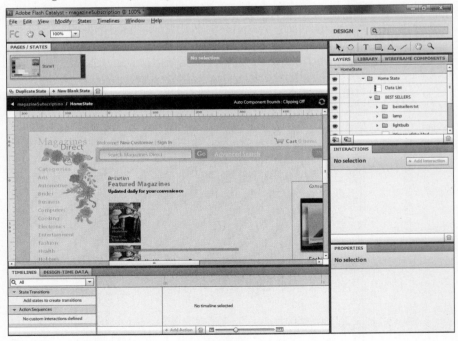

2. Double-click the data list to return to its editing mode (see Figure 24.7).

Returning to edit the data list

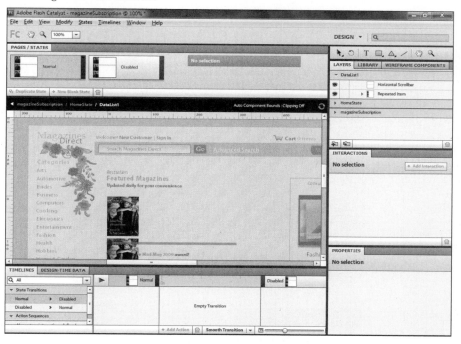

3. Click on the repeating item.

4. On the Properties panel, click to expand the Layout section (see Figure 24.8).

5. Click the horizontal alignment button to change the list orientation to horizontal (see Figure 24.9).

FIGURE 24.8

The Layout section of the Properties panel for the repeating item, showing the default settings

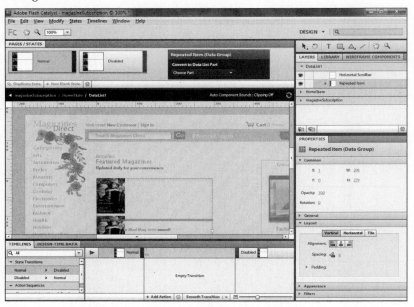

FIGURE 24.9

Changing the list orientation to horizontal

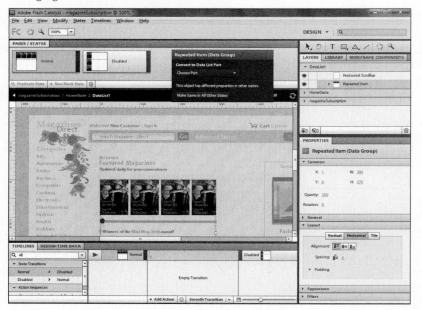

6. Click and drag to change the horizontal spacing value (see Figure 24.10). There is no correct amount of horizontal spacing for data items; rather, as you scrub the value pay attention not to the actual value but instead to the artboard, as you will see the value being applied to the data list directly. Scrub until the list is showing the amount of spacing that looks good to you.

Changing the spacing in the list

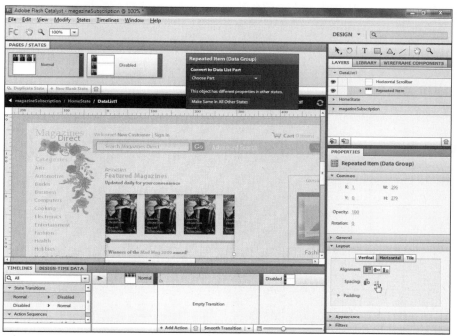

7. If necessary, use the Select tool to resize the data list to fit the items (see Figure 24.11). The size adjustment will only apply to the Normal state of the data grid.

8. Click Make Same on All Other States on the HUD to apply the size adjustment to the Disabled state as well (see Figure 24.12).

FIGURE 24.11

Resizing the data list

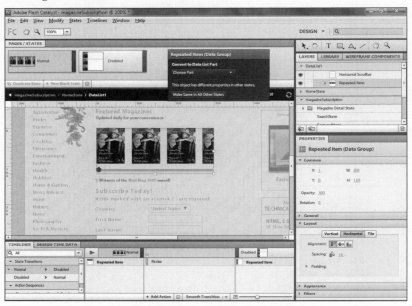

FIGURE 24.12

Applying the size adjustment to other states

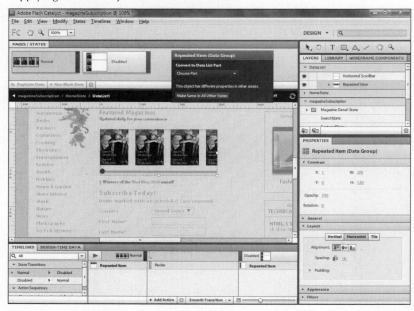

The data list will now be set up to your liking. In this example, you have adjusted it to be a horizontal list and have better spacing. You do not need to do anything to get the scrollbar to work. A data list component will automatically detect if a scrollbar component exists within it and use it.

Set Up Design-time Data

When showing the initial design to your client or boss, you likely added different items to represent the data. In the Magazines Now design, five magazine titles were displayed. When you convert the artwork to a data list, you will have the same item — whichever piece of the artwork you designated as the repeating item — displaying multiple times in the list.

If you need to show the design comp to a client or boss at some point before handing the comp off to your Flex developer, you will likely want to have the list continue to display varying data as it did initially. Fortunately, Catalyst includes a Design-time Data panel that allows you to simulate the actual data that will eventually be used in the application.

1. **If necessary, double-click the data list component so that you in its editing mode.**
2. **Click the Design-time Data panel's tab to display it (see Figure 24.13).** The panel shares the same space as the Timeline. The panel displays the information from the repeating item in the data list in a spreadsheet-like table.

FIGURE 24.13

The Design-time data panel

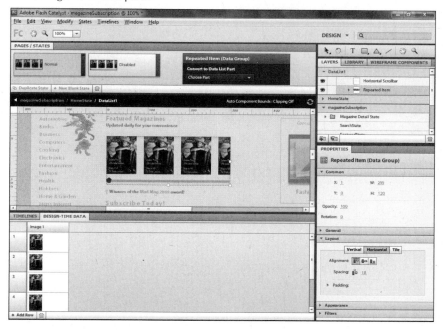

3. **Click on any cell that contains text to edit the text directly.** This example data list only contains images. Changing the images involves loading a new image from the library.

4. **Click the image in the second row to display the library dialog box, select the appropriate image (see Figure 24.14).**

5. **Click OK.**

The library dialog box launched from the design-time data panel

Note

If you do not have an image you need in the library, you can load it by clicking the Import button at the bottom of the dialog box.

On the Web

You can download all of the magazine images from the book's Web site (www.wiley.com/go/flash catalystbible).

6. Repeat Step 5 to change each of the other images (see Figure 24.15).

The design-time data panel, showing the different images

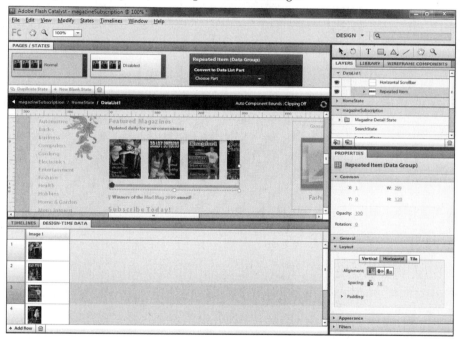

7. Click the name of the application to exit editing of the data list.

8. Choose File ➪ Run Project. The project opens in Flash Player, allowing you to scroll through the data list and view the sample data (see Figure 24.16).

FIGURE 24.16

The project running in Flash Player, showing the sample data

Cross-Reference

See Chapter 22 for more details on running the project.

Your data list is now set up. You have a set of repeating items, laid out horizontally, with a custom scrollbar.

Summary

In this chapter, you set up a data list in the project and added design-time data. You learned how to:

- Convert artwork to a data list
- Configure the data list's parts and set up the repeating item to display correctly
- Add design-time data to mimic the real-world data that will eventually populate the list in production

Importing Your Project into Flash Builder

In order to finish the Magazines Direct project, you will need to import it into Flash Builder, where either you or a Flex developer will add any additional functionality that cannot be handled by Catalyst. You can also run the project from Flash Builder to preview it.

Once the project has been opened and edited in Flash Builder, you will no longer be able to open it in Catalyst. However, if you keep a backup copy of the original project, you can open that in Catalyst, make needed changes, and then merge those changes back into the Flash Builder project.

Beginning the Import Process

Catalyst creates FXP files. An FXP file is actually nothing more than a zipped Flex project, which can be opened directly in Flash Builder. Therefore, there is nothing special you actually need to do in order to export your file to Flash Builder; it will automatically be in a file format supported by Flash Builder.

However, it is a good idea to make a back-up copy of the project so that it can be opened later by Catalyst if changes need to be made.

On the Web
The exercises in this chapter assume that you have completed the exercises in chapter 24. If you have not, you can download a version of the project as of the start of this chapter from the book's Web site (www.wiley.com/go/flashcatalystbible).

1. In Catalyst, choose File ⇨ Save As.

2. Navigate to the folder into which you wish to save the back-up copy of the project.

3. If necessary, rename the project.

4. Click Save (see Figure 25.1).

Saving a back-up copy of the project

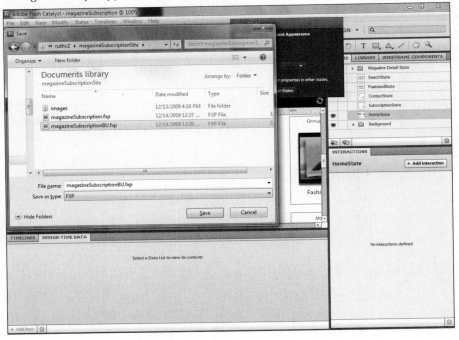

Note

If you'd prefer, you can also create a backup copy of the project using Windows Explorer or Finder on the Mac.

5. **Open Flash Builder.** On Windows, choose Start ⇨ All Programs. If you purchased Flash Builder as a part of a suite, there will be a folder representing that suite that should contain Flash Builder. Otherwise, look for an Adobe folder. On a Mac, use the Applications folder to launch it (see Figure 25.2).

FIGURE 25.2

Flash Builder immediately after launch

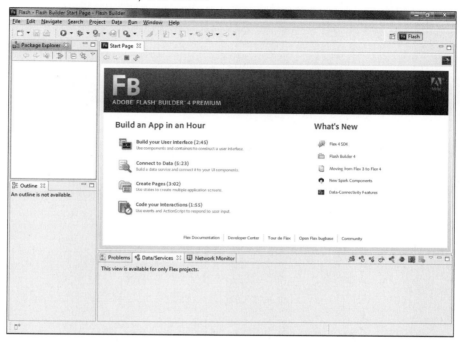

On the Web

If you do not have a copy of Flash Builder, you can download a free trial version from www.adobe.com/products/flex. The trial is fully-functional, but will eventually time-out and stop working.

6. In Flash Builder, choose File ⇨ Import Flex Project (FXP), as shown in Figure 25.3.

7. Click the Browse button to browser for a file to import.

8. Navigate to the directory that contains the original FXP project from Catalyst.

8. Click Import.

9. On the Import Flex Project dialog box, click Finish (see Figure 25.4). The project will be imported into Flash Builder.

FIGURE 25.3

Selecting the Import Flex Project menu command

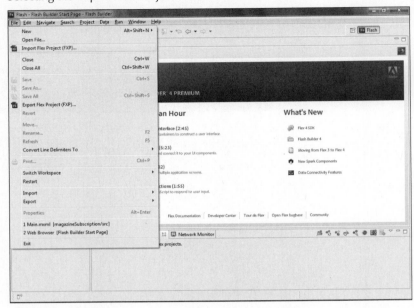

FIGURE 25.4

The Import Flex Project dialog box in Flash Builder

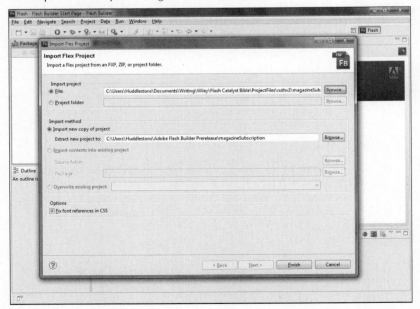

10. Expand the package in the Package Explorer in Flash Builder to examine the project's files (see Figure 25.5).

FIGURE 25.5

Examining the project's files in the Package Explorer in Flash Builder

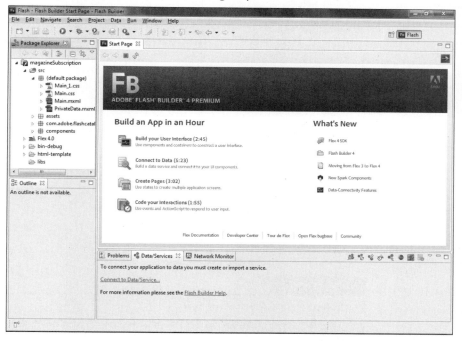

11. **Open** `Main.mxml` **from the Package Explorer.** This is the primary file created by Catalyst, and represents the starting file for the project.

12. **If necessary, click Design to view the project in Design mode.** The view of the project in Design mode should closely resemble Catalyst's view (see Figure 25.6).

13. **Click Source.** This switches to Flash Builder's code view, where you can edit the code for the project.

14. **Examine the code that was created by Catalyst (see Figure 25.7).**

FIGURE 25.6

The project in Flash Builder's design mode

FIGURE 25.7

The project's main file in source view

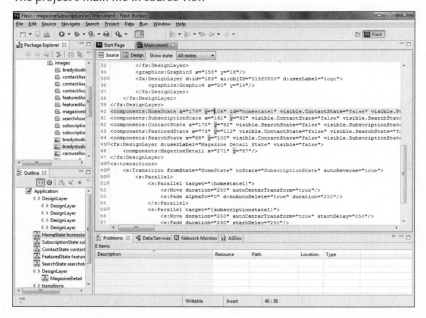

There will likely be less code in this file than you may have anticipated, as it does not contain all of the code for the project. Every component is contained within its own, independent MXML file.

15. **In the Package Explorer, click the arrow to open the CustomComponents folder.**

16. **Double-click one of the custom components to open it.** In this example, the SubscriptionAssets component has been opened.

17. **Examine the source code of the component (see Figure 25.8).**

FIGURE 25.8

The component's source code

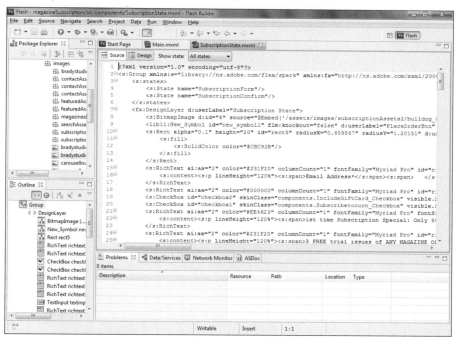

18. **Click Design to switch back to Design mode.** Again, the component appears in Flash Builder in a manner very similar to what you saw in Catalyst (see Figure 25.9).

You have now imported your Catalyst project into Flash Builder and examined some of the elements of the project.

FIGURE 25.9

The component in Design mode

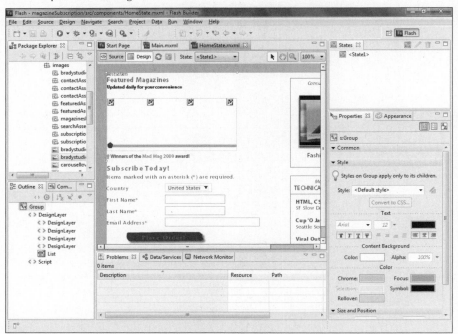

Running a Project in Flash Builder

Just as you can run a project in Catalyst to view how it will appear to your user, you can do the same in Flash Builder. The key difference is that, by default, Catalyst opens the project in a stand-alone version of Flash Player, while Flash Builder defaults to opening the project in a Web browser.

1. **In Flash Builder, ensure that you are viewing the project's main file.** When you have multiple files open in Flash Builder, you can switch between them by clicking the tabs in the top-left corner of the editing window (see Figure 25.10).

2. **From the Flash Builder toolbar, click the Run button (see Figure 25.11).** Its icon is a green circle with a white arrow. You can also choose Project ➪ Run Project or press F11. Flash Builder builds the project.

   Depending on the size and complexity of the project and your computer's resources, this process may take some time. A Build dialog box will display the progress while the project is built, or compiled (see Figure 25.12).

FIGURE 25.10

Returning to the main application file

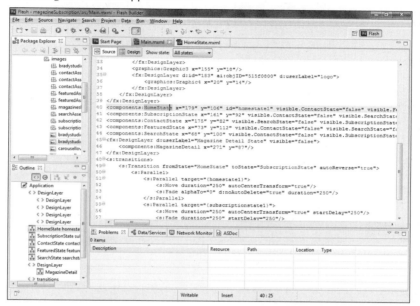

FIGURE 25.11

The Run button in Flash Builder

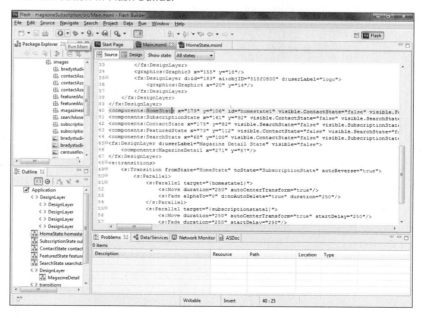

Running Components Directly

You cannot directly run a component. If a component is the active file when you run a project, Flash Builder will actually run the project's default application file. In these examples, that is not likely to be a problem, as projects created in Catalyst will only have a single application file. However, complex applications that have been created or edited in Flash Builder may contain more than one application, so attempting to run the project from a component may result in an application other than the one you expect actually running. Thus, you should get in the habit of making sure that you always return to the main application file before running the project.

Once the build is complete, the project will open in your computer's default Web browser. It should be fully functional, so you can click buttons, change states, fill out forms, and otherwise use the project. When you finish testing the application, you can return to Flash Builder to continue working on it.

FIGURE 25.12

The project running in the browser

Merging Changes from Catalyst into Flash Builder

Once a project has been opened and edited in Flash Builder, you will no longer be able to open it in Catalyst. In an ideal workflow, this would not be necessary; the design phase of the project will have been completed in Catalyst, and all that will remain will be editing it in Flash Builder.

However, ideal workflows rarely, if ever, apply in the real world. The unfortunate fact is that there will be times when edits need to be made to the visual interface of the project, and it may be easier to complete those edits in Catalyst rather than in Flash Builder. Therefore, you can open a back-up copy of the project in Catalyst, edit it, and then merge those changes into Flash Builder. Follow these steps:

1. **In Catalyst, choose File ⇨ Open Project.**
2. **Select the back-up copy of the project.**
3. **Click Open (see Figure 25.13).**

FIGURE 25.13

Selecting the back-up copy of the project to be opened in Catalyst

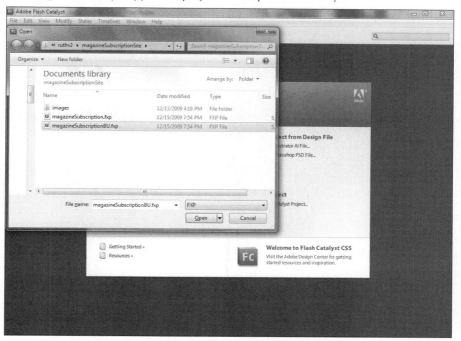

479

4. **Make any needed changes to the project.** In this example, the heading text in the HomeState component is being changed (see Figure 25.14).

Editing the project in Catalyst

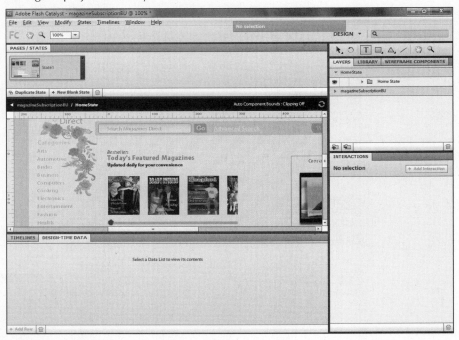

5. Choose File ⇨ Save to save the project in Catalyst (see Figure 25.15).

6. **Choose File ⇨ Save As to create a new back-up copy of the project.** Once the changes are merged into Flash Builder, you will be unable to open the current back-up to the project in Catalyst for further edits, so you should make a new back-up. Of course, you could pass the new back-up off to Flash Builder, and continue using the current one as your Catalyst file.

7. **Type a new name or navigate to a new location to save the back-up (see Figure 25.16).**

FIGURE 25.15

Saving the project

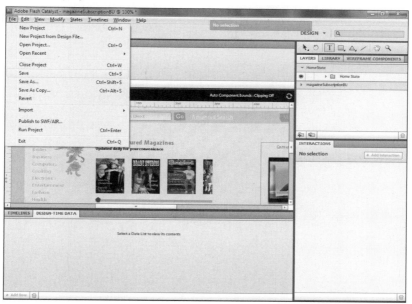

FIGURE 25.16

Saving a new back-up of the project

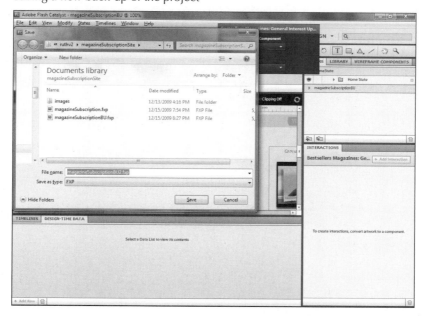

8. **Switch to Flash Builder.**

9. **Choose File ➪ Import Flex Project (FXP).**

10. **Click Import new copy of project (see Figure 25.17).**

11. **Navigate to the location of the new file from Catalyst.** The changes will be opened in Flash Builder as a new project.

Importing a new copy of the project

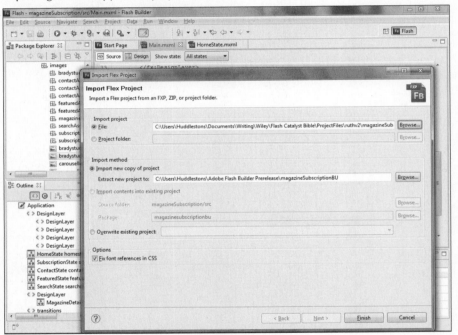

12. **To merge those changes into the existing project, right-click (⌘+click) the new project in the Package Explorer.**

13. **Select Compare With (see Figure 25.18), than select the original project.** If it is the only other project currently open in Flash Builder, it will be the only item on the list.

    Flash Builder examines the code in both projects and display a dialog box detailing the differences it discovers between the two. Depending on the size and complexity of the files and your computer's resources, this process might take some time to complete.

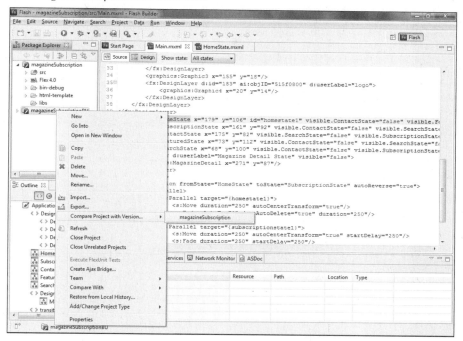

FIGURE 25.18

Selecting the Compare with command

14. Expand the src folder, then the components folder, and then double-click `HomeState.mxml`. The component opens and the first difference between the files is highlighted.

15. **Click Next Difference to move to the next change.** If necessary, scroll to the right to see the highlighted differences (see Figure 25.19).

16. **Click Copy All from Left to Right (see Figure 25.20).**

FIGURE 25.19

Changes highlighted in the code

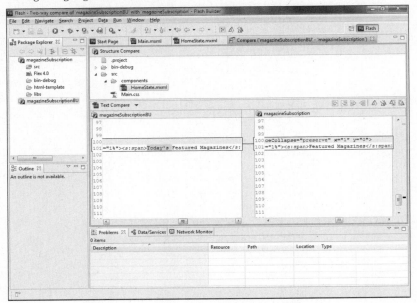

FIGURE 25.20

Accepting the changed code

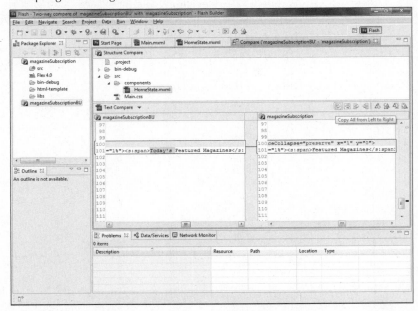

17. Click Close on the Compare window's tab (see Figure 25.21).

Closing the Compare window

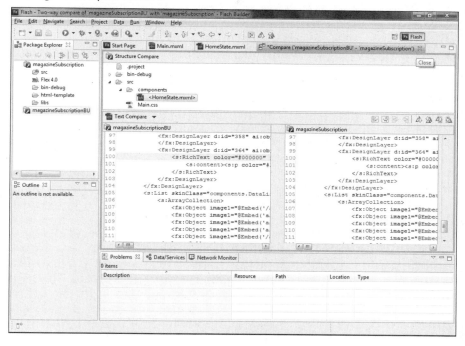

18. Click Yes to save the comparison (see Figure 25.22).

19. Right-click (⌘+click) the project in the Package Explorer and select Close project (see Figure 25.23).

FIGURE 25.22

Saving the file comparison

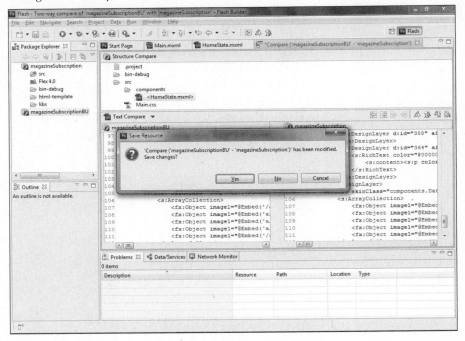

Closing the project ensures that you will not accidentally begin editing it, instead of the other version of the project. You may want to actually delete the project from Flash Builder by right-clicking (⌘+clicking) it and selecting Delete project.

Should you find yourself making multiple edits in Catalyst that need to be merged with Flash Builder, you will need to develop a clean naming convention for the new projects to avoid confusion. You may also want to treat the files to be merged as temporary files, deleting them immediately after merging into Flash Builder, so that you only keep two copies of the project:

- The copy being edited in Flash Builder
- The back-up for editing in Catalyst

You should also work with your Flex developer to attempt to limit the number of times changes need to be merged; for example, you may not want to send the developer a new copy of the project for every change, but instead wait to try to combine several changes together.

FIGURE 25.23

Closing the new project in Flash Builder

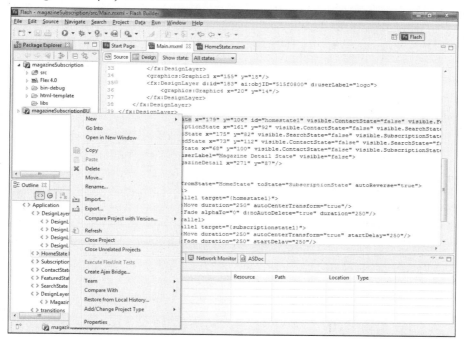

Summary

This chapter showed the workflow between Catalyst and Flash Builder. You learned:

- How to import a Catalyst project for editing in Flash Builder
- Run the project in a Web browser
- Make changes in Catalyst and merge them back into the Flash Builder project

Connecting Your Project to Live Data

Your design comp likely contained a representation of data. In your Catalyst project, you converted that representation into a data list and, with the help of the Design-time Data panel, displayed sample data. Now, you will be able to connect the project to live data, generated by the server.

Flex projects run entirely on the client's side; that is, they run in Flash Player through a Web browser or on a user's desktop via AIR. As they do not run on the server, they have no direct access to server-side resources such as databases.

In order for your application to display live data, you need a script running on the server that can communicate with the database, retrieve the desired data, format it appropriately, and send it to Flex.

You can write this script in any one of a number of languages and rely on varying technologies. Whether you or your developer is proficient in Adobe ColdFusion, PHP, Microsoft ASP.NET, Ruby on Rails, or almost any other server-side technology, you will be able to leverage it to get data into your Flex application.

Setting Up a Local Testing Server

A local testing server is a Web server installed on your personal computer that you can use to simulate live connections with the database. While there are quite a few steps involved with downloading, installing and configuring the server, the process is fairly simple and will enable you to test your pages and further develop your applications as needed.

Why ColdFusion?

As mentioned in this chapter's introduction, ColdFusion is one of many possible application servers that would work for your Flex application. This book uses ColdFusion for this example because, as both ColdFusion and Flex are Adobe products, the two share a special relationship. As you'll see in the upcoming examples, Flash Builder handles ColdFusion a bit differently than it does other server-side technologies. This relationship makes connecting to a ColdFusion service far easier than connecting to a PHP or ASP.NET service. As the purpose of this book is not to delve completely into server-side technologies, but rather to merely demonstrate how this process works, showing the easiest solution seemed best.

The other reason this book uses ColdFusion is that it can run in a completely self-contained, stand-alone environment; thus, it was not necessary to provide step-by-step instructions on downloading and installing a Web server or database as well. This built-in Web server in ColdFusion can only be used for development purposes on a local machine, while the built-in database, Apache Derby, can be used in either development or production environments.

Download and install ColdFusion

Adobe ColdFusion provides a set of powerful, easy-to-learn and easy-to-use tools for developing data-driven Web applications. As a commercial product, it does need to be purchased by your company or Web host in order for it to be deployed on a live, production Web server. However, Adobe makes a Developer Edition available, free of charge, to be installed and used in testing environments.

1. Using a Web browser, go to www.adobe.com/products/coldfusion.
2. Click Get the Trial (see Figure 26.1). A login screen appears.

Note

The most recent release of ColdFusion as of this writing is version 9, released in October of 2009. The process shown in these steps will work with ColdFusion MX7, ColdFusion 8, or ColdFusion 9, so if you have already installed one of those earlier versions, you need not re-download and reinstall ColdFusion 9.

3. Log into Adobe's Web site in order to download software. If you have an Adobe account, type your username and password. If you do not have an account, you can click the link on the page and create a free account, and then return to this page and log in (see Figure 26.2).

FIGURE 26.1

The Adobe ColdFusion home page

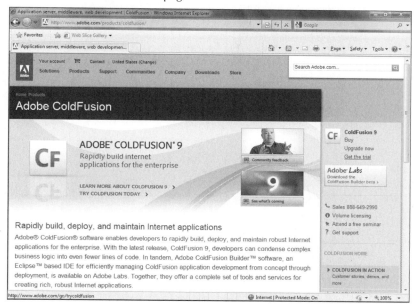

FIGURE 26.2

The login page

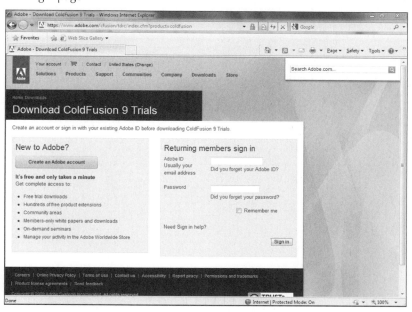

4. **Select the version of ColdFusion that is appropriate for your operating system and click Download (see Figure 26.3).** The File Download dialog box appears.

The download page for ColdFusion

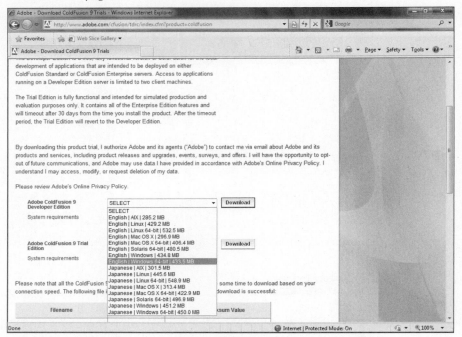

5. **Click Save (see Figure 26.4).**

6. **Navigate to a directory on your computer into which you want to download the file and click Save.**

7. **When the download completes, navigate to the directory into which you downloaded the file and double-click it to launch the installer.** The first step of the installer informs you that ColdFusion is going to be installed.

8. **Click Next (see Figure 26.5).**

FIGURE 26.4

Saving the download

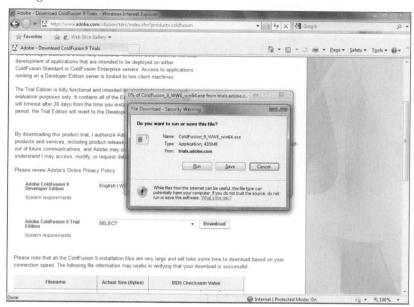

FIGURE 26.5

The first step of the ColdFusion installer

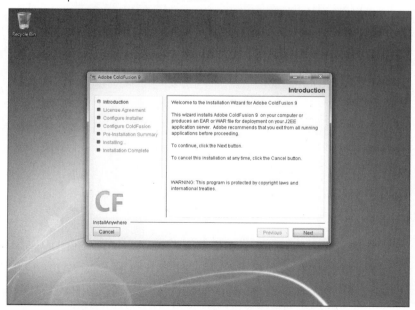

9. After reviewing the license agreement, click Next (see Figure 26.6).

The ColdFusion license installer license agreement

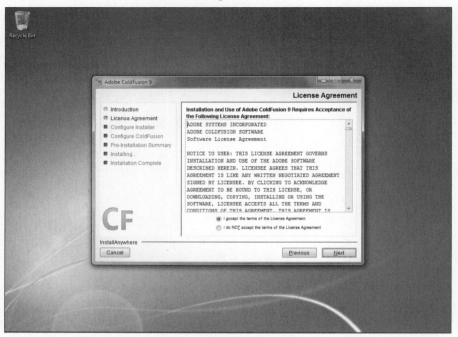

10. Click the option to install the Developer Edition.
11. Click Next (see Figure 26.7).
12. **Select a configuration for ColdFusion.** For a local testing server, Server configuration option, which is the default option, works best.
13. **Click Next (see Figure 26.8).** The next screen displays a list of subcomponents to install with ColdFusion.

FIGURE 26.7

Choosing to install the Developer Edition

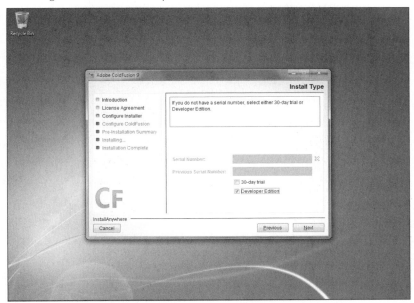

FIGURE 26.8

The Server Configuration screen

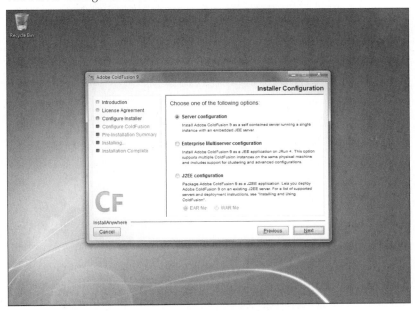

14. Leave the default selections and click Next (see Figure 26.9).

The Subcomponent Installation screen

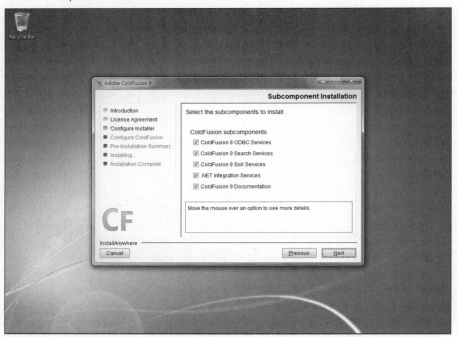

15. **Select the directory into which you want to install ColdFusion.** Unless you have a particular reason to choose something else, leave it at the default.

16. **Click Next (see Figure 26.10).** The next screen allows you to specify that you will be using the stand-alone version of ColdFusion.

17. Select the Built-in web server (Development use only) option.

18. Click Next (see Figure 26.11).

FIGURE 26.10

Choosing the installation directory

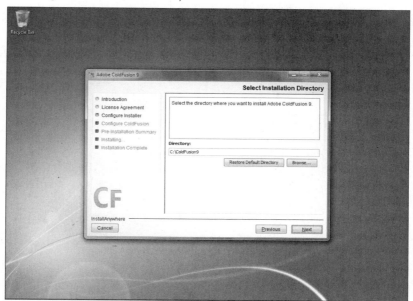

FIGURE 26.11

Setting ColdFusion to use its built-in Web server

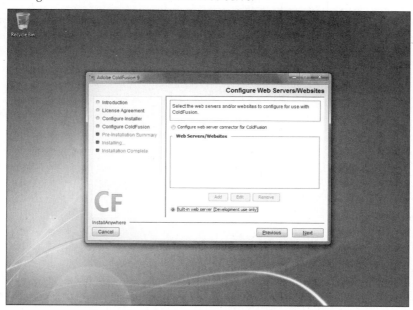

19. Enter a password and type it again to confirm. This password will be used by you when you need to log into the ColdFusion administrator to configure your server, so be sure to use a password that you will remember (see Figure 26.12).

ColdFusion uses the Remote Development Service to allow external editors such as Adobe Dreamweaver and Adobe ColdFusion Builder to have access to the server to simplify development. On a development or testing machine such as the one you are setting up, you should enable RDS and set up a password to control access. You should not enable RDS on a live production server.

FIGURE 26.12

Entering a server password

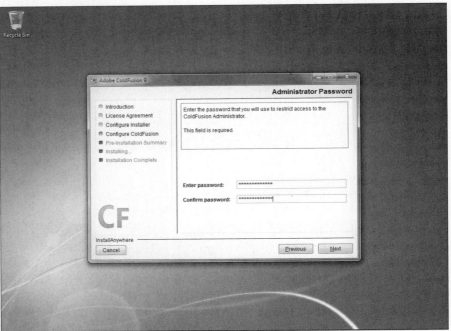

20. In this case, select the Enable RDS option and type, then confirm, a password (see Figure 26.13). The installation wizard offers a summary of the settings.

21. When you are ready, click Install (see Figure 26.14). The installer will likely take several minutes.

FIGURE 26.13

The Enable RDS step of the wizard

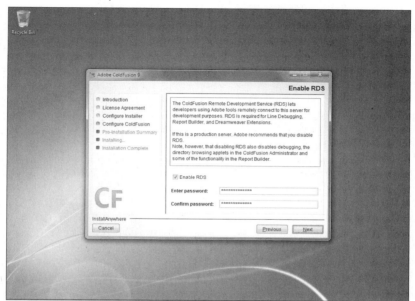

FIGURE 26.14

The summary screen of the installer

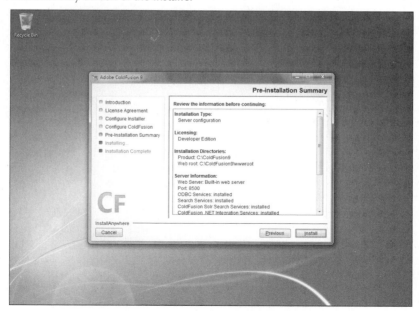

22. Once the installation is complete, launch the ColdFusion administrator to complete the configuration (see Figure 26.15).

FIGURE 26.15

The Installation Complete page

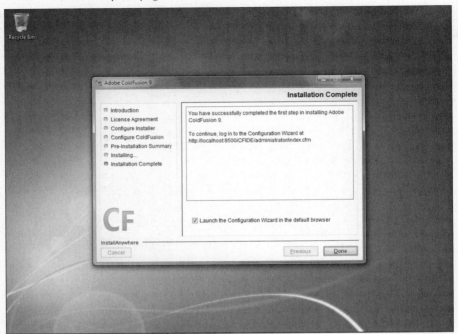

23. **Click the link provided to launch your Web browser.** After a few minutes, the installer will complete and display the ColdFusion administrator login screen (see Figure 26.16).

24. Log in and explore the administrator if you wish, using the password you created during the installation process (see Figure 26.17).

FIGURE 26.16

The ColdFusion administrator login screen, which displays when the installation and configuration are complete

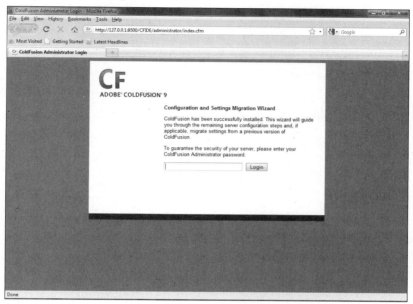

FIGURE 26.17

The ColdFusion Administrator home page

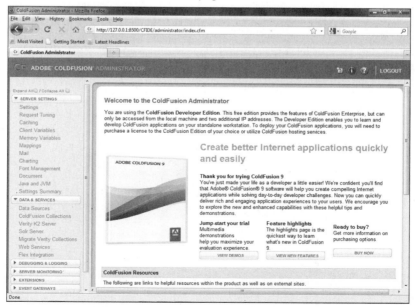

You have now installed ColdFusion on your computer, and are ready to begin using it as a back-end resource to connect your project to live data.

Configuring the database

After ColdFusion is installed, you need to set up and configure a database to use for your application. Many relational database systems exist, from desktop applications such as Microsoft Access to enterprise-level solutions offered by Oracle. One of ColdFusion's strengths is its ability to work with almost any database system.

Learning to effectively create, use and administer a relational database is a complicated task that is well beyond the scope of this book. Fortunately, ColdFusion includes a powerful database system, Apache Derby.

Derby offers many of the features found in expensive, enterprise-grade systems such as Microsoft SQL Server, but as an open-source solution, it is available free of charge. However, it does entirely lack a user interface. Therefore, it is necessary to create your own front end to the database. In this case, you can use ColdFusion to create that front end.

On the Web
You can download the ColdFusion files for configuring the database from the book's Web site (`www.wiley.com/go/flashcatalystbible`).

1. Download the ColdFusion database configuration files from the book's Web site (www.wiley.com/go/flashcatalystbible).
2. Once the files are downloaded, unzip them into the ColdFusion Web root. If you used a default installation on Windows, the root will be at `c:\ColdFusion9\wwwroot`, while on the Mac it will be at `Applications/ColdFusion9/wwwroot`.
3. Open a Web browser and type `http://localhost:8500/catalystbible dbconfig.cfm` in the browser's address bar.
4. Press enter.
5. Enter the ColdFusion administrator password you set up while installing ColdFusion.
6. Click Set Up Database. The ColdFusion page will create the necessary settings to configure the database, as well as creating the tables needed for the remainder of the examples here and populate the database with sample data.

   Once complete, a confirmation page will be displayed.
7. When you get the confirmation page, you can close the browser (see Figure 26.18).

FIGURE 26.18

The ColdFusion database configuration completed

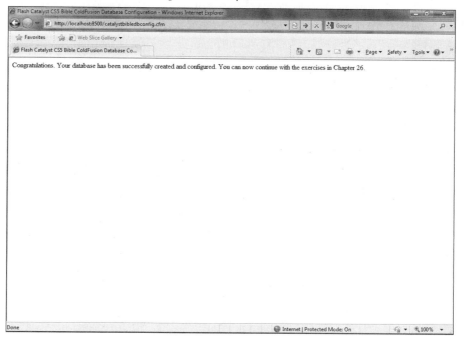

Changing the Project Type

When you create a project in Flash Builder, you must choose when you initially set up the project whether it will be *static* or use *server-side resources*.

Catalyst provides no such choice: All projects are assumed to be static.

Set up the project

When you import a Catalyst project that will need server-side resources into Flash Builder, you need to first convert the project to the appropriate type.

1. **Open Flash Builder.** If necessary, open a project created in Catalyst or import a new Catalyst project (see Figure 26.19).

FIGURE 26.19

Flash Builder with an open project created in Catalyst

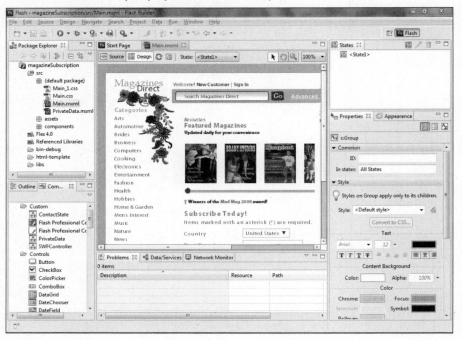

Cross-Reference

See Chapter 25 for details on importing Catalyst projects into Flash Builder.

On the Web

The following exercises assume that you have completed the steps in Chapter 25 to import the project. If you did not do those exercises, you can download a version of the project for this chapter from the book's Web site (www.wiley.com/go/flashcatalystbible).

2. Click the Data/Services view, located by default at the bottom of the Flash Builder interface.

3. Click the Connect to Data/Service link (see Figure 26.20) to launch the Flash Builder Wizard that will step you through the process of connecting to a server-side resource. The first step of the wizard allows you to choose the type of service to which you want to connect (see Figure 26.21).

FIGURE 26.20

The Connect to Data/Services link in the Data/Services view in Flash Builder

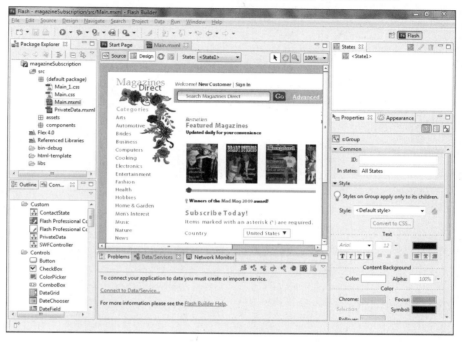

4. **Click ColdFusion.**

5. **Click Next.** You will be alerted to the fact that your project is not configured properly (see Figure 26.22).

6. **Click Yes to open the settings dialog box to change the configuration.** The Project Properties dialog box opens, with the Flex Server screen selected.

7. **From the Application server type drop-down list, select ColdFusion.**

8. **If necessary, select the Use remote object access service option.**

9. **Select ColdFusion Flash Remoting.**

10. **Set the ColdFusion installation type to Standalone.**

11. **Select the Use built-in ColdFusion web server checkbox.** Assuming that you installed ColdFusion using the defaults, the Web root and Root URL text boxes should have the correct paths pre-configured.

FIGURE 26.21

The first step of the wizard, where you select the type of service

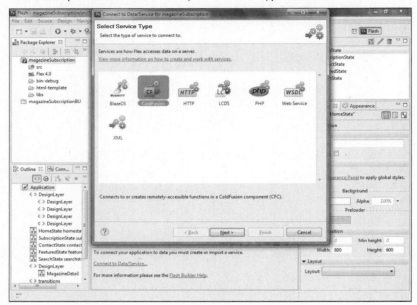

FIGURE 26.22

The configuration warning dialog box

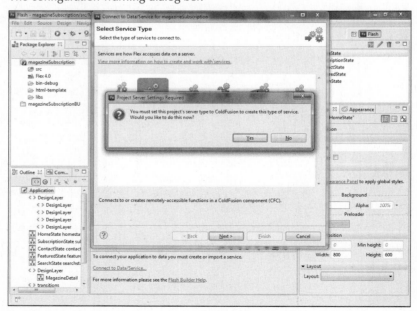

12. **In the Compiled Flex application location, type the location where you want the file to be deployed.** It must be within the Web root.

13. **Click OK (see Figure 26.23).** Flash Builder displays the New Flex Service dialog box.

The Flex Server configuration dialog box showing the settings necessary to set up a ColdFusion server resource.

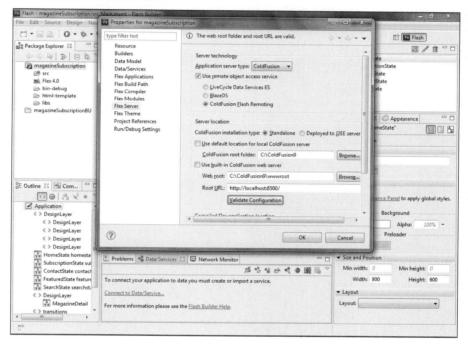

Cross-Reference
The Flex 4 Bible contains more details on setting up the server configuration. You can also look in the Flash Builder help files for more information.

14. **To specify the location of the ColdFusion Component (CFC), which will be responsible for retrieving the database information, click Browse and navigate to the directory that contains the CFC you downloaded from the book's Web site** (www.wiley.com/go/flashcatalystbible).

15. **Type** magazineList **as the Service name (see Figure 26.24).** Flash Builder should automatically enter services.magazines as the Service package and valueObjects as the Data type package.

16.   Click Next.

FIGURE 26.24

Configuring the ColdFusion service

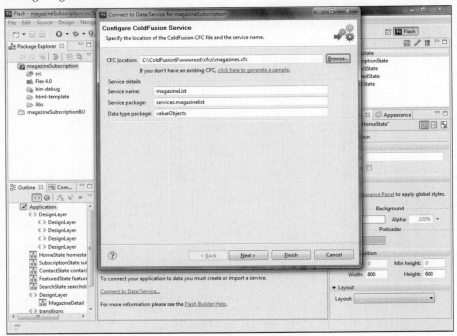

17.   **If you are prompted for an RDS username and password, type** admin **as the user-name and the RDS password you created when you installed ColdFusion (see Figure 26.25).** Flash Builder examines the CFC and returns a list of the operations, or methods, available in it. In this example, there is only one such method.

18.   Select the method (see Figure 26.26).

19.   **Click Finish.** Flash Builder creates a series of ActionScript classes to process the data returned from the CFC.

FIGURE 26.25

The RDS login screen

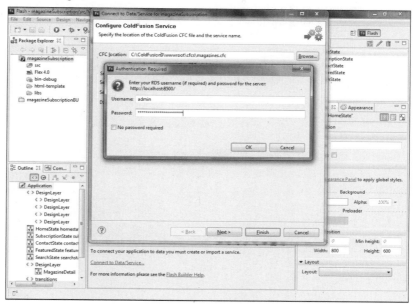

FIGURE 26.26

Selecting the Service Operation

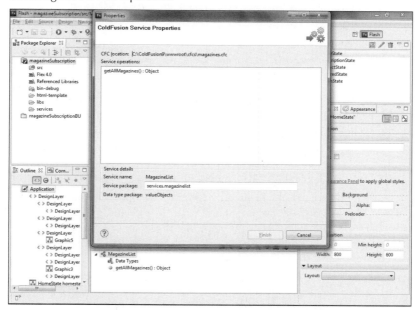

20. In the Package Explorer, expand the services package, then the services.magazineList package to see the ActionScript files created by the wizard (see Figure 29.27).

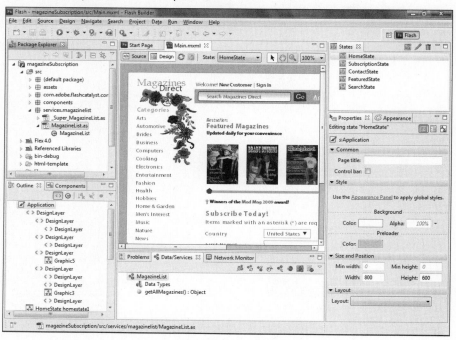

FIGURE 26.27

The ActionScript files created to process the data

Your project is now properly set up, and the necessary ActionScript files have been created.

Configuring the return data

You need to configure the type of data that the service will return so that Flex can properly process it. Once you have completed the steps in the previous section, the Data/Services view will display the getAllMagazines operation.

1. Select the getAllMagazines operation.

2. Right-click (⌘+click) the getAllMagazines operation and choose Configure Return Type from the context menu. You can also click the Configure Return Type button at the top of the Data/Services view. (see Figure 26.28).

FIGURE 26.28

Selecting the service and clicking the Configure Return Type button in the Data/Services view

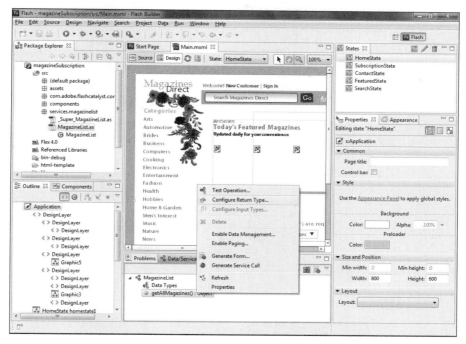

3. In the Configure Return Type dialog box, ensure that the option Auto-detect return type from sample data is selected (see Figure 26.29).

4. Click Next. Flash Builder needs to call, or invoke, the service to determine what kind of data will be returned. Some services will require that a parameter be sent to them; for example, a search operation would need a search string. The service used in these examples, however, simply returns all data, so you do not need to provide a parameter.

Flash Builder will therefore invoke the service and return a list of the data being returned.

In this example, the service returns a list of magazines and information about them. ActionScript can store multiple values in a single variable, as is needed in this case, in an *array*. Flash Builder will display a dialog box stating that it cannot automatically determine the property type.

6. Enter a name for the array, such as MagazinesData (see Figure 26.30).

7. Click Finish.

FIGURE 26.29

The first step in configuring the return type

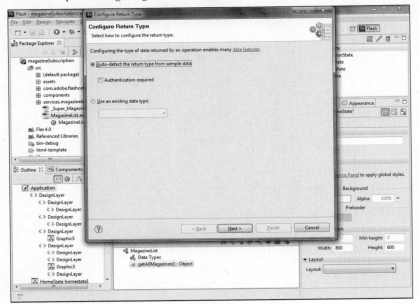

FIGURE 26.30

Entering the name of the property type for the data.

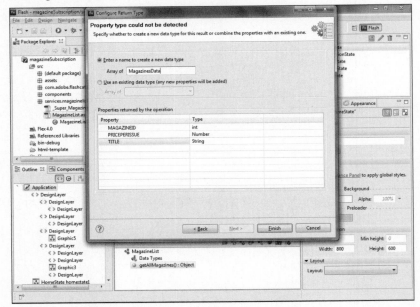

Caution

The name of the service and the name of the data type cannot be the same. In this example, the service name is Magazines, so the data type cannot be Magazines.

Binding the Data to the Visual Component

The final step in getting the data into the component is binding the data returned from the service to the component that will display it.

1. If necessary, open `Main.mxml` by double-clicking it in the Package Explorer in Flash Builder.

2. If necessary, click Design to view the file in Design mode (see Figure 26.31).

3. Check the States view in the top-right corner of the screen to ensure that you are in the HomeState.

4. Click on the data list component created in Catalyst.

FIGURE 26.31

Viewing the main project file's home state in Design mode, with the data list component selected

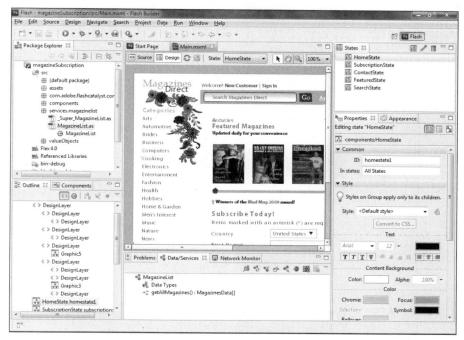

5. **In the Data/Services view, click the Bind to Data button (see Figure 26.32).** You can also drag the getAllMagazines operation from the Data/Services view and drop it on the list.

In Catalyst, you assigned sample data to the control. Flash Builder now needs to replace that dummy data with the real information from the service, so it will display a warning message confirming that you want to perform this operation.

FIGURE 26.32

The Bind control to data button in the Data/Services view

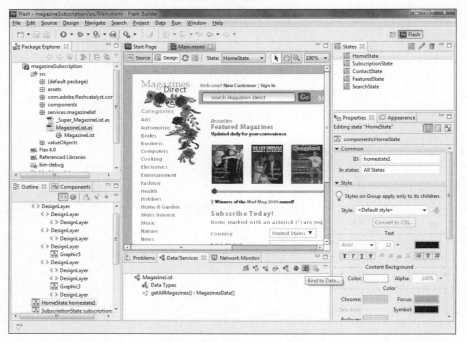

6. **Click OK.** A dialog box appears (see Figure 26.33).

7. **Confirm that the correct operation is being used.** The dialog box should already be filled out correctly, but if necessary, you can select the MagazineList service and getAllMagazines operation (see Figure 26.34).

8. **Flash Builder will want to automatically assign the data to a label, but click in the drop-down and select the empty option.** This enables you to use a custom component to display the data.

9. **Click OK.**

FIGURE 26.33

The warning that the dummy data is going to be replaced

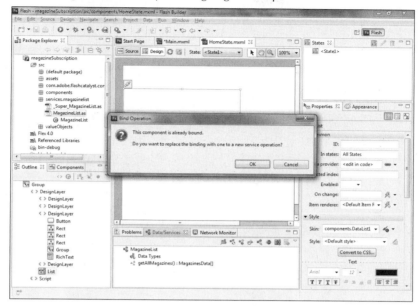

FIGURE 26.34

The Bind to Data dialog

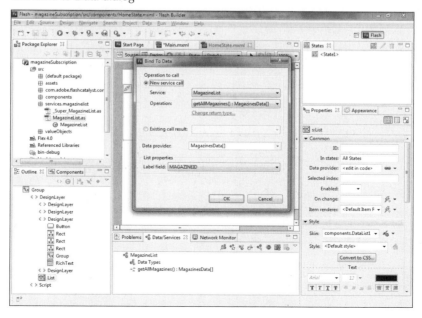

10. **Right-click (⌘+click) the data list control on the page and select Generate Details Form.** Another wizard launches that will enable you to set up the custom renderer for the data.

11. **Ensure that the Magazines data type is selected, and that the Make form editable option is not (see Figure 26.35).**

12. **Click Next.** The wizard displays the data being returned by the service.

The first step in the Generate Form wizard

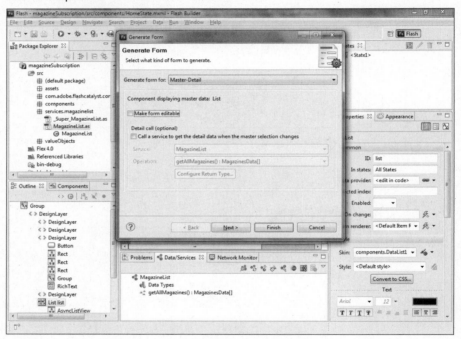

13. **Remove the checkmark in the box next to magazineID, as you do not want to display this.**

14. **Ensure that magazine_title and price are set to Text controls, while cover_picture is set to Image (see Figure 26.36).**

15. **Click Finish.** The form generated by the wizard is placed in the list.

16. **Click each text control and use the Properties view to adjust the font settings as desired.**

FIGURE 26.36

Configuring the display types

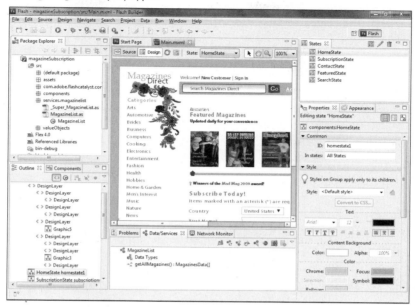

FIGURE 26.37

The completed data list, bound to live data from the server

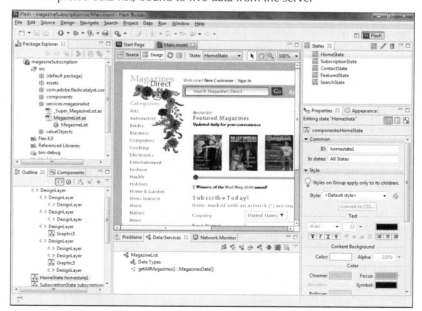

Summary

This chapter took you through the process of setting up a testing server on your computer and configuring your Catalyst project to display live data from the server. You learned:

- How to download and install ColdFusion
- Change the project type in Flash Builder to use server-side resources
- Set up the project to call a service
- Bind the data returned from the server to a component

Part VI

Appendixes

Keyboard Shortcuts

A s with most programs, Catalyst includes a host of keyboard shortcuts designed to speed up your work. Where the functionality is the same, Catalyst uses shortcuts from other Adobe Creative Suite tools, particularly Illustrator and Flash Professional.

Basic Commands

Tables A.1 through A. 8 list the keyboard shortcuts for the basic commands found in the program's menus. The tables are organized by menu category.

TABLE A.1

Keyboard Shortcuts for File Menu Commands

Command	Windows Shortcut	Mac Shortcut	Description
New Project	Ctrl+N	⌘+N	Opens the New Project dialog box to create a new, blank project.
Open Project	Ctrl+O	⌘+O	Opens an existing project by browsing to an FXP file.
Close Project	Ctrl+W	⌘+W	Closes the current project.
Save	Ctrl+S	⌘+S	Saves the current project. If the project has never been saved, this command does the same thing as Save As.
Save As	Ctrl+Shift+S	⌘+Shift+S	Prompts you to save the project with a new name.
Save As Copy	Ctrl+Alt+S	⌘+Option+S	Saves the project as a copy.
Run Project	Ctrl+Enter	⌘+Enter	Runs the project in Flash Player.
Exit	Ctrl+Q	⌘+Q	Exits out of Catalyst.

TABLE A.2

Keyboard Shortcuts for Edit Menu Commands

Command	Windows Shortcut	Mac Shortcut	Description
Undo	Ctrl+Z	⌘+Z	Undoes the prior command.
Redo	Ctrl+Shift+Z	⌘+Shift+Z	Redoes the most recent command that was undone.
Cut	Ctrl+X	⌘+X	Cuts the selected objects to the clipboard.
Copy	Ctrl+C	⌘+C	Copies the selected object to the clipboard.
Paste	Ctrl+P	⌘+P	Pastes the contents of the clipboard to the artboard. The objects will be pasted into the currently selected layer.
			Items cut or copied from within Catalyst will be placed at whatever spot on the artboard they were cut or copied from; items cut or copied from outside applications will be placed at the last point on which the artboard was clicked.
Delete	Delete	Delete	Deletes the currently selected item. Note that this shortcut is not listed on the Edit menu.
Select All	Ctrl+A	⌘+A	Selects all objects on the artboard. Items in hidden layers are not selected.

Keyboard Shortcuts for View Menu Commands

Command	Windows Shortcut	Mac Shortcut	Description
Zoom in	Ctrl++	⌘++	Zooms in on the artboard.
Zoom out	Ctrl+-	⌘+-	Zooms out on the artboard.
Fit Artboard in Window	Ctrl+0	⌘+0	Zooms to whatever magnification is necessary to fit the entire artboard in the window. The magnification will vary based on the size of the panels and the size and resolution of the user's screen.
Magnification ⇨ 50%	Ctrl+5	⌘+5	Sets the magnification to 50 percent.
Magnification ⇨ 100%	Ctrl+1	⌘+1	Sets the magnification to 100 percent.
Magnification ⇨ 200%	Ctrl+2	⌘+2	Sets the magnification to 200 percent.
Magnification ⇨ 400%	Ctrl+4	⌘+4	Sets the magnification to 400 percent.
Magnification ⇨ 800%	Ctrl+8	⌘+8	Sets the magnification to 800 percent.
Show Rulers	Ctrl+R	⌘+R	Shows or hides the rulers. The menu item will display with a checkmark if the rulers are visible, in which case selecting it again will hide them.
Grid ⇨ Show Grid	Ctrl+'	⌘+'	Shows or hides the grid. The menu item will display with a checkmark if the grid is visible, in which case selecting it again will hide it.
Grid ⇨ Snap to Grid	Ctrl+Shift+'	⌘+Shift+'	Turns the Snap to Grid feature on or off. The menu item will display with a checkmark if the feature is enabled, in which case selecting it again will disable it.
Guides ⇨ Show Guides	Ctrl+;	⌘+;	Shows or hides the guides. The menu item will display with a checkmark if the guides are visible, in which case selecting it again will hide them.
Guides ⇨ Lock Guides	Ctrl+Alt+;	⌘+Option+;	Locks or unlocks the guides. Locked guides cannot be selected or moved. The menu item will display with a checkmark if the guides are locked, in which case selecting it again will unlock them.
Guides ⇨ Snap to Guides	Ctrl+Shift+;	⌘+Option+;	Turns the Snap to Guides feature on or off. The menu item will display with a checkmark if the feature is enabled, in which case selecting it again will disable it.
Refresh Artboard	F5	F5	Refreshes the artboard.

```
TABLE A.4
```

Keyboard Shortcuts for Modify Menu Commands

Command	Windows Shortcut	Mac Shortcut	Description
Artboard Settings	Ctrl+J	⌘+J	Opens the Artboard Settings dialog box, from which you can adjust the width, height, and background color of the artboard.
Convert Artwork to Component ➪ Button	Ctrl+Shift+U	⌘+Shift+U	Converts the currently selected artwork to a button component.
Convert Artwork to Component ➪ Text Input	Ctrl+Shift+I	⌘+Shift+I	Converts the currently selected artwork to a text input component.
Convert Artwork to Component ➪ Custom/Generic Component	Ctrl+Shift+C	⌘+Shift+C	Converts the currently selected artwork to a custom or generic component.
Edit Component	Ctrl+E	⌘+E	Enters a component's editing mode.
Edit in Adobe Illustrator	Ctrl+Alt+I	⌘+Option+I	Opens the selected artwork in Adobe Illustrator CS5 for editing.
Edit in Adobe Photoshop	Ctrl+Alt+P	⌘+Option+P	Opens the selected artwork in Adobe Photoshop CS5 for editing.
Arrange ➪ Bring to Front	Ctrl+Shift+]	⌘+Shift+]	Shifts the currently selected sublayer to the top of the current layer's stack.
Arrange ➪ Bring Forward	Ctrl+]	⌘+]	Shifts the currently selected sublayer up one level within the current layer's stack.
Arrange ➪ Send Backward	Ctrl+[	⌘+[	Shifts the currently selected sublayer down one level within the current layer's stack.
Arrange ➪ Send to Back	Ctrl+Shift+[	⌘+Shift+[	Shifts the currently selected sublayer to the bottom of the current layer's stack.
Align ➪ Left	Ctrl+Alt+1	⌘+Option+1	Aligns currently selected items with the left edge of the left-most item in the selected items.
Align ➪ Horizontal Center	Ctrl+Alt+2	⌘+Option+2	Aligns currently selected items with the horizontal center point of the center item in the selected items.
Align ➪ Right	Ctrl+Alt+3	⌘+Option+3	Aligns currently selected items with the right edge of the right-most item in the selected items.
Align ➪ Top	Ctrl+Alt+4	⌘+Option+4	Aligns currently selected items with the top edge of the top-most item in the selected items.

Command	Windows Shortcut	Mac Shortcut	Description
Align ⇨ Vertical Center	Ctrl+Alt+5	⌘+Option+5	Aligns currently selected items with the vertical center point of the center item in the selected items.
Align ⇨ Bottom	Ctrl+Alt+6	⌘+Option+6	Aligns currently selected items with the bottom edge of the bottom-most item in the selected items.
Group	Ctrl+G	⌘+G	Groups the selected items.
Ungroup	Ctrl+Shift+G	⌘+Shift+G	Ungroups the selected items.

TABLE A.5

Keyboard Shortcuts for States Menu Commands

Command	Windows Shortcut	Mac Shortcut	Description
New Blank State	Ctrl+Shift+B	⌘+Shift+B	Creates a new blank state.
New Duplicate State	Ctrl+Shift+D	⌘+Shift+D	Creates a new state that is a duplicate of the currently selected state.
Share to State ⇨ All States	Ctrl+Shift+A	⌘+Shift+A	Shares the currently selected artwork with all states.
Make Same in All States	Ctrl+Alt+M	⌘+Option+M	Makes the attributes such as size and position of the currently selected artwork the same across all states.

TABLE A.6

Keyboard Shortcuts for Timelines Menu Commands

Command	Windows Shortcut	Mac Shortcut	Description
Smooth Transition	Ctrl+Alt+T	⌘+Option+T	Smooths the currently selected transition.
Play Timeline	Ctrl+Shift+P	⌘+Shift+P	Plays the currently selected timeline.

TABLE A.7

Keyboard Shortcuts for Window Menu Commands

Command	Windows Shortcut	Mac Shortcut	Description
Switch to Code or Design Workspace	Ctrl+`	⌘+`	Switches to the Code workspace if in Design, or the Design workspace if in Code.
Hide all Panels	F4 or Tab	F4 or Tab	Hides all panels to provide a full-screen work area for the artboard.
HUD	F7	F7	Shows or hides the HUD.

TABLE A.8

Keyboard Shortcuts for Help Menu Commands

Command	Windows Shortcut	Mac Shortcut	Description
Help	F1	F1	Displays the Adobe Community Help application for Catalyst. This shortcut is not shown in the Help menu, but it corresponds to the Flash Catalyst Help item.

Tool Selections

Catalyst, like Illustrator, Photoshop, and Fireworks, provides the ability to select tools by pressing a single key on the keyboard. Table A.9 describes these shortcuts. They are the same on both Windows and Macintosh.

Note

The Triangle, Hexagon, Octagon, and Star tools do not have a keyboard selector associated with them.

Tool Selection Keyboard Shortcuts

Tool	Keyboard Selector
Select	V
Direct Select	A
Transform	Q
Text	T
Rectangle	M
Rounded Rectangle	U
Ellipse	L
Line	N or \
Hand	H
Zoom	Z

Temporary Tool Selections

As with Illustrator, Photoshop, and Fireworks, you can temporarily switch to a few tools by pressing and holding certain key combinations, as shown in Table A.10. As soon as you let go of the keys, Catalyst will revert to the previously selected tool.

Temporary Tool Selection Shortcuts

Tool	Windows Temporary Selection Shortcut	Mac Temporary Selection Shortcut
Hand	Spacebar	Spacebar
Select	Ctrl	⌘
Zoom In	Ctrl+Spacebar	⌘+Spacebar
Zoom Out	Ctrl+Alt+Spacebar	⌘+Option+Spacebar

Note

Anytime you have the Zoom tool selected, you can press and hold the Alt (Option) key to switch to the Zoom Out tool.

Best Practices

W hile Catalyst can, at first glance, seem an easy program to learn and master, always remember that Catalyst is designed to be used in the middle of a designer-to-developer workflow. Following the best practices outlined in the following sections will help facilitate that workflow and minimize the potential conflicts between the designer and developer.

Designer Best Practices

From the very beginning of the design process, keep in mind that designing something that will eventually end up as a Flex application is a bit different from creating designs for print or even for traditional HTML-based Web sites.

The Web is not print

Many designers coming from a print background run into significant issues when moving to the Web by failing to grasp or acknowledge the differences between the media.

Even though Web sites may closely resemble print documents, particularly as both are made primarily of text and images, the Web is nonetheless as different a design medium from print as is video. Designing a television commercial would necessarily require a different design approach from designing a printed brochure. The same is true for Web sites.

For example, when a document is printed, it will always be precisely the same size. A designer of an 8½ × 11 newsletter knows that the document will always be those dimensions, and thus can plan exactly what size font to use and how big graphics should be.

On the Web, however, designers have no control over the size and resolution of the user's monitor. While Catalyst projects are at a fixed size, you cannot predict how much of a document will appear on a user's screen without scrolling, or how big or small the fonts may appear due to the user's screen resolution.

Design for interactivity

The project you design will eventually end up running in Flash Player. While a static design will certainly work, you can and should plan to leverage Flash Player's powerful animation capabilities in your application. After all, if you are not going to have any interactivity, there is little reason to use Catalyst and Flex at all: Your design would likely look the same in HTML and would possibly be quite a bit easier to create.

What separates Flex applications from their HTML counterparts is the interactivity and animation offered by Flash Player.

As you design, consider state transitions and how they might enhance your design. Think about what elements might be enhanced by the addition of action sequences. Plan to take advantage of a button's built-in states, and design Up, Down, and Over appearances for them.

Catalyst makes adding video and audio to a project a matter of a few clicks. Both, if used appropriately, can dramatically enhance the user's experience in your application.

Do not overuse interactivity

While leveraging Flash Player's capabilities can enhance an application, it can as easily detract from it. Use animation when appropriate, but do not use it merely because you can. Be sure that audio, video, and animation add something to the experience and are not in the project "just because."

Stay organized

Illustrator, somewhat unfortunately, makes it very easy to create projects with hundreds of layers with generic names such as *Path* or *Group*. When designing for print, these meaningless layer names are usually not a reason for concern, since the printer does not need to worry about working with the layers.

When designing for Catalyst, however, many layers with meaningless names can create headaches, as the layer's purpose might not be as clear when working in Catalyst as it was in Illustrator. Also, there is a possibility that while you understand what the layers represent, another designer or developer who need to work with the Catalyst version of the document will not. Be sure that you name your layers appropriately. Group layers logically and give the groups meaningful names.

Follow the same rules once you start working in Catalyst. Rearrange and rename any layers from Illustrator that were not grouped or named well initially. As you create new layers and sublayers, get in the habit of immediately renaming them.

Once you complete your work in Catalyst, you will likely be handing the project off to a Flex developer. While in an ideal situation the developer will have been involved in some way from the beginning of the design process, in many real-world situations the developer may be seeing the project for the first time when it is opened in Flash Builder.

Your Flex developer will not see or need to deal with layer names — keeping them organized will merely help you. The developer, however, will spend a considerable amount of time working with the components you create. Therefore, be sure to rename components as you create them. The developer may not inherently understand the meaning of the components or the roles they play in the application if the components do not have meaningful names.

An application that contains several forms named CustomComponent1 and CustomComponent2 will be much more difficult to work with than one with forms named ContactForm and SubscriptionForm. Follow the same rules with states, another element with which your developer will spend considerable time.

When you create a component from a layer in Catalyst, both the component and the layer will be given the same name. However, they are different elements, and either can be renamed later without affecting the other.

Remember that component and state names cannot contain spaces, and that the case you use will matter to your Flex developer. Most name components using Pascal casing, whereby the first letter of every word is capitalized, such as `FirstName` or `MagazineTitle`.

State names generally use camel case, which capitalizes the first letter of each word other than the first: `homeState` or `subscriptionState`.

Gain an understanding of Flash Builder and the Flex framework

If your role is and will remain a designer, it will likely be a waste for you to invest a large amount of time in learning Flex. However, you need to understand that as a Catalyst designer, you are designing for Flex. Just as a print designer can only get better at his job by understanding how commercial printers work, you will find that having an idea of how Flex works will help you better understand Catalyst and better understand the needs of your developer.

If you skipped over the chapters late in this book that covered those topics, go back and read them. I didn't write them with the idea of turning any designers into developers; rather, I intended to give designers a foundational knowledge of the technologies for which they will be designing.

Communicate

Unless you are the sole designer and developer, the single most important key to the success of your project will be communication.

If you are a designer, you likely have a very different background from your developer and almost certainly will have a different approach to the project. Any time you are unsure if something you are doing will adversely affect the developer's job in finishing the project, you should communicate with her to see what you can do to minimize or avoid that impact.

Developer Best Practices

If you are a developer using Catalyst for the design phase of your project, there are a few things you can do to maximize the effectiveness of the program. The same is true if your role as a developer will be to take a project that a designer created for you in Catalyst and finalize it in Flash Builder.

Gain an understanding of Illustrator and Photoshop

As a Flex developer, you may be as intimidated by Illustrator and Photoshop as designers who specialize in those programs are of Flex and programming. You need not become an expert in either, but gaining a basic understanding of how they work and what they can and cannot do will help you work better with the files you get from them.

If, as a developer, you skipped over the early chapters in this book on those tools, go back and read them. I didn't write them to convert developers to designers but rather to give developers an idea of what those programs can do.

Plan ahead

Many Flex developers have traditionally treated design as a sort of afterthought, believing that the functionality of an application was more important than its design.

In fact, neither function nor design is more important than the other: The best applications are those in which the design attracts users and aids them in accomplishing tasks, while obviously the functionality allows them to do those tasks.

When working in Catalyst, and even more so when working with a separate designer, carefully plan the application and its design. This will greatly reduce the number of design revisions that must be made and reduce the potential conflicts and frustrations between the designer and the developer.

Do not change skins in Flash Builder

Once you open and begin modifying a project in Flash Builder, neither you nor the designer will be able to open and continue modifying that design in Catalyst.

Inevitably, however, design changes will need to be made. Your designer can open a backup copy of the project in Catalyst, make the changes, and then send the changed project to you to be merged into your existing project. These changes will most likely be contained almost entirely, if not completely, in the skins and visual components.

Your task merging the changes will be made much easier if you refrain from altering these files in Flash Builder. That way, when you are merging the projects, you will know that any changes to the skins will be the revisions from Catalyst and can rest assured that merging those changes will not break anything that you have done in the project.

Communicate

As a developer receiving a design from a designer, the more you communicate with your designer, the better off you both will be.

If, in the initial design and planning phase, you see elements of the application that will be difficult to implement, speak up then. As the design progresses, stay involved so that you can deal with issues as they arise, rather than waiting for a finished but largely unworkable design to be delivered to you.

After you receive the project, continue to communicate changes you make to your designer. If she needs to make further changes to the Catalyst project later, she can have a good idea as to what you have done and how that might impact the decisions she will need to make.

Best Practices When Working in Catalyst

Whether you are a designer or developer, you may find the following hints helpful in working with Catalyst.

Do things in the right order

Optimize graphics right away when you import art into Catalyst. Optimized graphics are not only easier to work with, but also make Catalyst run more efficiently. Keep in mind that optimized graphics cannot be altered at run-time in the application; that is, your developer will not be able to write code that changes the graphic dynamically while the program runs in Flash Player. Therefore, any graphics that might need this capability should not be optimized, but all others should.

Cross Ref

See Chapter 8 for more information on optimizing graphics.

Convert objects to components before adding them to states. As much as possible, group elements into custom or generic components. Elements that do not make sense as components should be grouped into logical sets.

Cross Ref

See Chapter 9 for more information on creating components.

When setting up states, first define the location, visibility, and appearance for each element in the state. Then specify the transitions between that state and other states in the application. Finally, define the interactions on the components that will trigger the state changes.

Cross Ref

See Chapter 10 for more information on creating states.

Think about using components

You do not need to define a separate component for each element if those elements all serve the same basic purpose.

For example, rather than defining a separate text input component for each field in a form, you can define a single component and then reuse it. Doing so will not only minimize the file size of the project but will also make working with the project in Flash Builder easier.

Changes apply only to single states

Duplicate states can be copies of the original state as of the moment the new state was created. Any changes to the elements of a state after duplicate states are created only effect that state.

Changing an element on a state that exists on another state will cause a transition to be created for the change. If you alter something on a state and need that alteration to carry through to other states, be sure to choose Modify ➪ Make Same in All States.

Cross Ref

See Chapter 10 for more information on working with states.

Preview the project at regular intervals

Particularly when defining interactions and transitions, preview the project frequently to make sure you are getting the effects you want.

Cross-Ref

For more information on best practices in Catalyst, check out Chapter 5.

What's on the Book's Web Site

This book has an accompanying Web site (www.wiley.com/go/
flashcatalystbible) with the files needed to complete the
exercises throughout the chapters, particularly those in the hands-on
tutorials in Part V. The site contains a set of Zip files, the purposes of which
are each described in the Tables in this appendix.

All of the files should be extracted to your computer's hard drive. With the
exception of the ColdFusion files (see Table C.1), they can be extracted to
any location on your hard drive.

The ColdFusion files must be extracted into ColdFusion's Web root directory. See the readMe.txt file included with each archive that includes
ColdFusion files for details.

TABLE C.1

Finalized Project Files

File Name	Contents	Purpose
FinalCatalystProject.zip	magazinesDirect.fxp	This file represents the completed Catalyst version of the project.
		Readers can open this project in Catalyst to see the project in its completed Catalyst state, the point at which it would be just before being handed off to a developer.
FinalProject.zip	magazinesDirect.fxp cfcs/magazines.cfc	This is the truly finished project, after the completion of work in Flash Builder.
		The FXP file can be imported into Flash Builder and run from there, but you cannot open it in Catalyst. The cfc directory contains the ColdFusion component that returns the data for the data list.
ColdFusionSetUp.zip*	setup/createDB.cfm readMe.txt	The ColdFusion document in this package adds the necessary database connection to ColdFusion, creates the Derby database, and creates and populates the magazine table.
		The readMe.txt contains instructions detailing where to save the file and how to run it. This file must be run before the final project can be run from Flash Builder.

* This file does not contain the ColdFusion application server, which must be downloaded and installed separately from Adobe.com.

The files in PartII.zip, detailed in Table C.2, were created in the CS5 versions of the respective applications, and readers may not be able to open them in older versions of the programs.

TABLE C.2

Files for Part II

Contents	Purpose
chapter5/MagazinesDirect.ai	Contains endpoint file for Illustrator, discussed in Chapter 5.
chapter6/bradystudios.psd	Contains the magazine covers as layered Photoshop files, along with a JPG version of the Smithsonian image.
chapter6/carousellovers.psd	
chapter6/gardenstatuary.psd	
chapter6/knapford.psd	
chapter6/screamingzebras.psd	
chapter6/smithsonian.jpg	
chapter6/sombreromonthly.psd	
Chapter7/bradystudios.psd	Contains the Brady Studios magazine cover as a layered Photoshop file.

The files outlined in Table C.3 from PartIII.zip represent the starting and ending points of the project for each of the chapters.

Note that the starting project for each chapter is a duplicate of the ending project from the prior chapter in this file, so the file in chapter8/end is identical to the file in chapter9/start and so forth.

TABLE C.3

Files for Part III

Contents	Purpose
chapter8/ magazinesDirect.ai	Chapter 8 details importing the project and assets from Illustrator and Photoshop.
chapter8/bradystudios.psd	
	The files included are the Illustrator comp and a layered Photoshop magazine cover.
chapter9/magazineSubscription.fxp	Chapter 9 details making modifications to the individual parts of the application. The included file represents the beginning state of the project for the chapter.
chapter10/magazineSubscription.fxp	Chapter 10 details making modifications to the individual parts of the application. The included file represents the beginning state of the project for the chapter.

continued

TABLE C.3 *(continued)*

Contents	Purpose
chapter11/magazineSubscription.fxp	Chapter 11 details making modifications to the individual parts of the application. The included file represents the beginning state of the project for the chapter.
chapter12/magazineSubscription.fxp	Chapter 12 details making modifications to the individual parts of the application. The included file represents the beginning state of the project for the chapter.
chapter13/magazineSubscription.fxp chapter13/video.flv chapter13/audio.mp3 chapter13/homepagemovie.swf	Chapter 13 shows how to import and work with audio and video files. A sample video file, audio file, and Flash SWF movie are included along with the project, represented as of the beginning of the chapter.

Table C.4 details the files in PartIV.zip, which will help the user step through the chapters in Part IV of the book.

TABLE C.4

Files for Part IV

Contents	Purpose
Chapter14/magazineSubscription.fxp	The Chapter 14 folder contains a sample of the final Catalyst project.
chapter15/magazineSubscription.fxp	The Chapter 15 folder contains the final Catalyst version of the FXP. This matches the version from the /chapter14.
chapter16/magazineSubscription.fxp	Chapter 16's file likewise matches the files from Chapter 14 and 15
chapter17/magazineSubscription.fxp chapter17/end/deploy-to-web/assets/images/contactAssets/Image_0001.png chapter17/end/deploy-to-web/assets/images/contactAssets/phone_002.png chapter17/end/deploy-to-web/assets/images/contactAssets/rubber-ducks_devil.png chapter17/end/deploy-to-web/assets/images/contactAssets/rubber_ducks_housewife.png	The Chapter 17 folder contains, as with the other chapters, a version of the project at the start of the chapter. Also included are the deploy-to-web and run-local folders created by the exporting process. See the chapter itself for details on each of these files.

Appendix C: What's on the Book's Web Site

Contents	Purpose
`chapter17/end/deploy-to-web/assets/images/contactAssets/rubber_ducks_pirate.png`	
`chapter17/end/deploy-to-web/assets/images/bradyStudios.jpg`	
`chapter17/end/deploy-to-web/assets/images/carousellovers.jpg`	
`chapter17/end/deploy-to-web/assets/images/garenstatuary.jpg`	
`chapter17/end/deploy-to-web/assets/images/knapford.jpg`	
`chapter17/end/deploy-to-web/assets/images/screamingzebras.jpg`	
`chapter17/end/deploy-to-web/history/history.css`	
`chapter17/end/deploy-to-web/history/history.js`	
`chapter17/end/deploy-to-web/history/historyFrame.html`	
`chapter17/end/deploy-to-web/ framework_4.0.0.12112.swf`	
`chapter17/end/run-local/assets/images/contactAssets/rubber_ducks_housewife.png`	
`chapter17/end/run-local/assets/images/contactAssets/rubber_ducks_pirate.png`	
`chapter17/end/run-local/assets/images/bradyStudios.jpg`	
`chapter17/end/run-local/assets/images/carousellovers.jpg`	
`chapter17/end/run-local/assets/images/garenstatuary.jpg`	
`chapter17/end/run-local/assets/images/knapford.jpg`	
`chapter17/end/run-local/assets/images/screamingzebras.jpg`	
`chapter17/end/run-local/history/history.css`	
`chapter17/end/run-local/history/history.js`	
`chapter17/end/run-local/history/historyFrame.html`	
`chapter17/end/run-local/ framework_4.0.0.12112.swf`	

continued

TABLE C.4 *(continued)*

Contents	Purpose
chapter17/end/run-local/Main.css	
chapter17/end/run-local/Main.html	
chapter17/end/run-local/Main.swf	
chapter17/end/run-local/playerProductInstall.swf	
chapter17/end/run-local/rpc_4.0.0.12112.swf	
chapter17/end/run-local/spark_4.0.0.12112.swf	
swfobject.js	
textLayout_1.0.0.554.swf	
chapter18/magazineSubscription.fxp chapter18/magazineSubscription.air	Chapter 18's files include a copy of the main project file, along with the finalized AIR application.

The files detailed in Table A.5 (found in PartV.zip) contain the assets for the walk-through exercises in Part V.

TABLE A.5

Files for Part V

Contents	Purpose
chapter19/start/assets/bradyStudios.jpg	Chapter 19's /start/assets/ folder contains the images that will be imported into the Illustrator file, while the /end/ file contains the completed Illustrator design, which is also included in the chapter20/start folder.
chapter19/start/assets/carouselLovers.jpg	
chapter19/start/assets/garenstatuary.jpg	
chapter19/start/assets/knapford.jpg	
chapter19/start/assets/screamingzebras.jpg	
chapter19/start/assets/sombreromonthly.jpg	
chapter19/start/assets/Image_0001.png	
chapter19/start/assets/phone_002.png	
chapter19/start/assets/rubber-ducks_devil.png	
chapter19/start/assets/rubber_ducks_housewife.png	
chapter19/start/assets/rubber_ducks_pirate.png	
chapter19/end/magainzesDirect.ai	

Contents	Purpose
chapter20/start/magainzesDirect.ai chapter20/end/magazineSubscription.fxp	Chapter 20's /end/ file contains the completed Illustrator design, which is also included in Chapter 19's /end/ folder.
chapter21/start/magazineSubscription.fxp chapter21/end/magainzesDirect.fxp	Chapter 21's /start/ folder contains the same file as Chapter 20's /end/ folder, both of which represent the project's starting point for Chapter 21. The /start/ folder also includes the other two Illustrator files needed for the importing exercise in that chapter.
chapter22/start/magazineSubscription.fxp chapter22/end/magazineSubscription.fxp	The /start/ folder for Chapter 22 contains a copy of the project That matches the one in the /end/ folder in Chapter 21, while the /end/ folder contains a copy of the project as of the end of the chapter.
chapter23/start/ magazineSubscription.fxp chapter23/end/ magazineSubscription.fxp	The /start/ folder for Chapter 23 contains a copy of the project That matches the one in the /end/ folder in Chapter 22, while the /end/ folder contains a copy of the project as of the end of the chapter.
chapter24/start/ magazineSubscription.fxp chapter24/start/assets/bradyStudios.jpg chapter24/start/assets/carouselLovers.jpg chapter24/start/assets/garenstatuary.jpg chapter24/start/assets/knapford.jpg chapter24/start/assets/screamingzebras.jpg chapter24/start/assets/sombreromonthly.jpg chapter24/end/ magazineSubscription.fxp	The /start/ folder for Chapter 24 contains a copy of the project That matches the one in the /end/ folder in Chapter 23, while the /end/ folder contains a copy of the project as of the end of the chapter. Also included are optimized JPG versions of the magazine cover images.
chapter25/start/ magazineSubscription.fxp chapter25/end/ magazineSubscription.fxp	The /start/ folder for Chapter 25 contains a copy of the project That matches the one in the /end/ folder in Chapter 24, while the /end/ folder contains a copy of the project as of the end of the chapter.
chapter26/start/magazinesDirect.fxp chapter26/coldFusion/readMe.txt chapter26/coldFusion/cfc/magazines.cfc chapter26/end/magazinesDirect.fxp	The /start/ folder for Chapter 26 contains a copy of the project That matches the one in the /end/ folder in Chapter 25, while the /end/ folder contains a copy of the project as of the end of the chapter. Chapter 26 contains a /coldFusion/ folder, which contains the magazines.cfc file in a /cfc/ folder and a readMe.txt file detailing the proper placement and use of the CFC.

Index

Index

Index

Index

Index

Index

Index

O

object-oriented programming (OOP), 254–257
objects
    defined, 255
    properties, 256
On Video Load Complete, 245
On Video Play Complete, 245
Opacity setting, 69–71, 134
Open Project command (Ctrl+O, ⌘+O), 522
open-source applications, 37, 257, 502. *See also* Flex framework
opening files
    Flash Catalyst, 479
    Photoshop, 119–121
operating systems, 305–306
Optimize Artwork menu, 397
Optimize panel (Fireworks), 158
Optimized Graphics dialog box, 376
optimizing graphics
    converting artwork, 385–386
    Flash Catalyst best practices, 533
    imported graphics, 16–17, 188–189, 393
    Optimized Graphics dialog box, 376
    rasterizing, 364–367
Outer Bevel filter (Fireworks), 168
Outline view (Flash Builder), 283
outlines, text, 117
output folder, 262, 263
Oval Marquee tool (Fireworks), 155
Over state (buttons), 196, 198, 203, 223, 441, 442
Overlay blend mode, 81, 134

P

Package Explorer view (Flash Builder), 24, 277, 283, 307, 311, 473, 475, 510
packages, 279
packages (object-oriented programming), 256
Pages panel (Fireworks), 158
Pages/States panel
    buttons, 196
    Design workspace, 40
    editing components, 411
    resizing, 44
    view states, 19, 211–213, 215, 431
Paint Brush tool (Illustrator), 8, 9, 101

Paint Bucket tool (Fireworks), 157
painting tools (Illustrator), 101–102
panels. *See also* views (Flash Builder)
    Adobe CS5, 51–54
    Code workspace, 42–43
    collapsing, 45, 51
    Design workspace, 38–42
    Fireworks
        Access CS Live panel, 159
        Align panel, 158
        Behaviors panel, 160
        Color Palette panel, 159–162
        Common Library panel, 159, 171
        Document Library library, 159
        Find and Replace panel, 160
        History panel, 158
        Image Editing panel, 159
        Info panel, 160
        Kuler panel, 160
        Layers panel, 159
        Optimize panel, 158
        Pages panel, 158
        Path panel, 159
        Properties panel, 159, 164–165, 166
        Search for Help panel, 160
        Shapes panel, 159
        Special Characters panel, 159
        States panel, 159
        Styles panel, 159
        Swatches panel, 159, 160, 163–164
        Symbol Properties panel, 160
        URL panel, 160
    Flash Catalyst
        Design-time Data panel, 16, 41, 206, 207, 236, 465, 467
        Interactions panel, 16, 20, 21, 41, 444
        Layers panel, 16, 41, 78, 180, 214, 377, 411
        Library panel, 16, 41, 186, 296–297, 409, 410
        Pages/States panel, 19, 40, 44, 196, 211–213, 215, 411, 431
        Problems panel, 43, 275, 276
        Project Navigator panel, 42, 43, 275–276
        Properties panel, 16, 42, 66, 67, 71, 73, 79, 200, 206, 228–231, 235, 247, 248, 460, 462
        Timeline panel, 16, 17, 22, 220–223, 226–227, 232, 242, 447

Index

Index

Index

Index

Index

Index

Word, 1
workbench (FlashBuilder), 258
workflow
    design implementation, 35
    designer/developer, 295, 298
    Fireworks, 151
    Flash Builder vs. Flash Catalyst, 294
    merging changes from Flash Catalyst, 479
    overview, 3–5
    Rich Internet Applications, 47
workspace
    Fireworks, 157
    Flash Catalyst
        Code, 39, 42–43
        customization, 44–45
        Design, 39–42
        main, 38–39
    perspective vs., 282
World Wide Web
    deploying projects, 302–304
    development, 1, 2
    history, 29–30
    sizing projects, 63
WYSIWYG (what-you-see-is-what-you-get) environment, 259

X

XHTML, 32
XML (Extensible Markup Language), 31, 32
XML tags, 266
xmlns attribute, 266, 268

Z

Zoom blur filter (Fireworks), 169
Zoom in command (Ctrl++, ⌘++), 123, 523
Zoom In tool keyboard shortcut (Ctrl+Spacebar,
        ⌘+Spacebar), 527
Zoom out command (Ctrl+-, ⌘+-), 123, 523
Zoom Out keyboard short (Ctrl+Alt+Spacebar,
        ⌘+Option+Spacebar), 527
Zoom to 100 percent magnification shortcut, 123
Zoom tool
    Adobe CS5, 50
    Flash Catalyst, 64–66
    Illustrator, 322, 360, 361, 366
    Photoshop, 121–123
Zoom tool keyboard shortcut (Z), 527
zooming out, 22